Becoming John Updike: Critical Reception, 1958–2010

Studies in American Literature and Culture:
Literary Criticism in Perspective

Brian Yothers, Series Editor
(*El Paso, Texas*)

About *Literary Criticism in Perspective*

Books in the series *Literary Criticism in Perspective* trace literary scholarship and criticism on major and neglected writers alike, or on a single major work, a group of writers, a literary school or movement. In so doing the authors—authorities on the topic in question who are also well-versed in the principles and history of literary criticism—address a readership consisting of scholars, students of literature at the graduate and undergraduate level, and the general reader. One of the primary purposes of the series is to illuminate the nature of literary criticism itself, to gauge the influence of social and historic currents on aesthetic judgments once thought objective and normative.

BECOMING JOHN UPDIKE

Critical Reception, 1958–2010

Laurence W. Mazzeno

CAMDEN HOUSE
Rochester, New York

Copyright © 2013 Laurence W. Mazzeno

All Rights Reserved. Except as permitted under current legislation, no part of this work may be photocopied, stored in a retrieval system, published, performed in public, adapted, broadcast, transmitted, recorded, or reproduced in any form or by any means, without the prior permission of the copyright owner.

First published 2013 by Camden House
Reprinted in paperback 2015

Camden House is an imprint of Boydell & Brewer Inc.
668 Mt. Hope Avenue, Rochester, NY 14620, USA
www.camden-house.com
and of Boydell & Brewer Limited
PO Box 9, Woodbridge, Suffolk IP12 3DF, UK
www.boydellandbrewer.com

Paperback ISBN-13: 978-1-57113-937-5
Paperback ISBN-10: 1-57113-937-0
Hardcover ISBN-13: 978-1-57113-511-7
Hardcover ISBN-10: 1-57113-511-1

Library of Congress Cataloging-in-Publication Data

Mazzeno, Laurence W.
 Becoming John Updike: critical reception, 1958-2010 / Laurence W. Mazzeno.
   p. cm. — (Studies in American Literature and Culture: Literary Criticism in Perspective)
 Includes bibliographical references and index.
 ISBN-13: 978-1-57113-511-7 (hardcover : acid-free paper) —
 ISBN-10: 1-57113-511-1 (hardcover : acid-free paper)
  1. Updike, John—Criticism and interpretation. 2. Updike, John—Appreciation. I. Title.

PS3571.P4Z7825 2013
813'.54—dc23

2012045294

This publication is printed on acid-free paper.
Printed in the United States of America.

This book is dedicated to my colleagues in the English Department at Alvernia University, who were gracious enough to let someone who had "gone over to the Dark Side" back into the classroom where he could be reminded every week why he chose higher education as a profession.

Contents

Acknowledgments	ix
Introduction	1
1: Developing a Style, Experimenting with Form (1958–1967)	6
2: Making a Name on the National Scene (1968–1975)	27
3: Launching New Ventures (1976–1980)	50
4: Pulitzer Prize Winner, Vilified Misogynist (1981–1985)	67
5: Crowning Achievements (1986–1990)	90
6: Keeping Up the Pace (1991–1995)	114
7: America and Updike, Growing Old Together (1996–1999)	131
8: New Experiments in the New Century (2000–2004)	148
9: Facing the Unthinkable, Contemplating the Inevitable (2005–2008)	168
10: Final Volumes, Fresh Assessments (2009–)	182
Major Works by John Updike	195
Works Cited	197
Index	245

Acknowledgments

I MUST BEGIN by thanking Jim Walker and the editorial board at Camden House for endorsing my work once again. I would like to acknowledge also the cheerful support I have received from the staff at Alvernia University's Frank A. Franco Library, especially Roberta Rohrbach, who spent countless hours locating obscure materials and copying out reviews for a researcher who lives hundreds of miles away. Even in the age of the Internet, one cannot conduct responsible scholarship without the help of a great team of librarians.

Introduction

> *John Updike ... is probably the most significant young novelist in America.*
> —Peter Buitenhuis, 1963

> *In any reasonably discriminating age a young man of Mr. Updike's charming but limited gifts might expect to make his way in time to a position of some security in the second or just possibly the third rank of serious American novelists.*
> —John Aldridge, 1966

> *In Updike, one sees a certain cultural process in concentrated form: the accumulation of great formal, technical skill at one pole, and the severe weakening of the artist's understanding of history and social organization at the other.*
> —David Walsh, 2006

> *John Updike ... is certainly one of the great American novelists of the 20th century.*
> —Martin Amis, 2009

THESE FOUR STATEMENTS lay out the central problem I wish to tackle in *Becoming John Updike: Critical Reception, 1958–2010*. Both early and late in his career, Updike was a controversial figure in American letters: for some, a major voice in fiction, for others a pretentious mannerist who substituted florid stylistic flourishes for substantive insight. A cursory examination of a random selection of reviews listed in Jack De Bellis and Michael Broomfield's *John Updike: A Bibliography of Primary & Secondary Materials, 1948–2007* (2007) will confirm these generalizations. Certainly Updike is not the first writer to provoke widely divergent judgments among reviewers and the reading public, but the fact that he was recognized early by the academic community as a writer of some significance makes it worthwhile to see why these divergent judgments existed throughout Updike's career and how they may affect his future reputation.

Updike was no Herman Melville, toiling away on underappreciated masterpieces, dying an unrecognized genius. His early stories and verse were published in the *New Yorker*, where he worked as a staff writer between 1955 and 1957. Because he was, to a certain extent, a known commodity in literary circles, his first three books—a volume of poems, a collection of short stories, and the novel *The Poorhouse Fair*—were reviewed in widely read and respected newspapers and periodicals in America and abroad. In fact, despite some rather caustic criticisms, just a decade after Updike published his first book, some considered him one of America's premier writers. This is no idle claim. In 1969, in preparing a new edition of *This Is My Best*, veteran editor Whit Burnett (1970) asked successful authors to name the top one hundred living writers. Updike tied for eleventh place (with Truman Capote), behind giants like Tennessee Williams, Arthur Miller, John Steinbeck, and J. D. Salinger, but ahead of Katherine Anne Porter, John Dos Passos, James Baldwin, Saul Bellow, Bernard Malamud, and Norman Mailer. Perhaps most notable, Updike was one of only two writers under age forty (Edward Albee being the other) who made the Top Twenty.

Updike is one of the few writers to have his work reviewed in both popular women's magazines like *Vogue* and *Mademoiselle* and the scholarly journal *Foreign Affairs* (Whitaker 1979). At the same time, defying the trend for popular authors to be either ignored or dismissed by academics, Updike was recognized early in his career as a writer to be taken seriously. Clarke Taylor's *John Updike: A Bibliography*, published in 1968, lists a surprisingly large number of critical commentaries already available. B. A. Sokoloff and David Arnason's 1971 volume *John Updike: A Comprehensive Bibliography* and Michael Olivas's *An Annotated Bibliography of John Updike Criticism, 1967–1973* (1975) reveal the rapid pace at which criticism on Updike was being published. Perhaps most remarkable is the fact that, less than two decades after he began publishing, Updike was either the principal subject of, or a major figure discussed in, a dozen doctoral dissertations—although whether this is a credit to the quality of Updike's work or a sign of the times in academe is open to debate.

The work of these early bibliographers is extended in Jack De Bellis's *John Updike: A Bibliography, 1967–1993* (1994) and the monumental bibliography compiled by De Bellis and Michael Broomfield cited above, which lists nearly six thousand books, articles, reviews, and dissertations published between 1958 and 2007. A quick Google search, coupled with a glance at the Library of Congress catalog, reveals no slow-down since that date. In fact, a flurry of commentary appeared in 2009, the year Updike died. Much of this material is merely eulogistic, but that does not take away from the imposing fact that Updike was for his entire writing life the subject of intense scrutiny by reviewers and academic critics alike. At the same time, Updike seemed to pay attention to what others thought of him. That is not to say that he wrote simply to please the reviewers, but both directly (in his public and private comments) and indirectly (in the subjects of his novels and stories), Updike engaged in dialogue with reviewers and academic critics as his career progressed. *Becoming John Updike: Critical Reception, 1958–2010* is in part a record of the way Updike's career and reputation was shaped by contemporary commentary—a record of how he "became" the "John Updike" that, at his death, was almost universally hailed as a major voice in American literature.

Of course, the central question one must ask now that Updike has died is: "Will he last?" This book is based on the belief that he will. I agree with Andrew Rosenheim (2009), who observed just days after Updike's death that "the best of his novels" make him "one of a handful of American writers whose work in the second half of the last century will be read in the second half of this one." I think many of his short stories, selections from his nonfiction, and even some of his poetry will also continue to attract readers, especially academics interested in American literature and culture.

The aim of this book is to trace the growth of Updike's reputation and examine the reasons for his success. Because nearly everything I cover was written while Updike was alive, I have examined not only criticism in academic journals, but also reviews and assessments in periodicals and newspapers. This dual focus is undertaken with the clear recognition that reviewers and authors of academic studies have different aims. The successful reviewer is out to convince readers that a book or author is worth their time—particularly their leisure time—while an academic is more likely to approach a text to determine its aesthetic or cultural value. On the other hand, distinguishing between a "review" and a "critical article" is sometimes difficult. A surprisingly large number of reviews of Updike's work were written by academics, and even ones by journalists contain a good bit of critical commentary. In examining both kinds of documents, I have tried to address the following questions: Why did Updike's work appeal to critics early and throughout his career? When and why did he become a figure of controversy? How have changes in critical practice affected attitudes toward Updike's fiction?

I must also explain what this book does *not* do. First I don't attempt to summarize everything written about Updike's work. Doing so would produce a book too large and unwieldy to be of any use in assessing trends. I have routinely ignored notices, but often pay attention to brief reviews that comment on Updike's promise when he was young, or enduring value as he grew older. However, my decision to omit a work does not reflect on its quality, nor are briefly summarized works of less value to Updike scholars than shorter pieces that get more ink. Quite often I have omitted works when including commentary from frequent reviewers of Updike's work, especially when their judgments were consistent over time. Hence, one will not find mention of every review by Michiko Kakutani or William Pritchard, but I hope from the many that are included readers will get a sense of how these reviewers viewed Updike's accomplishments. Also, with rare exceptions, I have not included commentary from reviewers and scholars outside the English-speaking world. I have also chosen not to cover movie and television adaptations of Updike's fiction.

Although I was tempted (and encouraged) to explore another line of "commentary" on Updike's work, I have elected not to examine the responses to Updike's fiction that appear in the creative work of other novelists and short-story writers. Unquestionably, Updike has had an influence, positive or negative, on both his contemporaries and succeeding generations of writers. Some of them—Philip Roth, Norman Mailer, Joyce Carol Oates, David Foster Wallace, and Nicholson Baker, for example—reviewed Updike's work, and their observations are included where appropriate. What I have not done is attempt to trace the way Updike has helped shape the themes or styles of these and other writers whose work owes a debt to him. That would have made this book considerably longer and might have taken the focus off my principal objective, which is to show how Updike's reputation has been shaped by reviewers and critics. I suspect that a study of his influence on other writers would necessitate an entire new book.

What may be more controversial is my decision to forego lengthy analysis of many critiques of individual works in order to provide some sense of the scope of critical commentary. On occasion I have devoted two or three pages to a single work that is seminal (the Hamiltons' first books on Updike) or notably controversial (Frederick Crews's 1986 review essay), or written by someone who has come to be widely recognized as an expert on Updike (Donald Greiner or James Schiff, for example). My hope is that the selections I have included are representative of what was written at a particular point in time. I have also refrained from providing my own lengthy analyses of individual reviews and critical commentaries, desiring instead to let my readers get a sense of what these commentators have said directly from them. Where appropriate, however, I have made observations about ways critical practices prevalent at the time these critiques were written may have influenced judgments about Updike's work.

That brings me to my next point. I have organized the volume chronologically, partly to conform to the guidelines of the Literary Criticism in Perspective series, but also to demonstrate what I would describe as an ongoing conversation among reviewers and critics trying to make sense of Updike's contributions to literature and culture. This is certainly not the first study of Updike's reputation, but those that precede mine have examined Updike's writings while he was still alive and publishing; the chance existed that what he might do in the future would change critical opinion. Now that Updike is dead, unless his widow or his heirs uncover a blockbuster manuscript among his papers, we can be fairly certain that we have the entire corpus upon which we can now make judgments. In *Becoming John Updike: Critical Reception, 1958–2010* I hope to give my readers a sense of why Updike mattered to his first readers and critics, so that those who study his work in the future will have a sense of how we—not a royal "we" but an inclusive one, as I, too, was Updike's contemporary—judged him while he was alive.

1: Developing a Style, Experimenting with Form (1958–1967)

JOHN UPDIKE HAD THE DISTINCTION of being reviewed early and often.[1] It may be debated whether that was good or bad for a budding writer feeling his way through multiple genres to discover his voice and his message. It seems likely, however, that early notices of *The Poorhouse Fair* and *Rabbit, Run* made Updike realize he had chosen the right profession. It may also have convinced Knopf to continue as his publisher—no mean feat, when so many aspiring writers who land a contract with a major publisher discover to their chagrin that poor sales of a first book ends that relationship quickly. Early recognition no doubt affected what Updike chose to write and publish, especially as critics expressed growing dissatisfaction with what might be called the preciousness of his work. For a decade, reviewers urged him to be less myopic, introspective, and autobiographical, encouraging him instead to engage with major social issues. One might call the first ten years of Updike criticism the "decade of promise and anticipation"—promise generated by a style that even Updike's harshest critics recognized as special, anticipation generated by the hope that he would finally publish a novel whose subject would be worthy of his great facility with language.

Poems, Stories, Novel: 1958–1959

Updike's first published volume, *The Carpentered Hen and Other Tame Creatures*, was brought out by Harper in 1958 in the United States, and in 1959 in England under the title *Hoping for a Hoopoe*. Reviews in more than a dozen newspapers and periodicals offered genteel praise for Updike's talent as a purveyor of light verse (Osborne 1958) capable of amusing and delighting any reader "who doesn't want to work at poetry but merely to enjoy it" (Hough 1958, 12). Only a handful noted that he displays maturity of technique and ability to find substance in the trivial and mundane (cf. McCord 1958), or that his ephemera mask a serious and original poet who may well be heard from again (Bogan [1959] 1983, 256).

The following year Updike published his first novel, *The Poorhouse Fair*. It was also his first book with the firm Alfred A. Knopf. That relationship lasted for the remainder of Updike's career. Knopf was a respected New York publishing house, which may account in part for the many reviews that appeared on both sides of the Atlantic. The novel made the *New York Times* bestseller list during the week of February 8, at fourteenth place behind *Doctor Zhivago* (first), *Lolita* (second), *Exodus* (third), and a half-dozen works by then-popular authors like Frances Parkinson Keyes and Mary Renault.

No one made any claims that *The Poorhouse Fair* was light reading, although several reviewers saw the novel's comic aspects. Generally, those who thought highly of it praised Updike's exceptional facility with language and his ability to get outside himself to create this fiction—here was a twenty-six year old author writing confidently about old age. It was hailed as "a rare and beautiful achievement" (Chase 1959, 3), an "elegantly wrought little gem" (Corbett 1959, 30), a novel whose "intellectual imagination and great charity" mark it unquestionably as "a work of art" (Barr 1959, 4). One enthusiastic reviewer described it as "a first novel of assurance and achievement: truthful, perceptive and coloured by a spirit of sad, unillusioned comedy, perfectly in keeping with the subject of old age" ("Ways of the World" 1959, 157). Impressed by Updike's novelistic skills, Whitney Balliett ([1959] 1982) says he possesses "a poet's sensitivity for language" (42) and has avoided writing "a thinly veiled, self-purgative catalogue of an author's adolescence" that characterizes so many first novels. Phoebe Adams (1959) considers the novel "a well-controlled, neatly constructed study," written with "great clarity" and exceptional "precision of language" (101). Richard Gilman is even more euphoric, claiming that "what Updike has held lovingly and explored in his hand" is "more worthy to be made known than all the paper towers and dragons of our hyperbolic age" ([1959] 1983, 259).

Praise for *The Poorhouse Fair* was tempered by some who, like Granville Hicks, expressed reservations about Updike's trying to do too much with his brief tale. Nonetheless, Hicks believes the novel gives "some cause for hope" that Updike will produce something even more substantial in the future ([1959] 1970, 109). Fanny Butcher (1959), too, says that, although the novel's structure appears haphazard, Updike's "brilliant use of words" and "subtle observations" show great promise. Someday "we surely will have a really important book" from him (IV: 4). The notion that a great novel lay hidden somewhere inside Updike, just waiting to be written, became a cliché that lasted more than a decade.

However, several negative reviews of *The Poorhouse Fair* came from writers associated with the Jewish intellectual establishment. A word of caution is in order at this point, though. A careful look at the review by Norman Podhoretz (1959), a critic often cited as a leading figure among Updike's early detractors, suggests that Podhortez's reaction to Updike's first novel was more balanced than later commentators have suggested. Barely two years older than Updike, Podhoretz may have found the extraordinary praise being heaped on his younger contemporary hard to swallow. Calling Updike a "talented young writer," Podhoretz finds *The Poorhouse Fair* marred by "Mandarin elegance" (42), and chastises Updike for refusing to deal seriously with the problems that the story raises. Somewhat archly, Podhoretz suggests that "the last thing Mr. Updike wants is to get exercised over anything." If Updike is to become a good novelist, "he will have to give up his easy Olympian superiority and take the risk of defining his stand" (43). Blunt advice, perhaps, but hardly caustic. Actually David Fitelson (1959), author of the first of what would be a long string of negative assessments of Updike's fiction in *Commentary*, is more dismissive. Describing *The Poorhouse Fair* as "a heartfelt but not very successful try at a first novel" (275), Fitelson complains that Updike manages to expose quite a number of problems but is unable to deal with "ideas and the problems that ideas create" (276). Ironically, in 1960 Updike received the Richard and Hinda Rosenthal Family Foundation Award, then a prize of $5,000 awarded to a young novelist for a book of exceptional literary merit published in the previous year.

Updike's first collection of stories, *The Same Door*, also published in 1959, was not reviewed as widely as his novel, but on the whole was favorably received. Updike was again cited as a writer of great promise. William Peden (1959) believes this collection is "a significant book by a very talented young writer, as solid as it is refreshing" (5). Although Robert Healey (1959) finds the stories "somewhat less impressive" than *The Poorhouse Fair*, they show evidence of "the same sure ear for nuances and dialogue and style." While Updike's fiction may not suit everyone's taste, Healy thinks he is "definitely a highly individual talent" (3). However, Milton Crane (1959) warns that, while these stories exhibit "the same remarkable sensitivity and restrained, poetic eloquence that characterize all [Updike's] work," readers may find it hard to become interested in his characters, who sometimes "seem to be in great need of something to occupy them" (B3). This criticism would become a frequent refrain.

Three responses to *The Same Door* published in British weeklies give some idea of Updike's early reception across the Atlantic. David Lodge (1962) praises Updike's ability "to communicate the quality of a whole life in a few pages," and compares his method to that of James Joyce (628). Richard Mayne (1962) likes the stories but says he could not help being "haunted by a feeling of *déjà vu*" because of the remarkable similarities among them (606). Mayne also notes perceptively that many of Updike's stories "implicitly criticize" the American lifestyle (607). The reviewer for the *Times Literary Supplement* ("Fragments of America" 1962) is put off by how much Updike shows the effects of writing for the *New Yorker*, which forces a kind of false consistency on his work. The reviewer also notices something that would be a signature of Updike's work throughout his career: "The success of these stories seems to depend on a catching of the exact nuances of American scene and dialogue." While these qualities might put an English reviewer "at a disadvantage when judging them" (277), they would become increasingly more characteristic of Updike's fiction as his career advanced.

The Angst-Filled Anti-Hero: *Rabbit, Run*, 1960

Where *The Poorhouse Fair* received polite, if tempered, praise from people who thought Updike showed promise of greater work, *Rabbit, Run* (1960) was greeted with enthusiasm by many and a good deal of skepticism by others. Like its predecessor, *Rabbit, Run* reached an audience larger than most serious fiction, appearing on the *New York Times* bestseller list sporadically between late November 1960 and March 1961. More important for this study, however, the novel was the first to prompt widely different opinions of Updike's talent and potential. Therefore, it seems worthwhile to look at a number of reviews in some detail to understand the reasons for the controversy and identify the critical principles that would be used to judge Updike in the future.

Typical of those who found the book appealing is David Boroff ([1960] 1983), who calls *Rabbit, Run* "moving and often brilliant" (259), a "notable triumph of intelligence and compassion" with "none of the glib condescension that spoils so many books of this type" (260–61). Of course, Boroff admits, the "treatment of sex" cannot be ignored; while Updike's explicit descriptions are intended to expose "the psychic underside of sexuality," certain passages are likely to "shock the prudish" (262). Looking back over half a century, one might wonder what the fuss was all about. But in 1960, Updike's graphic descriptions posed special problems for critics and readers accustomed to more oblique descriptions of sexual activity.

The reviewer for the Roman Catholic publication *America* ("Run from Rabbit" 1960) was certainly among those shocked at Updike's frank portrayal of sex. Although *America* would eventually publish numerous positive critiques of Updike's work, its 1960 review of *Rabbit, Run* was among the most searing assessments of Updike's talent. Insisting that "style is not the only norm for judging books," the reviewer zeroes in on Updike's treatment of sex, calling it "revoltingly gratuitous, obsessively all-pervading and restless until it can sink to descriptions of perversion" (257). Additionally, Rabbit's refusal to take responsibility for his actions makes him unworthy of readers' time or sympathy. The reviewer urges critics to stop praising Updike's felicitous style, which is merely "precious and self-conscious," and instead "cut him down to size a bit by asking what his gorgeous prose is trying to say." In this novel, the prose says "a nasty nothing" (258).

Echoing these sentiments, Frank McGuiness (1961) calls *Rabbit, Run* just another "sour-tasting novel" that "sees life as a futile drag relieved by a series of satisfactory orgasms" (439). Elizabeth Hardwick (1961), however, expresses markedly different concerns about the treatment of sex in the novel. Anticipating Norman Mailer's critique of Updike for exploiting sex without trying to explore the nature of sexual relationships, Hardwick criticizes him for not having figured out how to use graphic descriptions of sexual activity for some aesthetic purpose. Ironically, the ecumenical *Christian Century*'s reviewer, Alfred Klausler (1961), urges Christians who might be put off by the explicit treatment of sex in *Rabbit, Run* to read the novel anyway. Despite the "startling," sometimes "clinical and scabrous detailing of the sexual act," the novel displays Updike's "prophetic voice crying brutally and coarsely in our stainless steel wilderness." Those who "have comfortable feelings about American life" will no doubt be disturbed by the novel (246).

Some caviled about Updike's handling of his materials, criticizing his overreliance on literary tradition (Southern 1960) and on evocations of pity to capture and hold readers' attention and sympathy (N. Miller 1961). J. M. Edelstein (1960) complains that, though "an interesting and exciting book" with a protagonist representative of a certain class of young Americans, *Rabbit, Run* "is not quite believable as a novel." Edelstein is also disappointed by Updike's failure to inspire: "A novel should tell us something not only of the human condition but also of human aspiration." That message is absent in *Rabbit, Run*, and readers should expect more from someone who has already become "a figure to watch in American letters" (17).

Criticisms like Edelstein's balance those which offer virtually unadulterated praise for *Rabbit, Run*. Joan Didion (1961) calls it "a pleasure, an original, a piece of sharp, controlled, *written* fiction" in which Rabbit "runs for good" in his innocent belief that he will find something better away from where he is (55). Whitney Balliett (1960) claims the novel is proof that Updike can write "poetic prose" and that he possesses "an X-ray imagination" (222). The *Times Literary Supplement* reviewer ("Enemies of Promise" 1961) describes *Rabbit, Run* as "a small-town tragedy" in which Updike has captured "the contemporary American dilemma" (648). Similarly, Richard Foster (1961) calls it "absorbing, serious, painful," a "beautiful rendering of man's self-entrapment" and a "memorable" account of "our obese American life of the fifties and sixties." Foster believes Updike is "an original in the best sense" (149).

Not only was *Rabbit, Run* praised as a fine novel in its own right; some thought it the best indication yet of Updike's potential. Granville Hicks calls it an improvement over *The Poorhouse Fair* because Updike has not tried to make the story carry a larger political message. Looking back over Updike's career to date, Hicks offers the confident judgment that "Updike has to be regarded as one of our important young novelists, a powerful writer with his own vision of the world" ([1960] 1970, 113). Similarly, while using his review of *Rabbit, Run* to defend Updike from charges of irrelevancy and triviality, Richard Gilman suggests that the novel is in tune with the times in its failure to offer grand solutions to human dilemmas. It is both "a grotesque allegory of American life, with its myth of happiness and success, its dangerous innocence and crippling antagonism between value and fact" and "a minor epic of the spirit thirsting for room to discover and *be* itself" ([1960] 1979, 15–16). Certainly, Gilman suggests, from a writer this capable so early in his career, much could be expected in the future.

Experimentation and Critical Reaction: 1961–1963

Updike's second collection of stories, *Pigeon Feathers* (1962), was reviewed almost as extensively as *Rabbit, Run* and produced the same level of controversy. Praise came from distinguished writers like Joan Didion (1962) and Granville Hicks, who says *Pigeon Feathers* shows that Updike, "growing steadily in stylistic power, in architectural skill, and in depth of feeling," is not "merely talented" but "bold, resourceful, and intensely serious" ([1962] 1970, 113). Bruce Cook (1962) feels these stories display "subtlety and depth of perception," and will further solidify Updike's "golden reputation" (186). The "sense of excitement in Updike's prose" convinces William Hogan (1962) that "along with Salinger" he seems to be "the talent to bet on" (39).

A more balanced assessment is provided by Christopher Ricks (1963), who notes rather shrewdly that, like much Victorian fiction, many of Updike's stories deal with "the loss of faith, and fear of death" (208). But Ricks thinks Updike often is unable to provide closure or depict places other than those he knows well from personal experience. Mary Ellen Chase (1962) expresses annoyance that Updike's verbal histrionics sometimes get in the way of communicating with readers. "Readers want to read and think, to be led to new understandings and perceptions," she says. "They don't want to be frustrated by cryptic and annoying words and images" (4). That sentiment is echoed by the reviewer for the *Times Literary Supplement* ("Bigger and Better" 1963) who says it is unfortunate that Updike has always been bedeviled by cleverness; "the least happy feature of his work remains a straining after effect in the writing, as if in an attempt to make this compensate for thinness of matter" (73).

More serious criticisms were aimed at the collection and at Updike himself. J. M. Edelstein (1962) complains that, as rewarding as these stories are, reading Updike can be "terribly frustrating, as if either something were missing or there was too much of a good thing" (30). Though Updike is a master at "exploring the mysteries of the commonplace," these stories leave

Edelstein "troubled" because they hint at "things unsaid" and a "sureness that smacks of slickness" (31). Edelstein thinks Updike is capable of more. Stanley Rowland (1962), however, is not so sure about Updike's potential. While acknowledging Updike's "fine craftsmanship and sharp perception," he finds all Updike's fiction displays a "littleness of perception" that stems from a severely limited vision of life (840).

Alfred Chester (1962) is even more caustic. Though Updike may be a competent writer, much of his prose simply gives "the impression that something important and of uncanny depth is happening"; but "I can assure you," Chester says, "nothing is being said" (77). Updike is not wholly responsible for his failings, however; the villains responsible for his sad performance are the *New Yorker* and Sigmund Freud. Captivated by the *New Yorker*'s "concept of the human being" derived from Freud as "essentially psychoanalytical," Updike sees humankind as trivial (78). The smarmy prose "reduces everyone to the size of a sacrificial lamb" (79–80). Chester thinks it a shame that a writer of Updike's talent should "lavish such craft upon these worthless tales" (80). While not as savage, Stanley Hyman (1962) modifies his initial judgment of Updike as "the most gifted young writer in America" (22) with a litany of faults. "He publishes too much." He "falls into cuteness when he has nothing to say." He is too subjective. His characters "fall into neat dichotomies." Though he has "a first-rate intelligence," considerable learning, impressive honesty, and "a true creative imagination," he needs to "slow down," "stay backstage," and "choose larger subjects and shape them more fully." If he would only do so, he "cannot help becoming a major writer" (23).

Perhaps the most balanced review of the book, and the most significant assessment of Updike's strengths and weaknesses at this time, is Arthur Mizener's ([1962] 1982). He calls Updike "the most talented writer of his age in America," but sees this gift as a curse as well. Because Updike is so facile with language, he sometimes lets wit take precedence over insight. Mizener is among the first to point out that Updike is essentially a romantic, who shares with other American romantics "an irresistible impulse to go in memory home again in order to find himself" (46). Mizener also suggests that Updike's focus on matters of organized religion are merely "accidents of his subject matter," and that his real interest in religion lies deeper, in the "religious sense of the sacredness of life itself" (47).

Updike returned to the novel in 1963. Possibly because *Rabbit, Run* had brought him attention—and notoriety—*The Centaur* sold well, appeared in the top ten on the *New York Times* bestseller list for ten weeks, and was reviewed in more than a hundred publications. Although Updike described the novel as a companion piece to *Rabbit, Run*, few reviewers bothered to read it from that perspective. Instead, most concentrated on Updike's experiment in imposing a mythological framework on a realistic tale. The obvious parallels to James Joyce's *Ulysses* were duly noted, but critics were hardly united in declaring Updike's attempt a success. Once again, the swelling chorus of praise for his talent was balanced by less effusive commentary that pointed out defects in construction, and by negative critiques that highlighted what some reviewers considered Updike's more general shortcomings—and the blindness of those who either failed to notice them or willfully ignored them.

One reviewer who has strong positive feelings about the novel, Charlotte Armstrong (1963), rhapsodizes about it as "a flood of sensory impressions" in which "style takes you by the nape of your neck, pushes your nose down into the story until you cannot lift your head" (M16). Granville Hicks considers it "a brilliant achievement" ([1963b] 1970, 119) in which Updike demonstrates "a mastery of language" that is "matched in our time only by the finest poets" (117). Preston Roberts (1963) calls Updike "a young and gifted writer who in his work has been managing more and more successfully to combine humor, realism, poetry and a profoundly tragic sense of life" (463). Similarly, in the first of what would be a long series of reviews of Updike's work, Edmund Fuller (1963a) claims *The Centaur* is "finer" and "more demanding" than *Rabbit, Run* (14).

The novel received favorable notice in academic journals as well. In the *Hudson Review* Roger Sale (1963) describes it as an advance over Updike's earlier work and calls George Caldwell "the largest, most interesting, and most novelistic character Updike has created." Though Updike still tends to overwrite and load down his work with set pieces, *The Centaur* gives evidence that Updike "may soon be not only a good writer but a superlative novelist" (147). The *Sewanee Review* also carried a critique of *The Centaur*—the first published commentary on Updike by Jack De Bellis (1964), who would become a leading Updike scholar. Reviewing eight recently published works, including Mary McCarthy's *The Group* and John Fowles's *The Collector*, De Bellis does not mince words in declaring Updike's novel the best of the lot (535).

The most controversial aspect of *The Centaur* proved to be its mythological superstructure. Some reviewers expressed admiration for Updike's use of myth to lend *gravitas* to his contemporary tale (Davenport 1963; "A Mythical Animal" 1963; Curley 1963), while Renata Adler ([1963] 1982) appreciates Updike's ability to work simultaneously in the realms of myth and realistic fiction, only occasionally allowing his exceptional "stylistic virtuosity" to impede the progress of his narrative (52). On the other hand, Peter Buitenhuis (1963) does not believe Updike has melded the mythological framework onto his story with particular skill. Nevertheless, this novel demonstrates that "Updike is boldly experimenting as he develops" and "confirm[s] the impression that he is probably the most significant young novelist in America" (26). However, several reviewers agree with Harold Gardiner (1963), who finds that Updike's use of myth "gets in the way of a really poignant story that could have stood much more firmly on its own feet" (340).

Other reviewers raised different objections, calling attention to what some would cite consistently as general failures in Updike's canon. Robert Taubman (1963) considers *The Centaur* a competent, sometimes brilliant mythic novel in the tradition of Joyce, but is bothered by the ordinariness of George Caldwell, who is really just a little man "ennobled" and "inflat[ed] into grandeur." In an otherwise fine novel, this kind of "sentimentality," Taubman says, is "like an organic lesion," even if well disguised (406). Vereen Bell (1963) complains about Updike's muddled presentation of theme. The myth may be intended to redeem George Caldwell from "the sad anonymity" to which he is "doomed" in life (71), but Updike fails to make his intentions clear, and as a consequence "*The Centaur* fails in its purpose" (72). Even less generous is Jonathan Miller (1963), who thinks Updike's heavy-handed use of allegory and stylistic virtuosity get in the way of what could have been a fine human-interest story.

Was this Updike's breakthrough novel, the "big one" that critics had been predicting since the publication of *The Poorhouse Fair*? Stanley Hyman ([1963] 1966), who had observed in his review of *Rabbit, Run* that Updike seemed on the verge of writing such a work, does not think so. Still, he concedes, it is "a bold and ambitious break" with naturalist fiction and "a big step forward" (128). Updike's ability to write "magical, incandescent" language gives Hyman the confidence that he will be reading a major work by him in the near future (132). On the other hand, Roderick Nordell (1963) is not convinced that there will ever be such a novel. While *The Centaur* provides Updike a chance to display "the much-praised virtues of his prose," it also reveals some of his "characteristic shortcomings—a certain preciousness, a fondness for the over-elaborate image, diminishing the force of an exactly right one nearby," and—a point worth noting—"an immature determination to spell out the dirty words and be lushly 'poetical' in erotic description" (7).

Three additional assessments of the novel, representative of a group which did not find Updike worthy of the praise he was receiving, reinforce Nordell's criticisms. Orville Prescott (1963) deplores the imposition of the mythological superstructure, which he finds little more than an example of "useless ingenuity" and "pretentious experimentation." Much of *The Centaur* is "marvelously dull," and only Updike's skill is able to make a few parts worth reading. Prescott wishes Updike would "stop posturing" and refrain from interjecting himself between reader and characters. Prescott also takes issue with the "numerous obscenities" in the book—"no more loathsome than in many recent novels," he admits, "but entirely unnecessary" (7). Richard Gilman identifies two major faults that stretch across all Updike's novels: his extreme self-absorption and his unwillingness to deal with the important issues that truly great artists tackle, "suffering, struggle, conflict, disaster, and death" ([1963] 1970, 63). Instead, Updike writes around them, substituting highly polished prose for real substance, deflecting readers from confronting significant issues that are hinted at but not given imaginative life in his fiction.

Unquestionably, the most negative review of *The Centaur*—and the most frequently cited early attack on Updike's fiction—is Norman Podhoretz's "A Dissent on Updike" ([1963] 1964). Podhoretz not only excoriates the novel for its thin story line, lack of character motivation, and clumsy imposition of Greek myth on a realistic story, but also goes on to list the reasons why he dislikes Updike's fiction. "Puzzled" by the "high reputation" Updike enjoyed after publishing only a handful of novels and stories, Podhoretz claims Updike has "no mind at all" (251); the "sentimentality" of his tales is somehow "legitimized by the veneer" of his "literary sophistication" (252). Podhoretz is at a loss to understand why respected critics and writers have such high regard for Updike, a writer who "has very little to say and whose authentic emotional range is so narrow and thin" that it may simply be ascribed as "limited to a rather timid nostalgia for the confusions of youth." Certainly, Podhoretz concludes, on the "list of the many inflated literary reputations" created in recent years, "Updike's name belongs somewhere very near the top" (257).

Podhoretz's review suggests that lines were hardening with respect to Updike's merits as a novelist. In *Waiting for the End* (1964), Leslie Fiedler, one of the most influential literary critics of the day, dismisses Updike as "that *New Yorker* writer much touted recently by those who want the illusion of vision and fantasy without surrendering the kind of reassurance provided by slick writing at its most professionally *all right*" (164). Those who found Updike's fiction compelling tended to dismiss such attacks. An example of that attitude can be seen in J. A. Ward's (1963) comments on *The Centaur*, published after many reviews had already appeared. Ward respectfully acknowledges the debate over the merits of this novel and Updike's fiction in general before launching into a lengthy and highly laudatory assessment of *The Centaur*. It is "undoubtedly Updike's finest book and a superlative novel in its own right," in which "the craft and the vision are completely of a piece" (110). The mythic method is employed with considerable skill; only when Updike "tries to show his characters in the process of changing" does the work become less than satisfactory (113). Otherwise, Ward says, the novel contains "many virtues, and they are of a kind rarely encountered in contemporary fiction" (114). Apparently members of the publishing industry agreed. In 1964 *The Centaur* received the National Book Award for Fiction.

Working in All Genres: 1963–1966

In comparison to his early novels, Updike's second collection of verse, *Telephone Poles and Other Poems* (1963), went virtually unnoticed. Slightly more than a dozen contemporary reviews offered polite praise for the volume (Lask 1963, "Rustic and Urbane" 1964); only a handful offered mild criticisms (Ricks 1964). However, the poet X. J. Kennedy (1963) says that while the volume contains "much trivia," it also "shows Updike to be on occasion a poet of rare depth and competence" (10). Edmund Fuller (1963b) claims *Telephone Poles* demonstrates that "Updike, already an important writer of his generation in prose fiction, may have the happy option of being an important poet, too" (15). When Updike brought out *Verse* (1965), a combination of his first two volumes of poetry, J. R. Adams (1965) observed that "the very restricted vision which imperils [Updike] as a novelist serves him admirably as a poet," and suggested his "diaphousness verse" has "something of its own wisdom" (A26).

Updike's next publication, *Assorted Prose* (1965), generated considerable commentary for a first collection of previously published nonfiction. Richard Mayne (1966) finds these essays "very high quality" (169), although he admits the work may not be to everyone's taste. Others judged some of the essays first-rate ("Updike, Lettrist" 1966) and deemed the collection valuable for its "quality" and its "compass" (Rogers 1965, 3). However, more than one reviewer found *Assorted Prose* disappointing, objecting to Updike's apparent willingness to shift his ground in order to be entertaining ("That Long Atlantic Crossing" 1966), or resurrecting the oft-rehearsed complaint that his "free-flowing but spare writing style" often "overshadows his subject matter" (Linford 1965, W9). Finding that the "voice" that comes through sounds too much like boiler-plate *New Yorker* prose, Jane Kay (1965) offers a recommendation that others would echo in the coming years: it would be better, she says, if "a primary author" like Updike would "publish only his foremost endeavors" (9).

However, in a rather tendentious defense of Updike prompted by the publication of *Assorted Prose*, Eliot Fremont-Smith (1965) suggests that critics' real problem with Updike is that "he is not an exotic. He is burdened with being, among other things, American, white, Protestant, and heterosexual" (39). Adding to their distaste is Updike's choice of subject matter—the ordinary activities of everyday people. And yet, Fremont-Smith insists, Updike handles his materials with seriousness and sensitivity, exploring "the extraordinary act of living" in a way that makes his works as exciting as any adventure story (39).

Updike's next novel, *Of the Farm* (1965), failed to crack the top ten on the *New York Times* bestseller list. Nevertheless, it generated the same sort of mixed reaction that greeted other works by Updike. The novel also prompted one of the most savage attacks on Updike and those critics who claimed his work had lasting value.

No one was more enthusiastic about *Of the Farm* than Peter Buitenhuis (1965): "When a book like this comes along, a critic must, before attempting anything else, raise his voice in a halloo of praise." Updike has "achieved a sureness of touch, a suppleness of style and a subtlety of vision that is gained by few writers of fiction" (4). The novel is "very clearly and very completely, a small masterpiece" (34). Roderick Cook (1966) calls it "an excellent book" that demonstrates Updike's triple talents: "the painter's eye for form, line and color; the poet's ear for metaphor; and the storyteller's knack for 'and then what happened next?'" (100). Wesley Kort (1966) says the novel presents the same human problem Updike deals with in all his fiction, "maintaining an alternative to deprivation and death." Updike performs the role of a "sacramentalist" in this work, giving us his "confession of debt to a concrete reality, his mother of the farm" (82). Florence Casey (1965) believes Updike shows considerable skill in handling a difficult theme, the "problematic aspect of freedom" that arises when one attempts to assert one's own freedom without impinging on another's. Casey may be in a minority, however, in suggesting that his style "appears almost too direct in comparison to the allusive zigzag that is now the common approach to description." Updike's "simplicity will probably require some readaptation of focus," she says, but "the book merits the effort since the verbal rhythms are easy and dazzling while the word is always proximate to the thing described" (15).

Nevertheless, once again several reviewers complained that Updike had achieved another small success only by remaining in his comfort zone (cf. "Mother's Boy" 1966, Culligan 1965). However, Granville Hicks thinks it wrong to ask Updike to tackle a great subject; one should instead appreciate a "sound novel" ([1965] 1970, 126) on a "small, manageable theme" (124). Yet even Hicks admits that, while he prefers "Updike's modest success to the messes some of his more ambitious colleagues have made," if Updike did "find a mighty theme and mastered it, I should rejoice" (126). Anthony Burgess concurs, citing as a special strength Updike's "willingness to let language draw our attention from his narrative" as a sign that "language means something to him" ([1966] 1982, 57). Books like *Of the Farm* create for Burgess a sense of great expectation—a feeling that Updike is about to break through from his small, limited successes to write an important book that will "justify [his] linguistic extravagance" and "exploitation of myth" (58).

Among those less enamored with the novel, Richard Sullivan (1965) finds it "oddly ineffectual" and "brilliantly weak." While "technically superb," it is "substantially disappointing," proof that "technique in itself, however exciting, is never enough" (6). Roger Sale (1966) believes

Updike is "badly in need of a new subject," as he seems to have exhausted the imaginative possibilities of his hometown and region. No reviewer can pretend, Sale says, that this novel is interesting; in fact, it "just manages to avoid falling into the class of the short but interminable" (129).

The most strident attack sparked by *Of the Farm* came from John Aldridge ([1966] 1987), who uses his review as an occasion to offer a scathing rebuke of the entire Updike corpus. Calling Updike one of those writers "around whom we have generated a flamboyance of celebrity quite out of keeping with the value of anything they have so far written" (9), Aldridge savages each of the novels in turn. *The Poorhouse Fair* is a dated, thin piece in which Updike substitutes excessive writing for substance. In *Rabbit, Run* Updike fails "to come to fresh imaginative grips with his materials" (11). Updike "must have been alone among living writers" to suppose he could create interest by "juxtaposing ancient myth and contemporary fact in fiction" as he does in *The Centaur* (11). *Of the Farm* is substantively bankrupt. In Aldridge's opinion, Updike "does not have an interesting mind," nor does he possess "remarkable narrative gifts or a distinguished style" (9). Only his descriptive prose is competent. But he possesses the vice of needing to write, and he continues to practice it despite having "nothing to say" (13).

As the foregoing discussion indicates, consensus on Updike's achievement was far from established. The root of the controversy reveals as much about reviewers as it does about Updike. Those who came with preconceptions about fiction either discovered a strong new proponent of contemporary realism, or simply another pretender using technique to mask his unwillingness or inability to deal with important issues. "The word on John Updike is not yet in," writes Joseph Epstein in 1965. "Thus far he remains a victim of the kiss-and-kick system of American reviewing" (23).

Updike followed *Of The Farm* with his third collection of stories, *The Music School* (1966). Although the volume was generally well received, one can sense the growing discontent among critics with Updike's apparent unwillingness to deal with what they considered larger subjects. Of course, some praised the collection highly (Weeks 1966), but qualified praise was more common. Bernard Bergonzi (1967) says that, although Updike is "too gifted for his work to be treated with anything other than respect," these stories seem too formulaic and the language "narcissistic" (28). Josephine Jacobsen (1966) observes that Updike frequently "pois[es] his story at the exact point where fiction meets fable and poetry." When done well, a story "becomes marvelously reinforced and luminous"; when done poorly, however, "a poetically brilliant metaphor" can overshadow the story line. Richard Hubler (1966) is impressed with Updike's "uncanny skill in choosing words" and "erect[ing] a mosaic full of small philological delights" through the use of colorful details. Yet Updike "does not choose to use the supreme gift of selective emphasis," and as a result his work seems to be less effective or moving than it might be (M28).

The major complaint about *The Music School* centered on Updike's failure to take risks in his writing. Some reviewers were circumspect in their criticisms, calling Updike an "anxious writer" who has "rarely found a form to match his anxiety and his large talent" ("Keeping It Short" 1967, 757), or hinting that Updike would make critics happy if he "did something stronger and deeper and more challenging than he has thus far written" ([1966] 1970, 127), or claiming "it will be a good day for American fiction" when Updike "loses some of his prudence" (Adams 1966, 5). Susan Dilts (1966) puts the case more directly: "The more one reads Updike, the more one wishes he would go out and do something." Were he to get out of his suburban rut, he could easily become "one of the most important writers of his generation." But if he continues down what seems to be his chosen path, Dilts warns, "he will continue to write superb prose—signifying nothing" (D9).

The growing consensus about Updike is expressed succinctly by two reviewers, one from each side of the Atlantic. British writer Simon Gray (1967) says the stories in *The Music School* prove once again that Updike "can 'do' almost anything"—but whatever he does, the work ends up being "resolutely and fastidiously minor" (840) because a surfeit of surface splendor prevents readers from seeing any character or situation too deeply. American critic Stanley Kauffman (1966) wonders rhetorically why Updike "is not a better writer than he is and why, among serious critics, he is not always taken seriously" (23). The answer, Kauffman says, lies in Updike's tendency to stay within the limits of what his polished technique will permit him to explore. He comes off as a "professional performer," a "miniaturist" in dealing with themes—qualities that prohibit his being considered a writer of "serious stature" (25).

Demands for Updike to tackle more important subjects did not go unanswered, of course. Peter Meinke (1966) urges him to ignore calls to step too far away from the subjects that had made him successful. Meinke believes stories in *The Music School* reveal Updike for what he really is, "a romantic writer with a great longing for the irretrievable past" (1512). Responding to those who have criticized Updike for being an inconsequential artist, Charles Samuels says that "in his best work, Updike infuses his story with meaning not by commenting on the action but by always finding the right gesture or word for his people so that their significance is the satisfying accumulation of all they have said or done" ([1966a] 1979, 194). Echoing Henry James, Samuels insists that "skill is not a dispensable adjunct to seriousness: it *is* seriousness: proof that the artist esteems his craft, his subject, his readers" (195). On that ground alone, Updike deserves to be considered a serious artist.

Before moving on from Samuels's critique, it is worth noting a curious observation he makes in a 1966 *Kenyon Review* essay about academic criticism of Updike. There Samuels complains that Updike "has scarcely received notice" in the "leading literary quarterlies" (1966b, 268). This is unfortunate, he says, because the "more discerning criticism" that would have been provided in these periodicals could have balanced some of the "knee-jerk reactions" to his work. Samuels seems to have missed reviews by Foster (1961) and Sale (1963), both in the *Hudson Review,* and one by John Thompson in the *Partisan Review* (1961). Samuels's view is rather elitist, too. He says Updike has had to "rely on little-noticed essays in academic periodicals like *Critique* and *Modern Fiction Studies*" (268). Times have changed, of course, and these journals now enjoy wider readership among—and influence on—academics.

Early Critical Commentary: 1962–1967

While reviewers were calling for Updike to change his ways, academic critics were already discovering a subtext in Updike's work that revealed it was neither ephemeral nor irrelevant. Barely five years after Updike published his first book and less than a decade after his first story appeared in *The New Yorker,* scholarly evaluations of his achievement began appearing. In an early critical assessment, Richard Murphy (1962) claims Updike writes of the real American experience better than any of his contemporaries. While the action in his fiction is slight, "his is an inner-directed eye"; hence, his tales "move forward not in a crescendo of climaxes but by the slow accretion of small and apparently random detail." Furthermore, Updike's protagonists look for "a simpler, more virtuous land, for an America that eroded with the frontier"; though they do not find it, they should be applauded for continuing to try (84). Richard Fisher's (1962) survey in *Moderna Språk* opens with the enthusiastic pronouncement that "in the person and writings of John Updike we have the most exciting thing that has happened to American prose fiction since 1929, when William Faulkner published *The Sound and the Fury*" (255). Fisher identifies several overarching themes in Updike's fiction, including "the role of the church and religion in the contemporary scene," which he finds "bothersome" because it is difficult to see "exactly what Updike wants to say about it" (259). But he insists that Updike is important not so much for what he has to say as for the way "in which he makes what he has to say a part of how he says it" (260).

The first extended analysis of Updike's fiction appeared in *Critique* in 1962. J. A. Ward, who tries to be evenhanded in assessing strengths and weaknesses, believes that calls for Updike to write something more substantial stem from a "traditional American respect for physical weight and philosophical profundity in fiction" (27). Ward respects a novelist's right to choose to be an observer and pundit regarding social issues. Hence, while Updike's selection of characters limits his possibilities, his recurrent them, "isolation," and the "common thread" running through his works, "the location of the human disease in the ego," elevate his work and make it worth critical attention (29). Curiously, while Ward praises Updike for "his rendering of the sensuous and the complex," he finds Updike's "repeated concern with theological problems" decidedly "less satisfying" (39).

In a second early appraisal, David Anderson (1963) observes that "a bewildered cult has developed" around Updike's work; these devotees consider him a most promising writer who has failed "to take on any major themes." Anderson contests this judgment, finding that Updike has successfully dealt with the themes of "middleness" and "individualism" but has added a new dimension missing from many writers of his generation (10). "His language, deeply influenced by the language of religion and theology, is a language of praise," while "his style is a search for form, a search for liturgy," based upon "a sense of ritual and ceremony" (11). Admittedly, Anderson says, some of Updike's writings are existentialist. Yet unlike most American writers, whose existentialism is shaped by "atheistic or agnostic" thinkers, Updike's is "explicitly Christian and specifically Kierkegaardian." As a Christian existentialist, Updike sees humankind struggling to overcome "the despair of spiritual alienation" by "realizing some kind of immortality" (12). While Updike may not have yet "solved the problem of finding a language to describe the immortality he feels man possesses," he may do so in the future. Ironically, when Updike writes his "big book," Anderson doubts "if many will recognize" it (13).

Guerin La Course (1963) echoes some of Anderson's conclusions, asserting that, even though the number of Updike's publications is relatively slight, "it would be hard to deny that Updike is carving an indelible image on American letters." Underlying all his work is "the persistent quest for love and its sometimes attainment" (512). Unfortunately, Updike tends to play it safe in his fiction, repeating his successes rather than experimenting with new subjects or new ways of approaching his central theme. What Updike lacks is some overarching vision—and La Course would like it be a positive vision—of human nature: "The reflective world of the man of letters must, by an intrinsic necessity, be braced and founded on a consciously chosen pursuit (if not attainment) of human values" (513). But Paul Doyle (1964) asserts that Updike has already demonstrated not only technical mastery but also a strong commitment to important recurring themes: a concern with individualism and twentieth-century American values and a strong "interest in spiritual aspiration" in a world filled with evil and corruption. However, Updike manages to "disguise his fundamental views" so well that "most reviewers complain that he has no philosophy or world view" (13).

Even at this early date, critics were offering judgments about Updike's place among twentieth-century American writers. William O'Connor (1964) suggests that Updike might have a greater future than William Styron because he seems to have found a suitable subject. Granville Hicks (1963a) suggests that Updike shares with Bernard Malamud and Herbert Gold a preoccupation with "the theme of redemption." Though Updike's early works simply point out "the need for redemption," in his more recent fiction he "has undertaken bolder explorations," trying to find ways for humankind to find purpose now that traditional faiths seem ineffectual and outmoded (236). In *The Sense of Life in the American Novel*, Arthur Mizener (1964) explains what he admits is sometimes a disconnect between Updike's style and substance. The problem, he says, lies in Updike's commitment to becoming a conventional success, which on occasion causes him to use a grandiose style for describing the life he knows most well (248).

One of the most negative early critiques is Norman Mailer's (1963). Mailer is skeptical about the validity of Updike's current high reputation, which he says has been built up by "literary bodyguards" like Mizener and Hicks. A candid assessment of *Rabbit, Run* reveals how wrong they are. Amid its pages one finds numerous examples of "imprecise, flatulent, wry-necked, precious, overpreened, self-indulgent, tortured sentences," the kind that "would be admired in a writing course overseen by a fussy old nance." Its ending shows Updike "does not know how to finish." Mailer says Updike "could become the best of our literary novelists if he could forget about style and go deeper into the literature of sex." While "Updike will never be great," he could be "a good writer of the first rank with occasional echoes from the profound" (67). But only, Mailer insists, if he decides to make a few critics angry.

Critiques such as Mailer's were balanced by ones like those of Michael Novak, then a rising star among Catholic and conservative scholars. In a review of *Pigeon Feathers*, Novak (1963a) claims Updike is "feeling his way toward the themes of death, of God, of our small suburban selfishness and our unexpected discoveries of realistic love" (577). In "Updike's Quest for Liturgy" ([1963b] 1979) Novak notes that, though barely thirty, Updike was already "awaken[ing] themes dormant in American letters since Hawthorne and Melville" (183). Novak is delighted to see a writer trying to "understand life in small American towns and suburbs as it is now lived" and treating religious matters seriously. The growing tendency toward secularism in America is making it "almost impossible for faith to take root," thus making Updike's self-appointed task even more laudable. "Even though he is so far limiting himself to his own experience," Updike is "beginning to make religion intelligible in America, and to fashion symbols whereby it can be understood." Sadly, most critics, secular in their orientation, "see only the dazzling words" in Updike's prose and "do not grasp what they mean" (191).

In a complementary assessment, Norris Yates (1965) stresses that "the need for God and for a divinely inspired morality is a major theme" in Updike's first three novels (470). Like other American writers (including Hawthorne, Melville, Faulkner, Glasgow, and Wolfe), Updike continues to look for God in the world even though doing so requires a "leap of faith." However, unlike "exponents of negation" (like Mailer and Joseph Heller), Updike "refuses to admit that the search for God is hopeless or unnecessary. Out of his unresolved conflict has come vital thought-content for much of his fiction" (474).

In less than a decade after Updike's first novel was published, teachers were incorporating his fiction into high-school and college courses. To assist them, in 1965 the *English Journal* published Thaddeus Muradian's explanation of Updike's philosophy. Muradian identifies four points representative of Updike's "message" (577) and clarifies how each works to reveal Updike's "Christian-Judaic outlook" and his belief that "man's salvation will be determined by the solemnity with which he lives life—his redemption will be measured by his truth to himself in this life and possibly by his hopes for the next life" (584). Writing in the College English Association's journal, Sister Judith Tate (1964) explains how Updike attempts to "shine his light on reality" in *Rabbit, Run* and *The Centaur* (44), two novels that are ultimately about "man seeking to love God" (50).

Among individual works, *Rabbit, Run* received the most attention from academic critics. The variety of interpretation is suggested by six essays. Dean Doner's defense of Harry Angstrom is based on the premise that Updike sees the real villain in society to be Humanism, which, with its attendant "denial of the Unseen" and its "insistence upon shared life and shared guilt," is responsible for "the quintessence of modern feeling, Angst" ([1962] 1979, 18). In his debut publication on Updike, Robert Detweiler (1963) argues that the spiritual crisis depicted in the novel is brought about not simply by the personal failings of the protagonist, but by the inability of society to minister to his needs. None of the institutions on which Harry should be able to rely are capable of providing him the faith he so desperately seeks. He fails in his "search for God" (22) because "his community has failed him" (24). Fred Standley (1967) describes the novel as quintessentially modern, "an image of life involving human actions and values as seen by a literary artist" intent on making readers contemplate their own lives as a result of reading the story (371). The novel undermines traditional religious and spiritual values by presenting people as "dehumanized and depersonalized" (373). John Stubbs (1968) argues that the novel documents Harry Angstrom's quest "to find external corroboration for his vague feelings of immortality" (94). Rabbit is a man given wholly to "intuitive feelings" (100), who hopes to find his assurance of immortality not in books but in relationships. By contrast, Gerry Brenner ([1966] 1982) says Rabbit is no quester but simply a "sensitive but not-too-bright, middle-class hero" (91) who cannot find guidance from time-tested principles and must resort to instinct to survive in his world. Marxist critic Sidney Finkelstein (1965) describes Rabbit's situation as one of "all-encompassing alienation"; decidedly unheroic, he is "defeated by a life so antagonistic, so impossible to understand" that "his struggles are only pathetic, impotent gestures" (244). Finkelstein says that Updike sees America as "a home of petrified humanity" (246).

The influence of existentialist thinking, a topic of great interest to scholars of this period, is the subject of several studies. David Galloway, who in 1962 completed the first dissertation to include a discussion of Updike's work, later writes about Updike's creation of heroes struggling to find meaning in a meaningless world. The quest is absurd, but Updike ennobles it in his fiction. However, Galloway cautions that, while Updike's heroes represent the writer's "optimistic assertion of man's ability to overcome his environment" ([1964] 1966, 49–50), Updike's "involvement with purely verbal and otherwise formal elements of prose" actually jeopardizes the effect he wishes to convey (50).

Updike is the final novelist considered in a group described by Howard Harper (1967) as writers of "classic fiction": works that "deal with universal questions in unique and interesting ways" (3). Harper traces Updike's gradually deepening interest in existential questions. Though Updike's early work appears rather wooden and dogmatic, more recent fiction "has a depth, an integrity, and an ultimate concern which have not yet been generally appreciated." Harper believes Updike has already secured "a permanent place in American literature," and the only question about his reputation that remains to be answered is "how big that place will finally be" (190).

Of course, not every academic critic thought Updike's work had merit. For example, Robert Phillips (1967) argues that Updike tends to wallow in nostalgia while "imposing his own wit and suprasophistication" on characters who could not possibly be so informed or urbane. Phillips suggests, however, that it is still possible for Updike to overcome these faults and erase critics' perceptions of him as a dilettante by writing "the 'important' book everyone has been saying he is destined to write" (40). Otherwise, his books may go unread by future generations, "unless he begins to find something more to say" (39). Along those same lines, D. J. Enright ([1965] 1966) sees Updike as part of a conspiracy of current fiction writers to undermine humanity. While Updike "would come nowhere near the top" of a "dirty-laundry list" of such writers (134), his fiction suggests he is "hardly an author at all" (135). His thin story lines cannot be disguised by his felicitous style. Worst of all, "though long ago he found a way of writing, as yet he doesn't seem to have found something to write about"—although, Enright adds somewhat sardonically, "he still has time" (140).

Two studies of Updike's fiction published in 1967 provide snapshots of critical opinion of his career before the publication of *Couples*, and also provide some insight into the methodologies and assumptions of the critical establishment at the time. Bryant Wyatt (1967) argues that Updike's primary theme is the "question of self-identity, embracing the inner gropings of the subject toward personal realization." This "psychological interest" motivates Updike to search for "the appropriate form in which to order and best delineate his intensely subjective and impressionistic materials" (89). Though Updike has not yet succeeded in melding form and content, when he does, his work is "destined to endure" (95). Like Wyatt, Richard Rupp (1967) tries to determine if Updike's popularity will last. Attributing Updike's appeal to "his celebrated style" (693), Rupp suggests that Updike has not yet learned how to capture his characters' capacity "to feel and to make *us* feel." At best, his characters are only "potentially interesting"; at worst "the style leaves an empty husk" (695). If Updike is to be truly successful, he must learn to "bring together the outside and the inside" (709) of his characters.

It seems appropriate to close this chapter with some observations on the work of Kenneth and Alice Hamilton. These Canadian scholars were prolific (if not always sophisticated) champions of Updike's works as serious explorations of religious issues, and their commentary influenced (for good or for ill) the shape of Updike criticism for years. They published individually and as a team, but maintained in everything they wrote a consistent outlook about Updike's mission as a novelist. The outlines of their approach are evident in Kenneth Hamilton's "John Updike: Chronicler of 'the Time of the Death of God'" (1967). Hamilton shows how the young writer has become a kind of prophet warning about the impending doom that will befall America should it continue on its path toward material comfort at the expense of spiritual nourishment. Updike's works constantly contrast characters who chase after material satisfaction but find no real meaning in their lives, and often run from their responsibilities. Though Updike may treat these figures ironically, beneath the surface he is raging against contemporary America's abandonment of religious values.

The Hamiltons have the distinction of publishing the first book on Updike, although their *John Updike* (1967) is little more than an extended essay. In it they provide a thematic and technical analysis of Updike's fiction typical of 1960s literary criticism. They are heavily influenced, however, by a belief that the source of Updike's inspiration lies in the theological writings of Kierkegaard and Barth. Early in *John Updike* the Hamiltons assert that "Updike remains something of a puzzle." He has been called by one critic or another "an intellectual" who intentionally distances himself from his characters, a "back-to-nature romantic" given over to "the thoughtless sphere of feeling," an "apologist for traditional

Christianity" and "a skeptical critic of conventional religion" (7). Already, it seems, the critics were drawing the battle lines that would eventually determine how Updike would fare in the eyes of posterity. Yet Updike would confound many of them with the publication of his next novel, a sexually explicit tale of couples in a small New England town that made at least some critics believe he had finally written the "big book" that would define his career and assure his place in the canon of American literature.

Notes

[1] My observations on Updike's publications through the 1970s are intended to complement rather than supplant the insightful summaries and excellent analysis of the reception of Updike's work provided by Donald Greiner in *The Other John Updike: Poems/Short Stories/Prose/Play* (1981) and *John Updike's Novels* (1984a), and by William Macnaughton in the introduction to his *Critical Essays on John Updike* (1982). Nevertheless, a review of criticism written during the period between 1958 and 1980 is important because many of the terms by which Updike continues to be judged are contained in works written during these years, and because the value of original judgments may be assessed differently after the passage of three decades.

2: Making a Name on the National Scene (1968–1975)

IN RETROSPECT, the period between 1968 and 1975 might be described as the "breakthrough years" during which Updike became a major novelist, introduced or returned to important recurring characters and themes into his fiction, and continued his exploration of the American scene. Of course, before 1968 Updike was well-known to a select group of readers and critics, many of whom had high regard for his work. While his audience among the general readership was considerable, it did not rival that of contemporary popular giants—writers like Leon Uris, Mary Renault, James Clavell, Irving Wallace, Mary Stewart, and Arthur Hailey. The publication of *Couples*, however, brought Updike to national prominence (or notoriety, perhaps). The novel made the *New York Times* best-seller list and remained there for nine months, rising to number one for a week—but held just below the top spot for two months by Arthur Hailey's *Airport*. Additionally, the publication of "View from the Catacombs" (1968), a profile of Updike in *Time*, then one of the most-read magazines in America with a circulation of five million, made him a national celebrity. The authors perceptively suggest that in *Couples* Updike may have found "the explosive expression of his theme that his work has always lacked." The novel may be "flawed by overwriting and undercharacterization," but no longer can Updike be considered irrelevant (66).

During the seven-year period between 1968 and 1975 Updike continued to work in all genres, publishing a collection of poetry in 1969 that takes its title, *Midpoint and Other Poems*, from the long poem that makes up half the volume. His 1970 collection of short fiction, *Bech: A Book*, introduced another character who would occupy his imagination for three decades. In *Rabbit Redux* (1971) Updike demonstrated that he was attuned to and interested in the larger social forces that shaped his characters' destinies. A fine collection of short stories, *Museums and Women* (1972), reminded the public that he remained prolific in this genre. Updike's foray into drama with *Buchanan Dying* (1974) may not have led to commissions from Broadway, but his 1975 novel *A Month of Sundays* was immediately recognized as a kind of companion piece to *Couples* in its frank treatment of sexual relationships. The novel was also the first installment of the trilogy that would become a contemporary commentary on that most American of novels, Nathaniel Hawthorne's

The Scarlet Letter. By 1975, there could be no question that Updike was a literary force to be reckoned with.

Couples: Controversial Bestseller, 1968

Contemporary commentary on *Couples* suggests not only something about Updike's success, but also quite a bit about expectations of the reviewing establishment at the end of a turbulent decade in American history. It would be too much to expect that reviewers would have agreed on the merits of the novel; after all, they had not been unanimous in their judgment of any previous work by Updike. Notable about reviews of *Couples*, however, are the extremes to which critics went in celebrating Updike's accomplishment or damning the book as a crass attempt at pandering to the public's base appetites.

Among the most enthusiastic reviewers is Eliot Fremont-Smith (1968), who calls *Couples* an "intellectual 'Peyton Place'" that displays considerably more insight and greater command of language. While some may take issue with it on moral or aesthetic grounds, Fremont-Smith believes Updike has created "a universe that in the end quite magically escapes the binds of time and place and point of view, the demands of reality and programmed myth" (39). Wirt Williams (1968) agrees, noting that while Updike has in the past been "a novelist of distinction but never of notable daring," in *Couples* he has "struck the heaviest blow yet in the candor revolution." Williams believes the novel will have profound impact on American fiction, because its scenes of explicit sexual activity are contained in a novel that is "incontestably first-rate: integrity of intent and artistry of execution shine from every page" (D43). William Kennedy (1968) describes *Couples* as a scathing expose of modern Americans' lack of values, making "the depravity of self-centeredness seem not only despicable, but criminal." Other novels may demonstrate how societies have collapsed under the weight of moral depravity, but Updike is probably "the first artist to place the blame so lucidly on sexual promiscuity." Kennedy says this is the "big book" people have been waiting for (19).

Predictably, the aspect of *Couples* that attracted most notice was Updike's use of explicit sexual materials, and it is both instructive and sometimes amusing to observe how critics finessed their assessments. Wilfrid Sheed (1968) justifies Updike's use of explicit sex as necessary for exposing the character of the people in exurbia and revealing the insignificance of their lives. Several reviews in religious publications actually praise Updike's treatment of sex, calling it "the tragedy" that lays bare the essential sadness of the people of Tarbox (Hill 1968, 757) and acknowledging that, while Updike's skill at depicting "acts and thoughts of sex" may "titillate" readers, the novel describes brilliantly "what American society has lost" when religion is no longer present in people's lives (Kort 1968,

1342). The conservative Catholic Michael Novak ([1968] 1982) praises the novel effusively, claiming Updike has faithfully represented the sterility of American middle-class life while treating his fictional couples "affectionately and respectfully" (60). Novak says the "lovemaking scenes" are "among the most beautiful and compassionate in our literature." Though the plot seems contrived, "Updike proves himself as a storyteller," fulfilling "the promise reposed in him" (61). Ever the controversialist, Novak insists Updike's "specifically Christian" sensibility makes him unpalatable to "the Jewish sensibility" and "the hard, pragmatic, secular sensibility" of the modern "critical establishment" (59–60).

In a curious defense of Updike's use of sexual scenes, the reviewer for *Times Literary Supplement* ("Community Feeling" 1968) suggests that Updike is trying to deal with a serious subject—the state of contemporary suburban American society—but his message is sometimes obscured by the routine of sexual excesses that are less titillating than boring. Similarly, Dennis Potter (1968) believes that if Updike could have controlled "the torrent of his prose" or "the fever of his phrases, we would all be hailing a genuine masterpiece." Instead, Updike wastes his efforts on the lives of squalid people from whom readers learn little (23). By contrast, Tony Tanner (1968) thinks Updike's treatment of sex, while graphic, is also profound, because he sees sexual relationships as having devolved into "a meaningless and rather cruel game" which his couples play incessantly. Tanner points out how Updike's naturalism is always "edged with an incipient dread" inspired by the ever-present sense that the world is dissolving into chaos, and that death for both the individual and the planet seems inevitable. Unfortunately, Tanner finds Updike's characterization faulty, his plotting crude, and his "fine writing" unable on occasion to "redeem the prose from the rather comfortable materialism visible beneath the religious pessimism of the author's pose" (659).

Curiously, some who had written favorably about Updike's earlier work were reluctant to praise *Couples*. Granville Hicks is disappointed; this book "isn't the major novel many of us have been hoping for" and "not different from what Updike has written before but simply more" ([1968] 1970, 131). Alfred Kazin (1968) says that "as a sociologist" of the new American society Updike "gets an A plus" (1). Yet his exceptional facility as a writer undercuts the impact of his social commentary, because "his easy power of style is always threatening to turn the book into an idyll" (3). Anatole Broyard (1968) writes that "if anyone had asked me which contemporary American writer was best equipped to write a definitive description of love and sex" it would be Updike. Yet the sex in this novel "seems only an antidote to boredom and emptiness" (29).

A notable number of critics attacked *Couples* and its author with a vengeance. William Gass (1968) says the book contains nothing new or profound, only unrestrained and ultimately meaningless couplings.

Edmund Fuller (1968) laments that Updike has "made sex more depressing than it has ever been in literature." Although *Couples* "is receiving much publicity" and "many copies are in bookstore tables," Fuller believes "the judicious will let them stay there" (16). Writing in *Commentary*, where negative reviews of Updike were virtually *de rigueur*, John Thompson (1968) suggests that *Couples* is actually a kind of vicious sermon against human sexuality, and Updike's continual parade of sexual activity is intended to suggest Satan-worship. Josh Greenfield (1968) says that, for all its "bright and fancy trimmings," *Couples* is a clunker, proving that "you don't have to be a bad writer to come up with an awful novel" (185). Greenfield somewhat archly predicts that the book will be "a whopping commercial success," which may in turn provide Updike the financial stability he needs to return to "a serious and important and worthwhile literary quest" (187). Stanley Hyman (1968) echoes Greenfield's judgments. "Just about everything" is wrong with the book: its "endless sexual explicitness," its sentimentality, its "portentousness," its "ham-handed and grandiose" symbolism, and—most surprising to him—its "bad prose" ([1968] 1978, 107, 108, 109). Like Greenfield, Hyman expresses hope that in future work Updike will "return to his normal scope and to the true country of his imagination" (111).

Two especially savage reviews were written by women. Michele Murray (1968) says *Couples* will be popular largely because readers are drawn into Updike's world by "a prose style which is now like tuberculosis," giving patients "a pathetic appearance of health" but ultimately killing them. "The emptiness of conception" is matched by a "falsity of execution." The characters are "little more than puppets" for Updike to manipulate; the story is "void of ideas." Updike "takes no risks," remaining content with "a sentimental view of sex" and evading "the hard questions he thinks he is answering about The Withdrawal of God or Our American Sickness or whatever it is that puff the book so full of its own wind." Updike's attempt to create "a metaphysics of sex" is neither "exhaustive nor brilliant"; instead, it "perfectly exemplifies the self-indulgence of a narcissistic and adolescent literature" (11). Reaching the same conclusions, Diana Trilling (1968) considers *Couples* "about as sodden a performance, both as a work of the imagination and as prose, as could come from an ambitious writer already established in the ranks of our talented younger novelists" (140). The redundant sex scenes "leave us no room for an imagination of the world from which sex is assumed to offer escape"; Updike's vision of society "is no wider, actually, than the beds he explores." As a result, *Couples* "does not rise much above pornography" (141).

Some of the earliest academic critiques of *Couples* attempt to place the novel not only within the Updike canon but within the American literary tradition. Several examples illustrate how critics of the period were wedded to traditional critical approaches (and in some cases, to social prejudices as well). Joyce Flint (1968) defends Updike's right to write about white, middle-class America and important issues such as "the loss of God, rejection of the Puritan notion of work as a 'calling,' adultery, abortion, and divorce" (346). However, Updike's characters seem lifeless, principally because "they feel so little about what happens." They reflect "the success of the liberal-humanitarian's dream of progress"—a dream Updike finds unpalatable (347). John Ditsky (1969) thinks the novel effectively presents "the inward- and outward-looking versions of humanity at its sexual nadir: the psychological and sociological aspects of post-Freudian erotic confusion" (111). Yet these insights alone do not make *Couples* a particularly good novel. "One cannot separate the intentionally ludicrous from the clumsily awful in this novel," which is further burdened by "heavy-handed didacticism" and Updike's failure to distinguish among his characters (113). John Peter (1968) calls Updike "the inevitable fictional product" of "New Criticism." Every sentence is carefully crafted, but "if you are old-fashioned enough to go peering beyond the brocade of words," you are "disposed to glimpse an emptiness" (120).

Couples did make some immediate difference in the way critics viewed Updike's fiction as a body of creative work. An examination of *Couples* is central to Henri Petter's "John Updike's Metaphoric Novels" ([1969] 1982), which identifies important common themes in his fiction: "the individual's consistency, human relations, man's attempts at grasping the meaning of existence, mind and spirit" (109). In "Quest for Belief: Theme in the Novels of John Updike" (1969), *Couples* clearly influences John Hill's conclusion that the central premise in Updike's fiction is "failure": his principal characters fail to find meaning in life because they no longer accept the traditional symbols of good and evil that have guided the human race for centuries. Hill's essay also reveals the datedness of critical inquiry, as its focus is almost exclusively on Updike's male characters, nowhere more obvious than in his discussion of Updike's treatment of sex. In the modern world, sex has been "stripped of inherent value"; but Hill says Updike believes "this basic aspect of life" could become meaningful again. "If man can accept woman as she should be, he may come to accept also the centuries-old values personified in woman, and thus he may be able to realize that his own life can have connotation beyond his immediate here and now" (174). No question as to who is the acting subject and who remains the passive object in this scenario.

Taking a broader view, David Lodge places the novel in the American tradition of Utopian fiction, modified by Updike and many of his contemporaries who stress sexual freedom rather than rationality as the basis for achieving the perfect society. Updike's novel is part of a "determined effort to render pornography redundant by incorporating its characteristic materials into 'legitimate' art" ([1970] 1971, 237). Updike's "new kind of community" is based on "values that run counter to those prevailing in society at large." This tradition, Lodge says, "can be traced right back to *The Blithedale Romance*" (241). After pointing out parallels between *Couples* and Hawthorne's work, Lodge concludes with an observation that can only be described as prescient: "The more one dwells on the comparison, the more plausible it becomes to see Hawthorne as Updike's literary ancestor among the classic American novelists" (243).

Writing Obliquely about Oneself: *Midpoint* and *Bech: A Book*, 1969–1970

Updike followed *Couples* with another volume of poetry, *Midpoint and Other Poems* (1969). The centerpiece of the book, the long title poem *Midpoint*, is the closest thing to autobiography that Updike published until 1989. Much can be gleaned about his views on life, art, and the concept of self from this pastiche in which he employs numerous poetic forms to construct an assessment of his life and accomplishments at what he perceives to be its midpoint. Reviewers tended to ignore the collection, however; the De Bellis bibliography (2007) lists a mere dozen reviews, and most of these are little more than brief notices. The long title poem generated mixed assessments. Ann Gates (1969) calls it "difficult, intense" and "highly personal" (9), but the reviewer for the *Times Literary Supplement* ("Answers to Questions Unasked" 1970) claims it exhibits "the kind of slapdash speed-writing collage that Ezra Pound made possible" (104). William Heyen (1970) finds many sections of *Midpoint* "technically impressive," but the "sensibility" behind the remaining poems in the volume "is seldom able to take itself seriously" (428).

Heyen's observations highlight a problem Updike was to have throughout his career: few people took him seriously as a poet. Elizabeth Matson (1967) discusses this phenomenon in an early critical assessment of Updike's poetry. Its readability makes it seem so "deceptively simple" that readers often fail to recognize "the sense and sensitivity" (157) of his work. Matson points out that Updike's "clever and subtle, sometimes ambiguous, often highly intellectualized" poems share affinities with the work of the Metaphysical poets (161). Unfortunately, few critics followed up on her observations, and more than forty years later most readers retain the impression that Updike was little more than a clever versifier.

Bech: A Book (1970) attracted considerably more attention. It appeared on the *New York Times* top ten list for eight weeks, although it never rose higher than seventh place. Many reviewers were generous with their praise. This "light and bright" book (Donoghue 1970, 524) "succeeds marvelously" (Lehmann-Haupt 1970, 43) in creating a believable figure who makes readers laugh and think at the same time. The extravagancies of style are devices employed to mock the growing trend in novel-writing that stresses postmodern tendencies of excessive focus on the self (Raban 1970, 494). Jack Richardson (1970) thinks *Bech* is a major advance for Updike. Most of his novels, Richardson says, "have no large aesthetic or philosophical frame from which the reader is meant to derive their meaning"; *Bech* is "lean, antic, and to the point," supported but not encumbered by "the lessons of tradition." It may point to a new direction in Updike's fiction, showing that he has "propitiously somewhat liberated himself" from older forms that no longer work (48).

Others assessments were less enthusiastic. The book is a "put-on" to show critics Updike can write the book they have been demanding (Kuehl 1970, 7). It demonstrates that Updike has not yet found "an organic center of life to write from" (Donovan 1970, 7K). Though it is a bold statement that Updike has the right to break the unspoken taboo that in America "only Jews write about Jews," the book fails because "at no point does Bech convince one that he is a Jew" (Braine 1970, 480). Readers are likely to find Henry Bech little more than Updike's mouthpiece, "the agent of a gleeful revenge fantasy" rather than "a wounded hero" ("On Not Rocking the Boat" 1970, 1183). The portrait of Bech reflects a failure of imagination, a reversion to stereotype and caricature that is beneath Updike's considerable talents (Ozick[1970] 1983, 114).

Thomas Edwards (1970) offers a decidedly different perspective on Updike's achievement in *Bech: A Book*. He suggests that, heretofore, Updike's reliance on nostalgia in his Pennsylvania stories has limited his imagination; furthermore, works set in other locales have not been improvements. The appearance of *Bech: A Book*, "perhaps his best and most attractive book," is most welcome because in it Updike demonstrates that he is able to carry off an imaginative excursion (1). Similarly, L. E. Sissman (1970) believes *Bech* may signal a new phase for Updike, and readers may soon see him "flourish even as he has not in his brilliant past" (104). Finally, Michele Murray (1970) offers what must have been for her grudging praise. Though *Bech* is decidedly minor, it is "enormously appealing" largely because Updike has "freed himself from both the purple prose and stupefying solemnity about sex which so disfigured *Couples*" (13).

Academic Criticism, 1969–1971

As fast as Updike was turning out new fiction and poetry, academics were producing new commentaries. Well into the 1970s, most employed methodologies typical of critical practice for a half-century or more: formalist and technical studies, character studies and psychological criticism, humanist and moral criticism. Three examples illustrate these practices.

In "The Use of Rhythm in Three Novels by John Updike" Margaret Gratton (1969) applies E. M. Forster's ideas about the way pattern and rhythm have "potential for extending the significance of a literary work" (3) to Updike's fiction. Gratton is interested in rhythm as the pattern "established by the repetition of certain fundamental human activities which collectively constitute the ritual of man's existence and the material for his art" (4). She argues that the "important rhythmic characteristic" of *Rabbit, Run*, *The Centaur*, and *Of the Farm* is "the fusion of traditional, sacred life rhythms with the profane rhythms of contemporary, middle-class American culture" (12). In an ethical reading of *Rabbit, Run*, Elmer Suderman (1969) argues that Rabbit's problem is not having to choose between simple right and wrong, but between "the right way and the good way, a choice far more complex" (14)—between following conventional standards or listening to his inner voice. Suderman believes Updike uses his protagonist to critique "a society where the good and the right are in conflict and where it is difficult and perhaps futile to try to find either" (21). In *John Updike*, the second critical book on the writer, Charles Samuels (1969) discovers in Updike's works not only superb craftsmanship but a consistent interest in religion and theology and the recurrent use of fictionalized autobiography. While he is not hesitant to criticize Updike, Samuels considers him a master of realism and one of America's major writers.

The appearance of Alice and Kenneth Hamilton's *The Elements of John Updike* in 1970 in some ways was a watershed in Updike studies. For the Hamiltons, publishing on Updike was something of a cottage industry. In addition to the works cited in the previous chapter, Alice Hamilton published a brief comparison of stories by Updike and James Joyce in the *Dalhousie Review* (1969). The husband and wife team wrote an extended analysis of *Midpoint* almost immediately after the poem was published (1970c) and collaborated on a review essay of *Bech: A Book* ([1970b] 1982) in which they urge readers to get beyond the humor to see the book as Updike's "first attempt to deal specifically with the writer's calling" (125). Three years after publishing *Elements*, they again collaborated to produce "Mythic Dimensions of Updike's Fiction" (1973), a study of Updike's use of myth as a structural and thematic device in works other than *The Centaur*.

Though the Hamiltons claim in the introduction to *Elements* that their aim is "simply to lay down some guidelines that might help readers approach Updike's work with some degree of sympathetic understanding" (7), their detailed exegesis of nearly everything Updike had written to date presents him as the author of a new gospel, tailored for contemporary audiences and filled with allusions to the Bible, Søren Kierkegaard, Karl Barth, and Paul Tillich. Updike's "good news" is often contained in the "deeper meaning" (16) found in the "countermelody of imagery" that gives his works a symbolic dimension (28). Reading Updike "becomes a kind of treasure hunt, where the prize is the discovery of a richness and complexity in the text which casual attention would leave unrecognized" (17). The Hamiltons uncover obscure allusions and buried parallels that reveal not only Updike's exceptional erudition, but their own as well.

According to the Hamiltons, the Updike gospel demonstrates how "every son of Adam"—gender-inclusive language had not emerged as the academic standard by 1970—must accept "the challenge of life as it opens before him," resisting the temptation to embrace the world, which will leave a person with only "bitterness and tears," and "walk the straight line of a paradox leading to where time and the eternal are reconciled" (25). Though they recognize and appreciate Updike's humor and his keen sense of pleasure in form and style, what interests them most is his treatment of love and marriage, his use of sex as a means of foregrounding deeper philosophical insights into the human condition, and his consistent focus on the decline of America as a result of its abandonment of its religious heritage and traditions. One could go on citing examples of the Hamiltons' strongly religious reading of the Updike canon. However, those provided should be sufficient to show why they believe Updike's body of work, regardless of its external concerns with social mores, is aimed at answering the eternal question: "Does the universe, blindly ruled by chance, run downward into death; or does it follow the commands of Living God whose Will for it is life?" For the Hamiltons, Updike's answer is an "unambiguous" affirmation of the Christian faith in that Living God (249).

The Hamiltons' insistence on a narrow Christian reading of the Updike canon had great influence over critical commentary for the next two decades. Yet almost immediately, some saw danger in their reductive approach. In a review of their book, John Aldridge ([1970] 1972) is appalled at what he considers the Hamiltons' outrageous claims made for Updike's ability as a symbolist and theologian. Their stress on the importance of deeper meanings comes at the expense of commentary on the sufficiency of the narrative that carries these meanings, and Aldridge is not certain Updike's fiction is always up to the task. Acknowledging that many reviewers were becoming increasingly more negative about Updike, Aldridge speculates that overpraise like the Hamiltons' may do equal damage: "One has reason to wonder whether [Updike] will be saved from his detractors only to perish at the hands of his admirers" (196).

Several more modest claims regarding the Christian and mythic dimensions of Updike's fiction appeared at this time. David Myers (1971) argues that *The Centaur* is not simply "a satire on the modern world" but more importantly "the tragic allegory of a Christian soul" engaged in a struggle "for truth and love in a world which is filled with indifference, hate and death, and which may be beyond redemption and without transcendence" (73). Myers reads the novel as a "Christian quest" in which narrative structure is based "not so much on the parallelism between Greek myth and contemporary reality as on the Christian allegory of the triumph of goodness over death" (77). Robert Detweiler ([1971] 1982) constructs a reading of *Couples* that stresses its mythic dimensions, pointing out parallels between it and two important Western love stories: Tristan and Iseult, and Don Juan. Equally important, in a prescient observation that foreshadows postmodern approaches to fiction, Detweiler highlights the effect of multiple points of view in the novel, noting that readers are forced to "grant the legitimacy of its pluralism, as in fact we are learning to accept the plurality of thought and custom in our many-angled modern world" (129). In another essay on *Couples*, G. F. Waller (1972) claims the novel is not simply a sexually explicit potboiler but a "major, even prophetic, novel" that explores the spiritual state of New England and by extension humankind in a world that no longer relies on traditional faith for guidance (10).

James Gindin (1971) comes to a different conclusion about the religious dimension of Updike's fiction. While Updike's overriding themes may be "mythical and religious" (44), the religious theme is a kind of straightjacket, because Updike has a narrow vision of both God and church akin to that of the early founders of America. As *Couples* amply demonstrates, Updike has high regard for "the old, non-urban, God-fearing American society" (46) in which the values of white Protestants are held in esteem. Others are made welcome only if they accept the truth of that vision. Hence, Gindin says, *Couples* is "anti-Negro, anti-Catholic, and anti-Semitic" (47)—a fault he ascribes to other Updike novels as well.

By the beginning of the 1970s Updike had achieved sufficient stature to be included in studies evaluating trends in American fiction. In *Bright Book of Life* (1971) Alfred Kazin describes him as "virtuoso" capable of writing about anything. Updike is an "intellectual novelist" (121), and, "in an era of boundless personal confusion, he has been a moralist without rejecting the mores" (124). Though not as fulsome in his praise, Tony Tanner (1971) says Updike "has maintained, and demonstrated, that middle-class existence is more complex than American literature usually allows." He is at his best in revealing the "compromised environment" in which most middle-class Americans live, giving over many of their personal freedoms to fit in with society (273). Though Updike recognizes that social systems such as ones he describes lend themselves to dissolution, he "holds out for growth," serving as a "subversive" force who refutes the entropic process through his art (293–94).

In 1971, Southern Illinois Press published two studies of Updike that helped solidify his reputation among academics. The first, Larry Taylor's *Pastoral and Anti-Pastoral Patterns in John Updike's Fiction*, explores

Updike's use of the pastoral as both a theme and an organizing device. Taylor sees Updike pitting the pastoral tradition, with its nostalgic fondness for a golden-age past, against the modern anti-pastoral age. Taylor is less interested in justifying Updike's popularity than in placing him within a tradition which stretches back to classic times and has strong roots in American literature. By tying him to figures like Emerson, Thoreau, and Faulkner, Taylor is able to state with some certitude that Updike's "penetrating vision," which "equals his poetic gifts of language," makes him "one of the most important artists of his time" (135).

Like Taylor's study, Rachel Burchard's *John Updike: Yea Sayings* (1971) proceeds from the premise that Updike is "one of the most important writers on the contemporary scene" (159). Interested in explaining the reasons for his popularity with the general reading public and the academic community, Burchard mines Updike's work for evidence of what she describes as his affirmative, Christian attitude. The theme running through all of his fiction is "man searching" (2)—not simply for human happiness, but for some sense of the essential goodness in humankind and the assurance that life is purposeful. Updike is a "unique" talent who has assimilated the work of theologians and other writers to produce fiction that provides a perspective on life which reflects both Christianity and modern skepticism (3–4). Burchard seems delighted to have found a novelist who can attract a large following by writing with certitude that "God exists"—the "most important" yea-saying of all (159).

Controversial Sequel: *Rabbit Redux*, 1971

Rabbit Redux, the first of Updike's sequels, rode the wave of notoriety created by the publication of *Couples* to a position on the *New York Times* top ten list in December 1971, where it remained until the end of March 1972. It also generated the same kind of controversy that had characterized reactions to *Rabbit, Run*, and *Couples*. This is "the complete Updike at last," says Anatole Broyard (1971), "an awesomely accomplished writer who is better, tougher, wiser and more radically human than anyone could have expected him to be." In an uncharacteristically emotional plea, Broyard importunes readers, "For God's sake, read the book. It may even—will probably—change your life" (40). Equally appreciative if less emotional, Richard Locke ([1971] 1983) calls *Rabbit Redux* "a great achievement, by far the most audacious and successful book Updike has written" (291). John Heidenry (1972) believes it is "the best American novel in a decade" and Updike "one of only three first-rate prose writers that his country has"—Mailer and Capote being the others (333).

English reviewers were equally appreciative. Julian Symons (1972) judges *Rabbit Redux* "the finest novel John Updike has written," an "unforgettable" and "horrific vision" of what is happening in American society (7). James Lindroth (1972) says "Rabbit gains dignity through his tribulation" (104). Updike, too, has grown, and while his writing "may have lost some of its early vigor," it has "gained an impressive, if somber, irony" (104). William Trevor (1972) suggests that *Rabbit Redux* proves the novel as an art form is not dead. The Rabbit novels present an unvarnished view of middle America, exposing its obsessions and revealing the "sense of emptiness, of death without God and loneliness in hostile space" that characterize the country's mood (462).

More measured in his assessment, Charles Samuels praises Updike for being able to absorb "some of the chief sources of our discontent," distilling them "into characters realistically impelled by conflicting motives" ([1971] 1982, 67); however, the book fails in "fathoming causes and asserting judgments" (64) for the malaise of modern society. Marvin Mudrick (1972) says the novel reveals Updike continuing to do what he does well—describing "American places and atmospheres, textures, idioms, items, the pathos of the consumer society" (151). Unfortunately, he has tried to do too much, and is not successful in carrying out his plan. Bernard Oldsey (1972) says this sequel to *Rabbit, Run* makes it clear that Updike's protagonist is intended as "a species of white American Everyman, fitting a niche somewhere between the comic Babbitt and the tragic Willy Loman" (54). And yet, "something is lacking, some force of insight" (56), that causes the novel to be less than it might, considering Updike's exceptional mastery of style and technique.

Like Oldsey, others found parallels between *Rabbit Redux* and important literary predecessors but still judged the novel wanting. Brom Weber (1971) says it is a humorless version of *Babbitt*, and its protagonist—"saint, anti-hero, existential man, God-seeker, whatever he is"—no more than "a dead end from which John Updike should make a turnabout" (55). Christopher Ricks (1971) notes similarities between the novel and John Dryden's *Astraea Redux* and its inspiration, the Greek myth of Astraea, the goddess of justice. But Ricks says Updike fails to deliver any kind of justice, instead providing only mercy for his lame hero. John Gordon (1972) says *Rabbit Redux* calls to mind the seventeenth-century poet John Donne, full of neat conceits and vivid metaphors that suggest—but never deliver—something momentous. Gordon thinks Updike has difficulty handling dialogue, cannot represent what is foreign to him (including women), and stumbles when trying to write about ideas. However, should he ever find "a really satisfying solution" to these problems, "it will not be just a book, it will be a national event" (59).

Numerous reviewers debunked *Rabbit Redux* as bad in concept, execution, or both. Edmund Fuller (1971) dismisses it as "sentimental slop" (12). Seymour Epstein (1972) brands it "a failed novel" (94) full of "Birchite nonsense" (95) against social changes that challenge WASP supremacy. Paul Theroux (1971) says the novel "is bad in all the ways

Rabbit, Run was bad" and "in some different ways as well." Calling the book "disingenuous and trite," Theroux concludes that "at best it is dull, at worst the shabby outrage of an imagination damaged by indulgence" (3). It "offers no pleasure, no insights"; it is not even a novel "in the most generous and imaginative sense of the word." Instead, it is a sad testament to "how coarse Updike has become, how accustomed to the book-club taste and how heedless of his craft" (10).

Once again, Michele Murray's review (1971) seems the most waspish. She trashes *Rabbit Redux* for its "loose-lipped slackness" and "customary purple passages" (many dealing—offensively, she implies—with sex), for the "meager weight" of serious purpose dribbled throughout a story much too long, and for Updike's failure to "create a common social reality." Updike simply "cannot create women characters," largely because "he is unable to see women as anything else but their genitalia." Puzzled by "the disparity between the book being praised and the limp specimen" she read for herself, Murray also attacks those who reviewed the book favorably. She notes, too, that all the ecstatic reviews have been written by men, who do not seem to "know the difference between a wholly created adult female character and a piece of mindless sex, so they sincerely take these pathetic projections for the real thing." Using Updike's own words against him, Murray concludes the book is no better than a milkshake at the Burger Bliss in Brewer, which "tastes toward the bottom of chemical sludge" (13).

Reviews like Murray's did not go unchallenged. Alice and Kenneth Hamilton (1972) weighed in on Updike's behalf, suggesting that the novel contains his prescription for the survival of the human race in a world that seems to be "deliberately traveling, like a spacecraft, toward nothingness" (741). Through Rabbit's adventures at this pivotal time in human history, Updike suggests that humankind needs to be led back to its roots and recognize that "time, rather than space, is the dimension of human meaning" (744); as one season passes into another, so may humans pass from madness to wisdom.

Several critics focused on the political dimensions of the novel, among them the Marxist Sidney Finkelstein (1972), who laments that Updike has caved in to mainstream ideology, conveniently eliminating the only true radical in the novel in order to preserve the imperialist order. While Updike may win critics' praise, he has abdicated the "special task" that creative writers can perform: to "trace the operations of imperialism" in order to show its effects on "human life and happiness" (30). Eugene Lyons (1972) asserts that this "jarring and offensive" novel displays Updike's "breathtaking ineptitude" (44), revealing his penchant to follow the trend of so many American novelists to "self-destruct as a serious writer" by striving for "both critical and financial success" while remaining "socially significant" (45).

Before moving on from this discussion of the reception of *Rabbit Redux*, it may be useful to reflect for a moment on the tricky business of trying to offer judgments about a writer's career while that person is still relatively young. *The Village Voice* decided to tackle the controversy over Updike by running competing views under the clever banner heading, "Says the Rabbit, 'What's Updike?'" Arguing in support of Updike, Dennis Delrogh (1972) calls him "the contemporary paradigm of a serious, old-fashioned novelist" (25). Lee Edwards (1972), taking the negative side, finds Updike's novels "competent and informative" (24) but hardly groundbreaking. Worse, Edwards suggests, Updike's penchant for concentrating on the pathological aspects of society merely to titillate is "a failure of morality, which ultimately cannot be divorced from a failure of art, on the one hand, and a debasement of the implicit contract between art work and audience, on the other" (26). This clever method of argument did little to fix Updike's reputation, and future publications would do much to alter both Delrogh's and Edwards's positions.

The problem of offering early judgments about Updike's career is also well illustrated in Gabriel Pearson's (1972) thoughtful critique of *Rabbit Redux*. Like many others, Pearson is impressed with "the return Updike has always managed to extract from the routines and low keyed tranquilities of contemporary living," bringing to them "a stylistic exuberance and verve which utilised all the resources of modernist prose without getting committed to the corresponding desperation." The notion that Updike's fiction shares characteristics of modernist literature would generate increasing discussion in coming years. Pearson displays some prescience in calling *Rabbit Redux* "a genuine sequel" to its predecessor—so much so, he suggests, that "one could read them—and this reviewer has—as one novel." Yet he seems premature in suggesting that "God, the ghost that still haunted Updike as recently as *Couples*," has finally been laid to rest in this novel, or that Updike is not bothered by his "vision of the American future" as a "monster's playpen with all our cowardly humanism burned out" (22). It may be too much to ask that critics be able to see clearly into the future, but definitive statements such as these are too often proven wrong.

New Short Stories and a Play, 1972–1974

In 1973 Richard Larsen observed that "the often acerbic critical controversy over the stature of John Updike continues, unabated by the publication of *Rabbit Redux*. It is still too early to tell, of course, how durable will be the total work of a writer so surprisingly fertile and inventive" (33). The controversy had some immediate benefits, however, as it assured Updike an audience for subsequent works. His next book, *Museums and Women and Other Stories* (1972) was reviewed extensively, and even made it into the top ten on the *New York Times* bestseller list for a week. Reviews were overwhelmingly positive: Updike continues "year in and year out, to produce fiction of superior quality" (Rohrbach 1972, 535); he manages consistently to keep his eye on "the flashpoint, the explosion of dark against light, the arrested moment when mortality illuminates life" (Dinnage [1972] 1979, 204); "the sorrow of some central hollowness has seeped into every corner" of the lives of Updike's middle-class suburbanites (Tanner [1972] 1982, 72). While the collection is not likely to quell debate about whether Updike is merely a fine stylist or actually a first-rate writer, these stories "are the work of perhaps the finest literary craftsman working in America today" (Kanon 1972, 78).

Critics on both sides of the religious and political spectrum found the volume rewarding. Writing in the left-leaning *New Leader*, Charles Deemer (1973) asserts that those who think Updike has nothing to say are wrong. These stories display his exceptional talents for making the lives of ordinary people meaningful. The Hamiltons' lengthy critique of *Museums and Women and Other Stories* (1974) offers a highly theological reading of the collection, prefaced by the claim that all of Updike's fiction is somehow designed to explore "the theme of a silent, upholding radiance" that offers glimpses of the eternal in a world that seems meaningless to most people (56).

However, Francis Hope (1973) thinks *Museums and Women* exposes one of Updike's major weaknesses: he writes too much, publishes too much of what he writes, and collects too much of what he publishes. A more judicious selection of stories, she says, would have produced a volume worth savoring. Another critique is worth noting for its observations on Updike's reputation. Richard Todd (1972), observes that Updike has a perennial interest in "the ironic contrast between history and the present moment," which tends to be spurred by his wistful memories of the 1950s when society seemed more stable. Still, Todd continues, "For all their recognitions of the religious impulse, their honoring of tarnished values, [these] are not stories in which moral choice occurs" (209–10). The "moral paralysis" which afflicts Updike's fiction is becoming more pronounced as the 1950s fade farther into the past—a suggestion that Updike may be on the way to becoming irrelevant.

Updike followed the release of *Museums and Women and Other Stories* with the publication of his only full-length play. *Buchanan Dying* (1974) dramatizes the life of Pennsylvania's only president, a figure in whom Updike had a lifelong interest. The work was mounted as a stage production in several locales but generated few good reviews. Stanley Weintraub (1974) tries to make excuses for it, noting that while it may fail "to come to life as a drama, it is an absorbing piece of writing by a contemporary master" who displays exceptional conscientiousness (26). Peter Straub (1975) dismisses it in a paragraph, describing it as "almost heroically boring"; Updike's "gifts for lyric social observation don't function in historical drama" (50). Irvin Ehrenpreis (1974) criticizes both the history and the dramaturgy, quipping sarcastically that "if Updike's play held one's attention, its unhistorical features would matter less." Sadly, "for all the scholarly apparatus" Updike's account remains "dubious history" (8). Curiously, renowned political historian Arthur Schlesinger, Jr. ([1974] 1983) thinks highly of the play, calling attention to the ability of fiction writers like Updike to illuminate the past in ways historians often cannot. Although Schlesinger finds some faults with Updike's dramaturgy and quibbles over his interpretation of history, he insists that "*Buchanan Dying* is infinitely more interesting than most of the trash that finds its way to New York these days" (295).

Doubling Up: Fiction and Nonfiction, 1975

In 1975, Updike exceeded his ambitious promise to publish a book a year, releasing a new novel and a new collection of nonfiction. By a wide margin, *A Month of Sundays* garnered more attention; nearly a hundred reviews were published. *Picked-Up Pieces* did quite well for a nonfiction collection, however, being the subject of more than four dozen notices. *A Month of Sundays* received mixed assessments ranging from the euphoric to the disdainful. A handful of reviewers felt the book was "light entertainment," a "Sunday sort of book" (Broyard 1975a), one that allows Updike to show off his love of language and pursue a "double interest in the scatological and the theological"—but "not an indispensable addition" to his canon (Baker 1975, 335–36). Several reviewers, however, found it more substantive. William McPherson (1975) welcomes it as another first-rate production from the man who "may be America's finest novelist" (1). Frank Lipsius (1975), who describes Updike as "the Rabelais of the American suburbs," says he has "hit[] his stride" in this novel where "indulgent invective" is "encrusted in shiny verbiage" (28). William Hill (1975) says "no other book of Updike's" has been "so terse and so provocative as this one, none so consciously stylish, none so bent on juxtaposing the earthiest of facts with the most celestial thoughts" (320). Peter Ackroyd (1975) argues that "the difficult texture" of the novel is "just the right medium for the monologue of a cramped but glistening soul." Though occasionally too conventional and didactic, it is "far more inventive and more substantial that anything which is currently being written and praised in England" (781).

The overtly Christian overtones of the novel elicited several commentaries. Cheryl Forbes (1975) calls *A Month of Sundays* a decidedly Christian novel—partly because, at its core, it is a satire of "wordy, modern Protestant theology" (16) in which the worship of words substitutes for the inadequacy of religious experience. Daniel Morrissey (1975) describes it as "Updike's neo-orthodox Christianity com[ing] full-blown out of his literary closet" (187), a "theological tour de force and a pleasurable, enriching book," a "compendium of Protestant faith" in which Updike puts forth his ideas about "the substance of things hoped for, his evidence of things unseen" (188). More pointedly, Janet Larson's review in *Christian Century* (1975) is preceded by a note from the magazine's editors, who observe that "readers have come to expect the combination of religion and sex in John Updike's novels," largely because "few contemporary writers of fiction deal as consistently or as explicitly with Christianity and sexual themes." Though the editors do not consider *A Month of Sundays* Updike's best work, they note that, since its publication, the novel had already taken on a cultural significance equal to that which *Couples* had achieved seven years earlier. In her review, Larson says Marshfield serves as Updike's "new classic fool, speaking for an adulterous generation in an age of waned faith" (445). Although Marshfield is ultimately a "literary failure"—too much enamored with an aesthetic brand of theology and not real enough (447)—Larson is encouraged by the novel's central question and the answer Updike gives: "Is faith possible in these days?" Despite Marshfield's "instant wanderings over a wasted life," the answer seems to be "a tentative Yes." But faith is placed in "an extremely transcendent God," not one immanent in the people who inhabit Updike's novel (446).

A Month of Sundays also attracted a fair share of disparaging reviews. Ronald De Feo (1975) believes Updike's "conscious effort to loosen up" has allowed him to "break free from the restraints of traditional narration" (679), but the experiment is not wholly successful because the overblown style gets in the way of plot and characterization. At best, the novel is "a thoroughly professional though diffuse performance by one of our most gifted writers, who has given us and, no doubt, will give us more satisfying and memorable books than this" (680). Similarly, George Stade (1975) believes Updike's attempts to bring together the sexual and religious themes in the novel are never quite successful. "Much there is to praise about this novel," Stade admits, but "it is not good enough, not as good as its own possibilities demand" (4).

Thomas Edwards (1975) thinks Updike has chosen an appropriate hero, since "ministers aren't bad surrogates for novelists"; furthermore, combining religion and sex in a single volume seems perfect for him. But the writing is "overwrought" (18) and Updike's interest in religion and in sex have not "come together to say something that is impressive or interesting about love," making it "a great deal more than disappointing self-indulgence by a very gifted writer" (19). Joan Hall (1975) agrees, finding the novel tedious despite the presence of some exceptionally well written sermons interspersed in the narrative. "For all its cleverness" the book is "shallow in a way that its sermons are not" (30).

Viewing *A Month of Sundays* from the perspective of Updike's growth as an artist, Edmund Fuller (1975) describes it as "by far the most interesting, but no less exasperating" of Updike's novels to date. Because Updike fails to deal with the serious theological issues he raises, the novel is "intellectually flashy but bankrupt." Fuller, who had been complaining about the direction of Updike's work for some time, concludes with the excoriating observation that "if this is all Mr. Updike has to show and tell, he might as well not have set his fingers to keys. He is not ripening as an artist, but decaying" (16). Benjamin De Mott (1975) also faults Updike for not living up to his potential. While his novels give readers great pleasure in learning about the faults and foibles of contemporary America, Updike "lacks a principle on which to build resistance" to the problems he describes so accurately (20). However, since Updike is still relatively young, it is "extremely hard not to look ahead" and "wonder whether, sooner or later," he will offer solutions instead of simply highlighting problems. Gilbert Sorrentino is not so hopeful. Calling those who hold Updike's work in high regard misguided in their appreciation, he blasts Updike's writing for the "twitches and quivers" that pass for "sublime style" ([1976] 1982, 77). From Updike "we are given wit and talent and we are given invention," but sadly "we are not given literature" (79).

A few reviewers, however, found more going on in *A Month of Sundays* than many of their contemporaries realized. In his lengthy review, George Steiner (1975) devotes considerable attention to the parallels between Updike's novel and *The Scarlet Letter*. Having no indication of Updike's ultimate intent with regard to Hawthorne's masterpiece, Steiner can only be described as having exceptional foresight. In another provocative review, Thomas LeClair (1975) argues that the novel is on one level "fictive criticism" (130), a response to contemporary trends in critical theory and a defense of "the novelist's old authority to tell real people about imagined people" (131). Where metafiction writers have "emphasized the arbitrariness, playfulness, and limits of language," Updike insists on its "referential quality" (131–32). In clarifying the "realistic aesthetic," Updike is arguing for "the imagination's ability to know others—the subjects of the novel and its readers" (132).

Ten years after publishing *Assorted Prose*, Updike again collected essays and reviews he had written for various publications in a volume with the rather deprecatory title *Picked-Up Pieces*. The relatively large number of reviews of *Picked-Up Pieces* indicates the seriousness with which both the reading public and academic world viewed Updike's nonfiction. John Russell (1976) notes that "best-selling novelists do not always appear to advantage in their occasional writings," but Updike manages to come off quite well. Doris Grumbach (1975) ranks Updike's nonfiction on par with his creative work, calling him "the best novelist-critic now writing." He not only "understands the act of criticism as well as, and often better than, any other American now practicing that perilous craft," but he also possesses exceptional "insight about the writing of fiction" and is a "graceful, inventive, joyous and affectionate writer" (C4). John Brinnin (1975) is even more enthusiastic. Reading the "lighthearted" yet "erudite" essays in *Picked-Up Pieces* makes one "party to an evening of civilized contention." Furthermore, the book is "held together by an inescapable moral force" and a "searching light of discrimination that suggests Updike belongs in the company of secular divines" (A8).

Robert Kirsch (1975) says the reviews in *Picked-Up Pieces* reveal qualities of Updike's personality not often evident in his imaginative work, which is often "too much a performance": qualities of generosity, sensitivity, empathy, and erudition. In these essays "Updike comes through as an appealing and rounded personality: the picked-up pieces fill out the authentic man" (G15). Anatole Broyard (1975b) also finds most of the reviews engaging and thoughtful, and concludes that "Updike is an unassailable refutation of the old saw that those who can, do, while those who cannot, critique" (37). Martin Amis observes that reading an Updike review reminds one that "the review can, in its junior way, be something of a work of art" ([1976] 2001, 369).

Others, however, expressed reservations. Calvin Bedient (1975) finds these essays delightful, consistently charming and only occasionally filled with moralizing. Yet he is critical of Updike's style: "his adjectives whiz right in, but at the art of the sentence and the paragraph he nods; his sentences lack tautness, and his paragraphs grow and grow, getting flabbier" (29). Alfred Alvarez (1976) raises a complaint heard frequently about Updike's nonfiction collections. He is puzzled by Updike's motives for preserving everything he had published in the preceding decade. Many of the reviews are affected and unhelpful, he observes, and will harm Updike's reputation as a critic. Unfortunately, "Updike seems to suffer from the narcissistic delusion that *everything* he has written is worth preserving. So if it is held against him, he has nobody but himself to blame" (30).

Academic Criticism, 1972–1975

Updike's stature was confirmed again in 1972 by the publication of Robert Detweiler's *John Updike* in the Twayne US Authors series. Following the format prescribed for Twayne volumes, Detweiler devotes a chapter to each of Updike's novels from *The Poorhouse Fair* through *Rabbit Redux* and to the major short story collections issued to date. The significance of the volume, however, lies in Detweiler's systematic examination of Updike's literary techniques, particularly his use of irony. Detweiler classifies Updike as a practitioner of "secular baroque," which he describes as "elaborate, texture-conscious, structurally balanced, highly controlled, mythically resonant fiction" that marks the passing of an ordered world (7). What is missing from this volume—curiously, given Detweiler's interest in the intersection of literature and religion—is any extended discussion of religious overtones in Updike's work. Detweiler is cautious in dealing with this topic because he realizes that religious references can be misconstrued or misrepresented—a fault he finds throughout the Hamiltons' recently published volume, which he describes as being "marred by religious symbol hunting and overattention to tenuous religions allusions" (176).

Detweiler's fine study was followed the next year by two books devoted exclusively to Updike. Joyce Markle's *Fighters and Lovers: Theme in the Novels of John Updike* (1973) is also notable for its lack of commentary on theological matters. Markle chooses instead to provide "a broad schematic of the central issues and values that characterize" Updike's fiction. Her assessment demonstrates how Updike approaches themes such as "the flight from death," the "need for 'Lovers'" (which she defines as "characters who can give a feeling of stature and specialness to others"), the "evidence [of] man's impact on his world," and the "sources" of a person's "sense of importance" and of one's "abilities and responsibilities in relating" to others (2). Markle concentrates on the artistic methods Updike uses to expose his themes and values—techniques that link Markle's study to formalist critiques of mid-century rather than to studies based on new critical theories emerging in the 1970s.

The second book, and one of the best early studies of Updike as a religious writer, is Edward Vargo's *Rainstorms and Fire: Ritual in the Novels of John Updike* (1973b). Building on his essay about *The Centaur* in *PMLA* (1973a), Vargo makes a two-pronged argument: first, that Updike is a religious writer who invests the everyday with sacredness through the techniques of ritual; and second, that most critics who have dismissed his work as trivial and mannered simply do not understand him. Updike sees his task as "a quest" to discover "the unseen and elusive ambiguity behind life" and a "search for the means to help his readers experience the transcendent realities of life" (1973b, 6). He wishes to "achieve a new creation through his imagination" by "bringing into focus" the "divinity present in every particle of the universe" (7). Hence, he highlights details to "invest the familiar objects and gestures of everyday experience with religious meaning," accomplishing this through "the sophisticated use of ritual, of which the three basic elements are pattern, myth, and celebration" (16). Far from being a simple realist, Updike has written "many-layered novels that cannot be judged by the standards of a rigidly naturalistic tradition" (173). What is unique about his fiction is his "continuous integration of the process, the function, and the *spirit* of ritual to express spiritual yearning in an apparently materialistic world" (175).

Vargo recognizes that objections about Updike's "lack of depth, flawed moral vision, and manipulation of detail rather than genuine human involvement" have been "voiced too frequently and too seriously to be passed over lightly" (4). He goes to some lengths to debunk these misguided notions about Updike's art, asserting that in portraying "the strivings of the inner self in opposition to the gray outer world" Updike is "truer to life as most of us live it than those critics who demand showiness in plot construction rather than imagery" (174). Additionally, Vargo says, behind all these negative criticisms lies a "streak of dishonesty," because these critics' real objection to Updike's work is more fundamental: "they are unhappy with Updike because he does not portray a kind of realism which refuses to accept any kind of spiritual reality beyond Man" (174). Vargo believes Updike has gotten it right in seeing that "even in twentieth-century America man instinctively turns to rituals to answer his fear of death and his need for ecstasy and wholeness" (179).

By the early 1970s academics had begun to recognize the importance of the Rabbit novels in the Updike canon. Clinton Burhans ([1973] 1982) argues this point forcefully: "Whatever else can be said of John Updike's writing since 1960, one judgment seems clear. *Rabbit, Run* continues to be his most popular and critically successful novel, the one work in which his artistic and intellectual voices sound their fullest and truest sense" (148). Several articles suggest the diversity of opinions about the values and intent of the developing sequence. Noting that many reviewers and critics find Harry Angstrom "a rather trivial character," Lewis Lawson (1974) argues that Updike's artistry cleverly conceals the ways he is able to use this ordinary man to make "a profound statement about the agony of being religious in an irreligious world which thinks itself religious" (232). Wiley Umphlett's (1975) analysis suggests that Updike is concerned with the divergent demands on modern people: urges that pull them toward a simple life compete with those drawing them toward more complex social situations and responsibilities. Rabbit is a modern-day equivalent of Natty Bumpo, James Fenimore Cooper's woodsman who is always escaping civilization into the romantic natural world of the American wilderness. For Rabbit, however, there is no wilderness into which he can escape, so his running becomes simply frustrating and ultimately meaningless.

In a somewhat unflattering critique of *Rabbit Redux*, Mariann Russell (1973) argues that Updike creates Skeeter only so that Rabbit can see "the living embodiment of the disturbing elements of his public and private life" (97–98); hence, the use of a black character is clearly subordinate to Updike's interest in white society. David Vanderwerken (1975) explores Updike's use of "the language and technology of space flight" as a unifying device in *Rabbit Redux*, creating parallels between the scientific community's flight to land on the moon with Rabbit's inner journey toward self-discovery (73). Rabbit's return to Janice at the end of the novel "is both a literal and a suggestive action," as it becomes "Updike's objective correlative for his personal hope for America's, and the world's future" (77). By contrast, Kermit Turner (1975) is a bit put out with Updike because his title character has not grown up and is still "not capable of rational thought or moral choice; he merely reacts on an emotional, visceral, or glandular level" (37). Far from advancing in knowledge or coming to some mature emotional balance, Rabbit continues as he was ten years earlier, perhaps worse: in this novel "he also is without a conscience, a sense of guilt, which he at least showed some signs of in *Rabbit, Run*" (40). The only way to take *Rabbit Redux* seriously, Turner suggests, is to see it as Updike's portrait of "the sickness of modern, permissive, secular society" (42).

Five years before George Hunt would publish his systematic study of the "three great, secret things" which Updike identifies in "The Dogwood Tree" as the sources of his fiction, Francis Kunkel's (1975) chapter on Updike in *Passion and the Passion* explores in some detail the connection between sex and religion in Updike's fiction. Kunkel argues that Updike is pleading for a return to traditional Christian values as a means of staving off what he sees as the inevitable collapse of modern society into moral anarchy.

Where these essays and others written contemporaneously treat Updike's work seriously, not everyone thought he deserved such attention. In a brief essay Keith Mano crystallizes the negative reactions to Updike's fiction in a series of acerbic comments such as "Updike's characters don't deserve a form letter obituary, let alone a novel," and "great issues aren't at issue in Updike's fiction" ([1974] 1982, 74). Updike never takes a position on important issues. All he has going for him is facility of style. Neither funny nor deep, Updike is "a middle class realist" who "should be unread" (75). That he *is* widely read is a tribute more to the poor standards of the contemporary reading public rather than to Updike's accomplishments. He "has very little to say," Mano concludes with a note of irony, "and no one writing in America says it better" (76).

Mano's comments notwithstanding, a snapshot of mainstream critical opinion on Updike can be found in the spring 1974 issue of *Modern Fiction Studies*, where editor William T. Stafford assembled eight articles and two notes on Updike's work. Joseph Waldmeir argues that both Rabbit novels are organized around the motif of the quest. Wayne Falke provides a revisionist view of Updike's religious dimension, challenging the Hamiltons' insistent readings of everything in the Updike canon as a kind of theological tract; instead, Falke says, Updike's fiction is "calling for a humanism that has little justification in theology" (65). Alan McKenzie and the duo of Paula and Nick Backscheider explore aspects of *Couples*, while John Vickery examines Updike's use of myth and history in *The*

Centaur. The shorter pieces by Albert Griffith and Alfred Rosa provide insight into a number of Updike's short stories. The level of interest among academics in Updike is highlighted in Arlin Meyer's "Selected Checklist of Criticism," which runs to thirteen pages of very small type.

Several essays in this special issue of *MFS* speak directly to Updike's reputation. Robert Regan takes a broader look at the Updike canon in what he calls "a radically new approach" which, "for the first time in the criticism of his controversial art," examines his "ubiquitous symbol of the center" from "a neo-Kantian point of view" (77). This sweeping claim seems to give the lie to those who believe Updike's work is all surface and no depth. How the dazzling surface of the fiction has worked against Updike is the subject of Robert Gingher's essay, "Has Updike Anything to Say?," an extended rebuttal of earlier critics who had found Updike intellectually vacuous. Updike himself may be to blame for questions about his *gravitas*, however, as Robert McCoy (1974) points out in an intriguing contribution on Updike's apprenticeship on the *Harvard Lampoon*. A cartoon drawn by Updike depicts a petulant youth standing before a large canvas on which he has drawn a tiny figure; in the caption, the youth tells his teacher, "Miss Gridley, I may have little to say, but I'm determined to say it well" (6).

A year later, Joyce Carol Oates ([1975] 1979) published an extended defense of Updike's fiction, suggesting that, despite the sense of the tragic created by many of Updike's works, his vision is essentially comic. Oates admits Updike has difficulty portraying women, tending to reduce them all to archetypes of the Female, the object of desire for his male characters. On the other hand, she insists it is unfair to charge Updike with being "too fascinated with the near-infinitesimal at the cost of having failed to create massive, angry works of art that more accurately record a violent time." Oates thinks "it is far more difficult to do what Updike does," she says, "because he accepts the comic ironies and inadequacies of ordinary life" and makes art out of them (68).

3: Launching New Ventures (1976–1980)

During the second half of the 1970s, Updike carried out further exploration of familiar themes, especially in short stories and the 1976 novel *Marry Me*. He also made what was for him a decidedly bold move. Although he had occasionally written of locales and people other than those from his native Pennsylvania and his adopted home in New England, his 1978 novel *The Coup* marked his first attempt to render an extended treatment of another region of the world and deal with characters whose creation tested his imaginative powers in ways his earlier fiction had not. Reviewers made much of Updike's venture into foreign territory, though it would be unfair to say that a sea change in critical opinion occurred as a result of his experiment. There was a noted shift in attitudes toward Updike's work among academic critics, however, as feminists began systematic analysis that exposed what they felt were his misogynist views on women. At the same time, critics began commenting on the conservatism that formed the foundation of Updike's view of America. The writer once seen as a bold new voice challenging the status quo was quickly becoming known as the spokesperson for establishment values.

Dabbling in Romance: *Marry Me*, 1976

Marry Me, which Updike subtitled "A Romance" and for which he provided alternate endings, could be dubbed a commercial success. Between November 1976 and February 1977 it appeared sporadically among the *New York Times* top ten bestsellers. Like its predecessors, it received mixed reviews, in part because Updike seemed to be covering well-trodden ground, in part because some reviewers did not understand his aims or his methods in employing the vehicle of the romance. No one was more positive about the novel than Edmund Fuller (1976), who had loved *Rabbit, Run* but hated *Rabbit Redux* and *A Month of Sundays*. Fuller celebrates *Marry Me* as a rejuvenation of Updike's talents, calling it "among the best novels of his prolific production" (22). Updike is "poignantly amusing, keenly observant, in capturing the terrible sadnesses of marriages in crisis" (22). Likewise, Peter Prescott ([1976] 1983) notes how clinically yet sympathetically Updike portrays the travails of married life. "The best written and least self-conscious of Updike's longer fiction," *Marry Me* "contains his most sophisticated and sympathetic portraits of women"; it is "Updike's best novel yet" (306). Edmund White (1976) also praises Updike for his "awareness of his characters' inner life" (L1). The tale, anecdotal as it may be, is related with a touch of "lyricism" that "quietly imbues every paragraph of the book." The power of the prose overwhelms readers, making them "stand at a distance and blink at this great talent" (L2). Judith Barnard (1976) praises *Marry Me* as a "mirror of our modern popular wisdom," an advance over *Couples*, in which Updike "tried to plot the sociology of marriage" but "didn't quite make it" (6). George Hunt (1977b) argues that a novel like *Marry Me* succeeds when readers find "the complex questions posed about the nature of goodness" compelling (18). The alternate endings of the novel press this debate by allowing readers to choose one that is aesthetically satisfying or opt for a "moral one" (19).

Marry Me was hailed in the British press as well. Calling Updike "a cautious and deliberate writer" who avoids "Bellow's airy nonsense and Heller's rambling blandness," Peter Ackroyd (1977) admires Updike's ability to reveal how "the variety and the colour of the present moment" is merely "a patina behind which murmur anxieties, fears and memories which no amount of Western opulence and rationality can heal" (22). Updike's ability to represent "stubborn reality" elevates him "above most of his contemporaries in the United States" (23). Malcolm Bradbury (1977) says that, though not likely to be judged one of Updike's best, *Marry Me* is nevertheless quintessentially Updike, who is "superb at intersecting between the revelation and the void." If in this novel Updike seems "imbalanced" in his sympathy for characters who hunger for "the redemption of sex, art, and religion," he remains a master at finessing "the literary text" and giving it to readers "with his usual richness" (569). Even Paul Theroux (1977) reveals a rare sense of respect for the novel. Although virtually every novel that preceded *Marry Me* had left him uneasy in some way, Theroux finds this story compelling and concludes that "Updike has never written better of the woe that is in marriage."

Unfortunately, several reviewers and critics who had previously written favorable assessments of Updike's fiction did not find much to like in *Marry Me*. Maureen Howard (1976) says that while Updike is "inventive, witty and bright," this novel is "not one of Updike's better performances." The supposedly passionate affairs fail to impress, because the two couples in the novel "are not only absurd, they are ordinary" (2). Alfred Kazin ([1976] 1982) seems to agree, suggesting that, while Updike is "always at his best in handling the social matters," the people in *Marry Me* are "just not interesting" (80). Updike "uses the same man over and over" in all his novels, one tormented by sex and God, even when the individual story does not sustain his argument. For all his stylistic ability, Updike is unable to create sufficiently differentiated characters to make his books interesting and new. Karl Miller (1977) believes the work proceeds with such uncertainty that it reveals a sad fact: "a very talented novelist" is "currently at sea" (38). Thomas LeClair (1977) finds the book filled with sentimentality and banal writing. It is as if by "flourish[ing] his now familiar theology *in extremis*" Updike thinks he can "compensate for lackluster characterization" (90). Christopher Ricks (1977) complains that, for all his expertise, Updike wastes his talents in creating a novel that is simply a bit of cunning trickery about one of his favorite subjects, "marital mesh and mess."

Even less forgiving, L. J. Davis (1976) says the book clearly shows "there is no development in Updike's work, no flexibility in his vision"; every new work simply repeats a theme presented in some earlier story. "*Marry Me* is a sort of *Couples Redux*, reduced to the point where it is hard to escape the feeling that he wrote it in his sleep or perhaps on weekends" (25). Brigid Brophy's (1976) savage critique begins by warning readers that "the book has a high saccharin content" (80). Furthermore, the structure is inadequate and the plot trite and lackluster, filled with clichéd descriptions of domestic activity, especially sexual activity. Brophy is particularly appalled by the double ending, in which the male protagonist seems to get the best of both worlds, domestic stability and adventure with another woman. She thinks Updike is not even a good enough "virtuoso" to be considered "excruciatingly awful" (80).

Finally, two appraisals prompted by the publication of *Marry Me* warrant special attention because they point to larger issues in Updike's fiction. In "Updike as Matchmaker," Josephine Hendin ([1976] 1979) observes that, unlike male warriors of old, "Updike's men have only their women to justify their aggression and define them as men" (101). In Updike's fiction a man's life is a "sophisticated Oedipal knot" in which he is "tied at both ends" (102). Many of Updike's male protagonists are constantly searching for a wife who will behave like their mother. Too often, however, real women do not measure up to the ideal these men are seeking; this deficiency (which is not the woman's fault) often leads to tragic relationships. But Hendin does not think Updike diminishes women in his novels; instead, he seems "more grateful than any other male writer for the nobility of women," and he often portrays them lovingly (106).

Richard Todd (1976) also has something to say about the male protagonists of Updike's fiction. He is not surprised that *Marry Me* may remind readers of *Couples* and *A Month of Sundays*, although he believes it has a "texture" that is "purely its own, wit intermingled with passion and sadness in a density Updike has not achieved before" (115). Like many other Updike novels, however, this tale of men in domestic relationships also deals with the loss of conventional religious belief and its replacement with sex. Todd invents a short-hand term to describe the central figures in many of Updike's works (Rabbit Angstrom being the most notable exception): the Updike Figure, "a well-educated" man "employed in a cerebral, well-paid, if not as often a satisfying way, a suburban sort, comforted by humility and an intimation of a divine order and wracked by longings that lie outside his domestic life" (115). Unstated is the comparison with another archetype of American literature, the Hemingway Hero. While future critics would come to similar conclusions about the protagonists of many of Updike's works, for better or worse Todd's term has not caught on.

Poetry and a Bold Experiment in Fiction, 1977–1978

Updike's third collection of poems, *Tossing and Turning*, appeared in 1977 to relatively little notice. While none of the few reviews was hostile, no one suggested that Updike was a major poet. A number noted Updike's limited range, though as Christina Robb (1977) observed, his "versifying hand is very graceful and does these few things very well" (25). Presciently, perhaps, Matthew Hodgart (1978), who describes Updike as "a master, perhaps the master in our time, of light verse," says no final determination of Updike's status as a poet will be made "until twenty years after his death" (1158).

The following year Updike dropped a bombshell on the literary world. *The Coup* was like nothing he had written before. While the novel displays the same wit, the same interest in sex, and the same sardonic look at American society as one might find in earlier work, the protagonist is not an angst-filled man from Pennsylvania or New England but a failed African dictator. Perhaps the novel's notoriety sparked the wide readership it garnered. *The Coup* occupied a spot on the *New York Times* bestseller list from January through April 1978, rising as high as number four. Those familiar with Updike's career may have seen hints that such a novel was on the horizon—he had been to Africa and written a handful of stories set outside his "comfort zone"—but the reading public at large was left scratching their heads about what to make of this radical departure from Updike's normal fare. Given these circumstances, it is no wonder that reviewers expressed strong feelings pro and con.

It seems appropriate to provide a generous sampling of reviews, which numbered well over a hundred, to give some idea of what readers appreciated and what troubled them. William McPherson (1978) calls *The Coup* "a very funny book as well as a very serious one," quite different from Updike's earlier fiction but clearly "the work of an intelligent and funny and passionate man" (1). Robert Towers ([1978] 1979) considers it one of Updike's strongest novels, an example of what a prolific and gifted novelist can do "when his imagination, as well as his language, is strenuously engaged" (157). Lee Milazzo (1978) says *The Coup* may be "Updike's finest work, both for its presentation of the 'exotic' Ellellou and for its description of the inchoate Third World" (5G). Peter La Salle (1978) notes how strange it is to see Updike turn to "such an alien setting" but believes the experiment "works wonderfully well." The "vividness of the African scene" seems to be the perfect subject for Updike's "rare gift of language." Updike's "gamble has paid off, proving his versatility beyond denial." It is likely, La Salle continues, that "such versatility" will keep him ranked as one of America's major novelists for many years (482).

Claire Tomalin (1979), too, notes that the novel is an "enormous" departure for Updike. Yet "with extraordinary virtuosity and elegance" he has "constructed a tangible country" and a convincing narrator through whom he can offer a different kind of critique of America (552). The novel is "rich in characters, landscapes, ideas and compression," a clear sign that Updike is able to go beyond personal experience and employ his considerable stylistic skills in a work of imaginative brilliance (553). David Evanier (1979) believes *The Coup* possesses "scope, verbal dazzle on every page, and a sympathetic, credible crazy" in its protagonist (490). Its "blend of comedy, satire, elegant prose, seriousness of purpose, highly credible characterization" and an imagination "that takes wing on every page" combine to "endow[ ] the book with eminence" (491). Anthony Burgess (1979) finds it "crammed with poetry of a beautifully recognizable kind" by a writer whose gift for language is "perhaps the greatest in American fiction since Nabokov." It is full of serious ideas as well, exposing both the evils of neocolonialism and "the intractabilities of Africa" while highlighting some of the unseemly aspects of American life and values (36). John Thompson (1978) is dazzled by the book, praising both its conception and execution. "With much nerve and surely with some luck," he says, "Updike invented his Africa not the way other white novelists have done," choosing to use an African as his central character rather than a white man who might interpret the land of darkness to outsiders (3). Judy Cooke (1980) says one "cannot overpraise the greedy sweep of the author's grand scheme." The novel is an advance for "Updike the moralist" who is "no longer working within that cold pastoral which dictated the range of some earlier satires." In *The Coup* "his targets are political, literary, and educational, and he hits them smack in the bull's eye" (22).

Even the conservative *National Review* publisher and political commentator William F. Buckley, Jr. (1978) took an opportunity to comment on *The Coup*, publishing a brief review in *New York* magazine in which he says the novel is "not to be missed" (93). Perhaps ironically, writing in the leftist *New Leader* Daphne Merkin (1978) also praises Updike for finally overcoming his ideological shortcomings. The novel is "a very witty book about the merchandising of ideology," Nabokovian in its satire and yet compellingly critical as social commentary. "It is almost as though Updike had to figuratively leave home" in order "to see most clearly into the frailties" of America. The result is a powerful novel in which Updike "comes closer than he has ever come before to matching the intention with the act" (22). John Ryle (1979) judges *The Coup* "among the most illuminating books written about Africa in the post-colonial era." He is particularly struck by Updike's ability to turn "the Western romance of Africa on its head," making America the "heart of darkness" into which the African leader Ellellou has seen (77).

Several fellow novelists were also impressed. Joyce Carol Oates claims this "immensely inspired and energetic" tale can stand beside, or even above, Nabokov's *Pale Fire* as a dark, surreal comedy ([1979a] 1982, 85). Beneath the surface sparkle, however, Oates detects "a passionate and despairing cynicism" (84)—a characteristic she believes is present in Updike's more recent critiques of contemporary America. "The novel is beautifully calibrated, persuasive and lustrous," writes Paul Theroux (1978). Though one might quibble over some of the details and inconsistencies, Updike's invented country is powerfully imagined and "the narrative is convincing because it is passionate and humorous in equal degrees, because it is skeptical and concerned, its dominant tone informed by a kind of horrible hilarity" (36–37). David Lodge (1979) calls the novel "a coup for its author, daringly conceived and brilliantly carried off," a work in which Updike's imagination is not confined to suburbia. It is "full of wry political wisdom," and manages "to extend our sympathies in the great tradition of the realist novel, while being thoroughly modern in its artfulness and ironies" (405).

Perhaps the highest praise for *The Coup* comes from Paul Ableman (1979), who calls it "the finest American novel since *Lolita*," one which "marks a significant stage in the evolution of American literature and, undoubtedly, in the career of Updike." While Updike may lack "the sheer dramatic power of Nabokov" and "the profound compassion" that "characterizes the very greatest writers," he has produced a naturalistic novel that is at the same time a social commentary on the human condition akin to the great eighteenth-century masterpieces. "Social historians of the future may well conclude that this book signified a new maturity in the political consciousness of America," while "literary critics will certainly go on regarding it as a superb work of art" (18).

Mark Dintenfass (1979) is a bit more circumspect. *The Coup* may not be "the 'great novel' people keep expecting Updike to write," but it is "a very good book." Although it has an exotic quality, "Updike has not journeyed all that far from Tarbox; he's simply found a new dark and gaudy mirror to hold up to it" (5:3). Edmund Fuller (1978) says the novel "seems to promise some coherent philosophical development that never materializes," but leaves the reader with a sense of Updike's "non-discriminating" distaste for both the Third and First worlds (28). Margaret Manning (1978) is also not wholly satisfied. While the novel is "intelligent" and "occasionally even profound," she says, it is also too "romantic." Colonel Ellellou, "whom Updike plainly relishes, will not do" (A8).

Numerous others found fault with the novel. D. A. N. Jones (1979) describes it as a weak parody of serious fiction that left him "bored, irritated, and uninformed" (390). Roderick Nordell (1978) feels that, while the prose remains "a jeweled instrument of description and comedy," the erotic descriptions seem "rather overdone" and the irony falls flat because Updike does not attempt to get beyond caricatures of Africans (21). Gene Lyons (1979) is disappointed with the book, but even more upset by the extended praise Updike received for a work Lyons believes is inferior. "That a symbolist reading of a long narrative can parse a Deep Hidden Meaning out of what is otherwise confused and even ridiculous," Lyons concludes, "is a symptom of a kind of cultural confusion about literary meaning" (120).

Larry Swindell (1978), however, offers a decidedly different reading of Updike's achievement. "There seems lately to have been a shift in the general critical stance toward Updike." While critics have finally begun to consider Updike a writer "not of promise, but of achievement," they have begun to carp that his works "seem all from the same mold." Swindell thinks *The Coup* "triumphantly shatters that mold." Though the novel is set in Africa, Updike keeps his focus on America, observing the country from "an African viewpoint" that is "peculiarly Updike's." Swindell believes *The Coup* "certif[ies] Updike as a satirist of absolute brilliance" (24G).

How *The Coup* might affect Updike's general reputation is addressed by two reviewers with decidedly different opinions. The influential British academic Frank Kermode (1979) uses his review to defend Updike against the "three main objections" leveled at him: he writes incessantly; he is "obsessed with the sociological detail of the American suburb" (ostensibly an unworthy subject), which he does with the smarminess of a Harvard-educated *New Yorker* staffer; and—the worst fault of all—"he is some sort of a Christian and lets it affect his work." Kermode dismantles each of these objections, demonstrating that Updike has what it takes to be a major writer: "a fine mind, poise, and a total indifference to bad criticism" (10). However, in a more tempered defense, Russell Hunt (1979) says that, while the "bracing whiff of irony" readers get from Updike may remind them of the work of Jane Austen or George Meredith, Updike is in "an odd position" among contemporary authors: "He's neither trendy enough nor revolutionary enough to occupy a position of real eminence." As a consequence, Hunt predicts that when future undergraduate courses in American literary trends are organized, "Updike probably won't even get a mention" (25).

Short Story Collections, 1979

In 1979 Knopf published two collections of Updike's stories. The first, *Too Far to Go*, a collection of previously published stories about the Maples, was issued to coincide with the release of a two-hour made-for-television movie based on these stories. The other collection, *Problems and Other Stories*, is largely an anthology of Updike's short fiction published since the release of *Museums and Women and Other Stories* in 1972. The appearance of the two volumes gave many reviewers a chance to reevaluate Updike's capabilities as a short-story writer and reflect again on the themes that interested him since he began publishing in the 1950s.

Three reviews offer some idea of the reaction to the appearance of *Too Far to Go*. Erica Jong (1979) praises Updike's talent and offers some harsh words for his critics. In her view, Updike is "the most skillful writer currently using the American language." Claims that he has "too much technique" seem "transparently envious" (36). Jong likes the way Updike transforms autobiography into art, and also commends his portraits of women, calling them "at least partly symbols for the ineffability of the life force" but also "real women" (37). Paul Theroux (1979) suggests that of all contemporary writers, Updike best understands the problems of modern marriage. But—*contra* Jong—Theroux faults Updike for failing to recognize or represent adequately the woman's point of view in relationships. Finally, William McPherson (1979) notes that, while these stories may represent quite graphically and accurately "the way we, or some of the more fortunate among us, live now" (E1), they offer no new insight because Updike has done all this before. "It seems to me," he says, that Updike "now faces a choice in his work: to recapitulate with another set of names the familiar story of peccadilloes in suburban paradise" or "go on to something else" (E6).

Problems and Other Stories received favorable notice in most major American newspapers and periodicals. Edmund Fuller (1979) describes the volume as "Updike at his best, sometimes his most ruefully funny," noting that, "in spite of his reputation as a novelist," Updike's "finest and most consistent achievements are in the shorter form" (24). George Garrett (1980) claims that *Problems* demonstrates why "Updike must be named among our short-story masters" (422). His only limitation is his inability to create characters outside his immediate circle. However, Margaret Manning (1979) believes Updike's use of autobiography is a particular strength. His talent is evident in the way he writes about personal crises, employing "one of the world's most felicitous prose styles" which is not only "lucid," "agreeable," and highly readable, but at times "radiant" and "dazzling" (A7).

Joyce Carol Oates (1979b) finds that in *Problems* Updike's "lyricism is restrained," the mood "nostalgic" but "not sentimental" (44).

The strongest stories are "those that deal with Updike's primary theme, the gradual loss of innocence that is our common fate" (45). John Romano (1979) calls *Problems* "a work of really awesome literary cunning" whose "satisfactions are profound, and the proper emotion is one of gratitude that such a splendid artistic intelligence has been brought to bear on some of the important afflictions of our times" (1). George Hunt (1980b) claims the "problems" Updike deals with are like those described by the philosopher Gabriel Marcel: "radical probings that generate an encounter with mystery, the mystery of manifold 'presences' and their absences" (187). Hunt finds it curious that people consider Updike old-fashioned, because his "most developed talent is that of psychological realism, the rendering of 'felt life'" (188).

Among those expressing minor reservations is Diana Loercher (1979), who thinks Updike's ability to provide "microscopic analysis of psychological scintilla" sometimes obscures rather than elucidates his themes. "Updike's prose is as tropical as ever," though "sometimes overripe." His descriptions are "delicate as flowers," his humor "brittle as glass." All this, Loercher concludes, "confirms the suspicion that Updike's greatest romance of all is with language" (7). Echoing these observations, David Evanier (1980) finds that, while the quality of the stories is uneven, Updike, "a wonderful writer" (231), continues to invest his stories—even those which reveal "lives wearing down"—with "a sad, natural, and unmistakable beauty" (234).

Others, however, offered decidedly different judgments. Although Abigail McCarthy (1979) considers Updike "pre-eminent among contemporary writers of the short story," excelling at presenting "the world of domestic conflict," she finds that these stories give further proof to his limitations. He is "simply not effective with major themes," relying instead on his ability to write repeatedly about "one theme—the cherished, weak, and vulnerable self and the hazards attendant on its indulgence" (97). Robert Towers (1979) admits that Updike has proven exceptionally adept at depicting "the tribal customs and artifacts of middle-class life" in America (18). But the stories in this collection are uneven, and only occasionally does an emotionally charged scene dazzle readers and make them "willing to shrug off the lesser stuff that prevents *Problems* from being one of his better books" (20).

British reviewers had the same range of reactions. Claire Tomalin (1980) describes the collection as "confessional fiction without a trace of heavy breathing," a group of "wicked, near-perfect stories by a writer too clever to need to explain anything." Russell Davies (1980) suggests that in these stories Updike has taken the "good old tripod of births, marriage, and deaths" that has served as the basis for much fiction and created tales in which characters find themselves "impaled in an increasingly puncturesome way" on the "nasty old trident" of "mistress, divorce, memory"

(771). Margaret Drabble (1979) says Updike has the ability to make his characters "stumble bravely on through the dark world, remembering past innocence and past delights" as they become guilty while growing old. Yet, "as always with Updike," there are "moments of exhilaration, phrases that redeem the prevailing sense of loss" (1). However, William Walsh (1980) considers *Problems* a minor achievement at best, largely because the material is "too insubstantial" to "show Updike at the height of his powers, displaying the glittering constellation of gifts he certainly possesses" (39). Rosemary Dinnage (1980) describes the volume as "a slightly sadder gathering than previous collections," and a bit "stodgier" as well. The fault may not lie with Updike, however; "we have come to expect so much variety and wit from Updike that we are disappointed if the magician does not produce new tricks each time round" (575). James Campbell (1980) thinks the problem is more substantial. The stories in this volume reveal one of Updike's important limitations: his work lacks "the tragic dimension" (821).

Academic Criticism 1976–1980

In 1966, Granville Hicks wrote that, while most of Updike's fiction is told from a man's point of view, "he almost always manages to do justice to the women" ([1966] 1970, 127). A decade later it would have been hard to find many critics who agreed with that judgment. By then feminist critics had turned their gaze on John Updike—and did not like what they saw. Typical of scathing feminist critiques is Mary Allen's "John Updike's Love of 'Dull Bovine Beauty,'" (1976). Allen describes Updike as "the cunning enemy who would affectionately lull all womankind away from anything that had to do with the life of the mind or self-respect or the joy of doing to a more appropriate and 'natural' imbecility" (97). His only strong women are domineering mothers who are in some ways responsible for creating his ineffectual protagonists. Contrasted with these strong but generally distasteful female figures are women who submit gladly to housewifery, finding adequacy in pleasing a husband and lover physically without being too threatening to his intellect or sense of freedom. Allen says Updike's "lyricism in behalf of the female body and his devotion to the idea of marriage" both depend on "an idea of the undeniably *stupid* woman" (110). Worse still, Updike "appears not to be fully aware of the extent to which he demeans the female character" (109). Instead, "under the guise of tolerant acceptance" of women's rights as humans, "his fiction insidiously goes about making female mediocrity and inertia seem inevitable, even lovable." In Updike's vision of the world, women who "do not fit this standard are not really human and must be rubbed out" (132).

Taking a more generous stance toward Updike, Josephine Hendin (1978) offers praise for his understanding of the predicament in which modern men find themselves. "No one has done more to explode male freedom as a myth than John Updike," Hendin says, noting that his novels portray a series of American men whose lives are "structured by women" (88). Many of his characters are unable to adapt to the changing post-war world in which freedom seems an empty slogan. Hendin thinks Updike connects "the decline of society with the decline of masculinity" (89). What his men do not understand is that they really need women to achieve happiness (on the human level) and salvation (on the spiritual). Furthermore, Hendin insists, Updike the novelist is not his characters. Instead, fully understanding his characters' plight, he writes "with hard beauty of men endlessly wandering the labyrinth of their own needs"—"without sentimentality," Hendin says, "but not without compassion" (99).

During the late 1970s, the extent to which academics were still eager to present Updike as an apologist for Christian values can be seen in Linda Plagman's "*Eros* and *Agape*: The Opposition in Updike's *Couples*" (1976). Plagman asserts that, more than any other novel by Updike, *Couples* is about "the Christian faith" and its "relationship to the forces of sex and death in contemporary society" (83). Updike "relies heavily on Biblical prototypes" to structure the novel in which various couples try unsuccessfully to create "a pre-Christian society" (83–84).

Using philosophical rather than theological tools, Gerald Galgan (1976) examines *A Month of Sundays* to discover Updike's answer to the question he had posed in a 1968 interview: "After Christianity, What?" Galgan believes "Updike feels compelled to examine the fate of Christianity in an age when the gods have absconded, leaving man to ponder his groundless experience." A sense of fatalism seems to underlie all of Updike's fiction. God's withdrawal from the universe has left humankind searching for meaning but doomed to be disaffected with any solution that fails to account for the deity. Ultimately, Galgan says, Updike suggests there is no "after" Christianity in America, because Christianity is "blood to the American soul," a kind of life force that gives meaning to the American experience (725).

In the first of her two articles tracing Updike's reliance on Kierkegaard as a shaping force for theme and methodology in his fiction, Sue Mitchell Crowley (1977) argues that stories such as "The Astronomer" are in some ways "glosses upon—skillfully arranged sets of footnotes to"—the Danish philosopher's ideas about "the self as a synthesis of finitude and infinitude" (1013). While Updike's professed reliance on Karl Barth may mask the influence of Kierkegaard, what appeals to Updike in Barth are ideas that Barth developed from his own reading of Kierkegaard. Crowley finds that the Kierkegaardian "synthesis" not only enables Updike's characters "to move from despair to hope, from fear to faith," but also gives Updike himself a useful vehicle for "ponder[ing] his own religious problems" (1016). Also interested in matters of religion, Paul Borgman (1977a) describes Updike as a "Christian storyteller" whose fiction provides "important clues" about the "peculiar challenge of redemption in an age of leisure." Updike's willingness to deal with the problems of an age that seems "bent on ridding itself" not only of God but of "human freedom and dignity" is admirable. But Borgman wonders if "there is not in the sexual affirmations" of Updike's protagonists "a too easy dismissal, after all, of the domestic tangle and detail he so carefully represents" (22).

Robert Johnston's "John Updike's Theological World" (1977), in some ways a corrective to the Hamiltons' strident insistence on the orthodox Christianity at the heart of Updike's writings, offers a counterpoint to Borgman's position. Johnston believes Updike is a Christian, but his writings do not support the kind of mainstream Protestant theology that the Hamiltons and others have imposed on them. His principal purpose is to expose the bankruptcy of modern society and suggest that, despite its present condition, humankind has the means of achieving redemption if it will affirm life. Johnston finds Updike a modern-day version of the writers of the Book of Wisdom in the Bible, who believe that "God's signature is written on the patterns of life for the person who will look" (1065). Similarly, in "The 'Wisdom' of John Updike" (1978), Johnston goes to Wisdom literature to find sources and parallels for Updike's handling of the mystery of the Divine. Again Johnston concludes that Updike is neither specifically Christian nor wholly secular, but is nevertheless deeply religious, having found evidence of God in the world around him—and in biblical texts that most Protestants do not recognize as canonical.

Another critic who appreciates Updike's serious treatment of religion and morality, Bernard Schopen ([1978] 1982), takes issue with those who would trivialize Updike's recurring concern with matters of faith. Schopen argues that Updike is interested in both faith and morals simultaneously, but that these operate in two different spheres in the modern world: "religious questions are those arising from the relationship between man and God," while "moral questions are those which concern man's intercourse with his fellow man" (197). Deeply influenced by Barth, who posits God as Wholly Other, Updike is able to take up both types of questions in his novels and hold them apart—often to the dismay of critics who, caught up in the secular values of the twentieth century, are uncomfortable with a novelist so unabashedly concerned about matters of theology. Joseph Wagner (1978) also attempts to demonstrate the pervasive influence of Barth on Updike's fiction. Taking examples from poems, short stories, and novels, Wagner demonstrates that the "concept of two gods, one who is worshipped in men's religions and the real, fundamentally Other God"—a central tenet of Barthian theology—is "clearly present" in Updike's works (62). That Other God makes His presence known infrequently, sometimes dramatically and at other times in a quieter, almost imperceptible fashion. For Updike, Wagner insists, accepting the reality of this Other God is something one must do "with an unquestioning Barthian faith" (68).

To serve as a counterweight of sorts to the suggestions of Barth's hold over Updike, Robert Waxman (1977) traces the influence of Pascal on Updike's fiction. Concentrating on several short stories, Waxman carefully discredits the idea that Updike's works are a series of "yea sayings" (as Rachel Burchard and others had argued), but instead reflect "the darkening metaphysical dilemma of modern man" caught, in Matthew Arnold's phrase, between two worlds. Waxman points out that Updike, too, is caught in a dilemma: he wants to believe in God but has serious doubts, and his fiction does not provide a satisfactory solution to his problem. Instead, Updike—and America—hunger for "a new revelation" that can restore joy to people's lives (210). Similarly, Victor Strandberg ([1978] 1982) finds running through all of Updike's work a serious examination of the "crisis of culture" described by Herman Hesse, who writes about the suffering that occurs when competing cultures or religions overlap. Updike "has confronted the problem of belief" in a fashion similar to nineteenth-century writers like Tolstoy and Tennyson, but "with the added authority of a mind keenly aware of twentieth-century science and theology" (175). Answering charges by critics who believe Updike's work is "poor, mindless, and irrelevant," Strandberg demonstrates how it provides answers to "the problems of nihilism and the changing of the gods," in the process insuring that Updike's "own name, while civilization lasts, is not likely to be forgotten" (193).

Updike's concern for religious issues was by no means the only issue that interested critics at this time. For example, in "Science, the Saving Grace of John Updike: *The Centaur* and *Couples*," Betsy Curtler (1976) describes how Updike's "attitudes toward science and his artistic adaptation of scientific materials" provide "substance and grace to the mythology of *The Centaur*" and influences "the sexology of *Couples*" (209). Updike's use of scientists and scientific materials "enrich[es] the novels and increase[es] our appreciation of the complexity in 'the way the world operates'" (218). Updike's interest in social issues also prompted a number of studies, among them one by Robert Alter ([1972] 1979), who has high praise for Updike's treatment of race relations in *Rabbit Redux*. Updike renders the attitudes of the novel's central character—"an average, unintellectual, politically conservative, working-class figure"—toward African Americans "without authorial attitudinizing" (246). Rabbit's attitude may be disconcerting, Alter says, but Updike deserves praise for his lack of patronization or sanctimony.

As might be expected, at this time critics were still interested in constructing close readings of individual texts and concerned with matters of technique, social commentary, and literary tradition. A notable essay of this type is Howard Eiland's "Play in *Couples*" (1979). Building on Alan McKenzie's (1974) essay on parlor games in the novel, Eiland constructs a detailed analysis of the use of games to show how both traditional sports encounters and the more intimate sexual games in which characters engage demonstrate the importance of ritual in society. While Updike's characters may be ordinary, they participate in a series of social encounters that reveal how life is "an emergent drama in which individuals more or less unwittingly enact variations of archetypal roles" (83). In another traditional critique, Terrence Doody (1979) uses *A Month of Sundays* to illustrate Updike's idea of reification, which he says is different from that espoused by Marx (who sees capitalism turning human beings into objects) or Thomas Pynchon (who feels people are becoming dehumanized in a world of technology). Doody says Updike's idea "is essentially theological, based upon an idea about the nature of God's existence" (204).

At the same time, the emergence of new literary theories was beginning to influence study of Updike's work. As an example, Robert Detweiler's "Updike's *A Month of Sundays* and the Language of the Unconscious" (1979) relies heavily on the work of Jacques Lacan, and to a lesser extent that of Jacques Derrida, to construct a reading of the novel. Perhaps even more provocative is Detweiler's suggestion that this novel, and subsequent ones in the Updike canon, may have been influenced, albeit unconsciously, by the work of theorists like Roland Barthes, whom Updike read in 1975.

Debates among Updike's critics were often lively and at times even strident. Witness James Mellard's "The Novel as Lyric Elegy: The Mode of Updike's *The Centaur*" ([1979] 1982), in which he argues that Edward Vargo is off base in his *PMLA* article in suggesting that the novel represents some sort of ritual. Mellard says the "art" of *The Centaur* "is essentially lyrical," even elegiac (217). Mellard finds the novel both aesthetically pleasing and morally uplifting: instead of representing the sins of the father being passed on to the son, *The Centaur* presents "the more benevolent idea that it is the wisdom of the fathers that is passed along" (229). In further reinterpretations of *The Centaur* Wesley Hoag (1979, 1980) argues that the "full connotative power" of the novel can be understood only "when read as an extended, fictionalized adaptation" of Albert Camus's essay "The Myth of Sisyphus" (1979, 446). Hoag provides an explanation of how George Caldwell is finally healed of the psychic wounds that arise from what Hoag calls Caldwell's mind/body split.

Critical attention to the Rabbit novels remained strong as well. Paul Borgman (1977b) argues that to see Rabbit as simply a "silly and troublesome boy-man" is to misread a novel that presents readers with an "unlikely and tragic hero." Taking his cue from the novel's epigraph,

Borgman shows how the tragic conflict occurs between "the motions of grace" and the forces of contemporary society that oppose the spiritual dimension of life (106). In a somewhat more speculative critique, Robert Hogan (1980) suggests that Updike may have modeled his protagonist on the Cathars, a heretical sect active during the twelfth century. Updike would have known of the Cathars, Hogan says, from reading Denis de Rougemont's *Love in the Western World*, a work that influenced him during the period when he was writing *Rabbit, Run*. With a bit of clever argumentation, Hogan shows how Rabbit's disdain for work, his distaste for "normal sexual relations" with his wife (236), and his zeal for perfectionism make him a descendant of the Cathars.

Though only recently published, *The Coup* attracted attention from scholars inside and outside the field of literature. Among the most intriguing of the essays published during this period is political scientist Irving Markovitz's "John Updike's Africa" (1980), in which he points out ways in which the novel fails to capture the problems of the Third World. Displaying familiarity with the Updike canon, Markovitz demonstrates how Ellellou resembles many of Updike's other protagonists in his "sense of self-indulgence and self-absorption" (537). Markovitz claims Updike is "one of the most deeply discontented and conservative of writers" whose "intellectual arrogance" leads him to despair about humankind's ability to improve its lot, and "this despair supports continued injustice" (537–38). Even though Updike gets many details about Africa right, *The Coup* argues for passionate acceptance of the status quo—or the shrewd sense to get out while one can, because heroics and grand gestures count for nothing.

Some critics turned to Updike's work for examples of what was happening in the larger world of twentieth-century literature. In *The American Novel in the Twentieth Century* (1978) Miles Donald examines several of Updike's novels to illustrate a trend toward the separation of narrative and character from meaning. Donald links Updike with Faulkner, describing them as novelists whose works consistently show "the contrary pulls of structure and the absence of structure" (73). Like Faulkner, Updike "shows great power and skill" with narrative, but his tendency to write of multiple characters and fragmentary experiences detaches the narrative from the central meaning of his novels. Viewed in this way, Updike's novels expose "one of the great problems of the twentieth century novel in general and the American form in particular": novelists can no longer trust conventional forms of narrative and characterization to convey meaning—possibly, Donald speculates, because traditional methods of conveying meaning have lost their force with modern readers. The result is the constant experimentation with form one sees in modern fiction, even in seemingly realistic works like Updike's.

Despite the serious and generally positive treatment of Updike's work by the critics cited above, evidence of the ongoing controversy over the value of Updike's art can be seen in John Gardner's *On Moral Fiction* (1978). Updike is cited for specific opprobrium in Gardner's Jeremiad against contemporary serious writing and listed among authors whose works are not likely to outlast the century. Though "on a few occasions, especially in *The Centaur*, he proves himself an artist" (100), Gardner says, Updike's work is generally devoid of morality or genuine concern for the human condition.

Books by two scholars relatively new to Updike studies continued the critical tradition of exploring the religious dimension of his fiction. The first, Suzanne Uphaus's *John Updike* (1980), carries a dust jacket announcement touting it as "the first book-length study of John Updike to be published in seven years"—a claim that is true if one does not count anthologies like Thorburn and Eiland's influential 1979 essay collection. Updike scholars would have been familiar with Uphaus's work already from her essays on *The Centaur* (1977a), which describes that novel as a mock epic, and on *A Month of Sundays* (1977b), which offers a preview of the discussion she develops at greater length in her book. Confining her discussion principally to the novels, in *John Updike* Uphaus explores the "common theme" she sees running through all of Updike's writing: "the profound religious searching" that emerges from a feeling of despair for humankind cut off from God. This "quest in which doubt fights desperately with faith" causes Updike to write about "two worlds, the natural and the supernatural" (5). Recognizing this aspect of his work can help readers understand its significance. Uphaus portrays Updike as a writer looking for the religious dimensions of everyday experiences, moments when one can feel the presence of God in the world.

The second book, *John Updike and the Three Great Secret Things* (1980), is the work of the Jesuit priest George W. Hunt, a frequent contributor to the Catholic weekly *America* and editor of that magazine for fourteen years. Early in his career Hunt wrote a number of articles and reviews, including an essay on Updike's story "The Astronomer" in *Christianity and Literature* (1977a), an examination of Updike's characters in *Thought* (1978), and lengthy essays on *A Month of Sundays* in *America* (1975) and *Critique* (1979b). Hunt demonstrated his ability to provide close readings of Updike's fiction in "Reality, Imagination, and Art: The Significance of Updike's 'Best' Story" ([1979a] 1982), in which he points out parallels between the novelist and fellow Pennsylvanian Wallace Stevens. However, Hunt's 1980 book established him as an important voice in Updike studies.

Taking his title from Updike's 1962 essay "The Dogwood Tree," in which Updike names the "three great secret things" that were to occupy him as a writer for decades, Hunt constructs a systematic study of the interweaving themes that give Updike's fiction its characteristic subjects and style. Hunt's work is permeated with discussions of theological issues, as he illustrates how Updike's understanding of figures such as Kierkegaard and Barth shape his work. Hunt also provides detailed explanations (some might call them justifications) of Updike's use of explicit sex in his novels. Hunt's readings stress the dual focus of all of Updike's fiction on moral and ontological questions lying at the heart of human existence and social relationships. Throughout his commentary, Hunt is not shy about providing what were then (and in some cases still remain) unpopular judgments. He considers *Rabbit, Run* one of Updike's weakest novels; to him, *The Centaur* is Updike's "finest book to date" (49). He has high praise for *Couples*, calling it a "radical departure" in Updike's handling of sex and claiming it "engraced" the bestseller list by upstaging the many "second-rate items" listed there (117). He considers *The Coup* a breakout novel because Updike ventures far beyond New England and Pennsylvania for his subject. Perhaps the greatest service Hunt provides to Updike's reputation, however, is his insistence that Updike is an artist who is constant in exploring important human themes while at the same time experimental in looking beyond safe boundaries to jar his audience into thinking about the "three great secret things" that lie at the core of humanity.

Finally, the appearance in 1979 of David Thorburn and Howard Eiland's *John Updike: A Collection of Critical Essays* in Prentice Hall's Twentieth Century Views series was a godsend to young scholars and students seeking an overview of Updike's career. The handful of essays in the collection had all been previously published, but having a handy reference guide provided easy access to secondary sources. Additionally, the inclusion of a book on Updike in this prestigious series leant further credence to the idea that Updike was being taken seriously by the academic community.

4: Pulitzer Prize Winner, Vilified Misogynist (1981–1985)

WHILE THERE MAY BE no *annus mirabilis* in Updike's career, it seems fair to say that the decade of the 1980s was not only one of his most productive but also, perhaps, his most noteworthy. The first five years were ones of significant accomplishment. He began by publishing the third novel in the Rabbit series, following that highly acclaimed work with a sequel to his 1970 book on Henry Bech. A year later he issued a hefty collection of his nonfiction before making a bold foray into feminist literature with *The Witches of Eastwick*. Consistent with his publishing practice, in 1985 he issued a collection of previously published poetry. Updike's new publications continued to generate considerable notice—even his poetry collection, *Facing Nature*, was reviewed in more than two dozen publications—while a growing number of academics added to the body of critical commentary on his work.

The overwhelming commercial and critical success of *Rabbit Is Rich*, discussed immediately below, cemented Updike's reputation as a major force on the American literary scene. One could like him or not, but it was impossible to ignore him. As Margaret Manning (1982) observed in a brief note about the republication of *The Carpentered Hen* in 1982, "If John Updike isn't already a national monument, he seems to be becoming one" (A19). By 1983, Updike had become such an iconic (if still controversial) figure on the publishing scene that Victoria Glendinning (1983) could begin her review of *Bech Is Back* with the observation that "a new John Updike novel, like it or not, is a publishing event" (83).

Rabbit Is Rich, 1981

In 1981 Updike returned again to familiar ground, the ongoing story of Harry Angstrom's life. *Rabbit Is Rich*, the third installment in the series, was a genuine best seller. It debuted on the *New York Times* list in late October and held a place among the top fifteen for five months—a notable accomplishment for a work of serious fiction, placed as it was beside more sensational fare like Colleen McCullough's *An Indecent Obsession*, John Jakes's *North and South*, and Robert Ludlum's *The Prodigal Daughter*. The book generated the greatest number of positive reviews of any Updike novel to date; many considered it the fulfillment of the great promise Updike had shown for more than two decades. For *Rabbit Is Rich* Updike received the American Book Award (the name for the National Book Critics Circle Award between 1980 and 1986) in 1981, the National Book Award in 1982, and the 1982 Pulitzer Prize.

Despite this acclaim, some did not find the novel worthy of the attention it received. Therefore, it seems best to begin a survey of its reception with these negative assessments lest they get lost in all the praise. Reasons for disappointment were numerous. While acknowledging Updike's considerable talent, Pearl Bell (1981) believes he fails to establish sufficient distance between his protagonist and himself, giving Harry Angstrom too much of his creator's ability to provide insight into the American character. The Rabbit series, she concludes, which began as a study of arrested development but devolved into programmatic social commentary, is not advanced by this third installment. James Ellison (1981) says that, where *Rabbit Redux* was a daring leap forward over its predecessor, *Rabbit Is Rich* seems overwhelmingly nostalgic and static, a "catalog of complaints" about contemporary times (112). Furthermore, the extensive social commentary is not well integrated into the plot. Carol Rumens (1982) finds the novel "sags under a weight of description" and, though the book accurately reflects the "extreme ordinariness" of Rabbit's character and "the consumerism of his society," Harry is an unsuitable hero (48). Paul Chipchase (1982) says that, though the book "is full of convincing news bulletins and preoccupied with the world economic crisis" and "not unfamiliar images of [Updike's] mother-country's supposed loss of confidence and well-being" (13), Updike fails to offer any conclusions about the matters he raises in the novel. Readers who were won over by Updike's "gentle early manner" can "only mourn the huge labour and ingenuity expended on this long charmless novel" (14).

These sentiments are echoed by a number of other reviewers, several of whom did little to hide their extreme displeasure. Among them is Howard Davies (1982), who seems bothered by Updike's continuing preoccupation with sex. Davies notes that Updike "has always written" with his (male) "readership's tastes"—that is, their obsession with sex—"firmly in mind." Somewhat sardonically, he observes that "it might seem a little prim and anachronistic to accuse Updike of obscenity" (41). Yet Davies is "sure, well, almost sure, that Updike's principal intention is not to arouse and deprave his readers" (42). As Davies's review indicates, being on the edge, where serious discussion of sex can easily fall off into pornography, has its perils. Equally put out by the novel, James Wolcott (1981) dismisses it as "grumpy and despairing, swollen with forlorn rue"; "no banners of joy ripple" from its pages. Its central character "is lashed to the mast of Updike's theme." The notion that "entropy reigns supreme" (20) is preached rather than dramatized in this "static" work where "characters droop" (21). Easily Updike's "most unattractive book" (22), this "stoically grim affair" has "its head in the stars and its feet in the gutter, and at neither extreme is Updike's droll talent comfortably at home" (23). Jonathan Yardley ([1982] 1991) calls the selection of *Rabbit Is Rich* as the recipient of the American Book Award in Fiction a travesty, evidence of the bankrupt "political and social prejudices of the literati" who pretend to be sympathetic of the plight of working-class people like Rabbit Angstrom while turning up their noses at them. Yardley believes the novel is "a creature of the moment," and confidently predicts that "a quarter century from now, if not sooner, it will be gone and quite forgotten" (15).

A greater number of critics provided more measured assessments. Robert Taubman (1982), for example, suggests that the Rabbit novels are like "a series of reports on the state of America." Updike's title character is "not himself an interesting character," but he has "archetypal status, and the scenes he plays are archetypal ones" (19). The only drawbacks Taubman sees are Updike's tendency toward sentimentality and his overuse of ironic juxtaposition, which "may be droll, cheeky, disagreeable, or just nullifying," but does not give "any depth to the novel" (8). Though David Williams (1982) praises the book as a "whopper," and calls Updike "a damn good writer" (201), he is disappointed that once again Updike makes "everyone in the book" so "nasty" and treats every situation "with unrelenting sourness" (202). John Leonard (1981), too, notes that "almost everybody in a John Updike novel runs away from death and circles back," and Harry Angstrom is no exception. The novel contains much that critics will not like: "the style is too rich," the "sex is ritualized and incessant," the novel "wanders, pauses, ponders." Yet for all that, Leonard insists, *Rabbit Is Rich* is "a splendid achievement" (C13).

In fact, several critics who had not thought highly of earlier novels in the series changed their opinion after reading *Rabbit Is Rich*. Roger Sale (1981) says that "Rabbit and Updike have a relation that may be unique in literature" (1), partly because Harry allows Updike to return home, if only in his imagination. Where Sale found *Rabbit Redux* "a poisoned book," the portrait of Harry in *Rabbit Is Rich* is "more attentive and sympathetic" (32). And while it may be too long, it is "the first book in which Updike has fulfilled the fabulous promise he offered with 'Rabbit Run' and 'The Centaur' 20 years ago" (34). Gene Lyons (1981), who panned *Rabbit Redux*, does an about-face in reviewing *Rabbit Is Rich*. It is undoubtedly Updike's "best work in many years," a "beautifully written, compassionate and wise novel by an at-last mature writer working at a level he has always had the capacity to attain, but seemed destined never to reach." Lyons says he never objected to Updike's choice of a hero or a locale for his commentary on American society. "A novelist," he says, "is entitled to whatever vision of the world he can make credible" (477). But where its predecessor was ham-handed, preachy, and filled with symbols that were substituted for real insights, the new novel is "not only right, but triumphantly right." That is not to say it is a "what's right with America" tale, but instead is an honest look at a segment of society often overlooked by writers of contemporary fiction (478). Lyons hopes the novel is a commercial and critical success, because "I don't think anybody would say [Updike] hasn't earned his due" (479).

Many reviewers echoed Lyons's judgments. Anatole Broyard (1981) calls *Rabbit Is Rich* "the best book I've ever read about an ordinary man" (43). Mark Feeney (1981) virtually gushes over it, claiming it is unquestionably "Updike's finest novel" (1). Andrew Holleran (1981) thinks *Rabbit Is Rich* should put an end to complaints that Updike has not been able to produce a major novel. Alfred Kazin (1981) calls it a strong performance, a book in which Updike's "own proud voice rings out with a new steeliness" about the problems of a country lost in its materialist excesses. Declaring it the best book of its kind since Sinclair Lewis's *Babbitt* appeared in 1922, Kazin says the novel is both "brilliant" and "chastening" (3).

The publication of *Rabbit Is Rich* also generated the first review of Updike's work by Michiko Kakutani (1981b), who would eventually become one of his harshest critics.[1] Though she thinks *Rabbit Is Rich* is flatter and stiller than its predecessors, and "not a pleasant book" (14), it seems to capture the protagonist accurately at middle age. Kakutani suggests that the three Rabbit books "constitute something of an epic," chronicling "not only the maturation of one aging athlete, but the evolution of America through three remarkable decades as well" (15).

Thomas Edwards says each novel in the trilogy takes on a particular cast: *Rabbit, Run* is predominantly religious, *Rabbit Redux* political, *Rabbit Is Rich* economic. The trilogy reveals some of Updike's particular strengths, notably his "illusionless but tender understanding of how families work" and his "sense of the sanctity of memory" ([1981] 2005, 111). In his appreciative review, Russell Davies (1982) says the novel shows how Updike has progressed as a novelist. No longer does he use Rabbit simply as a "demonstration model" (21) to show what is happening to middle America; he has now found a way to give his anti-hero shades of complexity, and in the process has made the waning of the American male a subject of some interest, if not tragedy. In his long review, V. S. Pritchett (1981) notes how Updike is able to chronicle the problems of small-town, middle-class America while still maintaining readers' interest in a guilt-ridden hero who is often incapable of living up to his responsibilities. Considered collectively, Pritchett says, the Rabbit novels are "a monumental portrayal of provincial and domestic manners" (206).

Ralph Wood ([1982] 2005) focuses on the trilogy's religious dimensions. Setting out to trace Updike's "naively Lutheran vision of life cast by God into an indissoluble ambiguity" (118), Wood describes Harry

Angstrom's movement through the three novels as a "spiritual advance," something he calls "the product of Updike's natural religion: his conviction that God is discovered, if at all, in the irresoluble dialectic of human existence" (123). The Rabbit novels convince Wood that Updike is "our finest literary celebrant of human ambiguity and the human acceptance of it" (124). Like Wood, Daniel Pawley (1982) sees *Rabbit Is Rich* as another installment in Updike's quest to expose the spiritual bankruptcy of America, a country where men like Harry can prosper materially but suffer pangs of guilt for their sins. The novels are a sobering reminder of the effects of "secular humanism" which is now "so widespread and rampant that no part of society is exempt from its presence and effects" (101). George Hunt (1981b) says the novel reveals once again that Updike possesses exceptional sensibility and skill in using ordinary people to raise moral issues about the nature of goodness. Updike's satiric treatment of his material, a point of contention with some critics, is actually restrained and developed under the "spiritual penumbra that ultimately envelops" all the "being and doing" in his novels (322).

Thomas Mallon (1981) discovers that, in a literary world filled with experimental novels spare on detail, Updike's social realism is a breath of fresh air. Careful and tender with his characters, Updike has "always taken his own readers' breath away by showing small instants of how people really live. No one since Joyce himself has made such a gorgeous marriage of dailiness and poetry." Updike "is one of our greatest living novelists, the one most likely to be read a hundred years from now, if the literary historians just get things right" (1358). Elliott Fremont-Smith considers the Rabbit novels a saga on par with the great questing books of ages past, and delights in the way the "respectables" ([1981] 2005, 319) got it wrong when they dismissed *Rabbit, Run* as a novel in which brilliant style is wasted on meager substance. And Fremont-Smith offers a prediction made by a number of reviewers who approved of the Rabbit novels: "In ten years' time" he expects to see another book about Rabbit, in which Updike will "tell us how Rabbit is to die" (320).

Another Sequel: *Bech Is Back*, 1982

Bech Is Back did not generate as much public buzz as *Rabbit Is Rich*, but did create as much controversy. A cadre of critics celebrated its appearance, among them Michael Ratcliffe (1983), who observes that "no funnier nor more entertaining account of celebrity life" has ever appeared; the book "is every bit as funny as its predecessor" (8). George Hunt (1982) says the book demonstrates Updike's "wry perspective" on "the world of the contemporary culture vulture" (314–15). Joseph Cohen (1982) believes Updike "has always felt a close affinity for Jewish writers." The Bech books are Updike's attempt to portray himself as a Jewish writer, just as the Rabbit novels allow him to appear as "the 'Wasp' writer par excellence" (7). Joseph Blotner (1982) says it is impossible not to see Bech as Updike's alter ego, created not only to comment on the Jewish literary establishment but also to express the annoyance Updike feels toward critics who misunderstand his work. John Podhoretz (1982) also thinks Updike has resurrected Bech to keep alive his running battle with critics unwilling to consider him equal to the Jewish authors he lampoons in the Bech books.

Among those less euphoric about the new Bech book, Clancy Sigal (1982) says that, where the first Bech book was "a sparkling, wicked act of revenge" against the commodification of writers, much of this one is tedious and reveals signs of Updike's pervasive misogyny. "Let him find a way to gently bury Bech," Sigal advises, "and have another, more gracious look at the ladies" (70). Similarly, T. R. Fyvel (1983) finds *Bech Is Back* less effective than its predecessor, which he calls "a neat piece of satire by an American WASP novelist about his Jewish colleagues." The sequel "lacks some of the original's sharpness," and often devolves into Updike's personal reminiscences projected onto "a vaguely Jewish hero."

Isa Kapp (1982) considers *Bech Is Back* a somewhat preposterous sequel to the very entertaining *Bech: A Book*. Kapp's more serious concern, however, is with Updike's reputation. He finds him too lightweight to deserve the serious attention he has received. "Too irritating a literary personality to be the logical candidate for America's best novelist," Updike relies on his enthusiasm for his country to cover over his scant intellectual acumen, and never displays "the analytical intelligence of the Jewish novelists who have so magnetized him" (5–6). Moreover, Kapp says with a hint of disdain, although "Updike has a genius for conveying chronic tensions between male and female," he would be well advised "to quit forever the (for him) lugubrious preoccupation with sex and marriage" (6).

As one might expect, Joseph Epstein's (1983) review in *Commentary* keeps alive that periodical's tradition of negative critiques. Epstein admits that he had stopped reading Updike's fiction, but the hoopla over the appearance of *Rabbit Is Rich* made him wonder if he should try again. However, reading *Bech Is Back* confirms his original judgment. Updike remains juvenile, his novels too stylized and insubstantial. He writes about sex as a cover for his lack of anything to say. Worse, Epstein continues, he seems not to really care about his characters or "about the decline of American power that he continually alludes to" in his work (57). Like Bech, he has become a celebrity rather than a writer, peddling only small truths if any at all. His "high reputation" is "part of the general swindle" that modern novelists perpetrate on a reading public less concerned with the quality of fiction than the escapades of authors (58). Kenneth Lynn

(1982) is even more caustic, casting aspersions not only on Updike's talents and but also on his moral outlook. While it may not have been apparent that "Rabbit's emotional immaturity" reflects his creator's state of mind, *Couples* made clear to the world that Updike is "the Hugh Hefner of American fiction" (1558). Lynn feels that, for all his pretentions to seriousness social criticism, Updike more accurately reflects the Playboy philosophy in his fiction.

Updike on Everything: *Hugging the Shore*, 1983

In 1983, Updike issued his third collection of nonfiction, *Hugging the Shore*. Its title is intended to acknowledge—or perhaps gently poke fun at—the hierarchy that exists among types of writing: while the novelist sails out into uncharted waters, the essayist is content to stay close to the shoreline. Not everyone agreed, however, that the essays and reviews in *Hugging the Shore* were either trivial or especially safe, and Updike began to be generally acknowledged, as Dennis Donoghue (1983) does in his review, by the "old-fashioned" term, "a man of letters." Men of letters, Donoghue says, "take the occasions of reviewing to reflect on the intellectual and moral issues that beset us" (1), and no one handles this task better than Updike (31). On the whole, Donoghue finds that Updike "delivers more than he demands," but warns that a reader may be lulled into trusting him when in fact he often avoids "harder questions" that ought to be asked about the books and subjects he discusses (32).

Many shared Donoghue's high opinion. Lorna Sage (1984) says Updike brings a "rare gusto and connoisseurship to the task," always finding "something in a book to arouse his interest"; as a result his reviews are lively and entertaining. Michael Dirda (1983) believes Updike is "remarkably, consistently good," thoughtful in assessing a writer's aims and placing a new work in the context of the writer's career. Furthermore, Updike "nearly always" discovers "new things to praise in even familiar writers" (1). Shaun O'Connell (1983) admits it may be tempting to see Updike's essays as "lesser works" when compared with his fiction (A13); however, he disagrees. "Unweighted by prohibiting critical requirements, Updike's essays lift, range and shine," he says, and his body of criticism is "unmatched in range, discrimination and eloquence by any American novelist since Henry James" (A15). George Hunt (1983) says that anyone reading the essays in *Hugging the Shore* cannot help but come away "astonished by the breadth and variety of subject and both chastened and sharpened by the generous intelligence of this uncommon common reader" (437). Stephen Becker (1983) calls the book "a whole university of literary perception, wit, elegance, and judgment." Updike is particularly valuable as a critic of "generally unread novelists who struggle in small or exotic countries, or novelists appreciated at home who do not travel well" (26). Furthermore, Becker says, he is a critic and not simply a reviewer, helping readers understand the literary scene by relating "the particular to the general." In a somewhat hyperbolic conclusion, Becker suggests that for people a thousand years hence who wish to understand the literary culture of the twentieth century, Updike's nonfiction might serve as the age's "Rosetta Stone" (26).

Others found the volume a mixed success. Joe Mysak (1983) says that, while *Hugging the Shore* is "not as sexy as Updike's usual productions" (not making it clear how one should interpret the meaning of the adjective), it includes gems that make the volume worth reading (1426). Martin Amis (1984) acknowledges that Updike's unfailing generosity toward other writers "isn't always the foe of good criticism" (48), but worries that Updike's view of twentieth-century literature is "a leveling one," not always discriminating among writers of considerably different talents (48). David Montrose (1984) judges Updike a highly competent but seldom great reviewer. He always does his homework, and although given to benign judgments, is capable of citing weaknesses. Unfortunately, Updike's "cardinal flaw" is to consider reviews merely ephemeral, thus opting to be more descriptive than analytical (23). He seldom "rises above the level of polished competence," and as a result his reviews "do not generally possess the discursive breadth, nor reveal enough of their celebrated author, to be of long-term significance" (24). William Riggan (1984) also considers most of the essays in the volume "little more than entertaining ephemera" (381). Though the reviews seem "thoughtful and genial," in many instances Updike is "clearly out of his depth" (381). As a reviewer, Riggan judges Updike "somewhere between the middle of the pack and the frontrunners," and the collection itself "considerably less than an integrated critical work and considerably less than a prizewinner by any standard" (382).

John Simon (1983) takes issue with judgments like Riggan's. Although he is disappointed with many of the "safe" reviews that Updike has written over the years (34) and admits volumes like *Hugging the Shore* may contain too much material that is not first-rate, Simon says that scattered amid the more tepid critiques is "so much of genuine worth." Most notable, Simon says, are the "generosity of spirit" Updike displays toward "writers quite unlike himself" and the "equally good and honest" efforts to be fair regarding work of "writers who so resemble him that he might easily have remained blind to their blind spots" (35). While Updike seems to revel in poking fun at "structuralists and semiologists" (36), Simon thinks he is open to forms of literature other than his own brand of social realism. Furthermore, his "intellectual curiosity and aesthetic catholicity" allow him to treat fairly a wide range of work ranging from science fiction to contemporary theology. At the end of his review, Simon raises an important question regarding Updike's status as a critic:

"How does Updike's reviewing compare with that of Edmund Wilson?" The comparison is necessary, Simon says, because "every serious author of short journalistic criticism in America must be measured against that August touchstone." And while Simon does not think Wilson has been dethroned, Updike "does not trail far behind" (37).

However, in long review prompted by the publication of *Hugging the Shore*, Sanford Schwartz (1983) offers a different perspective on Updike both as a critic and writer of fiction. The essays in this volume, while well written, make Schwartz think he is "in the company of a brilliant person who is running on automatic." Updike goes out of his way to make his work as a reviewer seem "inconsequential," and the reviews produce "a tethered effect." Schwartz believes the essays reveal a larger problem with Updike; he "flashes so many masks before his face that we barely know what he stands for." A "disembodied, playacting note" characterizes the fiction as well, and despite his claims for fiction as the more risky enterprise, "his fictional characters don't venture into deep waters." Schwartz finds Updike less a storyteller than a "journal keeper," continually describing and analyzing specific moments in order to avoid dealing with larger issues. His writing "lacks a hero—or a heroine." Though his women occasionally appear strong, "their strength is seen only in relation to weak men" whose faults Updike glosses over. Schwartz says Updike "makes you want to shake him," because one has a sense that beneath the veneer of irony and detachment are "powerful emotions" waiting to "pour forth." The mastery of language which has earned him so much praise "seems to be a cover" behind which he can hide. Ultimately it seems sad and unfortunate, Schwartz says, that Updike has "shaped a language for himself that doesn't do justice to his emotions."

Writing from a Woman's Perspective:
The Witches of Eastwick, 1984

Every Updike novel generated controversy when it appeared, but none more so than *The Witches of Eastwick* (1984). Updike described this story of three New England divorcees who seem to possess magical powers as his attempt to answer critics who said he could not write from a woman's perspective. Filled with salacious detail and bawdy humor, the novel hit the *New York Times* top ten list in June and remained there through the summer. Some reviewers dismissed it as light fare, describing it as "the stuff of a beach reader's dream" (De Mott 1984, 24) or "fundamentally a frivolous book, a silly book" (Slavitt 1985, 136). However, Gail Godwin (1984) wonders whether *The Witches of Eastwick* is merely "a wicked entertainment," or if Updike wishes readers to draw "some deeper inferences" from his tale. She seems hard-pressed to find any strong statement that would provide clues as to what Updike wants readers to take from the novel. This frustrates Godwin; she wishes Updike would "risk a bold plunge into profundity rather than continuing to flirt playfully around its edges"—even though "one has to admit, he does it charmingly" (29). Margaret Peters (1984) is less forgiving, claiming the novel offers no insight into "feminine psyches" and relies on stock solutions to solve problems raised by the story. It may be "raunchy" and "bumptious," enhanced by Updike's "ensorcelling prose," but "nothing very serious lingers when the magic is over" (28).

The "elephant in the room" with this novel, of course, is Updike's attack on feminism. Few reviewers ignored it, but decidedly different opinions emerged regarding its propriety or effectiveness. For example, Lee Milazzo (1984) suspects feminists will be disappointed to discover that Updike's witches find happiness only when they get new husbands; yet the novel again "demonstrates why [Updike] is America's most accomplished literary artist" (4G). Peter Ackroyd (1984) celebrates Updike's bravado in attempting to "expose the female consciousness in a way which few male novelists have attempted," and concludes that Updike's ability to use language to connect the "psychic world" with "the recognizable human world" is a distinct achievement (9). Craig Raine (1984) finds *The Witches of Eastwick* a "deceptively playful, intricate and absorbing look at feminism, evil and the cosmic set-up." Though "the supernatural dimension" of the story is not wholly convincing and the magic "terribly banal," Raine says Updike "shows that the feminist myth of the gentler sex—the idea that women would exercise power more responsibly than men—is simply sentimental." That may not sit well with some readers, but it is one of the reasons that this "toughly argued and provocative" novel, "a text for our times," is worthy of attention (1084).

But as a brief note in *Glamour* predicts, *The Witches of Eastwick* was "sure to enrage feminists" ("Mocking Feminism" 1984, 118). The backlash against the novel (and its author) ranged from general distaste to outright disgust and disdain. Linda Moyer (1986) seems almost apologetic for finding *The Witches of Eastwick* disappointing, because it is the first novel in which Updike tries to write from a woman's point of view. Additionally, the work operates on several levels simultaneously; it is a story about "creativity," a critique of the 1970s, and "a book about Updike's major theme, adultery in a small town." What makes Moyer "deeply uneasy," however, is the "deep misogyny, even gynophobia," that she senses in the story. And although she acknowledges that Updike is "one of the few male writers to ever pretend to enter the female sensibility with any depth or complexity," reading *The Witches of Eastwick* makes Moyer "feel like I'm traveling along with a voyeur" (144).

Merle Rubin (1984) is more direct. She says the novel has "a lingering aftertaste of misogyny thinly disguised as admiration for the mystery of woman." Ultimately, Updike's attempts to "re-mythologize" the

Feminine mystique are unsuccessful (21). Alice Bloom (1984) agrees, describing the novel as "malicious cliché tarted up as sniggering, smart humor" (624). *Nation* literary editor Katha Pollitt (1984) also pulls no punches in calling out Updike for his misguided views. For him, "sisterhood is strictly for women who don't have dates." Making his heroines witches—associated with forces of nature, a "flattering way of saying women are their wombs"—is "a pretty sexist idea" (773). His view of women is "the ancient misogynist one—women are promiscuous, amoral, treacherous and a power force for ill," while his view of men is "all the New Sensitivity." Updike maintains a traditional, patriarchal idea about women's place—not in the workforce, certainly—and remains oblivious to the "changes in sex roles" that began in the 1960s (775). Nina Baym (1984) adds her voice to this chorus, claiming that, if Updike meant this novel to be a "foray into feminine awareness," it falls short. Its witchcraft is a "gimmick" used to further degrade women, whom Updike considers nonpersons. It is impossible to tell whether Updike "believes his own nonsense" (165), but Baym senses the "hatred" Updike feels for any woman who tries to do anything serious outside of copulating (166). She is even more dismayed at the number of reviewers who have praised the book. Such judgments suggest that women still have a long way to go to be taken seriously—and it is unlikely that Updike will ever do so.

Despite the lore that has grown up around reactions to the novel, not all women found *The Witches of Eastwick* distasteful or its author reprehensible. Margaret Manning (1984) says that although she has "reservations about the novel," she has none about Updike, whose work "has been and will be" the "stuff of great literature" (B3). Rhoda Koenig (1984) chides feminists without naming them by "suppos[ing] that some people (and we all know who they are) will ask why the witches' powers are circumscribed"—and why they fall under the spell of the devilish Darryl Van Horne, whom Koenig finds less convincingly conceived than the three females (76). Ultimately, Koenig concludes, the novel "isn't meant to be read for its plot," or for "any deep pronouncements on the mystical conjunctions of the sexes" (77). Perhaps even more supportive are comments by Margaret Atwood (1984), who calls the book "a strange and marvelous organism" in which Updike manages to "transpose[ ] mythology into the minor keys of small-town America." One has to look beyond the rather implausible plotting to see this as a serious novel full of "bravura writing" that merits readers' attention (G1). And while Updike is rather hard on his women—as he is in other novels—the "skill and inventiveness of the writing" make up for ideological shortcomings (G40).

In a rather lengthy, thoughtful, and supportive review, Diane Johnson (1984) suggests Updike tries to negotiate between the position of the writer "who gets behind his creations most of the time" and the private citizen "who fears and dislikes" witches—or at least the stereotype that most Americans have of them. His "wonderfully well-drawn" trio are "basically nice women just trying to get along," although they do possess some extraordinary powers that aid them in their quest. The problem Johnson sees is not with Updike, but with the contentious times in which "a writer of either sex attempting to speak as the other is scrutinized for offense" (3). Johnson is willing to forgive Updike for minor errors in portraying women, because in the main he understands "what it means to be a woman, perceiving accurately enough the economic basis of the sexual struggle"; no matter how potent the witches' magic might be, it is "always vanquished by temporal power or, in the current parlance, patriarchal power" (4). Mary Rose Sullivan (1984) also argues that one must look past Updike's treatment of women to see that the novel is actually a moral tale in which Updike puts his interest in sex and art to use in pitting good against evil. Challenging feminist criticism of Updike's portrayal of women, Sullivan thinks the novel's strength comes from the "loving characterization of Alexandra." Surely, Sullivan says, Updike is "the only contemporary writer who could carry out the task he has set himself here, setting his moral tale, about magical powers, in an incontestably quotidian world" (113).

Claire Tomalin (1984) notes that the novel "has aroused some displeasure in America because it carries the suggestion that women become witches when they are left alone by men." She thinks Updike should be applauded for making women the central figures of his story. Furthermore, she says, he introduces the supernatural only as a means of highlighting human relationships. And while the book contains a certain amount of "silliness," it is "enormously enjoyable." Charles Berryman (1986) argues that, despite the proclamations of new literary theorists about the impossibility of moralism existing in fiction, Updike remains a moralist, using his fiction to expose important moral issues. Though Berryman acknowledges that some will find Updike's portrait of the witches objectionable, he believes the women are often used to represent the larger forces at work in society that can lead to good or ill, depending on how they are employed. The novel is a "convincing study of the power of evil that has fascinated the American imagination from the time of Salem," and Updike has returned "contemporary literature" its "dark inheritance" by tracing again "the common ground of art, adultery, and witchcraft" (9).

Berryman was not the only reviewer to explore issues other than Updike's treatment of women. Phillip Corwin (1984) describes the book as another installment in Updike's "continuous battle against the demons of the Enlightenment," a statement that *something* may exist which cannot be discerned by reason. Yet Corwin concludes that the novel is simply a demonstration of Updike's "artistic virtuoso" rather than an attempt to come to terms with "a great theme" (341). D. J. Enright (1984) is disappointed as well, largely because Updike "appears to have a rich subject" on which to employ his considerable talent but fails to follow through in creating serious fiction (29). At best the novel is "up-market entertainment"; Updike never really tackles questions of good and evil as one might expect in a novel like this one (30).

In his avowedly religious reading, Ralph Wood (1984) describes the novel as a "cautionary tale" (716), Updike's "most deliberate fictional attempt to confront the reality of evil and demonry in our time" (715). Wood believes the three female protagonists and their demonic male lover represent a kind of evil force in the world, one that celebrates "the *idea* of their own sexuality as the source of preternatural power." Although Wood argues that Updike is not condemning all liberated women as "hellkites," he does suggest that the novel provides a counter to arguments made by feminists. At the same time, he is disappointed that Updike seems to remain a kind of gnostic, believing in a God "so transmundane that he cannot be discerned anywhere in creation" (716). That disappointment looms especially large in Wood's mind because he is otherwise in sympathy with what he sees as Updike's insistence that in the modern world "iniquity cleverly clothes itself in the urge for heedless personal freedom" (717).

The academic critic Donald Greiner, writing for a wider audience in the *Charlotte Observer* (1984b), calls *The Witches of Eastwick* "a darkly comic novel of marital disorder and social ennui." The novel is highly ironic, and though the witches hold readers' attention, Updike's sympathies are not really with them but with "the anonymous citizens who plod 'through their civic and Christian duties.'" The dark comedy gives way to serious social commentary when murder occurs as a result of the witches' actions, demonstrating that the novel is no comic fantasy, but a work in which "satire and sadness mix" and "evil seems so potent that nothing can combat it except art" (5F). Greiner later expanded his argument in "Updike's Witches" (1988), noting that many readers and reviewers were "caught off guard by Updike's unexpected excursion into the skewed world of black humor" (20). While Updike may seem to be having a good time poking fun at feminism, at the same time he stresses "the blackness of the laughter" (23). And lest one have any doubts about Updike's intent in satirizing these women's lives, it is clear that "the natural order of things" in the novel is "conventional marriage" (24–25).

Another Collection of Poetry: *Facing Nature*, 1985

While the controversy over *The Witches of Eastwick* was still playing out, Updike issued a new collection of his poetry. The publication of *Facing Nature* in 1985 sparked another round of brief comments on Updike's unusual ability to write effectively in multiple genres (Ewart 1985, Rotella 1985). In a rather longer critique, the poet Vernon Shetley (1986) observes that Updike's "ambitions as a poet" have grown steadily, "to the point that his poems demand to be judged by the same standards one would bring to any body of serious poetic effort." But Shetley believes Updike is not a natural poet, and without a "tightly confined meter and rhyme scheme" his lines "quickly go limp" (297). On the occasions when he demonstrates technical competence, his choice of subjects does him in. Witness, Shetley says, the amusing but ideologically flawed ditty "No More Access to Her Underpants": "Hasn't this man ever heard of the Women's Movement?" (299).

Academic Criticism, 1981–1985

In the second edition of his Twayne Series volume on Updike, Robert Detweiler says that since he published the first edition in 1972, "Updike criticism has become something of a minor industry" (1984, viii–ix [unpaginated]). Detweiler explains this phenomenon by asserting that Updike has remained "one of the most accomplished stylists of the English language," improving as he ages. Updike's continuing interest in problems of sexuality, linked with his increasing concerns about American society, suggest to Detweiler that Updike will one day "generate still more compelling fictions of human intimacy to sustain us above the void" (186)—and, no doubt, more critical commentary would follow.

Criticism published in the first half of the 1980s continued the winnowing process that began in the previous decade to identify works more likely to interest scholars and students of literature and culture in the future. In a study that attempts to bridge the gap between informed readers and academic critics, Philip Vaughan (1981) suggests that Updike depicts the contemporary social situation better than historians, and hence his novels deserve attention not simply as literature but as carefully crafted assessments of "the many paradoxes, complexities, and mysteries to be found in our society" (v). In a similar study, Robert Nadeau (1981) deftly applies an interdisciplinary approach to what was by this time a well-rehearsed topic among Updike's critics: the novelist's attempts to come to grips with the *angst* of modern life. Arguing that new discoveries in science, especially in physics, regarding the nature of reality have helped shape the work of many twentieth-century novelists, Nadeau says Updike derives from this new scientific view of reality "a notion of duality that looms large in his moral and theological debates with the reader" (14). Nadeau refutes claims that Updike's fiction is grounded in the Platonic notion of a duality between ideal and real; instead, the central tension in his fiction exists between "the dualities of self and other" (99), a tension that mirrors the scientific tension between matter and energy.

Perhaps the most important advance in Updike studies were the companion volumes on Updike's work published by Donald Greiner. The first to appear, *The Other John Updike* (1981), covers everything but the novels. (The second is *John Updike's Novels* [1984a], discussed later.) In what he calls "the first sustained study of the other Updike" (1981, xi), Greiner looks to isolate recurrent themes and describe techniques Updike developed over the decades. The tone of Greiner's work reflects his genuine admiration for Updike, a writer who offers surprises at every turn. The excellent spadework done by Greiner in this volume is valuable in its own right for establishing Updike as an important voice in short fiction and nonfiction prose. It also serves as justification for future examinations of Updike's writing outside the novels. But Greiner is wise enough to acknowledge that "any summary statement" of Updike's achievement or his value to future generations would be "presumptuous," given how prolific Updike is (261).

Another important book appeared the following year. William Macnaughton's *Critical Essays on John Updike* (1982) not only brings together sixteen reviews, twelve previously published articles, and a chapter from a recent book; it also includes five essays written specifically for the volume. The new essays reflect the central interests of critics at the opening of the 1980s. George Searles encourages critics to return to Updike's first novel to see how this "much underrated book" is both "an impressive novel in its own right" and "a harbinger of Updike's subsequent works" that critique contemporary American society (231). Gordon Slethaug argues that the second Rabbit novel provides clear evidence of Updike's belief that Americans "need to learn that unrestricted freedom cannot exist"; true freedom is possible only "when hedged with rules and governed by responsibility" (252). In the third new essay, Kathleen Verduin focuses on the specifically Protestant ethic of Updike's fiction to identify correspondences between Updike's views on subjects such as religious orthodoxy and responsibility and those of seventeenth-century Protestant thinkers. Gary Waller points out how *A Month of Sundays* can reinforce a reader's prejudices about Updike either as a fine stylist with a deep understanding of the world or a dogmatist who reduces complex issues to stylistic parlor tricks. In the final new essay, Joyce Markle tackles *The Coup*, the novel most recently published before Macnaughton's volume went to press. Acknowledging that it represents a sharp departure from Updike's previous fiction, Markle explores the novel's many "puzzlements" (281) to help make sense of its themes and justify Updike's choice of such an unusual subject.

Where the essayists in Macnaughton's volume treat Updike as a major voice in American literature, two books examining trends in American literature consider him only a minor figure. In *American Fictions 1940/1980*, Frederick Karl (1983) claims Updike's "vision of America" lacks "the irony, distrust, and authorial suspicion that transform the ordinary into the extraordinary" (169); in short, it is "distinctly, almost provisionally, native." Additionally, Updike is out of touch with literary trends in attempting to portray American life realistically. "Fictional invention can hardly keep pace with actuality" in modern America, and as a result, although "Updike writes earnestly about marriage, movingly about separation, divorce, personal entanglements," his "treatment is already a reprise of newspaper and magazine stories" (170). British critic Malcolm Bradbury's more modest survey, *The Modern American Novel* (1983), gives only passing attention to Updike. Bradbury is perceptive, however, in noting that Updike's best fiction "mixe[s] a very precise formalism with a rising note of historical concern" (146), and that the "domestic world" he portrays "is always a register of political and historical change." As a result, while his work can appear "realistic and local," its "resonances are greater; his essential concern is with transcendental form and the pressure against it of a compelling but disquieting history" (147).

A majority of critics writing on Updike at this time employed methodologies now described as "traditional"—formalist analyses, character studies, examinations of technique. For example, in her extended examination of Updike's stylistic techniques in the short stories, Jane Barnes (1981) claims that "Updike seems to write the way spiders spin," constantly "weaving his webs to catch life as it passes, spinning, spinning as much to survive as to astonish." This lack of discrimination among his subjects is what makes some of the work of "the most prolific gifted writer of his generation" suffer from "uneven" quality (120). In a thematic study, Diane Bowman (1982) asserts that several of Updike's novels may be better understood if one sees their protagonists as Icarus figures. The flight of Icarus, she says, "is a flight in the double sense of the word—a flight from authority and repression and a flight towards freedom; it is also a flight which ends in a fall" (10). In another examination of Updike's style, Peter Balbert (1983) says that Updike employs "lively metaphor" and "verbal excess" because he distrusts "utopian appeals to reason and common sense." The everyday world "seems all entangled metaphor to Updike because it is divinely interconnected, analogized at every glance by the heavenly forces of creation" (266). Updike's regionalism is examined by Miriam Miller (1984), who argues that his descriptions of literal places under fictional names places him in the tradition of Joyce, Hardy, and Faulkner. While Berks County, Pennsylvania and its cities and towns may be employed for mythic purposes, they nevertheless provide a literal grounding for the action Updike describes.

Criticism of Updike's work continued to appear in unusual places. *Perspectives on American Business* published Albert Wilhelm's (1982) study of Updike's ideas about the status of work, in which Wilhelm argues that Updike's fiction offers a profound, ongoing indictment of American business. Susan Feinberg's (1983) Freudian reading of Updike's *Of the Farm* appeared in the *Journal of Evolutionary Psychology*, where Feinberg uses Freud's theories to explain the function of the mother-son relationship in the novel.

Critics were consistently interested in Updike's focus on issues of sexuality. One such study, Elizabeth Tallent's *Married Men and Magic Tricks: John Updike's Erotic Heroes* (1982), examines ways Updike's men respond to the women in their lives. Suggesting that Updike's heroes tend to see all women as wives, Tallent posits that "the single great domestic truth accessible to nearly all of Updike's characters is marriage; the single great uncertainty is posed by the possibility of adultery" (10). She says this age-old dilemma stands at the center of Updike's best fiction. In another study of matters of sexuality, provocatively titled "Updike's Womanly Man" Howard Eiland suggests that all of Updike's fiction "participates in the contemporary debate over sexual identity and difference" (1982, 312). "The single overwhelming question" that occupies Updike in most of his fiction is, "What, in present day America, is a man?" (313). While a definitive answer may not emerge, one thing is clear: To define oneself as a man requires that one do so in relation to women, as the self (for Updike, at least) is always both male and female.

Interest in the problems of sexuality posed by the recently published *Witches of Eastwick* prompted a surprisingly sympathetic reading by Kathleen Verduin (1985), who answers the rancorous attacks on the novel launched by feminists with a more measured critique that recognizes the novel's importance while still acknowledging the troubling nature of Updike's portrayal of women. Verduin says the novel's themes are "metaphysical as well as social and topical" (294), and her reading stresses Updike's interest in "sexual and religious questions at the core of human life" (295). In the novel, Verduin says, females ascend in power as males become emasculated by the declining power of the patriarchy. At the same time, women are also equated closely with nature, toward which Updike has habitually been hostile. While Verduin admits that Updike's depiction of women in the novel is "problematical," a sympathetic reader can see that Updike is trying to "sort out and reassess the dualistic polarization of the sexes," to show them hesitantly "reach[ing] toward each other, not this time only in lust, but as companions in a fallen and bewildering human condition" (315).

The religious and philosophical dimensions of Updike's work also generated considerable commentary during this time. Typical of this interest is George Hunt's "Religious Themes in the Fiction of John Updike and John Cheever" (1981), in which he outlines the difficulties faced by writers interested in dealing with matters of religion. Updike has solved this problem in part, Hunt says, by finding secular metaphors to describe religious experience. Doing so, however, has made his work unpalatable for some readers. Hunt insists that in Updike sex becomes "the only viable metaphor for man's search for personal and communal meaning" (249).

Two essays that examine the importance of Pascal as a source of inspiration for Updike provide insight into methods of philosophical inquiry employed at the time. John Martin (1982) says that Updike's view of Harry Angstrom "begins and ends with the apparent paradox" of the epigraph from Pascal's *Pensees*: must the Christian possess faith as "a prerequisite for grace and salvation," or does grace "allow[ ] a man to have faith?" (103). Martin says Updike presents Harry as "an Everyman facing a naturalistic world, and because he is, Rabbit perceives the needs of the spirit" (104). Similarly, Margaret Hallissy (1981) suggests that in *Rabbit, Run* Harry Angstrom is "Pascalian man" operating in an "atmosphere of moral ambiguity" who has "fallen from grace yet moved toward God" (25).

In an article exploring the relationship between religion and sexuality, Ann-Janine Morey-Gaines (1983) argues that Updike "persistently confronts the reader with a sexualized sacramentality that spotlights with demanding clarity the usually submerged tensions between religion and sexuality in American culture" (595). Relying on feminist theory and the theoretical work of Philip Wheelwright, Paul Ricoeur, George Lakoff and Mark Johnson, and Jacob Bronowski, and displaying a deep understanding of the Christian tradition of "body-spirit dualism" (596), Morey-Gaines mines Updike's *Rabbit, Run* to identify "specific metaphoric continuities that might extend our understanding of religion and sexuality in modern fiction" (597). She sees Updike creating "fictions of infinite regress" in which both men and women feel entrapped; questions about "sexual bodies and religious spirits" become inquiries into "female sexuality, male spirituality, and the fictions we perpetuate about both" (607).

Updike's protagonist in *A Month of Sundays* also prompted considerable critical commentary. Donald Greiner (1983) suggests that the novel may be read simply as a tale of a wayward minister or as a complex exploration of religious issues informed by Barth's theological writings. Marie-Hélène Davies (1984) portrays Reverend Tom Marshfield in a most favorable light, claiming the novel shows his evolution "from judgmental moralism to a truly religious vision of the world in which all are accepted for what they are" (65). Sue Mitchell Crowley (1985) explains how Updike, following Kierkegaard, creates multiple personas in order to engage in a series of indirect communications that allow him to "overcome the problem of fiction as confessional" (215). Through the creation of a series of dialogues, Updike examines serious questions: "How does one exist as a religious man in a world of temptation? How does one make ethical choices totally contrary to one's own deepest longings? Is there certitude of immortality which one may posit over against the all-consuming anxiety one experiences in the face of death?" (216).

As one might expect, the Rabbit novels remained the focus of many critical commentaries. Of course, many who had written about earlier works in the series were at times forced to revise their opinions as each new novel appeared. Critical commentary was not always confined to aesthetic, social, or existential issues. Michael Oriard (1982) includes a discussion of Harry Angstrom in *Dreaming of Heroes: American Sports Fiction, 1868–1980*, suggesting that *Rabbit, Run* and its sequel *Rabbit Redux* fit comfortably into the category he calls the "novel of age," stories of ex-athletes who cannot adjust to life after their glory days as sports heroes are past. More typical, however, is Jeff Campbell's (1984) argument that the sequence (then three novels) simultaneously traces "Rabbit's personal odyssey" and offers "penetrating analyses of the America of the fifties, the sixties, and seventies" (7). Where critics have usually seen Harry's personal journey as a metaphor for the society's journey toward entropy, Campbell suggests that the third novel ends with the hope of regeneration, symbolized by Rabbit's granddaughter, who "affirms the reality and renewability of human selfhood" (13).

Countering the growing appreciation for Updike's series and its hero, Edward Jackson (1985) argues that "it is doubtful that Rabbit 'grows' in his racial views" (444). When forced to face up to the presence of African Americans in his society, as he must in *Rabbit Redux*, Rabbit tends to back away uncomfortably. In *Rabbit Is Rich* Harry runs to the suburbs to escape the multicultural society that is overtaking his beloved Brewer. In the end, "Rabbit still fears blacks; he still feels uncomfortable around them, and, intermittently, he thinks of blacks in sexual terms" (451). In sum, Jackson suggests, Rabbit remains a racist.

Critical commentary on Updike's revisions to his work is relatively rare. But in the future, when scholars begin to explore that aspect of his creative genius, Randall Waldron's "Rabbit Revised" (1984) will offer a good model. Waldron examines variants in the texts of *Rabbit, Run* published in 1960, 1964, and 1970. He insists that a study of these revisions not only "demonstrates the integral place of the revisor's [*sic*] craft in Updike's meticulous artistry," but also "reveals that the text of reference for virtually all of the published commentary" on *Rabbit, Run* (the first edition) "fails to represent not only the author's final intention but also his original one" (52). His point is worth pondering.

Controversy about Updike's talent was perpetuated during this period by commentary on *The Coup*. In a negative assessment of the novel, Jack Moore (1984) expresses a concern that was becoming commonplace: Updike's satirical method has begun to poison his work. What is wrong about *The Coup* "and what is ultimately wrong about so many of Updike's novels" is that his technique "is not accompanied by the ability to make his audience care much about the characters he has created or about what happens to them" (61). A central confusion exists about the purpose of this novel and many others by Updike, who "never seems quite to have decided what kind of book he wants his to be: satire, tragedy, absurdist melodrama"—and never commits to any approach

(63). The desire to treat a subject seriously is not matched with an ability to do so; hence, when measured against truly great novelists Updike "falls short" because he cannot exercise "artistic control" to "master his undoubted talents" (67).

Arguing against readings such as Moore's, Kathleen Lathrop (1985) presents an eloquent defense of *The Coup* as a work of great imagination and insight. In it Updike "superimposes on this largely realistic background comic variations on the myth of the hero" (250), interpreting Ellellou's struggle to save his country as "a parody of traditional grail legends" (255). At the same time, the "underlying message" of the novel is serious: "Western technology and its attendant consumer ethic are reducing the earth to a spiritual wasteland in which the integrated man has been doomed to oblivion" (258). Lathrop thinks the novel is Updike's "most richly imagined critique of technological society" (261).

In 1984 Donald Greiner published the companion volume to his 1981 study *The Other John Updike*. In *John Updike's Novels* (1984a), Greiner attempts to "isolate and discuss the qualities that make Updike a great writer" (ix). Organizing his study thematically around broad categories such as "home," "created landscapes," and "faltering toward divorce," Greiner shows how Updike's use of metaphor, imagery, and symbolism illuminate character and theme. To those who believe Updike has not written any single book of monumental stature, Greiner suggests that the "exceptional quality of a long career sustained for dozens of books should be the final measure" of his achievement (3). Furthermore, Harry Angstrom has become an American icon, "a character worthy of joining the long line of fictional American questers from Natty Bumppo to Augie March" (98).

Greiner also celebrates the grace and wit that Updike displays in poking fun at his detractors; and yet, Greiner notes, despite the playfulness that sometimes spills over into the fiction, Updike consistently deals with serious issues about human relationships. Though Updike's principal interest is in human love in all its forms, the novels reflect other important concerns as well, including Updike's fascination with the act of writing and the intractability of language. As Updike continues to turn out one masterpiece after another, Greiner suggests, the carping of critics like Norman Podhoretz takes on a "foolish consistency" that "loses its sting as the attacks drag on with the years" (1984a, 29). Of course, as he acknowledged in *The Other John Updike*, Greiner recognizes that *John Updike's Novels* is at best a mid-career assessment. The appearance of future novels may end up confounding critics who have already decided what value should be placed on his work.

Greiner's third book on Updike published within a span of five years, *Adultery in the American Novel: Updike, James, and Hawthorne* (1985), advances from the premise that Updike has come to be recognized as "*the* author of the contemporary adulterous society." Greiner traces Updike's debt to earlier authors whose portrayals of adultery serve as models for his work. Updike writes about adultery, Greiner suggests, because it is "one of the most obvious signs of the shift in moral value" taking place in the twentieth century (3). Like Hawthorne and James before him, Updike uses adultery as a means of exploring personal and social relationships. By reading works by these three novelists one can see "the decline of religious sensibility and social propriety in the United States" (24).[2] In 1989 Greiner expanded his critique of Updike's handling of Hawthorne's *The Scarlet Letter*. He says Updike's trilogy is not a "direct reflection but a transformation" of the nineteenth-century novel. Tracing some of the key transformations, Greiner asserts that Updike's work is "both an homage to a masterpiece and a radical feat of intertextuality" (1989, 495).

Other scholars also demonstrated an interest in Updike's debt to Hawthorne. Samuel Coale (1985) concentrates on Updike's remaking of the romance tradition and the points at which he diverges from Hawthorne in his understanding of human nature. "Updike's vision is thoroughly unlike Hawthorne's," Coale says; his sense of alienation from the world and from God is less disturbing. For Coale, Hawthorne remains the dominant figure against which Updike struggles, only to end up emphasizing the enduring nature of Hawthorne's hold over the American imagination. Like Greiner in *Adultery in the Novel*, John Matthews (1985) incorporates commentary on Updike into a larger discussion of literary tradition. Interested in how intertextuality functions to inscribe limitations on writing, Matthews applies the theoretical work of Julia Kristeva to an analysis of works by Hawthorne, Faulkner, and Updike to demonstrate "how the Law of others' discourse manifests itself as literary contexts for each work" (147).

Mathews' work is a good example of how new theoretical approaches to Updike were uncovering hitherto undiscovered dimensions of his fiction. For the remainder of the century, interpretations based on traditional critical methodologies would be supplemented, and in some cases replaced, by ones employing new theoretical approaches to literary and cultural studies. To understand some of the differences in approach, it may be useful to examine George Searles's *The Fiction of Philip Roth and John Updike* (1985) before closing with a brief look at a second essay by Mathews that employs sharply contrasting methodologies.

Searles justifies his comparative study by noting that, while Roth and Updike are "highly skilled writers whose novels and stories richly repay close scrutiny," the two "have seldom been discussed in relation to each other." A comparative study, he insists, can "convey a fuller understanding of each writer's vision" and expose "the techniques employed in bringing that vision to artistic fruition" (2). Searles's rationale points to the kind of analysis that began in the 1920s and was dominant after the Second

World War. Approaching the work from a sociological perspective, Searles is interested in the way Updike's fiction is shaped by his upbringing as a white, Anglo-Saxon Protestant, by his approach to topics such as the family or romance, and by his use of techniques of narration and characterization that give his fiction verisimilitude. Hence, Searles's study is filled with observations such as: Updike is "deeply concerned with matters of religious and ethnic identity" which "strongly color[ ]" his artistic perspective (30); Updike's "suburban fiction" is sometimes marred by "thinness of characterization" (67); Updike's handling of the everyday "never becomes middling" because he "elevates and transcends" his material through his "use of language," making his reader keenly aware of "life's small wonders" (120).

Absent from Searles's study is any mention of the theorists whose work was influencing critical analysis at this time. This observation is not intended to suggest a flaw in Searles's approach; in fact, a look back at the criticism described in the preceding pages of this study makes it clear that conventional approaches have held the greatest appeal to critics of Updike's fiction. The lesson here might be that an artist's subject matter and his professed approaches to writing (e.g., realist, experimentalist, postmodern) drive critical practice as much as any new development in literary theory.

Although one might point to feminist critiques of Updike's fiction published during the 1970s or Robert Detweiler's essay on *A Month of Sundays* (1979) as the earliest examples of the application of new critical theory to Updike's writing, the work of John Matthews may serve as a particularly good example of how these methodologies influenced Updike studies. In "The Word as Scandal: Updike's *A Month of Sundays*" (1983), Mathews employs the work of French literary theorists and others to argue persuasively that Updike's 1975 novel can be read as a book about the nature of writing itself, and the ability of writing to create identity. Even a conservative writer like Updike, wedded as he is to the realist esthetic, is nonetheless passionately interested in exploring "*écriture*," Matthews says. *A Month of Sundays*, in its "doubling back and forth over the social and literary grounds of identity and articulation" gives readers "the sensation of selfhood as the trace of a systolic and diastolic rhythm" (354). While acknowledging the importance of theology and sex in the novel, Matthews deftly manages to present these as means rather than ends, describing how Updike uses two of his favorite subjects to explore the more pressing issue of the nature and value of writing itself and of writing as a means of constructing a self. Matthews and others employing these new methodologies were opening new windows into Updike's fiction and suggesting possibilities of interpretation that might easily be missed by those still using traditional modes of critical inquiry.

Notes

[1] To be accurate, this 1981 review is not Kakutani's first published work on Updike. Two months earlier in the *New York Times Book Review*, she offered some pithy observations on his work in "Be More Like Graham Greene, Dear" (1981a).

[2] Greiner's work on the relationship between Updike and Hawthorne caught the attention of the Nathaniel Hawthorne Society, which asked him to arrange an interview with Updike that would provide Society members first-hand information on why a contemporary novelist would be so bold as to re-cast an iconic American classic. The results of that interview, which was actually conducted by correspondence, were published in a 1987 number of the *Nathaniel Hawthorne Review* (Greiner 1987).

5: Crowning Achievements (1986–1990)

UPDIKE MANAGED TO GRAB and hold the national spotlight with the publication of *Rabbit Is Rich* in 1981 and *The Witches of Eastwick* in 1984. Viewed in hindsight, however, his work between 1981 and 1985 was prelude to what was arguably the most important five-year period in his life as a creative writer. In this period he completed his *Scarlet Letter* trilogy, released a collection of short stories that reinforced his reputation as one of the most skilled practitioners in that genre, and published a self-deprecating memoir that sparked lively commentary. The appearance of *Rabbit at Rest* in 1990 garnered for him a second Pulitzer Prize, linking him with Booth Tarkington and William Faulkner as the only novelists so honored.

And yet, some critics continued to belittle and disparage Updike's work. Charges that his sumptuous prose overwhelmed his slight subject matter and complaints that he was too concerned about matters of religion persisted in some circles, as did charges that his portrayal of women was misogynistic. Curiously, though, the writer once accused of being too solidly planted in the liberals' camp was now charged with strident conservatism, accused of letting his visceral love for country blind him to America's failings.

Religion and Science Collide: *Roger's Version*, 1986

After *A Month of Sundays* appeared in 1975, Updike hinted that he would be producing a series of novels recasting Nathaniel Hawthorne's *The Scarlet Letter* for modern readers, each told from the point of view of one of Hawthorne's principal characters. *A Month of Sundays* focuses on a modern-day Arthur Dimmesdale: Thomas Marshfield, a minister sent into rehabilitation for sexual misconduct. *Roger's Version*, published in 1986, recreates Hawthorne's hard-hearted physician and scholar Roger Chillingworth in the person of Roger Lambert, a theology professor who torments a graduate student trying to prove God's existence by using a computer. *Roger's Version* gave Updike the perfect platform to explore subjects of continuing interest: sex, religion, and science. While the result did not please everyone, it attracted sufficient readership to make the *New York Times* bestseller list for more than three months.

Those that liked *Roger's Version* could hardly find language strong enough to tout its strengths. Thomas D'Evelyn (1986) calls it "vintage

Updike" (23). Lee Milazzo (1986) thinks it is apt to "prompt wonder, puzzlement, and admiration"—and perhaps demand "a second or third reading" (11C). The book even received a recommendation from the editors of *Radio-Electronics* ("*Rogers's Version*," 1987), who say it is "sure to get you thinking about numerous topics ranging from computers to religion." Updike manages to examine a "wide a range of subject matters," and create characters "so real that occasionally you feel like stopping an argument to participate" (137).

Paul Gray (1986) suggests that, while it may be "a novel that only the author's most faithful followers will love at first sight," it is a "dazzling and sometimes maddening display of talent and erudition" (67). Eugene Kennedy (1986) also thinks *Roger's Version* is "not an easy novel," largely because theological concerns that have always been implied in Updike's fiction are central in this work. One senses "on every page Updike's restless search for the vantage point from which he might glimpse the signs of divine presence and mediation in our tumbling, dream-like condition" (2). John Batchelor (1986) believes this "wonderfully tricky and nakedly sharp-minded" novel poses a problem central to Christianity: "Can you love the loathsome?" (1).

In the first of what would become nearly a dozen reviews of Updike's fiction, Anita Brookner (1986) expresses admiration for this "extremely grown-up novel." Reading it, one gets the impression "of being inside a box of dazzling tricks, in which two cultures [religion and science] are eclipsed by many exotic varieties of information, each of them rendered in a sequence of intricate codes" (39). David Sexton (1986) finds the book "explicit" though not "crude," because for Updike "sexual intercourse and religion are both approaches to the mystery of human incarnation." In fact, he continues, "you could say that Updike's imagination oscillates between fellatio and Karl Barth," and in *Roger's Version* "he puts the two together" (6).

Despite these accolades, some reviewers were not sold on the novel. Though Mark Feeney (1986) finds it "luminously written, as well as consistently enlightening and often very funny," he is not certain if Updike intends it to be "primarily about ideas" or about the "dailiness that absent-mindedly shoves ideas aside." In either case, Updike seems to have substituted his considerable skill with words for "the hard and dirty work of moral, intellectual and devotional doubt" (A12). Similarly, Arthur Moore (1986) calls *Roger's Version* "a near miss" (444), arguing that it suffers from Updike's inability to carry off a novel built around ideas. Edward Abbey (1987) believes the eschatological questions raised by *Roger's Version* seem to have little relevance to everyday living or appeal to a wide audience. Dan Cryer (1986) agrees, noting that "the subject of God is as fashionable in American letters these days as hoop skirts and crinolines." Yet Updike continues to write "about man's search for meaning as though God had something to do with it." Still, he admits, Updike handles this intellectual hot potato with considerable deftness by grounding his obsession with God "in our sexual being" (16), imbedding discussions of the deity "in a narrative as funny and saucy as it is earnest" (13).

However, Robert Davis (1986) professes not to be hoodwinked by this "theological comedy" that seems calculated to displease "practically everyone who thinks about religion at all" (16). Davis calls Updike a cynical theologian who seems truly unconcerned with the ethical dimension of human character. "His sexually self-indulgent characters rarely have inner struggles or act on principle or identify themselves with positive goods that readers can share" (17). Davis does find merit in Updike's experimentation with point of view. Influenced, Davis says, by "advanced French theorists" (16), Updike has given his title character the powers of omniscience normally reserved for authors, a technique unsettling for readers accustomed to more conventional fiction.

Reading the novel from a feminist perspective, Ann-Janine Morey (1986) finds it a "contrived" reworking of *The Scarlet Letter*. Updike's "excursion into computer language is tedious." His "language of sexuality," with its focus on anatomy, borders on the pornographic. The theological discussions are more interesting, especially for "those who delight in tracing theological themes in literature" (1036), and the novel worth reading for what it reveals about Updike's own theology. But Morey is particularly bothered by the presentation of women, who remain "objects in and of Updike's text." Repeatedly the novel speaks to "the male reader as a participant, the female reader as an observer or object." The "magnified silence of women" in the book "brings Updike ever closer to having created the pornographic ideal that Roger says he finds so inspiring" (1037).

Several reviewers complained about the book's technical deficiencies. Though "the merits of *Roger's Version* weigh against its peculiarities," Nicholas Spice (1986) writes, Roger Lambert is simply a veiled version of his creator and the novel another "installment in Updike's psychobiography, itself a form of exhibitionism" (8). Fredric Koeppel (1986) also thinks that the "inability to perceive where Roger Lambert ends and John Updike begins" destroys "the reader's ability to suspend disbelief" (J4). On the other hand, Lorna Sage (1986) says the real problem with Lambert, a "brilliantly bad example" of Nabokov's Humbert Humbert, is that he is "a paragon of self-awareness who outguesses any reader who tries to see round him" (1189).

Updike's handling of science and sex also came in for criticism. Rhoda Koenig (1986) finds this "chilly novel" full of "complex, clotted computer and science talk" that "sadly counterpoints the simplistic nature of the characters" (76). Adrianne Blue (1986) suggests that in *Roger's Version* Updike has made "a brave leap," bringing physics "into the centre of the mainstream novel." Unfortunately, she continues, he has "stubbed his toe," choosing to load the text with heavy doses of textbook language rather than translating the science into appropriate metaphors. Hilton Kramer (1986) laments that the novel shows off Updike's erudition without offering anything worthwhile about the serious problems raised about God and sex. Duane Mehl (1987) says that, where Hawthorne is more engaged in showing how "spiritual growth can arise from illicit sexual deeds," Updike presents these deeds as "a Götterdämmerung: the collapse of the Christian faith, tradition, and culture in American society" (53). *Roger's Version* may be read with profit as "a prophetic denunciation of American culture in the Eighties," but Mehl encourages readers to "skip the obscene descriptions of sexual perversity" (54). Rod Cockshutt (1986) "cannot say enough bad things" about a book he finds "disturbingly overwritten, pretentious, cynical and meanspirited." It devolves into a "kind of sexual obsessiveness and facile social satire." Updike bludgeons readers with trite revelations about characters he does not like, and seems to have abandoned the "playful eroticism" that characterized his earlier treatment of sex in favor of clinical accuracy.

Two reviews are worth noting for the broader perspective they provide on Updike's fiction. David Lodge's (1986) is actually an analysis of Updike's use of multiple discourses in the novel. Lodge identifies "five distinct discursive strands," four of which Updike uses successfully: the "discourse of theology," the "discourse of eroticism, or pornography," the "discourse of domesticity" (1), and the "discourse of physical description." But the fifth discourse—"that of science"—is challenging for most readers. In the end, though, all of these discourses are mediated through Roger, and hence "the question of his reliability becomes crucial." Because Roger seems too glib and too all-knowing, another key discourse—"objective report"—is suppressed. Despite this discomforting fact, one comes away from reading the book with "renewed respect for one of the most intelligent and resourceful of contemporary novelists" (15). Peter Forbes (1987) also extends his discussion beyond the novel to offer some observations about Updike as a writer. Forbes believes Updike's "feel for the textures of modern life is unerring": he is one of the first writers "to use in fiction material that is indisputably part of everyday life" (22). Similarly, Forbes is not surprised that Updike is interested in science and writes about it because "he has to see the whole picture" of human life (23).

Short Stories: *Trust Me*, 1987

Updike's short stories consistently generated less volatile reactions than his novels, and the 1987 collection *Trust Me* proved no exception. Gail Caldwell (1987), Theodore O'Leary (1987), and Adrianne Blue (1987) find these stories exceptionally luminescent reflections of everyday life. Marilynne Robinson (1987) says the best stories are "full of the deep humor very sad tales have when their burden is that we are all frail creatures in a mysterious and perilous world" (44). John Bayley (1987) compares reading this "marvelously good" (6) new collection to watching Olympic-class athletes. Neither "abstract" nor "cagey," Updike is intent on portraying a society that is "unflaggingly competitive" in social matters (7), and he manages to find humor in "the sadness of things" (6)—a quality that allows him to write uplifting prose about otherwise somber situations.

Of course, the usual criticisms surfaced as well. Anita Brookner (1987) finds the stories to be bland diversions, interesting in themselves but lightweight when compared to the novels. Yet she cautions that Updike tends to lull readers into a world where much more is happening than one might surmise from reading these nostalgic set pieces. Nancy Pate (1987), who admires Updike's ability to chart "the shifts and fault lines of our domestic lives" (F8), is disappointed that he takes few risks in these stories. Carolyn See (1987) suggests that, while Updike deserves some of the praise he has received, she "never saw a woman I recognized in any Updike story." She wonders, too, why readers "love his vision of domestic futility and cruelty so very much" (6). Michael Wood (1987) complains that Updike's "mind is larger than his fictional world." He seems to make his characters intentionally small and self-absorbed. Like "slightly spoiled children," they go through the world causing harm, and Updike seems unwilling to let them glimpse "the harm in their world and their part in causing it" (1106).

The stories in *Trust Me* prompted Jonathan Yardley (1987) to observe that, as Updike has aged, the center of interest in his stories has shifted, moving from accounts of "the relatively youthful" to ones about "middle-aged restlessness." The volume reminds him that Updike is "a far more accomplished and confident writer of stories than of novels." These stories represent his "most assured work" and "no doubt it is upon the best of them that his reputation ultimately will rest" (X3).

Completing the *Scarlet Letter* Trilogy: *S.*, 1988

With the publication of *S.* in 1988, Updike completed his *Scarlet Letter* trilogy. The third novel tells the story of Sarah Worth (the "S" of the title), a supposedly liberated woman who has left her husband and family to live in an Ashram in the Western United States. Although not as popular with the reading public as *Roger's Version*, *S.* managed to land on the *New York Times* bestseller list in March 1988 and remain there for six weeks. Like its predecessor, *S.* sparked lively responses that often provide more than mere critiques of the novel. One of the most insightful and provocative reviews is Alison Lurie's (1988). The problem with Updike, she suggests, is that he does not fit the conventional mold for American writers. American critics "prefer famous authors to suffer"; the "approved pattern is a meteoric rise like that of a Roman candle, exploding into brilliance at its apogee, and then descending and becoming extinguished in the glare of newer fountains of colored fire." One reason so many critics dislike Updike is that he rose early and stayed up. Lurie thinks Updike is "the Chekhov of suburbia," able to "make much of little" and to maintain "detached sympathy for his characters" (3). Unfortunately, Lurie says, *S.* is little more than "a clever but lightweight satire of New Agers and Hippies." The novel is not satisfying because once again Updike tries too hard to respond to criticism from feminists. Unfortunately, he cannot create a strong female protagonist because, Lurie says, in Updike's works "men are in the world to do, and women simply to be" (4).

Agreeing with Lurie, David Lipsky (1988) says it is no secret that Updike "wrote the book partially in answer to his female critics"; yet he believes *S.* has "a female lead as active and clever as any of his previous male leads" (58). Sarah Worth is "one of Updike's most sharp-eyed observers," and simply cannot be dismissed as "a final crystallization of Updike's negative vision of women" because she "behaves just as well and as badly as the men in Updike's fiction tend to" (59). Howard Mosher (1988) is also taken with Sarah, who despite her failings has "managed to hang onto a good-natured sense of humor and a battered but intact dignity rare in these times of drag-tail fictional anti-heroes." The book works equally well as a commentary on Hawthorne and "a fable of our times," but it is also "entertaining in its own right," a "comic triumph" (1).

Christopher Hitchens (1988) finds such claims suspect. He dismisses *S.* as one of Updike's "lighter efforts" (453), but not before making a number of sardonic criticisms of Updike's handling of the story, suggesting that his principal motive for producing the tale was to make money. Somewhat more generously, George Searles (1988) recommends that one not try to over-analyze *S.* because Updike intended it as comedy rather than social commentary. Sarah is something of "a caricature" (508)—which Searles admits will bother some feminists—but "exaggeration and distortion" are to be expected because of the work's genre (510). Like Searles, Anita Brookner (1988) thinks Updike has created a "foolish woman" (35) as his heroine in order to satirize religious cults. Brookner does not think Updike is being hard on feminists—Sarah comes off quite well, in her view—but in the end the novel is no more than "minor Updike, done with grace, wit, and an underlying seriousness, but sacrificing too much to make unimportant points" (36). Raymond Sokolov (1988) gives Updike credit for creating a woman of complexity and stature; but he believes the novel will probably "not endure" very long in readers' memories or on library shelves (28).

Treating the novel as more serious and potentially more enduring, Anatole Broyard (1988) admits that "Updike does seem to have some problem bestirring himself" to enter into the mind and voice of a female protagonist (7). The experiment, while not calamitous, is certainly not successful. Michiko Kakutani (1988) is decidedly less kind, describing the novel as both unconvincing and distasteful. Perhaps Updike intended to write "a persuasive novel about a woman" told from her point of view, but "there's a huge gap" between intention and accomplishment. "If Sarah Worth represents Mr. Updike's attempt to create a sympathetic heroine, it's hard to imagine what he'd come up with if he set out to depict a villain" (C29). Like Kakutani, Hope Davis (1988) finds patently specious Updike's claim that this novel is intended to paint women in a good light. And yet, Davis suggests, critics are likely to try to "justify in Updike what they might see in others as inexcusable" (21) because he has earned their respect. Davis's implication is that the reviewing establishment (mostly males) will simply applaud the novel as a comic masterpiece and avoid dealing with its more troubling connotations.

But some male reviewers were equally disturbed by the novel's portrait of women. Christopher Lehmann-Haupt (1988) considers *S.* blatantly misogynist. Rather than being a re-telling of *The Scarlet Letter* from a woman's perspective, as Updike intended, the voice in the novel seems much more like Updike's own. "The novel leaves one uneasy," Lehmann-Haupt concludes, and "ends up impressing one most of all as an ambivalent view of women coming straight from the author's heart" (C16). John Leonard (1989) claims *S.* is another attempt by this "Dennis the Menace" to "ingratiate himself" with feminists. Updike seems to be having fun lampooning the "wisdom of the East," but he does so "at the expense of Sarah and her upper-middle-class Radcliffe smarty-pants notions of what women's lib is all about." Sarah comes off as silly, which reveals something about Updike's attitude toward women. "Updike thinks he loves women," Leonard says, "but they emerge from the condescension of his novels, like the Jews in *Bech* and the Africans in *The Coup*, as merely cute, like poodles" (124).

Updike's inability to represent accurately and honestly any group outside the White male establishment is the principal criticism leveled at him by George Gessert (1990), who argues that in *S.* Updike seriously misrepresents and trivializes the Asian world and its religions. The novel reveals Updike's essential parochialism and his unwillingness, despite his scholarly research, to try to understand people different from the suburbanites about whom he writes with confidence. Instead, his works end up "faithfully reflecting a people who have been protected for so long that they do not recognize any limitations to their understanding of the world" (140).

A central question for many critics is how successfully Updike is able to capture the spirit of Hawthorne's *Scarlet Letter*. Merle Rubin (1988) finds the differences between Hawthorne's work and Updike's outweigh the similarities. Rubin believes no modern writer can "endow[ ] a character with Hester's heroic aura" (20); nevertheless, she praises Updike for his inventive style. "Sarah's voice," she says, "is Updike's parody of the modern, intelligent, liberated, upper-middle-class American woman" (20). Carol Iannone (1988) suggests that while Updike's trilogy is not always a faithful reinterpretation of Hawthorne's novel, it has merit for several reasons. The novel is a kind of "breakthrough" for Updike; "writing from a woman's perspective seems to have disciplined him" (57). Furthermore, she concludes, "the trilogy as a whole, for all its hesitations and compromising ambiguities, is to be welcomed not just for its many local artistic triumphs but for the hard questions it puts" to American society—"questions of renewal, of grace, of authenticity, of salvation" (59).

However, Carolyn See (1988) finds Updike's allusions to Hawthorne heavy-handed and his treatment of Eastern religions hopelessly reductive and condescending. His treatment of women is even more patronizing, making the novel nothing more than "a grand chance to laugh at women, religion, and the American West." The only thing about which Updike is serious, See says, is sex. Richard Gilman (1988), thinks *S.* is a "thin and halfhearted" exploitation of *The Scarlet Letter* (40), a novel in which "the satire is inconsistent" and moments of true feeling "rare." Updike is unable to conceive a female character sufficiently different from himself to make her believable, once again displaying his penchant for squandering his considerable literary talents.

Finally, John Lanchester's (1988) rather lengthy review of *S.* challenges critics like See and Gilman and offers some interesting observations about Updike's technical competencies. Lanchester believes that one of Updike's aims in writing *S.* is to solve two problems: "the problem of sufficiently varied texture and the problem of credible voice." Lanchester thinks this novel "goes a long way toward solving both of them" (20). He demonstrates how Updike is able to create a distinctive voice for his heroine—an important accomplishment, since Updike had been accused of creating characters who sound like him. *S.* is "a miracle of craftsmanly ingenuity" and "problem-solving," a "new departure in Updike's work in its twist toward the comic, and its willingness to embrace the fashionable assumption that what really motivates people is money" (21).

Writing Openly about Himself: *Self-Consciousness*, 1989

In 1989 Updike published a collection of essays that can loosely be described as a memoir. *Self-Consciousness* deals with issues important to Updike's formation as a writer, weaving autobiographical details into contemplative pieces that focus on the development of the "self." Specifically, these essays deal with Updike's "self," but concurrently, they also address the issue of what it means to be a subject in the visible world. The work was welcomed by many but panned by a number of critics who found it little more than slick self-promotion.

The reviewer for the *Economist* ("The Loathly Glass" 1989) says that by publishing *Self-Consciousness* Updike "has trumped the biographers" (98), taking "the fashion for intimate revelations of a novelist's life just about as far as it can go." The book succeeds because Updike is "such a fundamentally honest man in matters both small—and large" (101). Scott Donaldson (1989) asserts that the book provides insights into Updike's mind "in the way that biography almost never can" (8). Paul Baumann (1989) observes that in these "gracious memoirs" Updike explores his own defects, physical and literary, to make the point that the responsibility of "the self" is "to appreciate what has been given" by a God who truly exists, even if humankind cannot always connect with Him (439).

Taking a slightly different approach, Michael Wood (1989) suggests that *Self-Consciousness* offers at least a partial answer to the question, What "odd loyalty" confines Updike to writing about the "cramped and easy culture" of the East Coast? The answers lie in the remembrances Updike relates in this autobiographical memoir, and are worth contemplating if one wants to understand him. Anita Brookner (1989) also believes Updike has provided genuine insight into his life and offered readers an inkling of what it has taken for him to become a writer. The distinguishing characteristic of his fiction, Brookner says, is its sense of innocence—not because his writing is innocent, but because it "exudes a kind of fidelity to first impressions that has never faltered" (37). Mark Feeney (1989) thinks some may consider *Self-Consciousness* superfluous as autobiography, since Updike reveals so much of himself in his fiction; still, he finds the memoir highly enlightening. "More clearly than in any of his books," in *Self-Consciousness* "Updike betrays his obsession with mortality." Though Updike's "gorgeous prose" can sometimes "distract the reader" from what he has to say, the memoir exposes "a more nakedly human John Updike" than any of his previous books do. Reading it, Feeney says, "is a chastening, but also a moving experience" (B18).

Among those who saw *Self-Consciousness* as a kind of *apologia*, Mark Caldwell (1989) says that in this memoir Updike "stakes out a defense for himself" (F1) against critics' charges about the quality and *gravitas* of his work. Arthur Moore (1989), on the other hand, believes Updike is not using *Self-Consciousness* to answer his critics; instead, "he is primarily explaining himself to himself" (173). Curiously, however, "Updike seems oddly distant and disengaged when he gets around to an extended treatment of religion" (174). Also bothered by the book, Richard Eder

(1989) thinks that *Self-Consciousness* fails to be convincing as a memoir because Updike does not feel a "hunger" to confess. The book will not ward off future biographers, either, Eder says, because "Updike means too much to us to be left alone" (3).

Rhoda Koenig (1989) is among those disappointed with *Self-Consciousness*; she complains that Updike has provided only the sparest biographical details and managed to smother "nearly all unruly emotion" beneath "an eiderdown of lyricism" (66). Bruce Bawer (1989) says "much of this book is—to put it bluntly—boring." Updike emerges from its pages "at once a duller and more intellectually respectable sort than one might have expected" (A10). David Denby (1989) finds the memoir deficient because Updike is too reticent to open up fully. Instead, he comes off like "the Updike of the literary criticism, honey-tongued, encompassing, solicitous, a marvelously observant but slightly diffident companion" (31), the "patron saint of the sensitive who wish not to feel defeated, of the diffident and the retiring who wish not to relinquish life's pleasures, of the cautious who still demand to triumph" (33).

Among those even less besmitten, Martin Amis ([1989] 2001) says *Self-Consciousness* is full of cranky observations and contains some of the worst prose Updike has ever written. Richard Vigilante (1989) calls it "tedious, mundane, cliché-ridden, self-obsessed, and overwritten" (52). The only essay that is in any way compelling is the one of Vietnam, because "it is the only one premised on the author's taking an action" (54). Fred Inglis (1989) thinks Updike comes off as "a perfectly unconscious self made up of petty-minded vengefulness, high-pitched sanctimony, political silliness of a really worked-at variety and old-fashioned grandparental boringness" (59). Inglis takes Updike to task for his conservative political views, which may be the reason Inglis finds the book "appalling" (60), filled with "the kind of rotten emotivism, cruel irresponsibility and downright hypocrisy that is one potent formation in the political influence of a great and generous superpower" (61).

Finally, a more appreciative and forgiving Ralph Wood (1989b) believes this memoir reveals much about Updike, whom Wood sees as subscribing to Whitman's theory of "egotheism"—the "awestruck wonder and thanksgiving to God for the staggering miracle of unrepeatable life, the utterly unique self-consciousness that enables one to say 'I'" (526). That is the real theme of *Self-Consciousness*, a work that helps explain why Updike writes *what* he does and *as* he does. But Wood considers Updike's handling of theological matters disappointing, especially since he seems to tread lightly on conventional Protestant theologians' notions of sin and humankind's relationship with the deity. There is much about "man" in Updike's theology, but considerably less about "God." "It is tempting to wish," Wood muses, "that Updike might write a sequel in praise of God for who *God* is" (528).

Updike on Art, Part 1: *Just Looking*, 1989

Throughout his career as a reviewer, Updike wrote regularly about art—hardly a surprise, since he did postgraduate work at Oxford's Ruskin School of Drawing and Fine Art. In 1989 he issued his first collection devoted exclusively to art criticism, *Just Looking*, which received attention not only from the usual array of book critics but also from professional art critics and practitioners. Reviews suggest something about the limits of Updike's range of expertise—and that of his reviewers. Notices by critics not trained as artists or art historians tended to be favorable, though some reviewers expressed reservations. For example, Christopher Lehmann-Haupt (1989) praises *Just Looking* as a book of "original and perceptive" critiques, "instructive and full of intelligence" (C18). Jerome Donnelly (1990) finds Updike's unpretentious approach to art criticism refreshing, noting with approbation his ability to blend a keen eye for art "with a consummate articulation of what that eye sees." Donnelly feels Updike's preference for representational art is one of his strengths, because it allows him to "compare artistic rendering with actual reality" (180). Craig Raine (1990) says Updike's "engagingly unpretentious" approach can be "misleading," because Updike has a much wider knowledge of art than he lets on, and occasionally provides "inspired" descriptions of individual works (12). However, Raine concludes, *contra* Donnelly, that Updike is too naïve to be a truly effective critic, because he does not understand the subtle complexities of nonrepresentational art.

The assessments of those professionally trained in the arts are somewhat more critical. In a generally favorable review with the clever title "What MOMA Done Tole Him," Arthur Danto (1989) suggests that, while most of the essays hold no "great urgency for those whose concerns with art connect with the great critical issues of today," on occasion Updike manages to say "something deep" about works other critics refuse to comment on, either out of ignorance or fear (12). Mark Rudman (1990) finds compelling Updike's precision in recording "what makes a painting memorable to him" without ever becoming too effusive about works he values. At the same time, however, Rudman finds that *Just Looking* lacks "the edge of demonic insight that characterizes other writers' great writings on art" (104).

Art critic Hilton Kramer (1989) complains that *Just Looking* represents a trend in which "'literary writing' about art" turns painting and sculpture into something akin to literature. Updike is unable to provide cogent commentary on nonrepresentational art, and his comments on realistic works are not much better. Only two pieces "can claim anything in the way of intellectual authenticity," neither of them really art criticism: Updike's account of early visits to New York's Museum of Modern Art and a character study of cartoonist Ralph Barton. Except for these articles, *Just Looking* "is nothing but a celebrity gift book" (9). Similarly, Deborah Solomon (1989), another art critic, questions the depth of Updike's knowledge of art. He rarely gets beyond surface details in describing individual works and offers few "sharp or decisive" critical judgments (70). Despite his "wonderful writing," Solomon laments, the essays do not have "the weight or the urgency one expects from a first-rate writer." Instead, "the book as a whole gives off an air of self-congratulation," and Updike's "modesty" seems "ostentatious" (71).

Bret Waller (1990) of the Getty Museum suggests that Updike's bias for representational art blinds him to the subtleties of abstract work. Most of his criticism is actually a description of his personal associations with the work under review. *Just Looking* offers some insight into the way people relate to works of art, but as "art criticism, or even as high-class art journalism," it is "pretty insubstantial" (26). That judgment is challenged by Carter Ratcliff (2001), whose review of the reissued volume of *Just Looking* defends Updike's right to be an art critic. Ratcliff provides an insightful critique of Updike's conservatism, the reason he seems to minimize the achievements of postmodernists and promote realist art against abstractionism. However, Ratcliff believes the art world is made healthier by Updike's articulate conservatism, because it forces those who are advancing the arts to refine their values.

The Series Ends: *Rabbit at Rest*, 1990

Critics had predicted it, and while many of Updike's devoted fans dreaded it, few were surprised when in September 1990 Updike issued the last of his novels about Harry Angstrom. *Rabbit at Rest* recounts the final months of Harry's turbulent life, ending with his collapse (appropriately enough) on a basketball court where he tries unsuccessfully to recapture a moment of his youth in a pickup game with youngsters less than half his age. The novel was a popular success, landing on the *New York Times* bestseller list in mid-October and remaining there through Thanksgiving. *Rabbit at Rest* was awarded the Pulitzer Prize for 1990.

Undoubtedly, praise far outweighed criticism. Chilton Williamson (1990) dubbed *Rabbit at Rest* "not just the best of the Rabbit novels" but "probably the best of all its author's novels." In it, Updike "has achieved the serious writer's aim: namely, the perfection of his unique peculiarities of style, and their perfect reconciliation with one another" (51). Jonathan Raban (1990) believes that "from now on it is going to be hard to read John Updike without seeing all his earlier work as a long rehearsal for the writing of this book." *Rabbit at Rest* "is one of the few modern novels in English" that "one can set beside the work of Dickens, Thackeray, George Eliot, Joyce" (1).

The towering figure of Harry Angstrom elicited numerous comments. Sven Birkerts (1990) thinks it is a tribute to Updike's artistry that "on one level Rabbit is but a shallow and reactionary male of his class and era," but on another he is "a sweet and watchful soul, as deep in his affectionate perceptiveness as the man who made his world" (4). George Searles (1990) observes that while Harry is not a particularly likeable character—too reactionary, full of racial and class prejudices, jingoistic in his patriotism—*Rabbit at Rest* succeeds on two levels: as the continuing saga of the life of a man undefeated in spirit by the commonplace travails of his ordinary life, and as a "documentary of a society sinking in its own vulgar excesses" (21). Michiko Kakutani (1990), a critic often quick to bash Updike, finds *Rabbit at Rest* a "rich and rewarding novel" (C17), a fitting conclusion to Updike's "Kodachrome-sharp picture of American life—the psychic ups and downs, enthusiasms and reversals" that the country experienced from the 1950s through the 1980s. In this novel Updike "is working at the full height of his powers, reorchestrating the themes that have animated not only his earlier Rabbit novels but his entire oeuvre as well" (C13). William Pritchard (1990) praises *Rabbit at Rest* as a fitting close to Updike's thirty-year love affair with a character who is in some ways his alter ego, in others his diametrical opposite. Pritchard is certain that, although Rabbit is "put to rest" in this final installment, "the book that did it to him will be around as long as people continue to look to American novels for the stuff they can't get elsewhere" (27).

Fellow novelist Joyce Carol Oates ([1990] 1999) believes that the Rabbit novels collectively constitute "Updike's surpassingly eloquent elegy for his country" (165). Josh Getlin (1990) also claims Harry's story is "writ large against the backdrop of a changing society"; this final novel "paints a dark picture of the American middle class in decline" (E12). Mark Feeney (1990) says one can easily say "grand things" about the Rabbit novels because they are "a matchless record of middle-class life in twentieth-century America" and social comedy about "the treachery of the American dream." Although Harry Angstrom comes across as "a heel," readers have spent so much time inside his head they cannot "help but become attached to him and begin to see the world as he does" (B45). Ralph Wood ([1990] 2005) insists that, through Rabbit, Updike has "let us absorb the ethos of our time" (159). That is not to say, Wood insists, that Updike intends to exonerate Rabbit for his sometimes immoral or egotistical behavior. But he does reflect accurately "our carnal condition" (162).

Looking at Harry's development through the four novels, Rand Richards Cooper (1991) probes Updike's interest in questions of faith and doubt. Where *Rabbit, Run* foregrounds those concerns, *Rabbit Redux* seems concerned exclusively with social issues. *Rabbit Is Rich* is "a persuasive return to the themes of Harry Angstrom's inner life" (318).

Beneath its "playful comedy," however, "lies an accumulating bleakness" (319). The novel is filled with presentiments of Harry's mortality, which are fulfilled in the final book in the sequence, "the novel Updike has been waiting all his career to write." Updike makes Harry face death "without benefit of faith" (320). Hence, Cooper suggests somewhat provocatively, "*Rabbit at Rest* should be seen as the final campaign in a losing battle for faith, bespeaking substantial spiritual gloom not only for Rabbit, but, one senses, for his creator as well" (321).

Reaction to *Rabbit at Rest* on the other side of the Atlantic was generally positive as well. Zachary Leader (1990) finds it the best statement of Updike's vision of America and Americans. Martin Amis says it is as if Updike loaded the bases with his first three Rabbit novels then hit a grand-slam home run with *Rabbit at Rest*. Amis is impressed with Updike's ability to make the lives of ordinary Americans "worth examining." Furthermore, his extraordinary ornate style gives grandeur to the life of Rabbit and, by extension, to ordinary people who tend to sing unheard "until the novelist intercedes" ([1990] 2001, 32). The reviewer for the *Economist* ("God Bless America" 1990) notes that, while Rabbit seems to be a "manifest failure" in every aspect of his life, few readers who "have come to know this complex slob" will be happy to see him die. The "complex, startling, revealing ambiguity" found throughout the Rabbit series is what makes Updike "so great a writer about contemporary Americans"—or, more accurately, "about contemporary American men" (157).

Anita Brookner (1990) finds *Rabbit at Rest* a fitting close to a four-volume saga that has begun to "look dangerously like a masterpiece." The books are a record of contemporary American history, a taxonomy of the country's "fall from grace" (28). In the Rabbit novels Updike "has produced something extravagant and inimitable which makes most other contemporary fiction pall and shrivel in its wake" (29). Hermione Lee ([1990] 2005) says that, while the Rabbit novels seem to be solid and accurate portraits of America, they also possess a certain elusive strangeness because of Updike's insistence on stressing the metaphorical nature of the real (171). In the final novel, Harry's memory "fuses with the narrative's metaphors to make an elegy for our world" (173).

A number of reviewers—from both sides of the political spectrum—stressed the sociopolitical dimensions of the Rabbit novels. Louis Menand (1990) says Updike intends the series to be an expose of "American egotism—the overdeveloped shell and the soft blob of need it protects" (93). Charles Bremner (1990) believes the novel "has touched a raw nerve," causing many to wonder "whether Updike has gone too far in depicting the demise of the selfish, superficial Rabbit as a metaphor for the America that was born in the abundance of the post-war decade" and "ended with the 1989 revolutions" that eliminated Communism as a viable bogeyman to energize US political, economic, and military interests (23). In an op-ed piece in the *Washington Post*, conservative political commentator George Will ([1990] 1994) praises Updike for making readers interested in "this emotionally stunted, intellectually barren, morally repulsive egotist, whose self-absorption lacks even the fascination of large scale" (401). Will believes the novels can best be read as "a cautionary tale for America the sclerotic, its arteries clogged by dumb consumption." Yet, while America may be mortal, her demise is not imminent—and he quotes Updike for support, noting that the novelist once said that "people run down, and they confuse their condition with the world's" (402).

The litany of praise excerpted in the preceding paragraphs should not obscure the fact that *Rabbit at Rest* had its critics. Some were like Bruce Manuel (1990), who admits that, on one level, Rabbit's story "reads like a national tragedy." Ultimately, however, Harry "lacks the dimensions of a truly tragic character" (13). Dean Flower (1991) finds the central deficiency in the novel not its protagonist but its author. *Rabbit at Rest* is "the most uninspired" of the tetralogy, largely because Updike has become "sentimental" and failed to achieve sufficient "critical distance" from his protagonist, a flaw that reveals a diminution of Updike's artistic powers (321). Garry Wills (1990) expresses serious reservations about the value of the Rabbit novels. The "compulsive tidiness" of Updike's scheme "tries to make up in comprehensiveness what it has increasingly lost in plausibility." Wills believes that "Updike began with the aim of saying some hard true things about what is wrong with America." However, "by succumbing to his own stylistic solipsism," he ends up "exemplifying what is wrong. Description makes up for analysis; detail for design; inclusiveness for rigor; and mere length for moral heft or grip" (14).

The publication of *Rabbit at Rest* served as the springboard to a series of consistently negative critiques of Updike by James Wood (1990), the young (just twenty-five at the time) British critic who would become a major voice in critical practice over the next two decades. Wood says Harry Angstrom is "the swine before which Updike casts his pearls." In the series, Updike "turns America and everything in it into a vast foodstuff, instantly and deliciously consumable." The consistent thread running through the novels is the "singularly average" quality in Rabbit's character, a quality Updike equates with America. By the fourth installment, however, "the Rabbit series has become something of a joke, an enterprise that teeters (deliberately) on the edge of parody" (25). Wood appreciates Updike's efforts to elevate the saga of his pedestrian protagonist into something significant by exposing the triviality of his life. Sadly, Wood concludes, the effort is a failure.

Wood's is a minority view, however, and it seems appropriate to close this section with comments from a writer who expresses what was becoming the general sentiment about Updike at this time. On the occasion of Updike's appearance for a public reading in Memphis, Fredric Koeppel published companion pieces critiquing the novel and profiling its author. In the first, Koeppel says that had Updike written nothing else besides the Rabbit novels "he should be celebrated as a great American author" because these books "stand as a magnificent group, both for their plumbing of the American psyche and for the sheer glorious accumulation of their writing" (1990a, G2). In his profile of Updike, Koeppel declares that Updike's characters "seem universal, not specific to the white middle class of the Northeast," and hails Updike as "our most interesting, our most various, our most compelling fiction writer, the one who most beautifully holds a mirror to our faces" (1990b, G2). Certainly not every reviewer or critic would agree with Koeppel's judgments, but it is likely that his view is representative of the majority of readers who had followed Harry's progress over three decades.

Academic Criticism, 1986–1990

For years after Richard Rupp's 1967 essay on Updike's weaknesses appeared in the *Sewanee Review*, relatively little negative criticism of Updike made its way into any scholarly publication. A handful of unflattering reviews by academics were carried in newspapers and popular magazines, but by the 1980s the academic establishment seems to have embraced Updike as a writer of substance. One strong dissenter from academe, however, was Frederick Crews (1986), who used the considerable space and flexibility afforded by the *New York Review of Books* to present one of the harshest critiques of Updike's achievements ever published. Reviewing *Roger's Version*, Crews surveys Updike's entire career in an effort to explain his popularity and identify his strengths and weaknesses. Crews notes that while a considerable number of reviewers (and a meager handful of academics) bemoan Updike's narrow focus and preoccupation with sex, "a formidable array of critics, most of them English professors," consider Updike "a powerful social chronicler, a master of physical texture and psychological nuance, a profound moralist, a symbolist, a Christian philosopher, in short a living classic whose accession to the Nobel podium is already overdue." Crews poses the question: "Who is kidding whom?" (1986, 7)

Crews quickly reveals which side he is on. He is dismayed by his fellow academics' high opinion of Updike, suggesting they have been duped by a writer whose mastery of style conceals significant shortcomings in other areas. Most of Updike's novels "revert to a few central, urgently autobiographical preoccupations." Academics are right in saying that understanding Updike's religious position is central to "any broad comprehension" of his fiction; but over the years Updike has "grown more eccentric and brittle as the range of his sympathies has contracted, radically divorcing his notion of Christian theology from that of Christian ethics." His "adoring critics" are hesitant to acknowledge this drift, as it might mean expulsion from "the pietistic fold" (7).

Since the early 1970s, Crews continues, Updike's novels have become more mannerist, filled with "a combination of rant and facetiousness," in which he casts aspersions on everything he does not like about the post-Eisenhower world (10). By the mid-1980s his "sensibility has appreciably calcified, leaving him at once morally obtuse, politically inflexible, and crabbedly protective" of his belief in the me-first generation. Nowhere is this more evident, Crews says, than in *Roger's Version*, "the coldest and most self-conscious of his novels" (11). The book becomes an excuse for Updike to "cast malevolent suspicion on every group that strikes" him as "potentially disruptive" to the ideal society he envisions for himself and like-minded individuals (12).

Perhaps the most damning critique Crews makes of Updike's later fiction is that it calls for "white readers" to "wake up—not, however, to social injustice, but to the fact that their homes, jobs, and persons cannot be indefinitely safeguarded against the covetous have-nots." This "show of class-based misanthropy cannot be dismissed as a passing aberration," since it has been evident in Updike's work since *Rabbit Redux* appeared in 1971. While one might claim that Updike is a chameleon writing in the style and voice appropriate for each tale, beneath these voices lies the real Updike, a "morbid and curmudgeonly" figure "starved for a missing grace, playing an unfunny hide-and-seek with his readers, reluctant to confide his anguish yet driven to express both a lurking nihilism and a doctrinal obsession that barely keeps that nihilism at bay." Updike dwells "on the sunny outskirts of his mind," Crews says, because "a certain bleakness" is present "at the center" (12).

Predictably, Crews's assessment prompted rebuttals from some of the academics he skewers. In Letters to the Editor in the February 12, 1987 issue of the *New York Review of Books*, Amherst English professor William H. Pritchard (1987) and Bangor Theological Seminary's George Hunsinger (1987) challenged Crews's method and motives. Pritchard accuses him of cherry-picking his evidence, "eviscerate[ing]" Updike's work by "rip[ping] out illiberal, unright-thinking utterances from a number of novels" to justify claims about Updike's misanthropy. Crews suppresses any recognition of the sense of pleasure one might get from reading Updike's work "in favor of a sternly moral disapprobation" of his ideas (41). Hunsinger attacks Crews's understanding of the theology that informs Updike's work, claiming his assertions about Barth are "riddled with factual errors" (41). In the same issue of the *Review*, Crews replies to Pritchard and Hunsinger, parroting their format in ripostes that make Pritchard seem like he has his head in the sand and Hunsinger to have misunderstood not only Updike but Barth as well.

Had the editors at the *New York Review of Books* wished, they could have allowed this debate to carry on for some time, as both Pritchard and Hunsinger appear capable of going toe-to-toe with Crews on these issues (and possibly others as well). What is truly ironic, however, is that, two years after Crews issued his lengthy condemnation, one of Updike's longstanding adversaries publicly reversed his position. In a 1988 essay, Norman Podhoretz admits that his 1963 judgment of Updike was perhaps too dismissive, and certainly premature. Over the years, Podhoretz says, Updike has managed to "get his weakness for stylistic pyrotechnics under control" and become a writer capable of holding up a mirror to society (A23).

Crews's judgment not withstanding, favorable critical commentaries continued to proliferate. In *Updike's Novels*, Jeff Campbell (1987) presents an interpretation of Updike that he says is based not on critical presuppositions but on Updike's own description of his ideology and values. Campbell finds the source of Updike's world view in *Midpoint*, the long poem in which he "sets forth in his own words his outlook on life and art" (13). There, Updike proclaims his belief in the importance of the individual and the reality of the world; posits an essential dualism in which there is an "interpenetration and interdependence of mind/spirit and body/matter" (31); and affirms the importance of mystery and faith in giving meaning to human life. Although Campbell quotes infrequently from other critics, his occasional references to the Hamiltons indicate his similar interest in the religious dimensions of Updike's fiction.

In *John Updike*, a relatively brief study intended for students, Judie Newman (1988) offers some suggestive interpretations of Updike's fiction, organizing her commentary around broad themes: the social ethic, the world of work, the aesthetic sphere, and what Newman calls the politics of the imagination. The novels she chooses to discuss are in her view ones that "demand extended treatment" (6). Although Newman breaks no new ground in her discussion, she stresses the need for a more comprehensive examination of the social dimensions of Updike's fiction and for a more detailed analysis of his use of science and technology. Newman's volume on Updike is one of twenty-five monographs in the Macmillan Modern Writers series. According to the general editor, they are devoted to figures such as Proust, Camus, Conrad, Faulkner, and Joyce who "created the modern novel and to those who, in turn, either continued and extended or reacted against and rejected, the traditions established during that period of intense exploration and experiment" (Newman 1988, vii).

In 1987 Harold Bloom issued the first of several collections of criticism on Updike. *Modern Critical Views: John Updike* (1987) contains ten previously published essays and book chapters, including Mary Allen's rather hostile "John Updike's Love of 'Dull Bovine Beauty.'" A revised version appeared a little more than a decade later in 2001, the same year

Bloom issued a volume on Updike's short fiction in his "Major American Short Story Writers" series. That collection contains considerably more excerpts, but most are short, and analyze only five stories. Bloom himself seems to have mixed feelings about Updike's achievements. He calls Updike "a major stylist" but says his "literary production has been vast and varied"—code, no doubt, for uneven and sometimes downright second-rate. In fact, in the Introduction to the collection of short-story criticism, Bloom (2001) suggests that Updike is at his best as a short story writer, because as a novelist he "overly contaminates his principal longer narratives with his own beliefs and opinions" (9).

Other critics, however, were assertive in defending Updike's virtues. Keith Opdahl (1987) calls Updike "Saul Bellow's heir in American fiction," and says he is "even more of a realist than Bellow" (1). John Fleischauer (1989) notes that Updike's "distinctive style" has been a major reason he has "occupied a place near the center of the American literary scene for over twenty years" (277). Updike uses adjectives, metaphors, diction, imagery, and even syntax to create a sense of ironic detachment and avoid having his stories become sentimental. The "richness" one experiences in reading Updike comes not from "the stature of his characters but from the milieu in which they act," a milieu highlighted by the stylistic devices he employs (285).

The issue of Updike's reputation was far from settled, however, as Peter Conn (1989) makes clear in his brief, unflattering discussion of him in *Literature in America*. Citing as Updike's principal themes "religious questions" and "the difficulty of investing fiction with seriousness in a culture of multiplying counterfeit," Conn undercuts any positive judgments with a number of barbed observations. For example, he suggests that Updike's novels are "larded with mythology" and other allusions that turn his fiction into "an anthology of solemn reference that often misfires by merely confirming his suburban sufferers in their smallness." Updike's "intentions" in his sexually explicit fiction "at least professedly, are not to titillate but to explore" (484). Many of the stories and novels "are excuses for Updike's expenditures of talent" in which banal characters are "overpowered by the prose" (486).

Interest in Updike's fiction by scholars employing new critical methodologies began to grow substantially during the 1980s, and their commentaries provide new and in some cases radically different ways of thinking about Updike. For example, the influence of French intellectuals is evident in John Neary's 1986 essay in which he claims Updike is not a "simple unselfconscious formal realist" (228) but a writer concerned about the creation of a self-conscious self. Neary applies Emmanuel Levinas's "dualistic philosophy of otherness" (229) to produce a reading of *The Centaur*, which he says deconstructs the traditional *Künstlerroman*, but not strictly in a Derridian sense, largely because it provides an ethical solution to the problem of "bridg[ing] the gap between human beings without denying their autonomy" (244). Similarly, the writings of J. Hillis Miller and Kierkegaard provide the theoretical framework for Neary's 1989 study of the Rabbit novels, in which he concludes that, for all their "reputed 'realism,'" Updike's novels "have a good deal of the Nietzschean volatility of more trendy, deconstructionist writing" (109).

Robert Siegle (1986) provides a brief but thought-provoking reading of *Rabbit, Run* in *The Politics of Reflexivity*, a book grounded in poststructuralist theory (and filled with the language that characterizes many of the new critical methodologies). As much as Updike expresses a desire to write conventional narrative, Siegle says, the many instances in which the narrator's or the character's reflections on the social web that entangles Rabbit demonstrate how *Rabbit, Run* "pushes the limits of the romantic novel's effort to happen more or less uncritically within the framework of the protagonist's achieving selfhood." Thus, despite Updike's "lack of interest in explicitly reflexive techniques in the novel, the work becomes at a deeper level a reflexive hollowing of the nucleus of late modernist narrative" (156).

Two other essays further illustrate the trend toward new critical readings. Francesco Ancona (1986) examines father-son relationships in Updike's fiction by applying Lacanian psychoanalytical theory regarding the role of the father as the "guarantor of the Law" (81). Raman Selden ([1989] 1993) suggests that by examining Updike's story "Should Wizard Hit Mommy" from "the point of view of narrative theory," especially structuralist theory (201–2), it is possible to develop a more nuanced reading and come to a deeper appreciation of Updike's accomplishments in constructing the tale for the "implied reader" that he envisions (206).

As might be expected, those engaged in gender studies found fertile ground for criticism in Updike's work. While reviewers railed against Updike for his chauvinist views, academics were paying closer attention to his treatment of women *and* men. Typical of such studies is George Bodmer's (1986) examination of Updike's male characters. Bodmer finds that, viewed through the lens of gender, male protagonists in Updike's fiction often find themselves prisoners of a patriarchal tradition, unable to cope with societal changes that are giving women new freedoms. When under stress, most resort to traditional male pursuits rather than attempt to understand the changing social dynamic. Bodmer is silent, however, on whether he thinks Updike shares the values of his characters.

Francine Prose (1988) tries to explain feminists' dislike of Updike by placing him in a larger context—that of male novelists trying to write about women. In the past, she says, "one privilege of being a writer" has been the freedom to "describe life from the point of view of both sexes." At present, however, "perhaps because the sex war has so escalated that we cannot trust even our imaginations to cross the battle lines," one can no longer expect men to write with such insight about women (18). Prose believes "the gap between the sexes has finally become unbridgeable"—a conclusion she reached by her experience reading Updike's *S*. "Updike's mistake"—a flaw shared by other male writers—"is to assume that women see themselves the way men have decided they do" (19). A few men are still able to capture female character accurately, Prose says, but Updike is not one of them.

The religious dimensions of Updike's fiction remained of interest both to literary critics and theologians. One important study on this topic is Ralph Wood's *The Comedy of Redemption* (1988). Relying on Barthian theology, Wood demonstrates how, like a number of other Christian writers, Updike is a "comic artist[ ] in the theological sense of the term" (2). Wood calls Updike "an ironist of the spiritual life" who sees human existence as a "tragic conflict of opposites" that by God's grace "can nonetheless be affirmed as good" (178). Wood even makes sense of Updike's "absorption with sex," claiming Updike shares Kierkegaard's view that "eroticism" is "an attempt to fend off death more than to seek pleasure" (180). Wood calls the Rabbit novels an "American saga" and Harry Angstrom a figure "no less definitive for our cultural consciousness" than Twain's Huck Finn, Faulkner's Ike McCaslin, or Hemingway's Nick Adams (207). Rabbit's travails are those of all modern Americans, and the novels in which he is the protagonist "attest that the surest way to hurt oneself and others is to live as if the purpose of life were to have a good time." On the other hand, when one accepts the fundamental paradoxes of life—"inescapable linkages of joy and sadness, comedy and tragedy, carnival and labor, faith and doubt"—one finds happiness serendipitously, as these paradoxes are resolved "by the gracious God of life" (229).

However, Wood could be critical of Updike when the occasion demanded, as evidenced by his review of a number of books about Karl Barth and Updike's *Roger's Version* (R. Wood, 1989a). Treating Updike's novel as a kind of theological text, Wood suggests that Updike "systematically miscomprehends the mature Barth," a failing that is not just a "theological error" but also "a severe detriment to his fiction as well" (30). Although Wood's interpretations may at times be reminiscent of earlier commentary by the Hamiltons, he displays a level of sophistication and an appreciation for the subtleties of Updike's fiction that make his commentary more valuable in advancing ideas about ways Updike explores theological issues in his fiction.

In *Breaking the Fall* (1989) Robert Detweiler turns to Updike's fiction for examples of how, in the age of postmodernism and poststructuralism, it is still possible to read contemporary fiction from a religious perspective. Detweiler demonstrates how the sermons in Updike's fiction, particularly those in *A Month of Sundays* and *The Witches of Eastwick*, reveal that in "postmodern fiction" the "boundary between fiction and nonfiction is blurring increasingly," as writers like Updike intermingle other literary genres into their narratives. Detweiler believes Updike uses sermons ironically, often putting them in the mouths of unreliable characters and creating not certainty but suspicion, standing for "the unreliability of all discourse" (114).

Among the more provocative studies of Updike as a social chronicler is an essay by Thomas Henricks (1988) with the somewhat misleading title "Social Science Meets Updike: The Passion for Sport as Personal Regression." Interested in the way sports functions in literature and life, Henricks turns to Updike because he considers him one of "five great commentators on modern social life"—the others being historian Johan Huizinga, psychologist Erik Erikson, philosopher Lawrence Kohlberg, and psychologist and educational reformer Jean Piaget. Henricks argues that Updike's fiction illustrates how, psychologically and symbolically, sport "involves a regression to the themes of youth, themes which serve as a foundation for the consciousness of later years" (132).

Of course, nowhere is Updike's concern for social issues more evident than in the Rabbit novels, where the sweep of America's post-war history forms the backdrop. Dilvo Ristoff's (1988) *Updike's America*, informed by the work of many contemporary theorists including Frederic Jameson and Kenneth Burke, provides a reading of the first three Rabbit novels that reveals the role history plays in shaping them. Ristoff also argues that the best way to understand these works is to look not at Harry Angstrom as active agent but at the scenes in which he is placed, because the "scene-oriented approach" allows one to "account for the fundamental tensions" (9) in the novels. The novels are not simply the story of Harry Angstrom's life; because of the "synechdochic mode" in which the Rabbit novels are cast, they become the story of "middle America" as well (8). One cannot "read the trilogy and not see three different decades of American history being brought to life" (157). Constructing an argument similar to Ristoff's, Kerry Ahearn (1988) argues persuasively that in the Rabbit novels Updike is able to unite "method and idea" to create stories in which the protagonist is balanced against a "social milieu larger than family" but "smaller than community" to create "a drama of opposites in the individual versus social, and the attendant spiritual versus mundane" (62).

In a carefully developed argument that relies heavily on contemporary psychological theory, Brooke Horvath (1988) shows how Harry moves through various stages of what psychologist Sam Keen has described as "erotic psychological development" (78). Horvath views Rabbit as a figure representative of his times, although he is never quite able to get free of his essential conservatism to become fully human. On the other hand, Horvath argues that Updike is not the quintessential WASP, as others have charged. His body of work is "severe in its critique of contemporary society," and his characters "can be seen as seeking, principally through love, a way back into contact with the spiritual dimension both they and their culture lack" (74). In another psychological reading, Jack De Bellis (1989) argues that Rabbit's actions in *Rabbit, Run* are motivated by his unconscious Oedipal complex. Pointing out how Rabbit secretly longs to return to a time in childhood when he was sheltered from the harsh realities of the world by his mother, De Bellis demonstrates how subtly Updike weaves larger patterns into his story to provide insight into Rabbit's seemingly irresponsible behavior.

The Rabbit novels also serve as grist for Marxist critics' ideological mill, as evidenced by Raymond Mazurek's (1989) challenge to Updike's political conservatism in "'Bringing the Corners Forward': Ideology and Representation in Updike's Rabbit Trilogy." While Updike may purport to represent the impact of contemporary history on the silent middle class, Mazurek believes he fails to provide any figure who can truly speak with authority about the real causes for America's decline. Instead, Updike simply attributes the decline to Rabbit's alienation and powerlessness without examining the root causes for those conditions. Rather than critiquing American society, Mazurek says, Updike has become "increasingly involved in telling the American middle-class what it wants to hear" (159).

Three essays illustrate how traditional critical approaches were still viable for providing insight into Updike's Rabbit novels. In "From Babbit to Rabbit" (1988), Gilbert Porter considers Rabbit as a literary descendent of Sinclair Lewis's George Babbitt and Arthur Miller's Willy Loman. These figures are representative of a type in America, the materialist who aspires to live out Ben Franklin's maxim to "fill his sack and maintain his virtue" (185). Despite Rabbit's steady rise to materialist success, he never finds that elusive something that would make life meaningful. In this he shares with Babbitt and Loman the tragic quality that marks figures who pursue commercial success without ever achieving spiritual fulfillment. Richard Bolton argues in "Cars of Our Years" (1989) that Updike uses the automobile as a device for measuring American progress in the Rabbit novels, where characters "measure or interpret their gains and losses, material and personal, through and by cars" (98). In the culturally diverse and fragmented society that America has become, cars have replaced "the Bible, Shakespeare, and McGuffey" as the common "cultural referents" for measuring "common experiences" (103). Victor Lasseter (1989) makes the case that *Rabbit Is Rich* recreates "the grim world of American naturalistic novels," so much so that its title is ironic (429). Lasseter catalogs ways the novel resembles classic naturalist works like *Sister Carrie* and *McTeague*.

Finally, Updike's conscious and ambitious efforts to re-tell Hawthorne's *Scarlet Letter* made it inevitable that traditional influence studies would be undertaken to determine the extent to which Hawthorne affected all of Updike's fiction. For example, Patrick Shaw (1986) claims that Hawthorne's "Young Goodman Brown" is not only an important source for "A & P," but that this "prototypical psychosexual drama" deals with topics that "become a central concern of Updike's art," evident in novels such as "the recently published *The Witches of Eastwick*" (323). However, Raymond Wilson (1989) pleads that the question of influence not be pushed too far. Focusing on *Roger's Version*, Wilson argues that Updike intended the novel to be read first on its own terms, without reference to Hawthorne's novel. Looking beyond Hawthorne for sources of influence, Cushing Stout (1990) demonstrates how intermediary works such as Harold Frederic's *The Damnation of Theron Ware* shaped Updike's attempt to re-vision *The Scarlet Letter* for his twentieth-century audience. An important point to be noted about these studies, and others during the period, is that scholars found Updike worthy of comparison with Hawthorne and other important American writers, and deserving of study in his own right.

6: Keeping Up the Pace (1991–1995)

After the success of *Rabbit at Rest*, few would have held it against Updike if he would have eased up on the grinding publication schedule he had set for himself more than three decades earlier. Yet in 1991 his name graced the spine of another hefty collection of nonfiction, *Odd Jobs*, and a year later he published a new novel, *Memories of the Ford Administration*. If there was a break, it came in 1993 when he collected the poetry he had been publishing since the 1950s into a surprisingly large volume. He brought out another novel in 1994, *Brazil*, and followed up later in the same year with a new collection of short fiction, *The Afterlife and Other Stories*. However, none of these works received the kind of superlative reviews that greeted *Rabbit at Rest*. In fact, both new novels were routinely dismissed as inferior to Updike's best work. Some reviewers suggested that Updike's creative powers were fading.

Ironically, however, when Nicolette Jones (1994) asked a group of writers and critics to identify the greatest living novelist writing in English, Updike ranked second, behind Saul Bellow. Jones quotes a number of the responses she received in her *London Times* article; these give some indication of what Updike's contemporaries thought of him. Anita Brookner praises Updike for his "easy and lucid command of the language." John Carey calls him "an extraordinarily fine novelist" (Jones 1994, 8). Ian McEwan admires his "exquisite" prose and his "very fine intelligence." Blake Morrison notes how, though living in the shadow of Bellow and Roth, Updike is better than both at tapping into "the common energies." Moreover, Morrison believes Updike "will last longer than many more high-minded writers—just because of his energy" (9).

Writer for Hire: *Odd Jobs*, 1991

Odd Jobs is a nine-hundred-page compendium of Updike's essays, reviews, and occasional pieces published during the previous decade. In places as divergent as the *New York Times* and *Playboy*, critics by the dozens had something to say about this collection. Comments typical of those who liked the book are those by William Trevor (1992), who praises Updike's ability as a stylist, critic, social chronicler, and philosopher. Trevor describes Updike as someone who celebrates the ordinary events of life while remaining detached enough to critique literature, art, and other matters with skill and accuracy. Despite its length, there "isn't a dull page" in this "long, pleasantly rambling book" that takes on the travails and tragedies of the world with "no whiff of defeat, no sense of compromise" on the part of its author (30). Galen Strawson (1992) calls Updike "a powerful and responsible reviewer and essayist," although he is "perhaps sounder on the methods of fiction than on its metaphysics (and ethics)" (26). Although Updike seems to distrust postmodernism, Strawson says "the cumulative impression of *Odd Jobs* is one of seriousness, straight-dealing and vivid reasonableness" (26).

The reviewer for the *Economist* ("A Master of Craft" 1992) notes that while most collections of previously published essays are simply a version of "recycling," *Odd Jobs* is "an honourable exception." Updike, whose interests seem "catholic and international," uses assignments as a reviewer or essayist as a means of educating himself, and in the process "educates the reader" (100). Sounding a similar note, Nicholas Mosley (1992) recommends *Odd Jobs* as a "guided tour of recent world literature" (12). Malcolm Bradbury (1992) says "the sheer capaciousness" of the volume is "extraordinary"; these "sharp, central assessments" reveal Updike's "edge of distrust for postmodern adventures." Moreover, Bradbury says, Updike provides a great service "in our deconstructive world," where many critics seem "bred, like rottweilers, for aggressive purposes only," and where "much serious criticism is avowedly 'posthumanist' and increasingly designed for developing some grand theoretical or ideological agenda"—or securing some academic advantage (5).

Surprisingly, given his penchant for heaping scorn on Updike, James Wood (1992) is quite positive about *Odd Jobs*. He says Updike's judgments "have a subtlety acquired through years as a novelist." Those he reviews should be happy, Wood says, because Updike is both gentle and insightful. His "four books of criticism must surely be the finest engagement with the contemporary novel by a living practitioner" (21). Michiko Kakutani (1991), another routinely critical reviewer, finds *Odd Jobs* "dazzling," evidence of Updike's "delight in the magic of writing" (C29). Martin Amis calls Updike affectionately a "psychotic Santa of volubility" ([1991] 2001, 384) who can write lucidly on almost any topic. Additionally, these essays are "proof of Updike's magnanimity" (386) and the volume "a torrent of fine phrased justice" (387) in which Updike praises whenever possible and only gently reproves when necessary.

However, another discriminating critic, Denis Donoghue (1991), is less sanguine about Updike's achievements. He says readers of earlier Updike collections will like *Odd Jobs* because Updike once again looks at classic and contemporary writers and a host of other topics besides. But Donoghue objects to Updike's obvious preference for realist fiction, not because Updike is not entitled to privilege one form over another, but because he never explains why he relishes this type of literature. "I wish he would take one of his (God knows) many occasions to address the question of realism, and not merely dispose of it by a wave of his authoritative hand" (5). Also a bit frustrated with *Odd Jobs* is Bruce Bawer (1991), who says that while the reviews are filled with "beautifully phrased insights" and reflect Updike's impatience with sham, the essays seem too much like polished exercises in which Updike "continually and contentedly bit[es] off less than he can chew" (A12). Similarly, Rhoda Koenig (1991) considers the volume no more than a minor accomplishment, too full of reviews that do not really help one understand a particular book or its author. Updike is needlessly kind to second-rate writers; "the passion" that drives him to write "does not give voice to a parallel intensity of attack against those who betray the seriousness of this enterprise" (131).

Back to Buchanan: *Memories of the Ford Administration*, 1992

Memories of the Ford Administration did not achieve the immediate success of *Rabbit at Rest*, and its fate at the hands of later critics suggests that it may end up being relegated to the list of minor works in the Updike canon. With benefit of hindsight, it may even be appropriate to see the novel simply as another indulgent attempt by Updike to make something out of the life of Pennsylvania's lone president, James Buchanan. Yet contemporary reviews were considerably more sympathetic than later commentaries on the novel might suggest.

Merle Rubin (1992) calls *Memories of the Ford Administration* "a vivid, fascinating, and rather wonderful recreation of a bygone age" (13). Charles Johnson (1992) observes that the novel "is quintessential Updike, an exploration of a modern American terrain of desire, guilt and moral ambiguity that he has made distinctly his own" (11). Christopher Lehmann-Haupt (1992) calls it a "slyly amusing novel" (C25) and wonders if it might signal a change in direction for Updike's fiction toward more historical materials.

Balancing this praise are a number of reviews like the ones by Galen Strawson (1993), Richard Eder (1992), and Bruce Bawer (1992). Strawson considers *Memories of the Ford Administration* "a brilliant imperfect book, a swollen modern short story about promiscuity and emotional disorder" (19). Eder, playing off the title of Updike's last book, suggests that a more appropriate title for this novel would be "Updike at Rest." Though "bracing and pleasurable" in many aspects, it covers ground familiar to Updike's readers and fails to offer the kind of close-up look at people and relationships that readers have come to expect from Updike (3). Bawer concedes that "old Updike hands will find themselves on familiar turf" because the novel's "elegiac tone" and "cynical view of wedded bliss" will bring to mind other Updike works, particularly the Rabbit novels (1). Bawer appreciates what he calls "Updike's preoccupation with textuality, the difficulty of knowledge and the relation of act to fancy"—issues central to the deconstructionists, whom Updike and his protagonist scorn. Yet while the novel brings to light one of Updike's enduring concerns, the seriousness of art, it "also displays the usual Updike liabilities: glibness, caution, lack of fire." At this point in his career, Updike "seems adrift in nostalgia and narcissism" (9).

Anita Brookner (1993) expresses even more serious reservations about a novel she describes as Updike's foray into postmodern writing. It "lacks the captivating fluency of Updike's earlier and more recent novels," and the historical sections seem little more than "a mass of undigested material" reproduced "in its entirety." As Updike has grown older, Brookner says, his work shows signs of growing "more majestic"—at the cost of intimacy in describing everyday life. Taking the opposite position, Theodore O'Leary (1992) admires Updike's talent as a historical novelist but finds *Memories of the Ford Administration* "misshapen." The sections on Buchanan are "particularly effective," but Updike fails to reconcile "Clayton's messy private life" with Buchanan's career. O'Leary offers a prescriptive judgment that reveals his own bias: "The serious purpose of Updike's novel," he says, "should have been to acquaint us with a neglected president" (K9). Alfred Kazin (1992) suggests that the novel displays Updike's "indifferen[ce] to politics," making his book "a pussycat on the central subject of American decay at the end of the twentieth century" (46). David Lipsky (1993) seems annoyed with Updike for publishing this banal tale, which demonstrates to him that Updike is "pursuing acedia—the terrifying condition of not much caring about anything—with alarming determination" (58). Lipsky ticks off a list of faults: Updike has recently abandoned good fiction for preaching; he is too exposed in this novel, and as a result it seems pretentious; the novel's best parts are stolen from earlier works. "Updike is still the most talented writer in America," Lipsky insists; he need not "wander off into the twilight of inconsequence" (60).

An Assemblage of Verse: *Collected Poems*, 1993

The overwhelming success of Updike's fiction can sometimes cause one to forget that his first published work was a collection of poems, and that throughout his life he kept on writing poetry while attending to his other work. In *Collected Poems, 1953–1993* Updike brought together his previously published volumes with nearly six dozen fugitive pieces to produce a collection that ranges from light verse to serious commentary on a variety of subjects. That *Collected Poems* was reviewed in more than two dozen periodicals and journals is a measure of the seriousness with which critics were taking Updike's work. Assessments of this collection, however, followed established opinion about his poetic talents and did little to advance his status. Among those who found more substance in the volume was the reviewer for the *Economist* ("John Updike: His Other Hand" 1994), who says these poems reveal that Updike is "a poet of great talent, whether as light versifier or in more serious mood" (92). More typical is the muted praise of Mark Ford (1994), who thinks Updike is "best approached as an occasional poet, in both senses of the word" (21), and the judgment of X. J. Kennedy (1993), who says Updike's best poems are "feelingful, sharply observed, and craftily made" but likely to "strike present-day champions of cool, shapeless poetry as hopelessly tender, polished, and reactionary" (62). James Wood (1994) admits Updike has a good eye but says he has no ear and no sense of how to create individual lines. He "tends to produce happy homily," yet because he has "deep talent," even his slightest efforts often contain "some valuable deposit." And "every so often" he manages to produce "a real work of art" (22).

Mythic Love with a Latin Flair: *Brazil*, 1994

By the 1990s most readers of Updike had come to consider *The Coup* a magnificent anomaly in the Updike canon. Only in rare instances did Updike venture out of his comfort zone so boldly as he had done in that novel. Not surprisingly, then, *Brazil* caused something of a stir when it appeared in 1994. The story is set in South America and has clear affinities with the medieval romance of Tristan and Iseult. Updike seemed to invite all kinds of controversy with his interracial lovers, explicit sex, overt parallels to classic literature, and exotic setting. Although *Brazil* was not well received by a majority of reviewers, it received some positive assessments at the time of its publication, and has subsequently been treated with some seriousness by academics. Therefore, a glance at contemporary reviews seems warranted lest the novel be written off on hearsay evidence as a disaster.

An unusual collection of reviewers found merit in the novel. Christopher Carduff (1994) calls it a "richly patterned metaphysical cliffhanger," a "dark, disquieting meditation on what it is to be male and female, black and white, rich and poor, at one with the world and at odds with every man." It is also an example of what "a contemporary master" can do when he dares to "re-invent himself before our jaded eyes" (78). Rhoda Koenig (1994) describes *Brazil* as "the most absorbing and unsettling novel, apart from the Rabbit books, that [Updike] has written for some time." Updike's language makes these sometimes insubstantial characters believable, as does the cast of minor figures who add substance to this work of "endless and astonishing fertility" (63). Writing after a number of reviews had appeared, Richard Stern (1994) recognizes that the novel "has attracted a considerable quantity of disdain" (40), but believes critics have misunderstood Updike's intent—to create a modern version of the Tristan romance by modeling not only his story but also his language on his medieval sources. Hence, the novel reveals something of Updike's willingness to experiment.

Brazil also received a highly favorable review from Ruthmarie Mitsch (1994) in the scholarly journal *Arthuriana*. Mitsch calls the novel a capable "reformulation of the dilemmas faced in the pursuit of Eros" (200) in which Updike uses the Tristan and Isolde myth effectively in a postmodern context to "problematize[ ] in new ways the meaning and limits of love and desire." While some scholars may find the "manipulation of an essential myth" to be "too transparent, too facile," Mitsch believes that Updike succeeds in transforming the classic tale so that it can "speak across generations, across cultures, across geographies" (201). However, the novelist Barbara Kingsolver (1994) feels that the book's principal characters "never quite realize the epic valor of their namesakes of medieval legend and Wagnerian drama," appearing "not merely doomed but also adolescent and wildly foolish" (1). Despite being put off by Updike's rather conservative, sometimes chauvinistic world view, Kingsolver nevertheless finds it "hard to resist the depth of his mind and the seduction of his prose" (26).

Andrew Billen (1994) makes the intriguing observation that *Brazil* represents a kind of liberation for Updike because he has moved away from the realism that has caused "his words" to "pound against the cages of his plots" (29). On the other hand, Christopher Hitchens (1994) says in *Brazil* Updike "has sketched a stark picture of hardship, cruelty and struggle, redeemed in the last instance by the power of love." Despite the strengths he sees in this novel, however, Hitchens agrees with those who have faulted Updike for being out of touch and callous in his portraits of women and people in the third world.

Gail Caldwell (1994) says that the "legion of loyal fans knows by now that there's Updike and there's updike"—the writer of major novels and the author of whimsical fictional excursions (A1). *Brazil* falls in the latter category. The novel seems playful at best, yet when Updike "stops sounding churlish or capricious and delivers the sui generis insight its creator possesses," *Brazil* offers "a glimpse of its own potential: fiercely ironic and brazenly true" (A17). Tom Shone (1994) also thinks *Brazil* is a kind of holiday excursion for Updike. Calling it "the most bizarrely uncharacteristic novel Updike has yet written," Shone thinks most of the novel's faults can be excused because Updike "wanted a holiday from himself." Unfortunately, he suggests, the reader "may have the same sort of politely fixed expression people adopt when shown others' holiday snaps" (21). Erich Eichman (1993) disagrees with even this modest praise. Although Updike occasionally "challenges himself with offbeat subjects," Eichman thinks he has failed to carry off his bravura performance in *Brazil*, a novel "neither magical nor transporting" (28). Part of Updike's problem is that he does not give himself over to the genre of magical realism which he apes in this work, but remains grounded in "the realist tradition of which he is a contemporary master" (30). Eichman also wonders about the reaction of subscribers to the Book of the Month Club, which featured *Brazil* as a main selection.

Some reviewers were less forgiving. Merle Rubin (1994) calls *Brazil* "a North American fantasy projected southward" in which "a great deal of beautiful writing" is wasted on "a story that is little more than a collection of clichés about women, men, blacks, whites, Indians, settlers, love, sex, class, and money" (15). John Bayley (1994) thinks Updike can get away with writing a novel like *Brazil* only because "in the literary climate of postmodernism" writers need not employ verisimilitude. Unfortunately, Updike seems lost in the world he describes, unable to create coherent characters or a plot that holds readers' interest. Rand Richards Cooper (1994) proclaims Updike's "experiment" a "disaster" (19). The descriptions of sex border on pornography, the handling of gender relations stereotypical, the "treatment of racial contraries" depressingly predictable (19–20). Similarly, Michiko Kakutani (1994b) calls *Brazil* a "decidedly unhappy" experiment in stretching the imagination beyond the familiar realms with which Updike deals so well. Despite a few "passages that sparkle," the novel is filled with contrived descriptions and heavy-handed adaptations of source materials into the narrative; its main characters are little more than "flimsy racial caricatures" in a novel that is "ugly" and "repellent" (C19). Gayle Kidder (1994) finds Updike's attempt to refashion medieval romance into a modern tragedy "thoroughly embarrassing" and "relentlessly depressing." The novel would be "quite laughable" if it were not "so unutterably boring" (4). Alicia Miller (1994) laments that *Brazil* is "the kind of fiasco that leaves you wondering if someone else is writing [Updike's] material." Had anyone but Updike submitted this manuscript, "it might never have been published" (13).

It may be too early to determine where *Brazil* is likely to stand in the Updike canon, but two judgments by academics writing soon after the novel was published suggest that it will remain controversial. In a brief but provocative commentary, Lloyd Eby (1994) argues that the novel's grounding in pagan-spiritualist theology makes it unique in the Updike canon, because Updike is able to offer a fresh perspective on questions he has always tried to address in his work. This "marked departure" from earlier work has allowed him to "break out of the iron box that made up his previous religious-sexual cage" and transcend "the misogyny, the 'class-based misanthropy,' and the 'ill will toward the marginal' that [Frederick] Crews and others have accused him of harboring" (319). In contrast, Earl Rovit (1994) claims that, since Updike's investment in *Brazil* is minimal, "the reader need not care much" about it either (679). A chance to write about this novel is Rovit's excuse to express his ambivalence about Updike, a writer who has wasted his exceptional talent on detailing the squalid side of family life, creating protagonists who "have such little aptitude for shame" (680).

Contemplations of Mortality: *The Afterlife and Other Stories*, 1994

By the 1990s earlier notions that Updike's short fiction simply exhibited the characteristics of slick *New Yorker* fiction had largely given way to more appreciative assessments of his skill in handling the form. Updike's ninth collection, *The Afterlife and Other Stories*, received substantial praise and little negative criticism. Among the more enthusiastic reviewers, Peter Kemp (1995) calls it "a magnificent new collection" full of stories that are "masterpieces of steady delineation" and psychological insight. "Updike has never written with more poignancy and power, more passion and compassion, than he does in these often piercingly perceptive pages" (13). The collection will aid in assuring Updike's own place in the afterlife as a major writer. Jay Parini (1994) seems awed by Updike's ability to write so much and so well; of the selections in *The Afterlife*, he says "Updike has rarely written more affectingly, more from the center of his being" (7). Even Michiko Kakutani (1994a) finds these stories engaging, filled with characters that command "sympathy and compassion" and "epiphanic moments" that are "quintessential Updike" (C17). Rosemary Dinnage (1995) thinks the collection might help make up for Updike's previous two novels, because "when he gets his hands on the short story the master can do no wrong" (20).

Nicholas Clee (1995) says that in these stories Updike "returns to some familiar subjects" (21) but uses them for a new purpose, to explore the problems of aging. Similarly, Lee Milazzo (1995) believes stories in *The Afterlife* signal "a subtle shift in the tenor and tone of [Updike's] short fiction," collectively "display[ing] a special glow from the delicate tints and shades that illuminate a later life that proves to be as wondrous as the tossing and turning that preceded it" (8J). Brooke Allen (1995) suggests that unlike earlier autobiographical stories, these tend to "eschew[ ] childhood reminiscences in favor of revisitations" (63) in which protagonists ponder aging and its attendant failures (particularly failures with women). The fact that his fictional alter-egos tend to be "ruthless and selfish" is the result of "Updike's lifelong attempt to record reality as he sees it" (64). Ian McEwan (1995) is not surprised that so many of these stories deal with aging and its effects; after all, for many years Updike has been "richly trouble[ed]" by "mortality and all its insults" (13). Tracy

Simmons (1994) notes that as Updike himself has aged, he invests his work with "deeper shades and brighter tints." And while he "might not be the most profound American writer living, he is among the last of the craftsman-writers," for whom "the story's the thing, not empty experimentation." The stories in this volume pass the most important test for fiction: "they bear re-reading" (64).

A cautionary note is sounded by Jonathan Yardley (1994), who suspects that many readers will find that these stories, delightful as they are, cover predictable ground: Updike's fascination with boyhood memories. Still, he says, "when Updike is good, he is very good, but he is always Updike, which is to say that mannerism triumphs over matter" (6). Philip Hensher (1995) points out some of the weaknesses that are often overlooked or unacknowledged because Updike has such a "deft way with sentences": Updike cannot create strong plots or even memorable scenes. His excellence lies in style, not construction. As "brilliant" as Updike is, he seems in the end little more than a talented "tour guide in the dangerous ordinary terrain of human feeling" (35). Finally, in a review both caustic and condescending, Natasha Walter (1995), a British writer and feminist activist, rehearses all the reasons Updike should be relegated to the large pile of irrelevant has-beens that litter the closet of American literary history. While no one can deny that Updike writes "sumptuous prose," his "thoroughgoing misogyny" makes it "difficult to read his work without wondering over the narrow artistic vision that so empties and objectifies half of his characters." The only reason not to be too hard on him at the moment, Walter says, is that his "heyday is past," his once-shocking exposes now little more than "dinky Seventies period pieces." Updike knows he is no longer the spokesperson for American culture, but his "narrow artistic range cannot grasp the world's new possibilities" (27). And now, Walter says, even his mastery of style is failing him.

Academic Criticism, 1991–1995

During the last decade of the century, critical commentary on Updike grew significantly. The first publication to receive considerable attention during the period, however, was not strictly a critical commentary but a quirky personal essay by the writer Nicholson Baker. *U & I: A True Story* (1991) is described as a commemoration of Updike, but it could be more aptly described as an exploration of Baker's response to the work of an older, more established writer (Baker was thirty-four when he wrote the book, and had published only two novels at that point in his career). As a form of reader-response criticism *U & I* can be instructive, but it provides only minimal critical analysis of Updike's work.

To gain a real sense of how the ground was shifting with respect to Updike studies, it may be useful to compare the 1991 special issue of *Modern Fiction Studies* with the one published seventeen years earlier (Stuckey 1991; Stafford 1974). Five of the eight articles in the Spring 1991 issue rely much more heavily on modern critical theory as the foundation for exploring Updike's fiction. Matthew Wilson tests Frederick Karl's thesis that American literature is not conducive to the production of sequels by examining Updike's use of traditional themes of isolation and social communication in the Rabbit tetralogy. Basem Ra'ad challenges conventional mythic readings of Updike's fiction. In a critique of *Rabbit, Run* Derek Wright revisits ideas put forth by Tony Tanner and Mary Allen to explain how Updike constructs in his landscapes "an extraordinary rhetoric of constriction to register his protagonist's constant negotiation of clutter in an oppressively commodity-packed world" (37). Barbara Leckie examines *Marry Me* to determine whether, in a world where "adultery has been publicly legitimated," it can "maintain its transgressive, liberating, and for Updike, quasi-religious status" (62). The influence of Roland Barthes is evident in John Duvall's discussion of *Roger's Version*, which contrasts the "texts" of religion and pornography that interest Roger Lambert equally (82). Sanford Pinsker argues that the Bech books are a commentary on the contemporary literary scene. Malini Schueller constructs a postcolonial (and not always sympathetic) reading of *The Coup*. While employing widely different methodologies and not always agreeing on the value of Updike's fiction, these essayists demonstrate that critical evaluation of his work was no longer limited to a narrow range of social topics or aesthetic and formalist issues.

The relationship between *The Scarlet Letter* and Updike's re-telling of Hawthorne's classic in three novels is the subject of extensive critical work by a major new voice in Updike studies. James Schiff, whose 1990 dissertation analyzed Updike's reworking of *The Scarlet Letter*, extended his examination in two important articles in the *South Atlantic Review* (1992a) and *Studies in American Fiction* (1992b). Schiff incorporates much of his earlier works into *Updike's Version: Rewriting The Scarlet Letter* (1992c), a detailed and well-reasoned discussion of Updike's "bold and intriguing project." Schiff argues that "any reconsideration of a canonical text by a major literary figure such as Updike warrants attention, particularly in light of so much contemporary interest in intertextuality" (1992c, 2). Schiff's interest lies in exploring "the specific critical questions and problems that arise when a contemporary novelist attempts to retell an earlier story that has achieved mythic significance" (11). After an exhaustive explanation of why *The Scarlet Letter* deserves to be called a myth rather than simply a romance, Schiff devotes the majority of his study to analyzing "the dialogue" between Updike's texts and Hawthorne's novel (17). At the same time, he provides insight into some of Updike's specific themes, especially his interest in "the American self, divided and unhappy, struggling to re-form and reconceive itself" (19).

Schiff admits that while the landscape of America has been altered significantly since Hawthorne's time, Updike is able to point out some persistent problems: adultery, women's place in a patriarchy, "conflicts between matter and spirit, individual and community," and "the need to shake off the past and reinvent both the world and the self" (1992c, 122). Schiff argues that Updike offers "a freshly conceived response to human behavior in America" (124). Rejecting "the traditional body-soul division in Hawthorne," Updike promotes an "acceptance of the body" as inextricably linked with spirit; through that acceptance, "the American self can rise from its middle-class malaise, recover wholeness, and experience joyous faith in the divine" (124–25). Schiff suggests another motive in Updike's decision to rewrite Hawthorne: by doing so, Updike inevitably causes his own work to be linked to one of the iconic texts in American literature. Therefore, "the final question for many becomes whether Updike is worthy of Hawthorne's company" (128). For Schiff, the answer is "yes."

Despite the growing dominance of new critical theory in shaping textual analysis, many of Updike's critics continued to employ conventional methodologies or blend these with newer approaches. As an example, in "Native Fathers" Jan Clausen (1992) explains why Updike's novels captivate her even though they grate against her feminist sensibilities. Clausen argues that Updike's "relentless verisimilitude" relies on "*visual* realism" that "feeds America's ever-growing appetite for pictures of itself" (48). In his passivity, Updike's most iconic character, Harry Angstrom, is a symbol of the nation, because "doing nothing aligns him with vast and crushing power"—the consequences of which, Clausen says, Updike conveniently fails to show (51). In "Marriage, Endings, and Art in Updike and Atwood," Judith Spector (1993) links Updike to a tradition extending back to early novelists like Samuel Richardson who deal with marriage. While many early novels examine the arduous journey toward matrimony, Updike is more interested in the humdrum life after marriage and the struggles couples undergo trying to keep their union intact.

In "Where is Yoknapatawpha County?" (1993) Karl Zender uses Updike's early work as a counterpoint to Faulkner's late fiction. Though separated by a generation, the two share a common purpose for writing: to "rescu[e] moments of experience out of the ongoing rush of time, so that these moments can later be relived" (292). Zender argues that, like Faulkner, Updike came to understand that the locale in which he grew up could "serve as a worthy subject for art"; by representing the region and its people through intense observation and with loving disposition, the "factuality" could acquire "the intensity of symbol" (293). Jerome Klinkowitz (1995) pairs Updike with Kurt Vonnegut in an assessment of "the path American fiction has taken" since 1960 (152), suggesting that the two have more in common than most critics suppose.

Klinkowitz believes Updike's fiction has accommodated critical trends while remaining accessible to a wide audience. Sanford Pinsker (1995) argues that much of the power of the Rabbit novels can be attributed to the way Updike, like James Joyce before him, uses his central character as a kind of cultural barometer. "Joycean resonances" pervade the Rabbit novels "not only in lyrical descriptions of the cultural landscape" but more importantly in "the ways that culture filters into, and around, an individual consciousness" (95). Aleksei Zverev's (1995) assessment of Updike's debt to Nabokov provides a useful summary of Updike's comments on the importance of the Russian novelist as a mentor, but also notes the many ways in which Updike's fiction differs from Nabokov's.

The influence of the movies on Updike's fiction inspired several intriguing essays, including two by Jack De Bellis. In "The 'Awful Power'" (1993), De Bellis explains how Updike appropriates Stanley Kubrick's *2001* to add resonance to plot and characterization in *Rabbit Redux*. De Bellis's more general assessment of Updike's relationship with cinema explores the way Updike's "lifelong devotion to film" influences his fiction (1995, 169), which on a broad thematic level "is filled with the same quest for distraction coupled to a tone of nostalgia for the aesthetic and moral guidance of film" (176). De Bellis says Updike found in the movies "new worlds that fed his creative fires and helped him discover not only a 'debonair style' but the protean nature of identity" (179).

Ordinarily, commentary on individual novels provides some hints as to which works may be of interest to scholars in the future. One of these was *Marry Me*. In "From Vermeer to Bonnard" Malcolm Magaw explains how frequent allusions to art and artists are carefully crafted to "let the reader in on the private and sometimes subliminal associations" of the novel's main characters, allowing Updike to share his "objective perceptions of them," thereby "sharpen[ing] the reader's perceptions" of their "idiosyncrasies" and "motivations" (1992, 139). Magaw says that in *Marry Me* Updike demonstrates how "the art of fiction" can be "transfused with borrowings from the other arts" to create an organic whole that is itself a new work of art (150). Magaw extends his analysis of the same novel in "The Geographical and Spatial Correlative in Updike's *Marry Me*" (1995), in which he explores the "carefully designed network of geographical, topographical, and spatial motifs and metaphors which serve as symbolic correlatives to the complex workings" of the protagonist's "abnormal psychology" (250).

As might be expected, numerous critiques of the Rabbit novels were published. The continuing use of *Rabbit, Run* in college classrooms served as the impetus for Stanley Trachtenberg's collection *New Essays on Rabbit, Run* (1993). Trachtenberg's lengthy introduction and four companion essays are intended as guides for understanding the text and placing it historically and critically in the American literary tradition.

Trachtenberg notes the importance of the figure of Harry Angstrom as a vehicle for Updike to comment on the changes to American society during the thirty years in which the Rabbit series evolved. Philip Stevick provides an assessment of the "two voices" in which the novel is written, representing "two epistemic grips on the world, two sets of rhetorical resources, played off against each other in a contrapuntal or dialogic way" (33). Sanford Pinsker surveys the novel's social and historical milieu. Erik Kielland-Lund describes the European reaction to *Rabbit, Run* and Updike in general, concluding that the "Americanness" of the novel lies in its "ambivalence." The "insistence on continuing the open-minded quest for answers to the fundamental question of human life," he says, "in society and in the universe, may ultimately be the most significant American tradition that *Rabbit, Run* upholds" (92).

Without meaning to downplay the value of any of these essays, the one contribution to Trachtenberg's collection that seems to do most to advance critical understanding of Updike is Stacey Olster's discussion of his treatment of women. Olster takes issue with Mary Allen's characterization of Updike as a misogynist capable of creating only "dull, bovine creatures." Instead, she says, Updike's portraits of women are shaped by his propensity to "think of women's bodies in mythologized forms" (101). In *Rabbit, Run,* Harry's tendency to cast all women as mythic figures and imbue them with unattainable attributes leads to his disillusionment and creates feelings of misogyny. Women in the novel are aware of Rabbit's unrealistic expectations and "recognize the inevitable failure to which mythologizing impulses are doomed" (109). They adjust to the circumstances in which they find themselves rather than protest against them; but Olster insists this does not imply that Updike endorses their actions, or that they are somehow "content with their condition" (111).

The appearance of *Rabbit at Rest* in 1990 prompted critics to examine the sequence for larger patterns and greater thematic statements. Stacey Olster (1992) makes a compelling case for seeing the Rabbit novels as Updike's historical chronicle of the decline of America's fortunes during the second half of the twentieth century. Thomas Hicks (1992/1993) describes the novels as Updike's epic, an investigation of "the mystery of individual destinies." Read as a single unit, the tetralogy reveals several qualities of Updike's writing and thinking. There is no "complacent optimism that the world can be improved." There is the realization that "when God dies, only sex remains as divine"; the absence of God in contemporary times has allowed Eros to become "the engine that drives the human machine" (68). Cristina Kirklighter (1994) explores once again the nature of Harry Angstrom's quests, suggesting that he is caught between two worlds—one demanding that he act responsibly, the other offering him freedom to discover things about the world and himself.

Roger Johnson (1995) uses *Rabbit at Rest* as a kind of sociological document and views Updike as an anthropologist gathering data about the state of contemporary society in order to understand what is wrong with it. Rabbit is a kind of Everyman attempting to find something he feels is missing in a society that seems to provide everything in the way of material gratification.

Over the years individual short stories received considerable attention from critics, but Robert Luscher's *John Updike: A Study of the Short Fiction* (1993) is the first book to offer an extensive analysis of Updike's short fiction. In an earlier essay, Luscher had written about the Olinger stories, claiming they form a sequence that seeks to recapture the past while simultaneously bidding it fond farewell ([1988] 1995). Now in the preface to his book Luscher argues that, unlike the novels, Updike's stories tend to focus on one principal theme, "the ongoing struggle against time's diminishment" (1993, x). Challenging critics who are unhappy with Updike for never producing "a big, important book on a controversial subject," Luscher insists that "the cumulative weight of his short fiction may embody an achievement on par with the one they seek—and in a form that may be more congenial to the author's gifts" (154).

During the 1990s, criticism grounded in new theoretical approaches enhanced understanding of Updike's imaginative enterprise. For example, in 1992, John Neary used Updike's fiction to illustrate a larger argument that "the novel as a genre exists within the tension between something and nothingness" (177), which he equates loosely to the realist and postmodernist trends in contemporary fiction. Employing theories about the nature of literature and culture, especially Derridean deconstruction, Neary contrasts Updike and John Fowles as representatives of opposing approaches to literature, though he admits that neither is slavishly realist nor experimental. Neary explains how Updike's affirmative vision of the world shapes his fiction both thematically and aesthetically. Hence, part of the intent of *The Centaur* is to deconstruct the conventions of the *Künstlerroman*. The employment of explicit sex in *Couples* allows Updike to undercut the conventions of the Victorian novel even as he employs them as an ordering principle. Though Updike seems to vitiate his own affirmative vision of the world in the three novels that recreate *The Scarlet Letter*, those who do not see the essential affirmation in this trilogy have missed the point. Updike ultimately upholds traditional values, ones founded on "connection" and "presence" rather than "dissociation and absence" (197).

One of the best examples of new critical readings is Ramchandran Sethuraman's "Updike's *The Centaur*" (1993a). Employing the theoretical work of Lacan, Sethuraman provides "a more productive way" to read the novel by "break[ing] through the binary opposition" espoused by Donald Greiner in his earlier critique of *The Centaur* and challenging other critics who have offered more conventional readings of the text. Sethuraman attempts to "hear the speech of the unconscious in the slidings/hesitations in the narrative itself, the dream text, and slips of the tongue" (41). In "Writing Woman's Body" (1993b), Sethuraman reprises this approach, using Lacanian psychoanalytic theory to supplement a feminist critique of Updike's first Rabbit novel. Updike's works also serve as texts for psychologist Leo Schneiderman (1992) to demonstrate how writing fiction "involves access to deep layers of the unconscious and to discordant ego states reflecting contradictory internalized object relations" (149). Schneiderman argues that Updike's fiction "does not look closely at the relationship between society's condition and individual suffering" because "the tragically flawed self is the focus of his fictional world." Updike believes "the writer's proper mission" is to "chart the chaos of individual lives in a universe that was created according to a grand but mysterious design, in which, possibly, private pain signifies something beyond itself" and has the potential to lead people to faith (159).

In an equally intriguing article Peter Powers (1994) revisits Updike's personal struggles to produce art by recasting his self-identified trilogy of concerns—sex, art, and religion—as the "intertwined issues of gender, theology, and aesthetics" (329). Powers believes that Updike's professed adherence to Barthian theology conflicts with "the historical scene" of his writing "and the aesthetics that flow from that scene." As a consequence, Powers says, "Updike's overt theological position functions as a kind of nostalgic scar rather than as a motivation for or description of his practice as an author" (330). The "awareness" that writing was "no longer the great self- and male-affirming activity that it at least once pretended to be" causes Updike great concern (333). "At the center of Updike's fictional world" is not the great Unknowable Deity (the "male phallus"), but what Powers calls "the stylistics of natural theology," a belief in "the basic goodness of human will and reason" (341). The "heterogeneity of Updike's prose, the stylistics of excess, the acute sense of the loss of father and the loss of creative power" all undermine traditional notions of God—and the authority that passes to the male writer from God. If one accepts this conclusion, Powers says, then "the critique of Updike's masculinism must proceed on some other grounds" that the traditional feminist critique of patriarchy (344).

Updike's novels also serve as useful examples for Matei Calinescu (1994) to show how readers deal with "(intra) textual and intertextual secrets" (444). Calinescu develops a theory of "rereading" fiction, or specifically "rereading for the secret," based on earlier work by Frank Kermode and Umberto Eco, which allows him to explain how Updike uses Hawthorne's fiction to encode his own work with meanings available only to the most erudite readers. Some may be put off by the notion of Updike as an arcane writer, but Calinescu, a distinguished critic whose works on philosophy and theory received international acclaim, offers a reading quite different from mainstream interpretations. Where Updike has often been seen "as a (belated) realist or naturalist and a master of what one might call transparent writing," some of his major novels "display at least one significant modernist/postmodernist trait, namely, a tendency toward the oblique rewriting of works by earlier novelists." The result is that the "transparency of his style" can be seen as a means of "hiding—sometimes only half-hiding—a rich intertextuality" (445).

Salah El Moncef's lengthy essay on *Rabbit at Rest* (1995) makes extensive use of numerous French, German, and Russian theorists to explore "the gigantic metaphoric mosaic" that constitutes the novel. In it, Thelma Harrison's disease represents "the symptomology of postmodern economy as Updike retraces it in the dialectical movements of the *psyche*, the *soma*, and the *societas*" (69–70). El Moncef demonstrates how, in addition to being a complex narrative device that helps tie together the elements of the story, "the underlying metaphoric equation of the effects of psychosomatic economy (cancer, gastric disorder, stress) with the motifs of (toxic) pollution and anal accumulation is also a crucial device in *conceptualizing* the parasitical nature of late capitalist reproduction as it appears in the process of general commodification" (78). However, El-Moncef believes the novel falls short in truly representing the problems of capitalist society because it looks for simplistic, external forces as corrupters of society rather than recognizing (as Foucault does) that the corruption arises from within.

Before concluding, a look at three works can help illustrate new directions in Updike studies and changing attitudes toward his work. The first represents the kind of scholarly work that would pave the way for future study of Updike's canon. Editor James Plath's *Conversations with John Updike* (1994), a collection of thirty-two interviews Updike granted between 1959 and 1993, brings together material of interest to those fascinated with the writing process and to scholars wishing to trace the relationship between Updike's work and his professed attitudes about writing. Plath argues Updike's interviews "affirm Updike's status as a major American writer, one whose Rabbit tetralogy may indeed loom as large over time as Melville's whale" (xiii).

In "Updike Ignored" (1995), James Schiff presents "the first sustained treatment of Updike's critical prose" (535). Schiff's careful analysis of Updike's motivation for writing criticism and the principles he applies to that endeavor is a major contribution to Updike scholarship in its own right. Of greater interest to a study of Updike's reputation, however, is Schiff's explanation for the academic world's failure to pay attention to Updike's nonfiction, even though reviewers have had much to say about it. Schiff believes the academic establishment has ignored Updike's critical writings largely because "academia has constructed a variety of theoretical schools, and critics who fail to operate within one of them or to generate an elaborate theoretical framework of their own are usually ignored." Even worse for Updike, "critics not affiliated with a theoretical school are seen as somehow simplistic and old-fashioned" (533). Additionally, because much of Updike's criticism is contained in book reviews, it is often overlooked, since the academic establishment generally considers reviews superficial and written for commercial motives. When one gets beyond these prejudices, Schiff says, one finds that Updike is a critic worthy of academic study.

Finally, in a brief reminiscence on his long-time love affair with Updike's works, Tom Roberts (1995), senior news editor for the conservative *National Catholic Reporter*, notes that Updike has been "a most unlikely companion" for a quarter century (28). Roberts says his "pleasure had always been mixed with a certain edgy disagreement," a desire to "argue with him," especially when Updike goes beyond "the familiar ground of Pennsylvania" to engage a "wider world." In these works, Roberts says, Updike serves as "a teacher of voyeurism and cultural pluralism." Additionally, Updike's people, especially those that wrestle with matters of faith, seem weighed down by sorrows; they suffer from "self-imposed wounds," and are "always hurting one another" (29). In spite of these problems, Roberts says he intends to keep reading Updike, because he believes readers can learn much from Updike's insightful portrayal of ordinary people living in the modern world. One need only look back at Michelle Murray's caustic critiques of Updike's work, published in the same journal two decades earlier, to see how far Updike had come in winning over critics.

7: America and Updike, Growing Old Together (1996–1999)

ANY THOUGHT THAT UPDIKE, approaching sixty-five, might slow down as the century moved toward its close was quickly dispelled by the publication in 1996 of what some have come to regard as his finest single novel, *In the Beauty of the Lilies*. That work was followed in succeeding years by another novel, a new collection about Henry Bech, and a fourth compendium of nonfiction. At the same time, however, a new generation of reviewers, raised after the post-war years of American prosperity and the angst-ridden years of the Cold War, was beginning to describe Updike as a literary dinosaur. Throughout the last decade of the century but even more pronounced in the final five years, these newcomers—critics and authors alike—found Updike's style mannerist without being provocative and his focus on everyday Americans of limited use as a subject for literary art. His brand of literary realism was considered old-fashioned and his emphasis on sex no longer shocking, only quaint. It fell to a group of admirers among reviewers and academics—some of longstanding, others newly come to Updike's writing—to advocate for him as one of the most important American writers of the twentieth century.

America under the Microscope:
In the Beauty of the Lilies, 1996

The publication of *In the Beauty of the Lilies* convinced many that Updike still possessed the powers of narration and keen insight that had characterized his best early work. This saga of four generations of a twentieth-century American family was quite a departure from Updike's normal mode of writing, covering a much wider geographical sweep and a much longer timeline than any of his previous novels. On the whole, reviewers approved, and despite its length (some five hundred pages), readers bought it. The novel appeared on the *New York Times* bestseller list in mid-February 1996 and, after falling out for a week, remained there through most of March. It was the last time an Updike work would achieve this level of popularity.

Praise for *In the Beauty of the Lilies* came from an unlikely source, Michiko Kakutani, who calls it "dazzling," not only Updike's "most ambitious novel to date," but "arguably his finest" (1996b, C1). It "possesses the hard, diamond radiance of a fully imagined work of art" (C32). This novel is "a work of astonishing breadth and intellectual depth," says Jay Parini (1996, 240). Though not flawless—Updike tends to get bogged down in research, and his rich, metaphoric language sometimes gets in the way of the story—this "profound and gorgeously written novel" explores important questions: "What has happened to God in our time, and how has His seeming disappearance affected our lives? How, indeed, are human beings to survive without a sense of genuine spirituality?" (247). George Steiner (1996) believes *In the Beauty of the Lilies* assures Updike's place beside American writers such as Hawthorne and Nabokov in chronicling the devolution of America, a movement Updike sees as tied closely to the country's abandonment of religion and God. "One puts down this novel," Steiner concludes, "with the intimation that America is, very near its center, the saddest country on earth" (106).

British reviewers were equally enthusiastic. Julian Barnes (1996) describes the novel as "domestic and epic, *intimiste* and magisterial." While it reflects Updike's disenchantment with America, it is not simply "a piece of dismayed authorial valetudinarianism." Rather, in this "novel of accumulated wisdom," Updike demonstrates that he is "in full control of his subtle, crafty and incessantly observing art" (9). Ian McEwan (1996) calls *In the Beauty of the Lilies* "the most readable and enjoyable" of Updike's books since *Rabbit at Rest*, a work that carries on the "grand nineteenth-century ambition to make of the novel a version of society" and capture in one book "the American century" (15). Noting its similarities to Galsworthy's *Forsyte Saga*, Peter Kemp (1996) says the book is brilliantly conceived and executed. "What keeps this often magnificent novel alive with appeal," Kemp concludes, "is its sturdily delicate portrayal of the small-scale human comedies and tragedies acted out against its panoramic back-projection of America's shifting visions and versions of paradise" (2).

Quite a number of reviewers concentrated on Updike's handling of religion. Ross Feld (1996) says that by dealing with "ancestralism" Updike has been forced to "stretch[] himself wider than he's gone before with his very nuclear families" and to question the religious impulse in a way he had never done before. "Can it really be," Feld asks, that a writer once "fascinated by the hard theological requirements of Karl Barth" is now "suggesting that religion and the movies are mirror images of illusion and disillusion both?" (9). Fredric Koeppel (1996) believes the ironic title is a "bitter jibe" at America, which has failed to live up to the "prospect of a New World paradise"; instead, "God has marched on, all right, straight out of the picture" (G4). James Wall (1996) reads the novel "partly as an account of the decline of religious faith in America, and partly as a reflection on Updike's own angry, personal struggle to find religious meaning." Whereas all of Updike's novels reflect his "multilayered theological struggles," in this one Updike is at his best in dramatizing the conflicts that bother him as well as the country at large (251). Brooke Allen (1996) suggests that Updike's focus on religion saves *In the Beauty of the Lilies* from becoming just another four-generation saga. She also makes an intriguing suggestion: "Protestantism is [Updike's] creed of choice" not because he believes in it but because "it happens to be the manifestation of the religious impulse that is specific to his own country and century" (57). Though not one of Updike's best works—"it feels too planned, too structured"—it is "of interest as the attempt of a considerable writer to give shape to America's ever-fascinating spiritual struggles" (60). Merle Rubin (1996) agrees in part, suggesting the novel can be read as "an extended meditation" on the shifting values in American society. But Rubin finds the story of the Wilmot family frequently overshadowed by "the more clichéd and over-rehearsed history of the changing American zeitgeist" (B3).

Updike's venture into the realm of historical fiction caught the attention of several reviewers, among them Mark Carnes (1996), who believes the novel is not simply a period piece depicting contemporary problems, but instead is a fine historical narrative: "Updike has become a historian, and a good one at that" (449). On the other hand, while John Crowley (1996) finds Updike's effort to chronicle generations of family experience quite impressive, he believes the novel "threatens to become a page-turner in a less than flattering sense," redeemed only by "Updike's astonishing ability to reproduce sensory experience" (1). Paul Gray (1996) admires Updike for producing so late in his career "the equivalent of an experimental novel," especially a historical novel, since many of these, "enslaved by chronology," become "little more than one damned thing after another." Nevertheless, Updike's novel "never catches fire" because "its central thesis—that movie theaters have become modern American houses of worship—is never really demonstrated in action" (78). A. O. Scott (1996) says that *In the Beauty of the Lilies* succeeds "when the sensuality of Updike's prose matches the sensitivity of his characters," and "falters when he tries to plot those experiences on the broad canvas of American history" (25). Though it may expose "the limits of Updike's literary imagination," it still makes a valuable contribution to the "historical romance of the American middle class that he has been tirelessly and cheerfully composing for nearly forty years" (28).

Others found considerably more flaws. Chauncey Mabe (1996) believes the novel is in need of "a bold and confident editor" (8D). Linda Hall (1996) feels that, though exceptionally well researched, the novel's historical portrait "is that of a *Time/Life* series," and the style seems to be "someone else's" rather than the one for which Updike has become justly famous (52). James Gardner (1996) suggests that Updike has taken on the task expected of American male novelists, to define the essential character of the nation. But the tale is too disjointed and displays too many affinities with postmodernism to be a convincing, realistic portrait of the national character (63). Richard Eder (1996) does not think the historical format suits Updike particularly well. One gets the sense that Updike is "skillfully sifting his research," reconstructing rather than constructing a narrative (10). James Wood (1996) says two of Updike's virtues—"his perpetual serenity and the richness of his prose" (29)—seem to work against him in this novel, which demands greater verve and active description of conflict, especially religious conflict. Instead, it seems overburdened by research, full of characters designed merely to "wander[ ] around in historical uniform, saluting the zeitgeist" (32).

Among the handful of truly negative critics, Mark Shechner (1996) says the novel demonstrates "what can happen to a writer" who works "with one eye on immortality and the other on immortality" (the repetition being intentional). Though this *tour de force* has "moments of grace abounding," on the whole it is "so mercilessly deterministic, so tightly scripted that the outcome is never in doubt." The book is "impressive," but on the whole "cold" (7B). J. Bottum (1996) dismisses *In the Beauty of the Lilies* as irrelevant, and laments that, "with each new and beautiful book, the significance of John Updike seems to fade further" (64). Though he remains capable of "forg[ing] gorgeous metaphors" and still possesses a "refreshing curiosity about the lives of real people across the social and cultural spectrum," he has never been able to fulfill "the promise of explaining ourselves to ourselves." His glaring inability shows up most notably in his attempts to render American religion. In fact, "Updike's theology has not advanced much beyond the adolescent schoolboy's discovery that the adults in his church are often hypocrites" (66). Still more severe is John Bellamy's assessment (1996) that the book is "a commercial potboiler of largely unremitting schlock." Despite its serious theme—that "the religious impulse may be damned or denied—but will always out," the novel is poorly wrought and sentimental, with some segments being "so programmatic that they could have been written by James Michener" (10).

Among the two hundred reviews of *In the Beauty of the Lilies*, two are of special note for what they say about Updike as a novelist and about the prejudices of some of reviewers and critics. In the first, Ralph Wood (1996) comments extensively on what he considers the "deeper problem" of Updike's work. His fiction is "imbued with spiritual passivity," and in every way he "abstains from judgment" (452). Updike believes in American exceptionalism, but not in the traditional sense; the nation is not "the 'last, best hope on earth,' as Lincoln declared"; instead, "our Union is uniquely blessed and cursed by God's absence." In fact, Wood says, "the Christ of Updike's fiction strikes me as stratospherically remote," and many of his narrators possess a "spiritual dryness and deadness of the soul that has lost its hunger for God," remaining "passive and indifferent before the things they describe." Updike should be praised for exposing the reasons why the "degeneration of American political and religious life is a pathetic inevitability." On the other hand, he seems "aridly indifferent about the ultimate outcome, offering no alternate vision of our common life" (457). Wood finds such indifference indefensible.

The second review of special interest is Gore Vidal's. Vidal's caustic attack on Updike seems to be prompted less by his disdain for *In the Beauty of the Lilies* than by his abhorrence of Updike's open support of conservative American values. Though Vidal claims never to have "taken Updike seriously as a writer" ([1996] 2001, 87), he begins by expressing his chagrin at what he believes are Updike's unwarranted criticisms of him. As a counter, Vidal launches a diatribe against Updike's politics, which he sees displayed throughout *In the Beauty of the Lilies*. Going back to Updike's 1989 memoir, Vidal looks for reasons that would explain Updike's ideology, noting how his stance on important political matters such as the Vietnam war seem both wrongheaded and particularly timid. Vidal's essay is full of satiric barbs such as "At times, reading Updike's political and cultural musings, one has the sense that there is no received opinion that our good rabbit does not hold with passion" (98), and Updike has "taken to heart every far-out far-right piety currently being fed us." Vidal is critical of Updike's style, finding that his extensive descriptions distract from his narrative. He also decries Updike's penchant for trying to be up-to-date in describing important historical events as simply another form of pandering. *In the Beauty of the Lilies*, an "inhuman novel" (112), gives further evidence that Updike's work "is more and more representative of that polarizing within a state where Authority grows ever more brutal" and its "hired hands" in the media more excited as "the holy war of the few against the many heats up" (113).

Philosophy of Sport: *Golf Dreams*, 1996

By the 1990s Updike was such an established giant that everything he wrote prompted commentary. Even his collection of essays on golf, *Golf Dreams*, was reviewed in dozens of newspapers and magazines. Michael O'Brien (1996) finds these essays "shrewd and funny," as Updike assumes the role of spokesperson for "the silent majority of the incompetent" multitude who play golf (11). Daniel Wackerman (1996) describes the collection as a combination of fine writing and entertaining reverie about a sport with which so many have a love-hate relationship. *Sports Illustrated* writer Michael Bamberger (1996) says these stories are more than sports tales. "Golf as a dream is a motif for Updike" in these anecdotes, and Updike's golf courses "are populated by people who would seem ordinary on the street but who on the links become larger than life" (12).

James Michie (1997) thinks Updike has scored a hole in one with *Golf Dreams*, capturing the essence of the game's hold on experts and duffers alike. He is charmed by Updike's ability to "take any cliché of golf literature" and "squeeze new humour, wisdom, even morality out of it" (41). Christopher Lehmann-Haupt (1996) says that golfers looking for answers as to why they love the game "could do worse than turn to John Updike," who seems to be able to articulate the joys and frustrations that come from the sport. Lehmann-Haupt is also delighted to see how the collection offers Updike a new venue for self-reflection—and for making golf a metaphor for other important matters as well. Putting a damper on these enthusiastic responses is Michiko Kakutani (1996a), who says Updike's essays are "infected" with "sentimentality" and pretentiousness; it as if Updike is trying "to make golf sound like some sort of Christian mission" (24).

Gazing into the Future: *Toward the End of Time*, 1997

Because Updike had come to be known as a chronicler of the contemporary scene, it must have come as something of a surprise to readers of his fiction to see him follow *In the Beauty of the Lilies* with another experimental novel. *Toward the End of Time* has been described as science fiction or a futurist novel, principally because its action is set three decades into the future. But its protagonist, Ben Turnbull, is typical of other Updike heroes in his preoccupation with matters of sex and aging. Although the novel was not technically a bestseller, it was reviewed widely and generated some of the same strong reactions that had greeted predecessors like *Memories of the Ford Administration* and *Brazil*.

Again, despite lore that has built up in recent years, *Toward the End of Time* was not universally panned. In fact, Anita Brookner (1998) calls the book "a classic for the twenty-first century, one that aptly reflects the fading glow of our own." The "exalted writing" in this novel proves again that Updike is "perfecting his own unique gifts" (39). William Pritchard (1997) describes the book as another expression of one of Updike's enduring themes, the notion that "we are here in the world to give praise." Here, however, the praise is tinged with melancholy. Joyce Carol Oates (1997) calls *Toward the End of Time* Updike's "most inventive novel." Similar to *The Poorhouse Fair* in many respects, the novel is "at heart a wholly realistic work," which Oates describes as "a cheerily bleak black comedy" (117). Margaret Atwood (1997) claims the novel is "deplorably good'; as "memento mori and its obverse, carpe diem, *Toward the End of Time* could scarcely be bettered" (10).

Among more tempered responses, Robert Stone (1997) suggests that, while *Toward the End of Time* "may not be among John Updike's greatest books," it "has a force that gets under your skin" (32). Michael Pearson (1997) admits the novel is "occasionally sluggish," but believes Updike once again demonstrates he is a "masterful stylist who can bring the unnoticed details of the world to brilliant life" (L10). James Miracky (1998) claims the novel's strength "lies in its presentation of a universe that is collapsing on two fronts": Ben Turnbull's "battle with mortality" and the author's "version of a world gone wrong in the not-so-distant future." Though Updike does not always succeed in connecting these "strands" and the protagonist seems "too much a creature of the late 1990s in his attitudes of sexism and technophobia," the book remains "a thought-provoking novel of poetic prose that moves the reader to an encounter with human limits that is sometimes painful but often profound" (26).

Dean Flower (1998) admits that it is easy to call *Toward the End of Time* "shockingly bad" and dismiss Ben Turnbull as a character "calculated to enrage women" (241). Yet a closer look at the novel reveals that Updike has a larger purpose for his protagonist. Updike may seem to like Turnbull, but that is because his tendency to "lavish verbal riches on his point-of-view characters has the unfortunate effect of his seeming to endorse them." Once one recognizes that Turnbull is not intended as a sympathetic character but rather "a lens through which Updike exposes contemporary moral failures," *Toward the End of Time* can be viewed as a dark portrait of contemporary society, bereft of any hope for "blessing" or grace (242). Similarly, while Brooke Allen (1997) finds numerous flaws, on the whole she thinks the book shows that Updike is still at the top of his form. The "enfant terrible" of the 1950s has "metamorphosed into the dirty old man" of recent work, still managing to present his vision of the world with "a high level of spirit, imagination and audacity" (14). Malcolm Bradbury (1998) argues that Updike's grand theme, "the winding down or wearing out of the world" (38), is made personal through the story of Ben Turnbull. The novel is a kind of "winding up," a leave-taking of "the youthful notions of sensation and sensuality" that have "furnished Updike with so many of his plots." This "book of universal ageing," Bradbury concludes, is "sad but moving," the creation of "a substantial writer whose earlier work helps us to make sense of what is here at stake" (38).

James Walton (1998) describes the novel as Updike's revolt against realism, combining as it does "magic realism, science fiction, science fact, nature writing, parallel-universe narratives and, less surprisingly, sex and golf." It also proves that Updike has not been influenced by "the acres of feminist criticism" aimed at him over the years (23). The novel may not be "top-drawer Updike," but it does not reveal any decline in his considerable powers (24). James Yerkes (1997) treats the novel as a metaphysical reflection in which the incessant sex serves a higher purpose: "There is no question," Yerkes says, that Updike regards Turnbull's "blind drive to fill all the holes as a compulsive surrogate expression of a religious quest for an absconded God" (1081). Ultimately, the novel is an exploration of Christian faith, which is "indeed about time—both its creation and its redemption, from beyond time" (1083).

Amid the numerous reviews, Richard Adelman's in *Science* (1998) stands out for several reasons. Adelman, a professor of biological chemistry, takes pleasure in seeing how Updike "uses literary images of science's sensuousness to enhance knowledge of human experience." Speaking from his dual experience as a scientist and a reader, Adelman notes that "emotional clarity can be as powerful as laboratory quantification" in helping to explain the aging process. As a result, he believes "all who care about growing old will discover treasure in this novel" (819).

However, *Toward the End of Time* had many detractors whose responses range from disappointment to outrage. Nancy Pate (1997) seems unhappy that Updike does not take full advantage of the futuristic setting he creates in this novel which is, at best, "minor Updike in a minor key" (F10). Robert Boyers faults Updike for producing a book that is not "about anything remediable, or about the way we live now." It is simply "the familiar Updikean dystopia," with "spiritual exhaustion" written "all over its pages" ([1997] 2005, 67). Gail Caldwell (1997) describes it as "quirky, sorrowful and willfully abrasive," an "odd mix of Updike's strengths and weaknesses" (P1); it is "dolorous, cantankerous," "occasionally funny," and at its core filled with regret (P4). Ultimately, though, Caldwell considers it an example of what she calls "little Updikes: eccentric detours on the creative journey" (P1). On the other hand, Michiko Kakutani (1997) asks, "how can such a gifted writer produce such a lousy book?" The novel is "sour, ugly and haphazardly constructed" (E1), its futuristic setting poorly imagined, its characters unworthy of readers' interest.

John Alden (1997) believes this dreary tale dressed up as science fiction contains "not a shred of vitality." Whatever Updike intends as the point of his story is lost in the "awful" writing and the "boring" account of Turnbull's self-centered account of his decidedly "inconsequential" life (13I). Celia Storey (1997) is even less charitable. Though she admits the book has passages of "great writing" and is willing to give Updike credit for experimenting with new forms of fiction, the story seems to "waddle toward failure." It is too long, and eventually begins to sound like "the melancholy ramblings of a vast, talkative fungus." Even the "excellent sentences wrought by an important American writer" will not keep most readers from falling "fast asleep" (J6). Finally, David Foster Wallace (1997), who insists he is "not one of these spleen-venting, spittle-spattering Updike haters" that exist in the under-forty generation, calls *Toward the End of Time* "far and away the worst" of the Updike novels he has read. It is "so mind-bendingly clunky and self-indulgent that it's hard to believe the author let it be published in this kind of shape" (1).

Another Series Ends: *Bech at Bay,* 1998

Updike closed out his series of tales about the fictional Jewish novelist Henry Bech with the publication of *Bech at Bay* in 1998. Once again Bech serves as a convenient mouthpiece for Updike to launch verbal bomblets against the literary establishment. The book was generally well received, although it did provoke some acerbic responses from those not keen on Updike's exploitation of Jewish writers or his attacks on critics and reviewers who had once disparaged his fiction. Among those delighted to see Bech return for a final encore, Jonathan Yardley (1998) claims the book is "a happy reminder" that "when Updike is good, he is very, very good" (3). David Lodge ([1998] 2002) finds it another example of how Updike is capable of rendering serious material in comic prose. Malcolm Bradbury (1999) believes the fictional Henry Bech has allowed Updike to comment on his Jewish rivals and display his "precise political observation" and "his gift for cultural satire" (37).

John Sutherland (1999) suggests that the Bech books are Updike's in-your-face response to the popular and highly regarded Jewish novelists who "have always felt free to build their fiction around non-Jewish protagonists" but "regarded the Jewish experience as very much a private preserve" (5). Bharat Tandon (1999) considers the Bech books great examples of Updike's deep understanding of the American literary scene. "No one has depicted with more fascinated disgust the process of commodity fetishism that transforms writers into literary lions," he notes. Updike does so without turning these stories into "an unpleasant exercise in navel-gazing." While the book "has the feeling of scores being settled and leave being taken," it is also a wonderful display of "Updike at play." Tandon says "this is the kind of work which gives *jeux d'esprit* a good name" (20).

Taking issue with those who value most highly Updike's autobiographical writings, Richard Brookhiser (1998) says the Bech books demonstrate that Updike is at his best when he chooses a subject "well removed" from his "own life experience." When Updike is too close to his subjects, he produces novels like *Couples*: "long, earnest, embarrassing, and indigestible." His "most sprightly work is enlivened by obvious fantasy, or pretense" (61). Similarly, Gail Caldwell (1998) thinks Bech is one of the most recognizable examples of Updike's ability—often unacknowledged by his critics—to get out of "the small back yard of old-WASP-guy-privilege" and try to understand people unlike himself (N4).

The Bech books strike Frank Kermode (1999) as "ample evidence of the author's intellectual energy, his skill in dialogue, his eye for detail." Bech is "a strange antitype, a funhouse distortion, of his inventor," and

Updike's decision to return to figures such as Bech demonstrate his "Trollopian fidelity to his characters" (23). Additionally, these books help "illuminate, by contrast, the author's scope and power when he is aiming very high," as he does in *Roger's Version* (24). While James Shapiro (1998) thinks "Updike has become a bit too fond of Bech," he believes "the sentimental, unreal universe of Bech is as vital to Updike's literary sensibility as the real, anti-poetic universe of Rabbit Angstrom." In fact, Shapiro concludes, "without Bech there can be no Rabbit" (7).

On the negative side of the ledger, *Commentary's* John Gross (1999) finds *Bech at Bay* amusing but not quite as effective as Updike might have wished. Clearly Updike "enjoyed himself fabricating a literary world tantalizingly close to the real thing, yet distorted at every turn by touches of parody and burlesque" (64). Updike's ability to create convincing Jewish characters is "an achievement" for a non-Jewish writer—"impressive as far as it goes" (65). But Gross implies that Updike is a bit too vindictive in his treatment of critics. Pankaj Mishra (1999) thinks the Bech books should be classified as "entertainments," part of the "less artistic part of the Updike *oeuvre*" (55). Eventually Bech begins to sound too much like Updike. "By letting his own private preoccupations with posterity infect Bech," Mishra says, "Updike loses the opportunity to offer Bech the same earthy integrity that Rabbit possesses, the integrity of a fictional character inseparable from his milieu and times" (56).

Man of Letters: *More Matter*, 1999

Updike closed out the century by issuing a new collection of nonfiction. Like its predecessors, *More Matter* is a hefty tome filled with reviews, essays, and occasional pieces, most published after Updike issued *Odd Jobs* eight years earlier. While a few negative reviews appeared, the volume is most notable for eliciting a growing chorus of praise for Updike's abilities in writing nonfiction. Michiko Kakutani (1999) hails the publication of *More Matter* as evidence of "Updike's remarkable versatility." While this collection is "less captivating" than earlier volumes of Updike's nonfiction, the best essays "manage both to edify and to beguile." As a result, *More Matter* "delights more often than it disappoints" (E8). William Pritchard (1999) identifies in these essays a persona that Updike has adopted for himself: "just a hard-working guy delivering the goods" (7). That self-deprecating pose does not keep Anita Brookner (2000) from declaring that Updike is perhaps the most gifted writer of the time, conducting his career "as if writing were a given, an entirely natural activity destined never to fail him." He is an amiable critic, "immediately sympathetic towards other writers," insightful and direct when necessary, and only occasionally quirky. "Updike seems, more than ever, an exemplum of all that a writer should be" (32).

Rather than simply reviewing the individual essays in *More Matter*, James Yerkes (1999a) looks at overarching themes in the collection. The major one seems to be Updike's concern over cultural issues. Yerkes sees him pleading for "more creative fiction writing" and less "banal cultural fixation," more attention to "religion and metaphysics" and "less preoccupation with a soulless postmodern secularity" (1132). While not every essay is first-rate, Yerkes says that as a whole the book is "a great feast of literary brilliance" (1134). Echoing those sentiments, Edward Pearce (2000) calls criticism of Updike's nonfiction as lightweight "a form of insolence" (64). Although Updike's bias toward realist fiction sometimes influences his judgments, his reviews "are the product not of vanity, but of inveterate involvement with books, films, art, politics," subjects "about which, unpontifically, he wants to talk—quietly." Pearce considers Updike's reviews "the record of the society and art of an age, left by one of that age's two or three great writers" (66). Greg Johnson (1999) goes even further in his praise, claiming *More Matter* reveals "the polymathic range" of Updike's interests, and confirms that he is deserving of the title "man of letters," which is "something of an endangered species in our age of jargon-ridden academic specialization" (L13).

On the other hand, Jay Parini (1999) has some misgivings about *More Matter*, finding it "overstuffed"; a "shrewd culling" might have improved the volume. Possibly, Parini speculates, "Updike's luxurious prose is not the best medium for serious thinking" (6). Adam Mars-Jones (1999) also wishes Updike would be more selective in preparing his anthologies. Instead, it seems to him that "every eight years, John Updike clears his desk, flosses his hard drive or decants his floppies, and publishes a collection of essays and criticism, in which his powers of description, evocation, and analysis are shown off on equal terms." James Wood (1999b) acknowledges that Updike "writes prose of extraordinary sumptuousness and great flexibility," but chastises him for "publish[ing] a book such as this one, with its serried trivia, its powdery bon-bons concealing sweet hollows" (41). Wood suggests that a "powerful will-to-power" drives Updike to overproduce (42). And while Wood concedes that Updike is certainly free to write about anything he chooses, he thinks Updike wastes considerable time on these journalistic efforts. "Thus," he concludes, "a serious writer undoes himself, mysteriously shedding his talents on tasks that are beneath him" (48).

In a lengthy and somewhat curious review, Bruce Bawer (2000) goes to extremes to praise Updike's capacity to turn out a mountain of insightful critical commentary and some respectable essays, before turning on him for his failure to be enlightened—i.e., liberal—in his political outlook. "Despite the remarkable facility and grace that characterize virtually every line of Updike's polished prose," Bawer laments, "there is something truly dismaying about the consistency with which he has dedicated himself to constructing a well-crafted *oeuvre* of late-Victorian proportions while devoting too little serious reflection to the question of what, in the end, really matters" (126). Echoing Bawer, the reviewer for the *Missoula Independent* ("*More Matter*" 1999) says *More Matter* "serves up both what we love and what we love to hate about our country's member of the old guard." While the volume shows how knowledgeable Updike is, it also reinforces the reputation he has "richly earned" as "the most staid, baleful, misogynist, and bourgeois writer to come down the American pike in a long time. Perhaps ever."

The publication of *More Matter* provided the impetus for Sanford Pinsker (2000) to offer some retrospective thoughts on Updike's career and some predictions about his reputation. Early in his career Updike struck "a note altogether his own" by chronicling "the satisfactions of ordinary life in thick, lyrical detail." Pinsker thinks *More Matter* does more than demonstrate Updike's ability to deal with multiple subjects; it also "reveals even more about what makes John Updike, writer, tick." Updike's genuine love for language infuses all his work, and as a result his words "outlive their specific occasion." None of the other novelists who have ventured into nonfiction is able to "return us to a time when literature mattered, when American culture, as it was then interpreted, was defined by serious books" (152). Essays like those in *More Matter* allow Pinsker to "safely predict" that people of the coming century will "come to value [Updike's] words even more" than those of the past one did (153).

Academic Criticism, 1996–1999

In the 1990s the editors at Twayne decided that, rather than simply reprinting volumes on important authors, they would commission new ones to reflect the revolution in critical study of the later decades of the century. In the case of living authors, new studies would also provide commentary on work written since the publication of the original Twayne volume. Given that freedom, James Schiff was able to make a significant contribution to Updike studies in *John Updike Revisited* (1998) by creating a useful guide to Updike's career. In some ways Schiff's study extends the work of Donald Greiner's *The Other John Updike* (1981) and *John Updike's Novels* (1984a), which attempt the same kind of comprehensive analysis of Updike's career. Organizing the new study topically, Schiff summarizes his own work on the *Scarlet Letter* trilogy, provides extensive commentary on the Rabbit novels, includes sections on "the marriage novels," comments on some short stories and Updike's historical fiction, and reprints his groundbreaking 1995 *American Literature* essay "Updike Ignored: The Contemporary Independent Critic." As a result, *John Updike Revisited* provides a useful starting point for those wishing to gain some understanding of what makes Updike one of America's most important writers.

The negative view of Updike at this time can be seen in James Wood's assessment in *The Broken Estate* ([1999a] 2000). Wood suggests that Updike is not "a great writer"—not because his prose is deficient but because he is unwilling to take risks intellectually, especially in areas of theology. "His fictions stage theological arguments which are foreclosed" (208), Wood argues. While works like *Roger's Version* seem to pose important questions about God's existence, Updike "rigs the entire novel" so that the answers seem predetermined. Similarly, *In the Beauty of the Lilies* is a "failure" because of "its inability to imagine atheism and the loss of religious faith" (210). Ultimately, Updike lacks real imagination and is forced to confine his vision to matters with which he feels comfortable. It is "a lost opportunity in American fiction that one of the few theologically literate novelists remains so unexercised by the tremor of faith" (215).

While it was common to find articles on Updike in journals specializing in criticism of contemporary American literature, occasionally a study appeared in an unlikely place that shed light on aspects of Updike's achievements that might have otherwise been missed. An interesting example of this phenomenon is Alain Corbellari's essay in *Tristania* (1999), in which he uses *Brazil* as an entrée for a discussion of Updike's use of medievalism. Corbellari is not the first to express an interest in this topic; nearly twenty years earlier in the same journal Michael Blechner (1980) compared Updike's use of the Tristan and Isolde myth in his clever short piece "Four Sides of One Story" to its treatment by C. S. Lewis and Owen Barfield. Corbellari's study investigates why and how Updike, a writer usually interested in contemporary issues, would use medieval materials. What he discovers is that references outside of *Brazil* are slight, and that even in this novel Updike is—to borrow a term from medieval criticism—more interested in "matter" than "sense," employing the tale of Tristan and Isolde for its value as a love story that he could update for his contemporary audience.

Several critics produced useful studies in the sociological dimensions of Updike's fiction. In his examination of the representation of families in contemporary American novels, Desmond McCarthy (1997) uses Updike's fiction as a counterpoint to depictions of family life in novels by other important American writers. Where many writers are optimistic that new social structures will improve family relationships, Updike seems decidedly pessimistic in believing that "significant social change invariably corrupts or degrades the institutions or practices being reformed"—including families (129). In another interesting sociological analysis, Peter Donahue (1996) argues that, in the short stories in *Too Far to Go*, the Maples' drinking habits do more than reflect the growing dissolution of their marriage. They also signal something about the larger community in which the Maples live: "Alcohol use, with all of its attendant behaviors, is linked to the specific gender roles and family dynamics of the middle-class suburban world" they occupy (361).

Cultural studies specialists were finding fertile ground in Updike's fiction for illustrating points about American literature and culture. Such is the case in Bettina Cornwell and Bruce Keillor's (1996) essay in *Empirical Approaches to Literature and Aesthetics*, a hefty collection designed to study literature as texts that reflect and comment on the real world in which they are produced. Cornwell and Keillor explain how the Rabbit novels demonstrate "the value of literature to the researcher interested in consumer behavior" and provide insight into changes in American consumers' behavior during the preceding three decades (560). In a similar vein, Kyle Pasewark (1996) analyzes the "thirty-year-long chronicle" of Harry Angstrom's life which "praises and indicts a culture uneasy with itself and its religion, demonstrating the consequences of an impossible but unyielding attempt to amalgamate God, redemption and several American dreams" (1). Examining what he calls the "religiocultural elements" (2) of the novels, Pasewark takes a careful look at the role religion plays in the Rabbit saga. What emerges from the novels, Pasewark suggests, is a vision of a particularly American religion: the worship of consumerism and the intense desire for freedom at all costs. As a result, "Rabbit's religion, a truly American religious mode of confident prelapsarian activity and freedom in various forms" is unable to "save him," but instead "hardens his heart" and makes his demise more pathetic than salvific (28).

The impact on academic critics of Updike's penchant for writing sequels can be seen in Joseph Waldmeir's "Rabbit's Four-Stage Quest to Learn the Way and Figure Out the Destination—Then Get There" (1996). Having written about the nature of Rabbit's quest in a 1974 *Modern Fiction Studies* article on *Rabbit, Run*, Waldmeir is forced to revise his initial conclusions based on evidence in the three sequels. While he still sees Rabbit being pulled by the competing forces of idealism and pragmatism, Waldmeir notes how Updike's view of his character seems to have changed; he is less detached from Harry and more determined to present him sympathetically, even while recognizing his intellectual and moral limitations.

Whereas early feminist critics like Mary Allen were generally unforgiving of Updike's treatment of women, the generation that followed were much kinder, or perhaps simply more evenhanded and dispassionate. Mary O'Connell's assessment in *Updike and the Patriarchal Dilemma* (1996) gives Updike credit for being ahead of his time in critiquing the modern concept of masculinity. "Long before" critics began to explore "the role of masculinity in male-authored texts," Updike "had begun work on the longest and most comprehensive representation of masculinity in American literature" (2). Unlike Allen, O'Connell does not assign blame for the demeaning portraits of women in these novels directly to Updike; rather, she says women in the Rabbit novels appear as they do because Harry sees them that way. Through these novels, "Updike has been analyzing and challenging socially constructed masculinity," revealing its "limitations and proscriptions as the source of a great deal of unhappiness for both men and women" (3). While the causes of Harry's failures may lie within him, "the *manner* of his failing derives from the defensive attitudes and behaviors that are part of his cultural inheritance as a male" (236). For Updike to have presented Harry or the women in his life differently would undermine his insightful portrait of the consequences of patriarchy in America. Examining this issue from a slightly different perspective, Sally Robinson (1998) argues that, especially in the middle novels of the Rabbit tetralogy, Updike tells the story of "a shift in the status of white heterosexual masculinity away from its position as the self-evident (and invisible) standard against which all identities are measure and found to be 'different'" (332). These novels present a view of the "growing crisis in white masculinity" by "foregrounding the dilemmas of visibility and invisibility" that are often suppressed in nonfictional accounts of this turbulent period (358).

The scholars contributing to Lawrence Broer's (1998) *Rabbit Tales* provide an enlightening collective assessment of Updike's achievement in his tetralogy. They share Broer's belief that Harry Angstrom is an iconic figure worthy of a place beside "Ishmael and Huck, Babbitt and Loman, Gatsby and Caulfield" in the American canon (xi). Contributors offer no noticeable dissent from Broer's sweeping claim that the Rabbit novels represent "not just the best of Updike's fiction, but a work of imagination rivaling Balzac's *Comédie Humaine*, Dos Passos's *USA Trilogy*, and Faulkner's Yoknapatawpha series" (1). To see how far criticism has come in revering Updike's Rabbit series, one need only to look back at the comments of critics like John Aldridge (1966) or the more recent dismissal by Jonathan Yardley ([1982] 1991), who seemed certain that the Rabbit novels would not be of interest for very long.

In 1998, Dilvo Ristoff followed up his earlier study of the first three Rabbit novels with an extended analysis of *Rabbit at Rest*, providing a new historicist assessment that shows how the novel not only reflects but also critiques contemporary culture. Ristoff claims that "Updike is today's great chronicler of the American life which started gaining sharpness of definition in the 1950s," drawing materials, metaphors, and themes from the world immediately around him—a world filtered through the media, which Ristoff says shapes Updike's view of the world, and hence his fiction (xiv). Similarly, with the advantage of having the entire tetralogy before her, Sara Anderson (1996) extends the work of George Hunt and

John Neary in offering a theological reading of the Rabbit novels, which she calls "an American epic illustrating the difficulty of retaining one's supernaturalism while growing up and growing old in a post-Christian world" (6). Anderson demonstrates how Rabbit sways and veers on his quest to find the unknowable entity that continually attracts him until he finally comes to rest, "embrac[ing] both the Barthian Something that wants him to find it" and the "something-as-opposed-to nothing"—the affirmation of life itself (23).

It may seem curious that many devout Christians embraced Updike's fiction, despite its extensive, graphic descriptions of sex. John McTavish (1996), a minister, offers an explanation for this phenomenon. Updike's subject matter is life, he says, "not in a vacuum, but life as it is lived on a real earth set under a real heaven." While Updike "doesn't pull his punches in describing earthly happenings," he also does not "shrink from letting heavenly realities such as judgment and grace illumine his characters' lives" (22). Updike does not press a Christian message on readers, but instead "confronts our doubts" and "depicts those little shiverings that move us to take, however, hesitantly, the leap of faith" (23). The penchant for reading Updike's work in religious terms also influences Sukhbir Singh's (1996) discussion of *Couples*, which Singh calls "a novel of spiritual awakening" that dramatizes Updike's belief that "the tendency of modern Christians to seek salvation through science, sex, and materialism has made their lives meaningless" (36). Demonstrating how symbolism works against the surface text in the novel, Singh concludes that *Couples* "affirms the Christian belief in spiritual chastity, sexual purity, and marital fidelity" (43).

The fifteen essays in James Yerkes's *John Updike and Religion* (1999b) provide further testament to the enduring interest academic critics have in the religious dimension of Updike's fiction. The book also provides good examples of the "disconnect" among readers and critics—both popular and academic—regarding the relative value of Updike's fiction. As Yerkes notes in his introduction, while many essays examine some of Updike's most respected works, others analyze "works considered by many establishment critics as among his worst"—*S.*, *Memories of the Ford Administration*, *Toward the End of Time*, and *Brazil*. That these novels could be worthy of extended analysis suggests something—either about the ability of reviewers to judge the quality of works immediately after publication, or about the doggedness of academics to find something of merit in every work by an author considered worthy of their attention. What unites contributors to this volume is a shared interest in what James Schiff describes as "a useful and fairly crucial question": "What exactly is the role of God in Updike's fiction, and how does one find this God?" (Yerkes 1999b, 51). Not every critic comes up with the same answers. Many broaden their examination to include queries into the importance of organized religion and related questions of theology. More than one is interested in how Updike's concerns about religion shape his characters' attitude toward domestic and political life. Some deal with influences such as the impact of Lutheranism, the importance of Barth, or the debt Updike owes to American romanticism. Among the more interesting approaches is that of Wesley Kort, who argues that "the center of religious interest" in Updike's work lies in the problem Updike's "narrators and characters have with their vocations." There is an expectation, Kort says, that work will connect people "with something of greater significance," an idea reflective of a strong Protestant ethic that has permeated American society for centuries (180).

What may be of even greater interest in Yerkes's collection is the attention given to those works Yerkes declares to be among Updike's failures. Despite the plethora of reviews declaring *Brazil* an execrable performance, Dilvo Ristoff insists that "much remains to be said about this intriguing text, especially with respect to Updike's treatment of its theme of eternal love and faith in a time and place of apparent godlessness, brutality, and permissiveness devoid of societal norms" (Yerkes 1999b, 65). Similarly, David Malone argues that those who have dismissed Updike's *Toward the End of Time* as failed realism or failed science fiction have missed "the richness and complexity of myth, philosophy, theology and social comment that blend and clash throughout the work" (82). George Diamond uses *Memories of the Ford Administration* to defend Updike's conservative political ideology. At times all this attention given to less well regarded works can be reminiscent of F. R. Leavis's strident insistence that *Hard Times* is Dickens's best novel (overwhelming critical commentary to the contrary), but these essays are cogent reminders that careful analysis can find the hand of a practiced craftsman and deep thinker beneath the surface of texts that do not immediately resonate with readers.

8: New Experiments in the New Century (2000–2004)

THE CONTINUING DEBATE over Updike's status at the beginning of the twenty-first century can be illustrated by the following three assessments. In his lengthy *History of American Literature* (2004), Richard Gray describes Updike as a master craftsman whose novels deal with problems posed by the "entropic vision" that characterizes modern life (615). But Jay Prosser (2001b) insists that, whatever Updike's supporters say about his talents, the decline in his reputation, though not "spectacular," has been "significant." Prosser believes this falling off is inevitable, because in his view Updike was never "America's most representative contemporary author"; instead, if he "was ever America's literary consciousness, it was a white consciousness" (579). By contrast, William Pritchard argues in *Updike: America's Man of Letters* (2000) that Updike is a unique figure in American literature: a man of letters in the tradition of Hawthorne, Howells, and Edmund Wilson, dedicated to the task of interpreting the world by examining his own life and extrapolating from it to explore American society and the American psyche during the latter half of the twentieth century. The debate over the value of Updike's work would not be solved during the next five years, either, as Updike published three new novels, a short story collection, and a volume of poems that would add bulk to his canon if they did not materially strengthen his claim as the country's pre-eminent writer.

One-Upping the Bard: *Gertrude and Claudius*, 2000

Updike's first work of the new century was unquestionably one of his boldest experiments. In the novel *Gertrude and Claudius* he creates a "prequel" to Shakespeare's *Hamlet*. The audacity Updike exhibits in linking his work directly with one of Shakespeare's greatest dramas attracted significant attention in more than seventy reviews. Among those who admired the novel, Ron Charles (2000a) says Updike has managed to create an elegant prequel, satisfying in its own right and "an insightful lead-in to *Hamlet*" (21). Gail Caldwell (2000a) exclaims, "What a piece of work is Updike!" His "intelligent little novel of whimsy" exposes his "intellectual curiosity" on every page (C4). John Freeman (2000) thinks Updike is "the perfect writer to riff on Shakespeare's tragedy, which he manages to do here without usurping the great play's rightful primacy." Richard Eder (2000) suggests that the novel redeems Updike's reputation after a string of failures and limited successes. Dazzling in its own right, it does more than entertain; it "illuminates questions about Shakespeare, about what a classic means and also the unexplored hills and forests that lie on either side of the path art pushes through them" (9).

In an insightful review, Katherine Duncan-Jones (2000) explains how Updike manages to defamiliarize readers from the story told in Shakespeare's play to create his own version that turns the Danish prince into a "postmodern anti-hero" and makes *Gertrude and Claudius* understandable if not admirable. With "brilliant scholarship and discipline," Updike manages to prepare the reader to dislike *Hamlet* for following through on his threats to avenge his dead father (3). Ron Rosenbaum (2000) also believes the novel is not just a takeoff from Shakespeare's *Hamlet* but a "rewriting" of the story of Eve and the serpent, a remarkable revisioning of "the origins of original sin in the lustful longing for originality" (22). Brooke Allen (2000) suggests that it takes every bit of Updike's superb writing skills to handle this bit of historical fiction that constantly alludes to one of the world's greatest dramas. But "Updike has never been afraid of taking risks" (an observation that would have been unthinkable in the early 1960s)—and when he succeeds, he produces a novel which "surpasses the intellectual exercise it might have been and becomes a living, powerfully physical work" (W13). John Bayley (2000) says that by "fitting together the older versions and joining them up with the text of *Hamlet*" Updike has created "an elegant little potpourri" in which he manages to "make us see *Hamlet* in three dimensions" (13). Although Felix Pryor (2000) finds *Gertrude and Claudius* "a trifle contrived," he approves of what Updike has done to create his own novel from the characters of Shakespeare's play. "Judged on its own terms," he says, "the book is a triumph," displaying Updike's exceptional stylistic gifts and allowing him to give free rein to his imagination (32).

Not surprisingly, James Yerkes (2000) calls *Gertrude and Claudius* a "beautifully crafted, captivating story," Updike's "best book since *The Witches of Eastwick*" (220)—quite a claim, considering that *Rabbit at Rest* and *In the Beauty of the Lilies* appeared between these two novels. Yerkes thinks *Gertrude and Claudius* helps refute charges that Updike is a misogynist. Yerkes believes "this novel "is alive because it poignantly mirrors the shadows of our souls as startled creatures caught in the light of reality" (221). Similarly, the renowned Renaissance scholar and new historicist Stephen Greenblatt (2000) sees domestic themes at work in the novel, as Updike attempts to answer some of the questions raised by Shakespeare's play, notably "Did she love her first husband? Did she have an affair with her brother-in-law?" And if so, did anyone else know of it? (34) Despite the novel's "late-medieval trappings" Updike's Gertrude "is a Danish Emma Bovary," into whose "impoverished world comes Claudius," who possesses all the qualities of a romantic seducer (37). What Updike manages to do in his novel is revive "a nineteenth-century tradition of imagining the lives of Shakespeare's characters before they make their appearance in the plays." While this kind of speculating has often been discredited by scholars, Greenblatt says Updike has made "a brilliant novel out of it" (38).

The accumulation of favorable reviews was nearly matched, however, by those that question Updike's methods or his achievements. Dan Hulbert (2000) considers *Gertrude and Claudius* "more like a daring academic exercise than a full-bodied, satisfying read." James Hopkin (2000) concedes that "if any writer has sufficient bombast to take on the Bard, it is John Updike," but wonders openly "whether or not such a full and frothy conceit can survive the rigours of a second reading." Millicent Bell (2001) is impressed with Updike's ability to imagine the lives of Shakespeare's characters before the time of *Hamlet*. But the novel's theme strikes Bell as reminiscent of Updike's other work, as its focus on "lust and treachery and ambition" bears striking similarities to other Updike stories about the "dangerous patterns in the lives of some well-placed, easy-living persons" (346).

Michiko Kakutani (2000a), who could not forgive Updike for novels like *Brazil* and *S.*, is considerably more sympathetic to *Gertrude and Claudius*, though she feels the novel provides a "decidedly warped reading of the characters in Shakespeare's play" (E1). She does feel Updike has done a better job creating a female protagonist than he had in previous novels, largely because Gertrude is "informed by the same dialectic between freedom and duty, passion and domesticity" that animates his best male protagonists. Ultimately, Updike seems less interested in "re-inventing Shakespeare" than in turning the story into a modern "tale of sexual jealousy and marital discord not unlike the ones he has told many times before" (E8).

While acknowledging Updike's right to recast Shakespearean characters, Norah Vincent (2000) thinks he has taken too many liberties with the principal personages of *Hamlet*. Turning the Prince into a spoiled brat and cavalierly dismissing Claudius's misdeeds "turns the plays and characters of Shakespeare into shadows of themselves, unworthy of the sublime poetry he wrote for them." Ultimately, she says, *Gertrude and Claudius* is a "disappointment to those who still find dignity and meaning in the tragic view of life" (58). The reviewer for the *Economist* ("Witty, Wise, Then Weary" 2000) is less kind, calling the novel a mistake, because Updike has the hubris to "invite[ ] comparison to the Bard," which offers "no surer route to being shown up." The "outsized passions" that characterize *Hamlet* "seem petty" in Updike's story, which is "no more majestic than the tawdry modern mid-life indiscretions" that constitute his customary material (3). The best that can be said of the novel is that it is "a diverting experiment that never quite rises above an able creative-writing exercise" (4).

The publication of *Gertrude and Claudius* prompted Martin Arnold (2000) to reflect on Updike's current reputation in England and America. He observes that *Gertrude and Claudius* "did not approach bestseller numbers," despite an unusually active world-of-mouth campaign promoting it. Instead, the public bought up Harry Potter and anything on the Oprah Book Club list. Even "bravura reviews" did not elevate the work's sales; to younger readers, Updike seems "remote." Notwithstanding the slip in popularity, however, Arnold is confident that Updike will be remembered because his books "are in libraries and on college syllabuses," and "there are a lot of doctorates in literature to be earned this century" from a study of his fiction (E3).

Rabbit Revived: *Licks of Love*, 2001

Updike's 2001 collection of short fiction, *Licks of Love*, is likely to remain of interest to scholars because it contains "Rabbit Remembered," a novella about life for Harry Angstrom's son Nelson after his father's death. Typical of most reviewers' responses is that of Gail Caldwell (2000b), who finds most of the stories overshadowed by the novella, which she calls "a thing of rich satisfaction" (M1). Michiko Kakutani (2000b) calls "Rabbit Remembered" a "sad-funny postscript" to the series, a work that "not only reconnoiters old ground but in doing so also manages to transform it into something stirring and new." However, she dismisses the other stories in *Licks of Love* as "superfluous and formulaic," covering familiar themes, as if Updike were "on automatic pilot" (E7). Francis King (2001) also laments that the relatively strong "Rabbit Remembered" has to share space in a volume with other stories "which are too frail to offer anything but token support" (42). By contrast, Ron Charles (2000b) thinks some of the short stories in *Licks of Love* "are among Updike's best," but is less sanguine about the merits of "Rabbit Remembered," which he says "isn't in the same league" as the Rabbit novels (19).

Zachary Leader (2001) admits that, while Updike's "coldness can sometimes invigorate, there is more of it in the current volume than usual"; virtually nothing "escapes the author's leveling irony." As a result, the "pleasures" afforded by the collection are "sometimes abrasive as well as bracing" (8). Xan Brooks (2001) is disappointed with *Licks of Love*, especially "Rabbit Remembered," which he says "feels false." In the Rabbit novels, Harry emerges as "a kind of feet-of-clay emblem for America itself: at first brimming with promise and a rude, restless energy, then sliding towards a frustrated fat-cat middle age." But in the new novella, Updike tries too hard to tidy up loose ends, and the work comes off as "too schematic a clean-up job." The greater problem Brooks sees is that, since the publication of *Rabbit at Rest* Updike has been "napping, turning out a few minor-key novels" and the "occasional misconceived folly."

Several reviews address the larger issue of Updike's accomplishments. Michael Dirda (2000) says "It's easy enough to be blasé" about Updike, since he has produced so much. While nothing remarkable happens in any of the stories, including "Rabbit Remembered," it would be a serious mistake to take Updike for granted. He is "our Flaubert," the "only major American novelist one could happily read just for his turns of phrase and handsomely tailored sentences" (X15). Less concerned about style than substance, James Wall (2001) says complaints that Updike "lacks a social conscience" and fails to deal with "the social conflicts that rage through the nation during Rabbit's lifetime" are without merit. Wall believes Updike is keenly interested in "recording the anguish of lives that can't invest emotion in others because their own lives lack meaning" (36). In a retrospective essay, Adam Mars-Jones (2001) says Updike is "one of the few writers you can genuinely imagine taking pride in giving value for money." Mars-Jones also thinks charges that Updike is a misogynist are misguided. Although his works contain "a number of sentences" that "seem almost specifically written to corroborate Levi-Strauss's idea that women are a medium of exchange between men," Updike has "not ignored feminism" and has shown himself "quite capable of writing thrilling pages from a woman's point of view" (15). If he has one failing, it is his inability to recognize and embrace homosexuality, especially male homosexuality—largely because it does not conform to his idea that men are fulfilled only in their relationship with women.

Paul Berman (2001) uses his review of *Licks of Love* to offer some cogent observations on Updike's accomplishment in the Rabbit tetralogy, which he calls "a single very long novel written in a traditional and even somewhat old-fashioned form" (4). Berman compares it to Whitman's *Leaves of Grass*, Balzac's *Human Comedy*, and similar books (including Marx's *Capital*) that try to say everything about society in a single work or series. In fact, Berman calls Updike too modest, writing "a nineteenth-century style giant opus that claims to be nothing of the sort; a book that embodies the huge and the grandiose and that, even so, trains your eyes on the modest and diminutive" (5). What Updike does best, Berman says, is "conjoin[] the here-and-now with hints of a thrilling, invisible reality" (6), giving readers a sense that the everyday world contains in it something deep and grand.

Adam Begley's review of *Licks of Love* (2000) is worth noting because in it he also comments on William Pritchard's *Updike: America's Man of Letters*. Begley considers himself a discriminating critic, able to recognize that the stories in *Licks of Love* are "decidedly uninteresting" except when Updike "slips into his Rabbit suit." Yet as Begley notes, Pritchard manages to praise the entire collection (313). "Will Mr. Pritchard encounter an Updike book," Begley asks sardonically, "just *one* book—he doesn't like?" Begley accuses Pritchard of ignoring "the clamor of anti-Updike critics" by insisting that Updike's ability to write "glorious prose" is proof enough that these critics are wrong in their assessments.

The appearance of *Licks of Love* provided James Wood (2001) yet another opportunity to highlight all of Updike's faults. Those include, first and foremost, writing too much. "It seems easier for Updike to stifle a yawn than to refrain from writing a book," Wood says. This obsession has led him to produce several bad books and fall into the unfortunate habit of substituting journalistic prose for high art. Updike has already published too much about the "distasteful and limited world" that interests him—a world where adultery, once a situation sure to create shock and spur interest, is no longer so intriguing to readers. Concentrating on themes that were important decades ago but not now makes Updike seem "not only dated, but provincial and minor" (30). He is also out of touch in his "impermeability to silence and the interruptions of the abyss," and his supposed Christianity is merely a pose that allows him to write about "pagans" in the language of pagans. To prove his point, Wood suggests that Updike's most effective novels are ones seen through the eyes of a pagan, Harry Angstrom. Yet even these novels about America's descent into a materialistic morass have a dated quality that makes stories like "Rabbit Remembered" of limited interest at best.

Interlude: *Americana and Other Poems*, 2001

Updike's 2001 collection *Americana and Other Poems* was generally well received. For the purposes of this study, however, the more important point to make is that several reviewers treated Updike as a serious poet. Christopher Bowden (2001) praises these poems for their "tough yet sensitive, stone-wall texture"; collectively "they tell us a bit more about our heritage than, perhaps, we already knew" (19). Paul Mariani (2001) celebrates Updike as a poet who finds possibilities for hope in everyday occurrences. John Eberhart (2001) says these verses show that Updike's poetry "has gotten heavier" (15) and reflect themes from his fiction—specifically, the intertwined concepts of faith and doubt. John Taylor (2002) gives Updike high marks for using his "considerable gifts" to attain "an epitome of vividness [and] liveliness." Furthermore, he is not afraid to "struggle to edge language, even clumsily, into some unexpected corner of possible truth" (294). Unfortunately, Updike's tendency toward verbal pyrotechnics and his penchant for avoiding introspection often cause readers to miss instances when he does become introspective. That happens more than once in the poems in this volume, which deal "rather often with intimations of mortality" (295).

Fiction about Art: *Seek My Face*, 2002

Although Updike had written about art and artists before, his 2002 novel *Seek My Face*, based on the life of Jackson Pollock and his wife, the painter Lee Krasner, is Updike's first attempt in fiction to conduct a serious extended examination of the nature of art. The experiment met with mixed success. Benjamin Markovits (2003) describes the novel as lightweight entertainment, "an afternoon's read" that puts a thin "coat of fiction" on facts about the New York art scene (42). By contrast, Galen Strawson (2003) feels it is a serious work whose central theme is "the connection between artistic creation, the beauty of being ('God') and self" (9). Adam Begley (2002) finds the premise of *Seek My Face*, the widow's explanation and justification of her life to a young reporter, "clean and powerful." The "essence and beauty" of the novel come from Updike's brilliance in "unpacking this plain truth" in "superabundant prose." Sadly, Begley says, some critics cannot appreciate the "playfulness Updike brings to his recreation of the New York School" (23).

Fellow novelist Ann Patchett (2002) finds reading *Seek My Face* "wonderful," because the novel is given over "so unabashedly to art" (T8); but the book "doesn't have much plot," and women are treated shabbily (T8). Charles Matthews (2002) thinks the novel goes on too long and relies too heavily on set pieces and "near-hallucinatory precision of detail," without using either technique to "propel the narrative or reinforce symbolic texture" (1). Both Nicholas Laird (2003) and Adam Mars-Jones (2003) believe Updike manipulates the story too much. Similarly, John Russell (2003) concludes that despite its "panoramic" descriptions and "deft and economical story-telling," much of the novel is "unconvincing" and Updike's portrait of America's pop-art world "shaky" and ill-informed (38).

Some reviewers expressed their displeasure more forcefully. Michiko Kakutani (2002) calls the novel "misbegotten" (E1); it is "impossible for the reader to find a single believable character" in it (E6). Ron Charles (2002) complains that, while Updike may be a "master at tracing the subtle currents of desire and disappointments that swirl around people trapped in a marriage or a career or an interview that runs too long," in *Seek My Face* such "moving moments are cramped in a structure that doesn't give them much air to breathe" (15). Focusing on the political dimensions of the novel, Aidan Campbell (2003) considers *Seek My Face* "a plaintive lament that American art is no longer as good as it used to be in Updike's youth." Updike "mourn[s] the demise of America's home-grown modernism that had to be annihilated to pave the way for the multicultural present." John Banville (2002) is kinder, admitting that the attempt to meld art history with fiction "is a fascinating but not entirely successful hybrid" (10). The book is marred by a "startling looseness in the writing" and a lack of sharp characterization (15). Yet in some scenes Updike excels in creating believable characters and vivid settings—qualities that keep the novel from being an abject failure.

Once again Updike's work found support among the Christian community, as two reviews in *Christian Century* attest. James Yerkes (2002) says *Seek My Face* further demonstrates ways Updike seeks to be "adventurously experimental." The juxtaposition of characters is designed to highlight one of the novel's "religious themes—the need to seek God in the world around us." *Seek My Face* is another testament to Updike's "lifelong consistency" in seeking to understand "the ineradicable religious character of human consciousness" (30). Mark Buchanan (2003) observes that, if Updike is "not a 'Christian' novelist" he is "certainly North America's most theological one" (42). He does not celebrate America's "sexual coming of age," but instead writes "elegies for a world where so much has been trampled, squandered, forgotten." Despite its seemingly secular veneer, *Seek My Face* reflects "Updike's concern for the loss of faith" (44).

Youth Remembered: *The Early Stories: 1953–1975*, 2003

The compendium of Updike's early stories re-issued in 2003 generated considerable nostalgic reverie, as critics who had read Updike over the years were able to look back on his first efforts with some sense of what those tales foretold about their author. Sebastian Smee (2004) remarks that, with the possible exception of the Rabbit novels, these stories "seem very close to being the best things" Updike has ever written, and "among the finest 20th-century writing by anyone" (33). Lorrie Moore (2003) calls the stories "focused, local meditations, suffused with Updike's brand of Protestant mysticism, a Christianity not of guilt and sin but of sorrow and beauty." These stories are early proof that "by dint of both quality and quantity" Updike is quite possibly "American literature's greatest short-story writer." Bernard Rodgers (2004) also suggests that Updike's most important legacy, along with the Rabbit novels, may well be the short stories. The collection is "a treasure," providing both a "wonderful introduction" to new readers and a "pleasurable reminder" of why Updike "has been a writer who truly matters to so many of us for so long" (234).

James Yerkes (2003) reminds readers that "exploring the extraordinary ordinary dimensions of our lives has always been John Updike's métier." While Yerkes finds the quality of the stories uneven, they still reinforce his belief in Updike's principal purpose as a writer. But Yerkes also points out another theme often overlooked by critics: the "astute exploration of the significance of literary art," something Updike has explored in his own criticism for decades (44). In his admiring review of *The Early Stories*, Louis Menand (2003) sees the collection as a kind of "shadow autobiography" in which Updike demonstrates his mastery at portraying "emotions of loss and nostalgia" (104). In superbly crafted stories like these, readers' satisfaction come from recognizing that they have been touched by the emotion embodied in the words. Lee Siegel (2003) finds that Updike has managed to do what few others writers have been able to accomplish: make the suburbs a subject of serious fiction. Those who accuse Updike of "partaking in the suburban mirage of happiness achieved" miss the point. Updike "turns that quality into a universal human delusion. He doesn't scorn the suburbs for their illusions; he cherishes the suburbs and their illusions for exposing a deep strain of human pathos" (16). Updike's great achievement is to have "take[n] the suburban chimera of happiness and transform[ed] it into a problem inscribed in human nature" (17).

Justin Cartwright (2004) uses his review to assess Updike's career. Cartwright catalogs several important strengths: an ability to translate the "preoccupations of an only child" into fiction, a persistent willingness to "grappl[e] intelligently with questions of faith and the afterlife," skill in creating tension between the material and the spiritual dimensions of the self, and commitment to dealing "honestly and unsparingly with the mechanics and the complications of sex and adultery" against the "low murmuring background of faith." Cartwright feels Updike has been done "grave injustice" by critics who dismiss him as a lightweight because he "deals with the ordinary" rather than with "more explicitly political or tendentious themes." In Cartwright's view, Updike is "one of the finest, most consistent, and most humane writers in English of the last half century" (16).

Of course, some reviewers were notably unimpressed. Michiko Kakutani (2003) calls the volume a "decidedly spotty production" marred by Updike's decision to include "virtually every short piece of fiction he wrote between 1953 and 1975." At best the collection serves as "a sort of index" to Updike's "evolution as a writer" (E31). Yet Kakutani somewhat begrudgingly admits that in his best works Updike manages to "bear witness to the mundane pleasures and pains of middle-class life," and to "preserve a time and a place through the sorcery of words" (E41).

Cynthia Ozick's retrospective of Updike ([2003] 2006), prompted by the publication of *The Early Stories* highlights the strength that lies in his felicity with language, a quality that more than compensates for his decision to write about ordinary life rather than tackle larger social issues. The urgency in Updike's fiction emerges not in his scenes depicting sex, which "seem as distanced and skeptical as a lapsed seminarian's meticulously recited breviary," but instead in ones dealing with matters of theology: "his God-seeking passages send out orgasmic shudders, whether of exaltation or distress" (50). Ozick believes Updike deserves to be spoken of alongside Faulkner, Fitzgerald, and Cather, "older masters who lay claim to territory previously untrafficked" and "make of it common American ground" (47). In Updike's case, "language in all its fecundity" is his native country, "and he is its patriot" (53). However, George Walden (2004) urges caution in predicting the lasting impact of Updike's fiction, speculating that his legacy is "likely to be affected by non-literary factors." American critics have accused him of "Old World preciousness," while Europeans who dislike America have faulted him "for being soft on the Great Satan." But what is really going on has more to do with ideological prejudice than critical assessment: "My own suspicion," Walden says, "is that what both sets of critics really resent is his failure to conform to their agendas, too cramping and conventional to accommodate the full expanse of his talent" (50).

"Tarbox" Revisited: *Villages*, 2004

Updike's 2004 novel, *Villages*, is eerily reminiscent of his 1968 blockbuster *Couples*, yet it did not attract the same popular readership nor garner significant critical acclaim. That is not to suggest, however, that reviewers were universal in their disapprobation. In fact, Justin Cartwright (2005) deems it "an extraordinary feat." Not since *Couples* has Updike been "so frank, indeed gynaecological, about sex." But this novel which explores the meaning of sex for a man of seventy becomes at the same time "a meditation on old age" (33). James Yerkes (2004) calls *Villages* "a retrospective coda to *Couples*" and insists that "there is no more gifted and insightful narrator of domestic experience, particularly of middle-class America in the 1960s and 1970s, than Updike" (32).

However, John Freeman (2004) suggests that the proper companion novel for *Villages* is not *Couples* but *Toward the End of Time*, the new novel serving as a more calming counterpoint to that dark and "mandarin" work. *Villages* is Updike's variation on the *Bildungsroman* in which the protagonist "does not emerge with a greater understanding of himself." Of course, Freeman admits, the novel's portrayal of women will give critics "plenty to gripe about," but one should not criticize Updike for choosing to write about men who view women as objects (G3). Somewhat surprisingly, Fay Weldon (2004) gives *Villages* an unqualified endorsement, even defending Updike from charges of misogyny: "Those who find the idea of female submission to the male distasteful" have not "lived through the sexual history of our times" as Updike has. *Villages* is "a wondrous sexual and social retrospective of small-town living over the last half-century." Weldon says that, while "some writers get more boring with age," Updike "just gets more perspicacious" (3). Writing in the left-leaning *New Leader*, Isa Kapp (2004) calls *Villages* a "high-strung autobiographical novel" in which Updike tells readers "about his own life and what he has made of growing older." Updike exhibits a "dismayed response to the decline of religion" (33), but gives his readers "an enormous gift: the guiltless pleasure of sex," thumbing his nose at "his church," which "cannot annul Nature's pronouncement" (34).

Updike's continuing insistence in focusing on sex did not impress every reviewer, however. Stephen Amidon (2005) says he may be the "sexual revolution's most meticulous chronicler" but he now seems out of touch with contemporary readers. *Villages* feels like "bitter-sweet nostalgia" for a past age, and may not sit well with a younger generation that does not see sex as the "liberating adventure" Updike and his generation did (51). On a related note, Walter Kirn (2004) suggests that the era in which novelists could shock readers by incorporating scenes of explicit sexual activity has passed. Updike seems to understand this, and while *Villages* "recaptures and concentrates the erotic essence of the earlier books," it "adds a mellow, retrospective tone" (13), serving as a kind of elegy to an earlier age.

The general attitude of a majority of reviewers is seen in comments by John Banville (2004), who finds himself apologizing for *Villages* because it falls "somewhat short of Updike's best work." But he says Updike has already created a body of work that warrants the praise he has received. Besides, "no one else I know of, simply no one, writes this well" (56). Peter Kemp (2005), too, admits that *Villages* contains flashes of the Updike who has justly earned his reputation as "modern America's peerless prose-poet of the everyday," but on the whole finds this novel "lackluster." One senses that this "jaded" work has been "recycled" from earlier novels and stories, making it "veteran, not vintage Updike" (52). John Keenan (2005) is more blunt. "Updike is running on empty," he says. "The customary brilliance" of his earlier work "has been replaced with a proficiency which drains emotion from his narrative." Sadly, Keenan concludes, "when all passion is spent, verisimilitude is no substitute." Adam Begley (2004) finds the novel "tired, timid, shaky"; though reminiscent of *Couples*, it pales by comparison. Although *Couples* is "by no means a perfect novel," it has "weathered well"; where it may have been "too thick," *Villages* is "too thin" and probably will not rank among Updike's best works (10).

That sentiment is echoed by Bob Hoover (2004), who sees *Villages* as yet another example of Updike's inability to plumb the depths of human existence. In Updike's work, the "mystery of our existence" has been reduced to "biology" or to "the hard-wiring installed in our computer brains." Sadly, Hoover concludes, "for all his ruminations on the American soul in a career spanning five decades, Updike has concluded that the mystery is no mystery at all" (B4). Max Watman (2004) is even more critical, claiming it is "difficult really to call these things Updike has written 'characters,'" and predicting that readers are certain to feel alienated by the book (54–55). Michiko Kakutani (2004) also dismisses *Villages* as one of the novels that results from Updike's "self-imposed quota of producing a new book nearly every year" (E33). Clichéd and formulaic, the work comes off as "narrow" and "claustrophobic," little more than "a weary exercise in the recycling of frayed and shop-worn material" (E43).

Academic Criticism 2000–2004

If reviewers did not agree about the quality of Updike's most recent publications, by the turn of the new century members of the academic community seemed to have made up their minds about his importance. During the 1990s Updike's work was the subject of twenty-four dissertations; between 2000 and 2004 fifteen more PhD candidates wrote about him. The number of articles proliferated as well, and several major books were published that significantly enhanced understanding of Updike as a craftsman and chronicler of the American experience.

Jack De Bellis's monumental *John Updike Encyclopedia* (2000) is a labor of love and significant scholarly acumen. Not only does De Bellis provide a detailed chronology of Updike's career; he also offers readers a handy alphabetical reference guide to, and descriptions of, all of Updike's works, major characters, and important topics through 1999. Many of the entries include thoughtful critical commentaries that combine factual details with analysis of works and characters. The only drawback is that the volume does not cover the last decade of Updike's life. Perhaps a second edition will provide a remedy.

A careful look at several more important or provocative critical commentaries published during this period illustrates the diversity of opinion among academics examining the Updike canon. Possibly the most extensive cultural and political study of Updike's work appeared in 2001. D. Quentin Miller's *John Updike and the Cold War* reads Updike's work through a historical and political lens. Though not the first to notice how frequently the Cold War exists as a shadowy presence in Updike's writings, Miller offers what is certainly to date the best systematic examination of the influence of this ideological conflict on Updike's work. Miller had already published a limited commentary on this topic in a 1997 essay, showing how the Rabbit novels provide "a striking example of the antagonism and resentment that can arise between parents and children in a world obsessed with the potential for its own destruction" (1997, 195). Now in his book (2001), Miller challenges critics who claim Updike seldom deals with large historical events, insisting that "for all his intellectual struggles—the theological, philosophical, literary, and scientific inquiries that give his work depth and solidity—Updike is first and foremost a social critic, and his legacy rests on his ability to depict contemporary America, which for most of his career was Cold War America" (7).[1]

Miller asserts that, beginning in the 1960s, "Updike increasingly places domestic problems alongside their global analogue: Cold War tensions" (39). The trajectory of Updike's work begins with the kind of anxiety produced by the Cold War, mirrored in the fractured social relationships that dominate his stories. As the country became more fractious over the next three decades, Updike becomes less certain about America's values and its future. By the 1990s his work takes on a tone of nostalgia for the period of the 1950s, when America seemed to know what it was about, defined and unified in its resistance to the evil represented by the Soviet Union.

Miller's political focus allows him to make sense of some of Updike's late work, which often deals with the future. While "history is in fact the driving force of Updike's work," Miller says, his "view of history is always a way of commenting on the present." Because the end of the Cold War made the present "maddeningly unknowable for Updike" (178), he looked to the future with the same sense of longing that he expressed in his nostalgia for the past. Assessments of works like *Toward the End of Time* give credence to Miller's central thesis that understanding Updike's reaction to the Cold War provides a useful key to unlocking the mysteries of his entire canon. Miller's study also demonstrates how critics who have the opportunity to consider the body of Updike's work (or in his case, almost the entire body of work) have the advantage of perspective in making judgments about it. No one writing about Updike in the 1960s or 1970s—even if he or she had noticed frequent veiled allusions to the Cold War—could have predicted its impact on Updike's writing.

Taking a more philosophical approach to matters of culture, in *Prophets without Vision*, a book about "crises of ideology and identity" in several contemporary American writers (11), Hedda Ben-Bassat (2000) relies heavily on recent theoretical work about the idea of Americanism and American literature to construct a reading of Updike's fiction that is historically situated and politically charged. In some ways, Updike serves as a convenient foil for Ben-Bassat's attack on Old Americanists who celebrate American exceptionalism. "Concerned with the destructive influence in America of self-ordained prophets" (52), Updike relies on Barth's "paradigm of prophetic subjectivity" to "deflate the titanism of American sublime, and offer an alternative model for twentieth-century American selfhood" (53). Updike's "confessional" writing situates Americans clearly among the common lot of modern individuals whose attempts to construct a self are often fraught with anxiety.

Updike's work also figures in Frank Farrell's provocative (perhaps even reactionary) study *Why Does Literature Matter?* (2004), which examines whether "older ways of reading can be defended" (1) in light of new theories about language, literature, psychology, and philosophy. Farrell's demonstrates how competing ideas of the self—including ideas about gender—permeate Updike's work, causing him to return frequently to the same topics, especially ones in which a child or teen features prominently.

Critics using both traditional and new approaches to Updike's texts added to an understanding of his earlier fiction and developed intriguing assessments of more recent work. For example, in an article in *Gothic Studies*, Avril Horner and Sue Zlosnik (2000) demonstrate how *The Witches of Eastwick* is part of the Gothic tradition, "in which conventional boundaries are destabilized by the intrusion of the uncanny" (136). Updike uses the tradition to create an "alchemy" of his own, one that is "creative rather than destructive, liberating rather than redemptive and comic rather than terrifying" (137). Horner and Zlosnik suggest, too, that the novel is aligned with "postmodern theology" in its attempt to dissolve boundaries between binary opposites such as life and death, good and evil, and masculine and feminine. Seen in this light, *The Witches of Eastwick* can be read as a fictionalized version of the Puritan fear that women might actually emerge as powerful figures in society. However, the authors caution, "whether Updike deconstructs or confirms misogyny remains open to debate" (142).

The Witches of Eastwick is not treated so kindly by Kim Loudermilk (2004). She acknowledges that Updike "really did try to investigate both women and feminism" in the novel, but "failed in both of his stated intentions." The novel actually "denigrates feminism and relegates women to their usual subordinate place" (102). One of the chief problems lies in Updike's selection of the witch as a symbol for the liberated woman, because the term has historically negative connotations that vitiate Updike's attempts to celebrate his heroines' freedom. *Witches* devolves into a celebration of male power, the sex scenes merely "male sexual fantasies" (109). Women who "escape patriarchal boundaries" (113) become evil, using their powers to undermine the concept of sisterhood. The three witches in the novel "conform and contribute to the worst stereotypes of feminists current today." Furthermore, they "neither work toward nor achieve social change," and are quick to "retreat into safely traditional roles" when given the opportunity (114).

That level of heightened rhetoric is absent from commentaries on *Memories of the Ford Administration*. While reviewers may not have been enamored with the novel, at least one critic, Kenneth Millard (2000), gives Updike credit for using it to grapple with the question of subjectivity. In an analysis informed by the theoretical work of Michel Foucault, Millard links the novel with Philip Roth's *American Pastoral*, E. L. Doctorow's *Billy Bathgate*, and Louise Erdrich's *Tales of Burning Love* to demonstrate how self-representation is called into question by the text itself. Updike's novel and those of his contemporaries "are notable," Millard says, "for scrutinizing their respective languages of representation while they tell their story" (231). Taking a notably different approach to the same novel, historian Paul Boyer (2001) finds that in *Memories of the Ford Administration* Updike manages to turn history to good use in creating fiction that is really about contemporary matters. The novel has special appeal for historians, Boyer argues, because one of Updike's central themes is "the self-delusion of historians in thinking that they can re-create a past time period" from the materials available to them (51).

Among more recent works receiving critical attention was *Gertrude and Claudius*. A mere three years after it was published, Henry Janowitz's (2003) article in *Hamlet Studies* treats Updike's novel as an "artful prequel" (193) to *Hamlet* in which Updike "completely inverts the characters of Claudius, Gertrude, the King of Denmark, and the basic nature of Hamlet" (194). Some of the changes sit well with Janowitz; others do not. What interests him most, however, is how Updike has ignored some earlier explanations of Hamlet's behavior (although Janowitz seems to ignore most criticism of the play written since the 1930s), pointing out how he has found his dramatic crux in what is essentially a dysfunctional family.

Elena Savu's "In Desire's Grip: Gender, Politics, and Intertextual Games in Updike's *Gertrude and Claudius*" (2003) manages to incorporate all the most popular buzzwords of contemporary theory. This mingling of critical approaches is justified, Savu says, because Updike's novel "testifies to what has become an important feature of postmodern aesthetics, the refashioning of canonical texts, through which novelists turn their literary forebears to new uses." In Updike's case, that means the "repositioning of Hamlet's mother as a desiring subject" (22). Savu reads the novel from a feminist perspective without bringing to bear all the negative baggage feminists have loaded onto Updike's work. As a result, she is able to claim that Updike's "engagement with Shakespeare's play integrates implications that express feminist values within the larger framework of textuality," giving readers a fresh perspective on Gertrude's motivations and her "struggle to redefine and empower herself by acknowledging the place of desire" in the construction of identity (23). Furthermore, Savu says, the novel "enacts the recovery of female experience from the realm of Shakespeare's play and, in a more abstract sense, from the realm of 'nonbeing' to which patriarchy relegates it" (24). Savu calls the novel an extended resistant reading of the play in which Gertrude becomes the most self-aware character who creates her own identity despite the many obstacles placed in her way.

In another study of Updike's use of older models, Derek Royal (2002) examines the narrative strategies Updike borrows from Hawthorne to recast *The Scarlet Letter* for modern readers. Concentrating principally on *S.*, Royal shows how Updike "foreground[s] narrative authority" by examining the role of the narrator, "an additional intrusive 'character' who stands between the real-world author and his story" (74). Recognizing this fact allows one to see that Updike is not simply a "mannerist realist," but an innovator capable of writing fiction that "foreground[s] metafictional aesthetics." Additionally, *S.* provides evidence that Updike has broken from realist tradition, turning not to postmodernism but to a pre-modern model for his work (75).

Among the many studies of the Rabbit novels, Marshall Boswell's *John Updike's Rabbit Tetralogy* (2001) is worth extended commentary. Boswell claims the four novels prove "in the end to be a unified, coherent work of the highest formal achievement" (2). Following a suggestion made by Updike in 1995, Boswell treats the work as a "mega-novel" in which Updike provides readers "a sustained, linear, and ultimately cumulative articulation" of his "dialectical vision" (3). Boswell devotes much attention to the creation of formal patterns that play off each other within individual novels and between novels. Acknowledging that Updike often presents dilemmas for which he provides no solutions, Boswell suggests that the novelist is following the method outlined by Kierkegaard: the practice of irony in which "the author's vision emerges indirectly via the unresolved tension produced by the interplay" of thematic elements that create sustained tension within the work as a whole (4). Updike is indebted to Kierkegaard, Heidegger, Tillich, and Barth (but only "those ideas and concepts associated with Barth's middle phase, the period of his dialectical theology" [16]) in creating these novels which, when read as a single, coherent work prove to be "the story of an education, specifically of Rabbit's gradual confrontation with the nothing aspect of Creation, with the God of Chaos and Death" (19). Incorporating materials from his earlier articles ("The Black Jesus" 1998, "The World and the Void" 1999), Boswell uses the central chapters of his study to demonstrate how each novel forms a part of this larger dialectic that eventually leads Rabbit to an understanding of himself and the nature of creation.

Boswell asserts that understanding how these novels form a single entity helps justify Updike's place among major American authors. "Posterity demands big novels, preferably with enough formalistic complexity and novelistic detail to sustain prolonged study" (2001, 232). Whereas no single novel in the Updike canon might rise to that level, the Rabbit tetralogy certainly does. In this saga about a "high-school educated car salesman" Updike manages to weave in "a fully coherent theological and moral vision" (233). Boswell defends Updike's vision of America that seems to privilege the average person by appealing to De Tocqueville's conception of the American character, which stresses the essential isolation of individuals in America's democratic society. He also challenges critics who believe Updike has been either naïve about, or too celebratory of, the American character. These critics fail to see the constant irony that calls into question every individual and social value even in the act of praising it. This ambiguity, Boswell insists, makes Updike's novels compelling reading, and the Rabbit tetralogy "Updike's most intoxicating achievement" (239).

Many shorter essays also explore the personal and cultural dimensions of the Rabbit novels. In *American Dream, American Nightmare* (2000) Kathryn Hume reprises arguments that present Rabbit as a quester searching for meaning in religion and in the American dream. By the end of the series he has soured on the idea of achieving his dreams, discovering they are unattainable. In this, Hume suggests, Rabbit stands for America itself, which was entering a period of great disillusionment as the century closed. Similarly, John-Paul Colgan (2003) examines aspects of Updike's "running report" on postwar American society "that are concerned with America's borders in both a literal and a figurative sense" (73). The "sense of containment" that permeates *Rabbit, Run* is gradually "infiltrated by a world beyond, an uncontainable world of news reports and international crises that challenge the instinctively inward looking characters" in these novels (73–74). At the same time, Colgan says, Updike's prose style is designed to contain; throughout the Rabbit novels, he employs language to "draw the outside world in" and "circumscribe" it (76). As Harry becomes more prosperous, he is increasingly forced to admit into his world unpleasant truths about America, namely that it is decaying. Ironically, foreign competitors and those who join with them—including Harry—are benefiting from America's difficulties. Harry's progress through life is emblematic of America's "progress" during the second half of the century—a gradual decline and a concurrent realization that no one, and no country, can "go it alone" (84).

Anne Roiphe's (2000) extended personal reading of the Rabbit novels almost lovingly describes her reaction to Updike's character as she encountered him in four novels over the span of three decades. Although a feminist, Roiphe finds much to admire in Updike's portrait of Harry Angstrom, whom she sees as a kind of American everyman. "Rabbit is an example of the twentieth-century contribution to the crawl of humankind toward whatever awaits us. Not to love him is not to love ourselves" (133). David Heddendorf ([2000] 2005), too, is intrigued by what he calls "a literary phenomenon that began life as a scandal and has achieved a kind of revered, grand-old-man status" (237). (Heddendorf might have made the same observation about Updike.) Heddendorf claims Updike's focus on sex, his interest in religious matters, and his determination to create a unique character arise from his belief that every person is an unrepeatable version of a self that at the same time shares much in common with the species. Hence, "to know and understand" what motivates

Harry is "to recognize ourselves in his disappointed faith, his alert and articulate pain" (242).

Concentrating on the women in the novels, Brenda Brown (2001) fills in what she says is a hitherto neglected aspect of the similarities between *Rabbit Is Rich* and Sinclair Lewis's *Babbitt*: parallels between the wives, who "represent the role of women in their respective societies" (55). Despite living at either end of the twentieth century, Brown says, these women are constrained by their societies and afforded little opportunity to develop individualized identities. In another study focused on gender issues, Kevin Goddard examines the construct of masculinity in *Rabbit, Run*. Goddard says Updike's novel offers a good case study of the way traditional concepts of masculinity were becoming undermined as gender roles shifted after the Second World War.

Textual studies of Updike's work are not common, although they may become more so as his manuscripts become available for study. However, their value can be seen in Donald Anderson's (2000) examination of textual variants in *Rabbit Redux*. Anderson speculates on why Updike decided to include in a 1996 revision of the novel a scene involving the Reverend Jack Eccles, who plays a prominent role in *Rabbit, Run* but does not appear in any other novel in the tetralogy. Anderson argues that Eccles' reappearance is used to "re-emphasize" Updike's vision of "the American paradox: that we torture ourselves to be what we are not" (335).

Updike's *Scarlet Letter* trilogy continued to attract significant attention as well. John McTavish (2000) revisits the theological dimension of Updike's fiction to show how Updike can be a "Christian novelist" without forcing "an explicitly Christian message onto the reader" (66). In a collection of essays designed to apply queer theory to constructs of heterosexuality, John Duvall (2000) offers a provocative reading of *A Month of Sundays* in which careful exploration of key passages reveals a decidedly unsure representation of heterosexuality, despite Updike's claims to the contrary. Concentrating his analysis on *Roger's Version*, Todd Billings (2003) shows how Updike "interweaves a diagnosis of contemporary American culture's 'loves' with theological reflection about the Incarnation" (203).

Several critics explored the influence of religion and philosophy on Updike in less well regarded novels. David Leigh (2002) argues that *Toward the End of Time* can be read as a fictional representation of "a theological treatise of the last things, namely, apocalypse and eschatology" (52). Leigh explains how Updike incorporates elements of apocalyptic writing to create his own ironic version of last days for both his narrator and American society. In "God and Pigment" Thomas Dicken (2004) argues that Updike's "strong nostalgic streak" is not an escapist mechanism, but rather a conscious strategy to help conserve meaning. Updike does not desire to "live in the past," but rather to "bring the value of the past with us" (73). That is one reason Updike is so enamored of visual art. Dicken says that *Seek My Face*, in which Updike "explores the work of artists as perhaps our closest approach to the Ultimate" (71), demonstrates that the permanence of art provides a bulwark against the transitory, which people experience so much in their everyday lives. In another philosophical inquiry, Thomas Engeman (2002) traces Updike's debt to existentialist philosophers Kierkegaard, Nietzsche, and Heidegger. Engeman demonstrates that, while Updike's novels "offer powerful reflections on the source of modern nihilism and its characteristic social manifestations," his "greatest interest" is in "Christianity's fate in modern and postmodern American society" (138).

Even Updike's memoir began to attract attention from academic critics, though not always for the same purposes. Mary Ann O'Farrell (2001) illustrates how Updike uses his medical condition, psoriasis, as a means of introducing a discussion of the more philosophic implications of the term "self consciousness." However, Jay Prosser (2001b) uses *Self-Consciousness* to construct a stinging critique of Updike's handling of racial issues in his fiction. While the memoir reveals Updike as supposedly self-aware about matters of race, Prosser believes his fiction continues to reflect his unconscious racism. The importance of skin—both its texture and its color—is the subject of another article by Prosser (2001a) in which he uses Updike's short story "Journal of a Leper" to "unpack the metaphorical valences of skin and superficiality, and the surface and interfaces between Updike's life and art, between autobiographical self and fictional other" (182). What Prosser discovers is a "substantive breach at the heart of Updike's *oeuvre*, a division between self and other" that Updike uses to "shape a white male self as American." Prosser argues that "at the core of Updike's stylization and apparent superficiality is a callousness toward the other" (191).

In part because of his psoriatic condition and his serious stutter Updike lived and worked away from the limelight. Nevertheless, over his lifetime he became a literary celebrity. Precisely how Updike achieved that status is discussed by Joe Moran in his book *Star Authors* (2000b) and in an article in *Auto/Biography Studies* (2000a). Moran argues that Updike played an active role in negotiating his own celebrity rather than having it thrust upon him (2000b, 10). Updike's desire to write and be read lies at the heart of his active pursuit of celebrity status. But Moran suggests that Updike's fame may not last. His penchant for writing almost exclusively about a small segment of American culture may ultimately cost him readership. Curiously, Moran also says that "Updike's star" has "descended within academia recently: as literary and cultural critics have sought to open up the canon to previously marginalized literary traditions, his work has been seen to focus too insistently on middle-aged, middle-class, white male angst" (84). One is prompted to wonder if Moran had looked at any annual bibliographies of literary criticism before he made this pronouncement.

Notes

[1] Similar charges of irrelevancy were leveled against Jane Austen by many early critics of her work. Only in recent decades, thanks to the work of cultural critics and new historians, is the influence of events like the Napoleonic Wars on her fiction being documented. To my knowledge, the affinities between Updike and Austen have not been explored in any detail, but it seems to me that—with the notable exception of their treatment of matters of sex—they have more in common than many have realized.

9: Facing the Unthinkable, Contemplating the Inevitable (2005–2008)

DURING WHAT WOULD TURN OUT to be the last years of his life, Updike continued the grueling pace he had set for himself, producing two collections of nonfiction and two novels: *The Widows of Eastwick*, a sequel to his controversial *Witches of Eastwick*, and *Terrorist*, a fictional portrayal of a Muslim extremist prompted by the events of September 11, 2001. The latter generated some of the most polarizing reviews ever written about his fiction. Despite the divergence of opinion expressed about these novels, however, the general acclaim for Updike's accomplishments tended to drown out—but not eliminate—criticism of individual books. While reviewers paid attention to these new publications, academics continued the winnowing process that was producing a clearer picture of what works will likely form the basis of Updike's lasting reputation.

Updike on Art, Part 2: *Still Looking*, 2005

Updike's second collection of essays devoted exclusively to art criticism appeared in 2005. The collection's title, *Still Looking*, intentionally recalls the first volume, *Just Looking*, and was similarly received. Sebastian Smee (2006) calls Updike "a model art critic" whose "gentlemanly tone" often disguises "sharp and unsentimental" judgments (47). Martin Gayford (2006) is delighted to see that "it is possible for a non-specialist to write about art with clarity, freshness of perception and, on occasion, damning, if urbanely expressed, judgment." Updike "wears his learning lightly, and takes his subject seriously," Gayford says. "There aren't many art critics around who can match that combination" (54). Serena Davies (2006) suggests that Updike's pose as "a gentleman-amateur reviewer" is actually a cover for his "considerable art-historical knowledge." Updike has the ability to "plumb the deepest motivations" of the artists he critiques, exploring the relationship between their work and "some of the fundamental artistic questions of the time"—in some instances, she says, "for the first time."

Terry Hartle (2005) judges the essays "uniformly thoughtful, focused, original, and provocative"—and best of all, "free of academic jargon and bias." While the "expert reader will not always agree with Updike's views," his essays encourage people "to look more closely and think harder about the artist and his place in art history" (15). Willibald Sauerländer (2006) also praises Updike for being "surprisingly well informed" about art while being able to avoid "the inflated jargon of professional art criticism and its theoretical capriciousness." As a result, "his essays on art give pleasure by the quality of his prose, whether one agrees with a specific judgment or not" (60). Sauerländer chastises the professional art world for its haughtiness, noting that "it is ironic that a great master of language" needs to remind curators, historians, and critics that a visit to a museum or to an art exhibition should be "a pleasure for the eye and not an hour of instruction and indoctrination" (64).

A number of professionals in the fields of art and art history agreed with Sauerländer. *Gallery & Studio* editor Ed McCormack (2006) believes Updike "writes more insightfully, not to mention with infinitely more grace, than most full-time critics" (10). His essays "harken back to the great tradition of belles lettres" practiced by Baudelaire, Flaubert, Apollinaire and others who wrote about art "before the territory was overrun by hordes of little clement greenbergs from the halls of academe" (the small caps on Greenberg's name are intentional). Early twentieth-century critics "brandished their degrees like bludgeons" and buried "lively discourse" under the "stupefying weight of their incomprehensible rhetoric," paving the way for "obscure postmodern theoreticians" who further "muddled the water." McCormack hopes that "future critics will take heart" from Updike's work "and make writing about art once again worth reading" (11). Similarly, writing in *Art Book*, Andrew Lambirth (2007) notes that, while the "fad for fiction writers" to "double" as "art critics" has tended to "make art literary," Updike's work does not function in that way. Instead, "he sees colour and form more as a painter does," and is often hesitant to press too hard for meaning in the images he observes (30).

However, British essayist and political commentator George Walden (2006) sounds a cautionary note. While it is "a relief to read a real writer" who chooses to write about art, one has to realize that Updike is "a patriot" who is "predisposed to think the best of American art" (51). Sometimes that leads to "perceptive judgments," but on other occasions Updike can be blinded to the accomplishments of European artists—or Americans like James McNeil Whistler who turned their back on the country.

Searching the Mind of the Other: *Terrorist*, 2006

In 2006 it would have been hard to imagine a more politically sensitive topic than the attack on the World Trade Center in New York City on September 11, 2001. Politicians, academics, artists, and everyday people around the world spoke and wrote of it incessantly, trying to make sense of the violence. While many looked for overarching ideological explanations, Updike turned his attention to the people affected by the tragedy. His first effort, the short story "Varieties of Religious Experience" which appeared in the November 2002 issue of *Atlantic*, examined the impact of the tragedy on several victims. In 2006 Updike narrowed his perspective and broadened his vision, publishing *Terrorist*, the story of a young man motivated to carry out acts of terrorism. The novel generated more commentary than any work since the publication of *Rabbit at Rest*. Nearly every review that praised Updike for creating an insightful portrait of a would-be jihadist was balanced by one that took exception to his stereotypical, ideologically motivated branding of Islam as a religion of violence.

Among those recommending the novel, George Hunt (2006) describes *Terrorist* as "a first" for Updike—a "contemporary thriller" and "a fine one" at that (23). Canadian writer Darryl Whetter (2006) also thinks Updike has done a superb job blending the conventions of the thriller into a "contentious novel" that is "equally attentive to the causes and effects of 9/11" (D5). The novel examines "the intersection of the personal with the political," making *Terrorist* "both psychologically and sociologically compelling" (D5). Gail Caldwell (2006) believes the novel gives Updike a chance to address once again questions of faith. In this "emotionally daring novel" he "applies his empathic powers" to provide "insight into the mind of a boy adrift in life who believes utterly in God," and who would do anything—to include committing violence—"in the name of religion" (E4). Tracy Simmons (2006) says that in this "bold literary effort to come to terms with the post 9/11 world" (50), Updike manages to make his young terrorist "a sympathetic subject" and deal with a faith that is "hopeless perverted." The result is a "horrific tale" that is "all the more dreadful for being plausible" (51).

John Leonard (2006) urges readers to be alert every time Updike "leaves his neighborhood" (71), because in works set outside his familiar haunts he stretches his imagination to make a larger point about the world. In *Terrorist*, Updike creates a believable protagonist in order to explore the implications of contemporary radicalism. Additionally, *Terrorist* must be read "as part of an accumulating literature in which serious novelists have tried to grope their way into the mind of the ultra"—a genre that includes works by Dostoevsky, Conrad, Malraux, and more recently Salman Rushdie. Updike's special contribution is to remind readers that "each fragile human being" is "an end, not a means" (72).

Such grandiose claims bother Adam Begley (2006). Updike's effort to get inside the head of the young terrorist may be laudable, but Begley says he mishandles the plot; "cloak-and-dagger" is not his strength (14). Mehammed Mack (2006) worries that Updike's attempt to enter "the mind of the young, angry, resentful Muslim"—an admittedly difficult task—may raise suspicions about Muslims in the larger community. Bill Duryea (2006) is more direct; he thinks Updike is simply "out of his element" in *Terrorist*, being perhaps the "least well suited" among notable novelists to portray a "person who would kill thousands of innocents." Although Updike tries mightily, bringing significant scholarly acumen to his task, the novel fails because he does not truly understand his protagonist. "For all the textual accuracy" of his portrait, "the book never achieves anything deeper than a rhetorical truth" (6P). Douglas Kennedy (2006) admits that Updike may be "one of those maddening polymaths who seems able to master quantum physics while simultaneously discoursing about American theological thought from the Massachusetts Bay Colony onwards"; nevertheless, the plot of *Terrorist* is "turgid" and the novel "a misjudged potboiler" (5). Doug Childers (2006) also believes *Terrorist* is "a miss." Despite its topical plot, Updike's focus on detail detracts from the pace of a novel intended as a thriller, and passages about the protagonist "read too often like jargon-based notes" (K3). Michiko Kakutani (2006) calls *Terrorist* "shopworn," its protagonist "completely unbelievable" and "cliché" (E1). Furthermore, Updike "manages to extract a fair amount of suspense" in this "maladroit" work only through "heavy reliance on unbelievable coincidences" (E8).

Yvonne Zipp (2006) has other concerns. While she applauds Updike for trying to help readers comprehend the idea of suicide bombers, she finds his characterization ham-handed and reliant on stereotypes. Zipp is certain that "American Muslims probably won't be lining up to shake Updike's hand" (17). Two who are not are Amitav Ghosh (2006) and Ibrahim Abusharif (2006). Despite Updike's attempts to "familiarize himself with Islam" (3), Ghosh says the novel offers no real insights into the way non-Americans think. It also fails to explain their values except in contrast to those of America, which is Updike's standard toward which he assumes all others should aspire. Abusharif questions Updike's motives for writing the book and challenges his knowledge of the Koran. Suggesting that Updike may be guilty of a literary form of ambulance-chasing, Abusharif describes the many ways *Terrorist* reveals Updike's ignorance of Muslim faith and traditions, and points out the dangers that such ignorance among westerners poses for the future of the world.

In his long review of *Terrorist*, Jonathan Raban (2006) suggests a different reason for the novel's failure to be convincing. The "burning-fuse plot," the novel's "credible hero," its "glowingly realized urban setting," and its "exhilarating narrative speed" can easily cause one to overlook its "deep, structural implausibilities." Unfortunately, in many respects the "painfully polite, self-conscious" and "intelligent" protagonist seems more akin to Updike than to radical Islamist militants (8), and he is never "exposed to the kind of intense political rage that has spurred terrorist attacks in the real world" (10). Almost apologetically, Raban says that, despite doing "so many things so well" and being "temporarily enthralling," Updike does not "imaginatively comprehend the roots and character of Islamist jihad against the West." As a result, *Terrorist* is "ultimately" an "empty, shaggy dog story" (11).

Jonathan Shainin (2006) also has serious problems with Updike's approach to terrorism. That Updike should view it "through the lens of religion" is not surprising, Shainin says, since faith has always interested him more than politics. Although Updike has done his homework to insure that Islam is represented appropriately, the protagonist is "infected with Updike's renowned mildness," and his attitude toward religion is more akin to his creator's than to jihadists'. "What convulses Ahmad," Shainin says, "is not the power of his faith but his fear of losing it" (29). Shainin concludes with a hint of disdain: "If only all our terrorists were so harmless" (30). In a more balanced review, Robert Stone (2006) argues that "in now old-fashioned sociopolitical terms," Updike's body of work can be described as an examination of "our struggle to maintain a viable center for our inner life while enduring the most revolutionary force in history—American capitalism." Stone finds one of the most interesting aspects of *Terrorist* Updike's juxtaposition of "imagined views about the way this country is and the way it appears." The novel describes the "moral exhaustion and reprobation" of America even as it suggests that its protagonist's solution for the country's ills is misguided (1). What *Terrorist* does best, Stone says, is "remind us that no amount of special pleading can set us free from history" (8).

Like Stone, Mark Steyn (2006) looks for deeper causes to explain his discontent with *Terrorist* but comes to a more demoralizing conclusion about its merits. Admitting that many writers have had difficulties in confronting the horrors of 9/11, Steyn nevertheless finds that Updike has "gone awry from the very first word." His protagonist is "little more than an Updike-esque aesthetic distaste for contemporary America filtered through some rather unconvincing Koranic prissiness." Worse, Updike "impos[es] the default literary voice of English letters—amused irony—on a world in which it is largely absent and, in its rare occurrences, life-threatening." In its "artifice of self-delusion" the book is "enough to make one despair of the novelist's art." *Terrorist* is "one of the most numbingly inadequate attempts to engage a major subject I've ever read." Similarly, Christopher Hitchens (2006), does not find *Terrorist* particularly convincing as fiction or compelling as an attempt to come to grips with the problem of terrorism. Claiming that the novel so repelled him that he "sent *Terrorist* windmilling across the room in a spasm of boredom and annoyance," Hitchens thinks "Updike has produced one of the worst pieces of writing from any grown-up source since the events he has so unwisely tried to draw upon" (117).

Terrorist prompted another attack on Updike by James Wood (2006), who suggests Updike "should have run a thousand miles away" from his subject—"as soon as he saw the results on the page." Wood asks rhetorically (and a bit snidely), "Does Updike reread his own prose?" In *Terrorist* Updike proves himself "relatively inept at the essential task of free indirect style, or trying to find an authorial voice for his Muslin schoolboy" (25). Ahmad is simply "Updike's serf," a "stiff stereotype" spouting the ideas his creator wants to propagate about the nature of terrorists and Islamic fundamentalism. The book is really about the nature of belief, Wood suggests, "a sort of Islamicized re-writing of *Roger's Version*, a much better Updike novel" (27). But even when Updike writes about religious matters, Wood says, he is disingenuous. Though "acclaimed as an unfashionably Christian novelist," he is more like "a pagan celebrant . . . than a religious explorer." He avoids dealing with the really tough issues surrounding the nature of faith, and instead uses his considerable aesthetic talents to "thank God for his creation by attending carefully to all its surfaces." But when tasked with coming to grips with "the otherness of Islamicism," he exposes his shortcomings (30).

Another caustic attack against Updike was launched by David Walsh (2006), who calls *Terrorist* a "poorly conceived and unconvincingly written" book with an "unlikely" protagonist whose transformation into a terrorist "fails every test." Using this novel as a touchstone for examining Updike's political attitudes and preconceptions, Walsh asserts that Updike conveniently separates his protagonist's actions "from any questions of US policies in the Middle East," ignoring (as "various right-wing pundits" do) the "predatory US foreign policy" that lies at the heart of the "rage felt in the Arab and Muslim world for the real machinations of imperialism." The novel also exposes Updike's "inability to come to terms in a profound manner with contemporary American social reality." While he describes in graphic detail the impoverished communities of northern New Jersey, he exhibits "disgust" for these people, holding them responsible for their own misery. Furthermore, his obsession with religion reveals another weakness, since interest in matters of faith merely highlights the regressive nature of post-war American society. In dealing with religious matters, Updike has exposed his provincialism and shrunk his scope of interest to people who think like him. Although Walsh offers some grudging admiration for the Rabbit novels, he concludes that Updike's career is an example of "a certain cultural process in concentrated form: the accumulation of great formal, technical skill at one pole, and the severe weakening of the artist's understanding of history and social organization at the other."

Given Walsh's critique of Updike's understanding of the forces of history, one of the more curious reviews of *Terrorist* is Warner Huston's (2006) in the *Conservative Voice*. While liberals had for years been bashing Updike for his conservative positions on matters such as the Vietnam war and American patriotism in general, Huston writes with disdain about Updike's inability to understand the seriousness of the threat to America posed by the rise of Islamic fundamentalism. *Terrorist* is simply Updike's attempt to capitalize on the public's fascination with terrorism. Furthermore, the novel demonstrates definitively that Updike is "past his prime." Huston says "the world"—at least the world outside the circle of liberals to which Huston says Updike belongs—"has passed by his internalized disdain for Christianity" and is concerned about more pressing matters. But Updike and his fans live in a fantasy world, incapable of "seeing the abyss they are pushing us ever faster towards" by their denial of the reality of the threat America faces.

It seems appropriate to conclude with a thought-provoking defense of Updike against his critics. Canadian journalist Robert Fulford (2006) admits *Terrorist* has its faults, mostly technical, but believes critics' problems with the novel may stem more from their own prejudices than from Updike's handling of the story. Fulford says "serious readers" seem to have "developed a sense of possession about 9/11" and are hesitant to let anyone spoil their preconceived ideas about what has become for them almost "sacred space" (A16). If critics like Kakutani and Hitchens are put off by Updike's portrait of a terrorist, it may be that Ahmad's simplicity and shallowness do not square with their idea of the exalted extremist ideology that must (for them) lie at the base of such abominable behavior.

Clearing the Shelves: *Due Considerations*, 2007

Updike stepped back from the political sphere after publishing *Terrorist*, collecting previously published essays and reviews for his next publication. Like its predecessors, *Due Considerations* generated a number of appreciative reviews while prompting only a handful of negative ones. The volume shows that Updike is "as good with nonfiction as he is with the made-up stuff," says John Barron (2007, B11). James Marcus (2007) finds Updike's criticism "refreshingly free of dogma." His "insatiable curiosity" leads him to find something of interest in a wide variety of books and make them appealing to those who read his reviews. In a more discriminating critique, David Heddendorf (2009a) says Updike's "essays and criticism express the nuanced sensibility that has distinguished a long career of book reviews and art commentary"; but they can easily give way to "the vulnerable musings of the average American" (xliii).

Surprisingly, Christopher Hitchens (2007), who savaged *Terrorist*, admires the "breathtaking" scope of Updike's critical acumen and his ability to remain aloof from the back-and-forth among thoughtful critics and the "dunces and frauds" that dominate American culture. On the other hand, Hitchens is not happy with Updike's constant insistence on being even-handed with everyone about everything. At some point, he says, Updike's "fair-mindedness" threatens to "decline into something completely passive, neutral and inert" (1). Victoria Brownworth (2007) also expresses annoyance that Updike rarely becomes exercised over any subject. Yet, despite misgivings about the "acutely clinical" nature of his nonfiction, Brownworth considers *Due Considerations* "a graduate course in everything from the art of language to the art of poker," a "small facet of glinting genius that cannot be ignored" (4F).

Lionesses in Winter: *The Widows of Eastwick*, 2008

In the last novel published during his lifetime, Updike returned to characters that had brought him a good deal of pleasure and considerable notoriety more than two decades earlier. *The Widows of Eastwick* (2008) continues the story of the three women first introduced in *The Witches of Eastwick* (1984), Updike's bawdy tale of female liberation. Older and presumably wiser now, the three women, all widowed, reunite to try to rekindle the spirit of sisterhood that had energized them years before. Unfortunately, both the characters and their author seem to have suffered something of a deceleration in the intervening years, and only a handful of reviewers celebrated the novel, while a greater number pointed out its deficiencies.

Among the few offering almost unqualified praise is Kai Maristed (2008), who thinks *The Widows of Eastwick* "offers more hard truths than escape." The central question is not whether good will triumph over evil, but "is there a meaningful difference?" Sam Tanenhaus (2008) enjoys this novel of "female empowerment" in which Updike "makes good sport" of "pseudofeminist cant" while at the same time evoking great sympathy for his female protagonists. However, where *The Witches of Eastwick* is a jaunty comedy "of the blackest sort," the sequel is "relaxed and contemplative," as Updike shows the witches trying to make amends for past sins. Caroline Moore (2008) finds that the novel's theme about "failing powers and the terror of death" is reflected in "a slackening of Updike's writing, particularly in the first half." Alison Lurie (2009) also is not pleased with the first part of *The Widows of Eastwick*, but she urges readers to persevere to the end, even though they are likely to find *Widows* "a sadder and more low-key novel than its predecessor."

Providing fewer excuses for the novel, Michiko Kakutani (2008) considers *The Widows of Eastwick* "deeply flawed" but "less tendentious" and "more emotionally credible" than its predecessor, which was in her view "a misogynist morality tale." Kakutani even has a few words of praise for Updike's handling of character, noting that when he "sets aside the magical mumbo jumbo and his petulant remarks about the witches' decaying bodies" he manages to present "compelling" portraits of "ordinary women, haunted by the sins of their youth, frightened of the looming prospect of the grave and trying their best to get by, day by day by day" (C1). However, Emily Nussbaum (2008) argues that, where *The Witches of Eastwick* was "a dazzling jolt of black comedy," the sequel feels "stuck, slack." The earlier novel is an accomplishment of sorts, because it is Updike's most successful attempt to "delve deeply into female psychology." By contrast, in *The Widows* he seems to have only "contempt" for his female characters. Similarly, Sarah Churchwell (2008) judges *The Widows of Eastwick* decidedly inferior to its predecessor, with which she has problems as well. In the 1984 novel, Updike's constant denigration of women is "offset by his cheerful lampooning of the male characters." Where that novel "was enriched" by the "ambiguity" of Updike's inability to decide if his witches are good or evil, the sequel has no such redeeming quality. "It is not only that Updike's plotting" has "stalled"; so has his "gender politics." In *The Widows of Eastwick* "female power" is simply "bad." Throughout the novel Updike "follows the standard pornographic tactic or projecting male self-regard on to female desire." Churchill concludes, with a barbed critique of the author, "it isn't only the witches who have lost their magic touch."

Women were not the only ones disappointed with *The Widows of Eastwick*. John Keenan (2008) says he "struggled" to make his way through "this tepid follow-up" to *The Witches of Eastwick*. The greatest problem is that the novel's characters are anachronistic—as is its author. Updike is unable to communicate effectively with the present generation and must content himself with writing "cosy remembrances of things past." Matt Thorne (2008) also finds *The Widows of Eastwick* a disappointing sequel to a book he describes as Updike's "only novel to have made a significant and lasting impact on popular culture." That "dark and unusual book" has "an occult power completely in keeping with its subject,"; it is "ebullient and exciting." By contrast, *Widows* is "portentous and dull," Updike's "very worst," an "unnecessary sequel which betrays an upsetting diminution of his once-formidable talents."

In the same month that Updike died, James Wolcott (2009) published a lengthy assessment of Updike's career as part of a review of *The Widows of Eastwick*. Calling Updike the literary descendent of Nabokov, Cheever, and Salinger, Wolcott believes the "newer generation of detractors" who have "reserved him a room at the retirement home" and the younger novelists who have "voiced disgruntlement" with him and his generation may be justified in some of their criticisms. Nevertheless, *The Widows of Eastwick* demonstrates that Updike is still the premier chronicler of America: "novelist, historian, social critic, civics teacher, randy theologian, anthropologist, dermatologist, photorealist illuminator"—a kind of "caretaker/pallbearer of the *New Yorker* tradition of scrupulous observation salted with a proper measure of irony, acerbity, dismay and regret, depending on the circumstance or site under inspection" (10).

Academic Criticism, 2005–2008

Whereas William Pritchard's *Updike: America's Man of Letters* (2000) provides an introduction to Updike's literary interests through a chronological assessment of individual works, Stacey Olster's collection of remarkably sophisticated essays, *The Cambridge Companion to John Updike* (2006), performs that task from a thematic perspective. Olster says the twelve contributions "foreground" the element of "evolution" (9) in the work of a major author whose career shows a pattern of development and experimentation often missed by those who think they know his work from reading a few novels or stories. These convictions naturally come through in essays like D. Quentin Miller's on Updike's realism and Donald Greiner's on Updike's exploration of the myth of American exceptionalism in the Rabbit novels. But they are equally discernible in Kathleen Verduin's essay on Updike's treatment of women and sexuality and Jay Prosser's analysis of Updike's writing on race and postcolonialism. Perhaps the most telling comment about Updike's versatility and keen sense of the state of affairs in fiction is offered by John Duvall in the concluding essay: "One almost wonders," Duvall speculates, if some of the fiction Updike published since the mid-1970s had "appeared under some other name," it might have been "hailed as postmodern"—not because Updike was definitively a postmodernist (he is too complex to be pigeonholed) but most notably because his "interrogation of the possibilities of faith," a subject dear to his heart throughout his career, suggests that he "stands much closer to postmodern conceptions of narrative, writing, and identity than has previously been suspected" (176).

Several intriguing essays published between 2005 and 2008 illustrate how the passage of time can affect critical judgments about individual works. One can see that phenomenon in the essays included in James Schiff's *Updike in Cincinnati* (2007), which is of interest as well to those who want to know Updike's views of his own work. Brief comments by William Pritchard and Donald Greiner on some of Updike's fiction reflect an awareness and appreciation of the writer's development over his career. A more striking example of how (to borrow a phrase from Updike's *Midpoint*) "distance improves vision" is John Parks's (2005) article on *Toward the End of Time*. Parks argues that the novel displays "the problematics" of the "will to faith in America since the Second World War." It reflects "Updike's career-long concerns: the possibilities of faith in a totally secular and materialistic world, the possibility of transcendence in a world sunk in its immanence, the consolations of love and nature" (151). Parks says the novel asks "what, if anything, lasts?" and provides the sobering answer that nothing does (152). Furthermore, it reveals that "the old covenant, the faith of the Bible and the church through the ages, is not viable in our scientific and enlightened age" (154). Ben Turnbull's continuous "yearning for the imperishable" dramatizes a "challenge to the Christian faith to rethink its outmoded cosmology" (157).

Another example of creative re-reading is Elisabeth Jay's (2005) commentary on *A Month of Sundays*, which comes to some decidedly unflattering conclusions about Updike's ideology. Jay's feminist critique shows how Updike makes readers feel comfortable with this attack on women unmitigated by any hints that the attitudes of the misogynistic protagonist might be wrong. Jay challenges several earlier readings as incomplete and evasive. Instead, she says contemporary readers, armed with the tools of new theories of reading, need not succumb to the temptation to become the "ideal readers" that Updike wants them to be. Fortunately, "the challenge presented by critical theory to monolithic institutions and totalizing narratives has provided us with the resources to provide reasons for the real dislike many women readers have experienced for this novel" (354).

A third example of essays that can materially alter perceptions of Updike's fiction is D. Quentin Miller's "Deeper Blues, or the Posthuman Prometheus" (2005). Miller's thoughtful and at times provocative analysis of the representation of computers in contemporary literature demonstrates how Updike deals with the "Frankensteinian implications of the machine that has ushered in what we have optimistically deemed the information age." But Miller asserts that Updike also "entertain[s] the possibility that computers can help humans understand some of our most perplexing problems" (381). His careful analysis of *Roger's Version* reveals Updike's genuine fascination with the possibilities that computers and artificial intelligence may offer to humankind if they are used properly.

Despite thirty years of revisionist reading prompted by critical theory, conventional readings of Updike's fiction remained a mainstay of the critical enterprise. Three can serve as representative of this trend. First, in "The Satanic Personality in Updike's *Roger's Version*," a reading influenced by the moralist tradition in critical analysis, Frank Novak (2005) lays out a careful (if at times tendentious) argument that Roger Lambert is "a fictional version of the satanic principle, a portrait of evil." The novel allows Updike to explore "the themes of transgression and guilt, truth and concealment, love and hatred" (4). Novak is convinced that, despite other critics' arguments that Roger is redeemed at the end of the novel, the protagonist remains throughout "insidiously, irredeemably evil" (9). If one reads the novel carefully, one can see that "Updike vividly evokes the satanic disposition and condemns it" (20). Because Lambert "demonstrates the emptiness and the horror of a life devoid of love and faith," Novak concludes, "*Roger's Version* is a profoundly moral and thoroughly Christian novel" (24).

Second, Sukhbir Singh's "Rewriting the American Wasteland" (2005) demonstrates that comparative analysis still proves a useful tool for interpretation. Singh shows that Updike's overtly mythic novel *The Centaur* also contains "striking parallels" to T. S. Eliot's *The Waste Land*, suggesting that *The Centaur* is Updike's attempt to seek "similar solutions to the current human predicament as Eliot's poem" (60).

Third, in a carefully constructed comparative analysis of Updike's Rabbit novels and Stephen Crane's "The Open Boat," Kelly Clasen (2008) extends arguments made by Victor Lasseter in 1989 that the Rabbit novels owe much to the naturalist tradition in American literature. They share a circular structure, a hero who senses his entrapment in an unconcerned universe, and a yearning for some sense of transcendence that remains unfulfilled. Perhaps most importantly, Clasen notes that "like the naturalistic hero of the 1890s, Harry [Angstrom] possesses a mediocrity and ambiguity that does not diminish his importance for us" (145).

As Clasen's essay illustrates, interest in the Rabbit novels remained undiminished. A notable contribution to our understanding of those works appeared in 2005, Jack De Bellis's *John Updike: The Critical Responses to the 'Rabbit' Saga*, the third and by far the most comprehensive collection of essays on the novels. De Bellis's introduction provides a snapshot of major themes that run through the series. His most important task, however, is to demonstrate that Rabbit is worthy of a place beside such memorable figures as Huckleberry Finn and Jay Gatsby in the pantheon of iconic American characters. The thirty-four essays and reviews in the collection give evidence of the continuing interest in Updike's development of Harry Angstrom's story and offer some idea of the varying critical perspectives employed in examining the four novels. The one original essay in De Bellis's volume, Irina Negrea's "'He. She. Sleeps'" (2005), on *Rabbit Redux*, focuses on the way the shift from print to other forms of media is emblematic of Rabbit's problem in adapting to a world that is becoming increasingly unfamiliar to him. Reliant on theories of culture developed by Marshall McLuhan and Jean Baudrillard, Negrea's essay illustrates how interdisciplinary study offers fresh insight into Updike's fiction.

Another thought-provoking analysis of the Rabbit novels is Brian Keener's *John Updike's Human Comedy* (2005). This study of the novels' comic dimensions helps flesh out the critical portrait of Updike, whom Keener says has been regarded for too long "primarily as a writer of high seriousness," interested principally in exploring "theological and philosophical" topics (1). While Keener acknowledges the presence of theological musings in Updike's work, he is more interested in answering the question, "Why would a writer as artful as Updike include so much comedy if it were not significant?" (7). Keener shows how, at least in these five novels, appreciating the comedy is essential to understanding Updike's answer to the question, What is a good person? The answer, Keener says, is: one who "lives a comic morality" (138).

A number of individual essays also expanded understanding of this important series. In "Updike's Golden Oldies," Judie Newman (2005) offers a postmodernist reading of the novels as spectacles. Relying on the work of Foucault, Debord, and others, Newman explains how cinematic technique and other elements of spectacle help shape the novels and illuminate Updike's indictment of modern society while highlighting his plea for human relationships based on love, not gratification. Employing the more traditional methodology of sociological criticism, in "Never the Right Food" Richard Androne (2008) demonstrates that paying special attention to references to food in the Rabbit novels allows one to gain a deeper appreciation of Updike's social commentary. Androne illustrates how "Rabbit's diet assumes the significance of cultural judgment" (330). Furthermore, Updike is following (perhaps unconsciously) a long tradition in literature that can be traced back at least as far as the *Iliad*. There the heroic feast becomes a symbol of community; in Updike's fiction, however, readers see only glimpses of community in a society where food is seldom quite right.

Although it may be too early to make predictions about the direction of Updike criticism for the coming two or three decades, the appearance of Peter J. Bailey's *Rabbit (Un)Redeemed* (2006) certainly marks a watershed—perhaps a turning point—in assessments of the religious dimensions of his fiction. No stranger to the circle of Updike's critics, Bailey had previously published essays on *The Centaur* (Bailey 1981) and *Self-Consciousness* (Bailey 1991). In *Rabbit (Un)Redeemed* he provides a systematic critique of Updike's fiction, informed but not overwhelmed by postmodernist theory, in which he posits that the central tension of Updike's best fiction stems from "egoistic impulses encountering, converging with, and often contending with religious belief" (20). Updike's Rabbit novels, as well as the revealing memoir *Self-Consciousness* and stories in the volume *The Afterlife and Other Stories*, are "compelling," Bailey says, because "their characters' preoccupations with personal oblivion oblige Updike to challenge his own assumptions about the at-one-ness of self and spirit and to place at risk his own Christian beliefs" (22).

Bailey's careful reading exposes what he calls "the reluctantly expanding secularism of Updike's aesthetic" (33). The loss of certainty leads to a feeling of terror—mirrored nicely in Rabbit Angstrom's name—inspired by the possibility that the universe has no creator. And because Updike shares Rabbit's fears, "the Rabbit tetralogy constitutes Updike's most significant literary configuring of that spiritual anxiety" (35). While not pushing for an autobiographical reading of the fiction, Bailey argues that in certain novels Updike is projecting his own sensibilities onto the characters he creates. Recognizing this fact, one discovers that, far from being consistent in affirming the presence of God and the hope of salvation, the arc of Updike's career actually points toward a gradual loss of faith. This radical notion turns on its head earlier readings of Updike's work—not only the strident exegeses of the Hamiltons, but many more recent critical commentaries as well. But only at this time, when Updike's career was drawing to a close, could a perceptive critic like Bailey see how a professedly Christian writer gradually begins to question the very idea of faith. After Bailey, it will prove difficult to sustain a critical reading of Updike that clings to the notion that his fiction is both optimistic and Christian in outlook.

It seems not too bold for me to conclude at this point that underlying many negative critiques of Updike's work is a distaste for two qualities that he exhibited consistently: his apparent refusal to take sides when writing about issues of morality, and a genuine humility about his gifts as a writer. Two essays written just before Updike died tackle these problems head-on. In "John Updike and the Waning of Mainline Protestantism" (2008), Stephen Webb argues that Updike's tendency to suspend judgment in moral issues is a result of the influence of a longstanding theological tradition that can be traced back to St. Augustine. The early Christian writer argues in his work that people choose to do evil not for evil's sake, but because they mistake it for good, making judgment difficult and perhaps even inappropriate. In "The Modesty of John Updike" (2008), David Heddendorf notes that, while many of Updike's critics describe him as smug, to sympathetic readers "one of the striking aspects of Updike's prose is its uninsistent, damped-down quality even when at its most dazzling" (108). For Updike, "writing is a humble act, the acceptance and use of a gift" (109). Unfortunately, even when Updike admits his own shortcomings and behaves modestly, some critics think he is simply acting. Heddendorf demonstrates how Updike's work displays the real modesty beneath his considerable talents.

Finally, in an article on the website of the National Association of Scholars, Peter Wood (2008), then the organization's executive director, speculates on Updike's place in the undergraduate curriculum. Wood believes "Updike is one of a handful of contemporary American writers whose work may be of lasting significance." Though not always easy to read, his novels "generally repay the effort it takes to read them." Furthermore, Updike is witty and ironic, "but never harshly so." His "mischievous good humor" and his "abiding intelligence make him a writer that civilized people should read." Still, Wood says, Updike's works are not likely to find their way into most course syllabi. No curriculum that "upholds some sense of sexual decorum" could possibly include most of his best work. And so the controversy continues.

10: Final Volumes, Fresh Assessments (2009–)

JOHN UPDIKE DIED on January 27, 2009. Before succumbing to lung cancer, he had been moved to a hospice in Danvers, Massachusetts, just a few miles from his home. While details of these last months may be made available in Adam Begley's forthcoming biography (Neyfakh 2009), what is remarkable for the purposes of this study is that, despite being terminally ill, Updike apparently continued to write. Within months after he died, Knopf issued a new collection of his short stories and a new volume of poetry. Two years later, editor Christopher Carduff assembled what is likely to be a final collection of his nonfiction.

Updike left behind a considerable archive of manuscripts, now at Harvard, among them two early unpublished novels (Tanenhaus 2010). However, unless some manuscript materials lurking among his papers turn out to be gems in the rough, it is likely that the Updike canon is complete. Hence, critical commentary on him is set to enter a new phase: assessments that for the first time can take into account the total body of his work. The initial direction those assessments are likely to take may be inferred from the tributes that poured forth after his death, and from some of the critical commentary that has appeared in the two years after Updike died.

A Sampling of Obituary Tributes

While not impossible, it is exceedingly difficult to find a truly negative commentary among the hundreds of obituary notices published during the months after Updike died. Obituary notices described him as America's pre-eminent man of letters whose talents as a comic writer and satirist are "not nearly enough appreciated" (Pritchard 2009), "our happy Proust, infinitely observant but not self-indulgently tortured" (Webb 2009), and "an American Balzac" (Mills 2009). Michael Dirda (2009) observes that the "metaphorical thickness" of his prose "quietly invests even the everyday with a kind of surreal strangeness" (B99). Marjorie Kehe (2009) says that, though Updike was often categorized as the "chronicler of suburban adultery," he should more appropriately be considered "an interpreter of the way that the tender and the tortured intertwine in domestic relationships." Though there are "glimpses of the transcendent" in his writings, the sublime is frequently "mingled with sadness that things and people are never quite as splendid as they should be."

New Yorker editor Roger Angell (2009) writes fondly of his long relationship with Updike, noting how Updike's writing is always "light and springy," his sentences "fresh painted," his tone "unforced." In all his writings he demonstrates he is "a fabulous noticer and expander." Using a contemporary comparison to express his admiration for these qualities, Angell says Updike "invented HD" (38). Writing in the *New Yorker*, Adam Gopnik (2009) acknowledges that it was the "great good fortune" of the magazine that Updike needed it—or indulged it. Updike's "reviews alone would have been enough to make a major career." His stories "provided a lyric, etched picture of a half century's domestic manners and longings." His novels cumulatively take on "the full weight of American social history, doing the classic job of the nineteenth-century novel as though no one had ever said you couldn't any longer" (35). Updike's religious faith and his patriotism may have "separated him from other writers of his time," but these were essential in shaping his central theme, "the American attempt to fill the gap left by faith with the materials produced by mass culture" (36). Gopnik compares Updike favorably with Sinclair Lewis, Edmund Wilson, Henry James, Proust, Nabokov, Austen, and Shakespeare. One could hardly ask for better company.

Pastor Jeffrey Johnson's (2009) tribute in *Christian Century* celebrates Updike as a man of faith, although Johnson admits many conservative Christians found the "sexually explicit content" of his work "vulgar or immoral" (12). John Buchanan (2009) notes that Updike was not always welcome among Christians, but in the end must be judged "one of the literary giants of our time" (3). Even a writer like Jonathan Gharraie (2009), who does not share Updike's commitment to faith, praises his "insatiable curiosity" that was "undiminished by caution or fear or the suspicion that the next generation was intent on robbing his own of its dignity and achievements." People who disagree with Updike's belief in "an everlasting self" can still believe that "his body of work is imperishable."

Sam Anderson (2009) believes Updike owes his success to a fusion of "two artistic virtues that rarely meet in the same person: a frisky, easy, improvisational energy and a rigorous workaday discipline." He had "the prose equivalent of a perfect baseball swing" (perhaps intended as an allusion to Updike's favorite baseball player, Ted Williams) that allowed him to write sentences "as funny, as stylistically bulletproof, and as present as any sentences have ever been." He did suffer from the "weakness of belletrism"—his work "tends to be apolitical, detached, comfortably rooted in its own exquisite self-consciousness." However, in a long personal reflection on Updike's achievement, Rand Richards Cooper (2009) argues that Updike was often "underappreciated" because many critics "resented the politics of a Johnson Democrat who abstained from Vietnam protest" (20).

Praise for Updike came from unlikely contributors, none more so than the polemic critic and disciple of atheism Christopher Hitchens (2009). Disappointed that "most of the celebrations and elegies" for Updike "were abysmally bland," Hitchens suggests that Updike was more complicated than most people realized. He was "a man of wry and reserved delicacy and elegance who would prefer very slightly to be wrong on account of the right reservations than right because of the wrong ones." A tribute appeared in, of all places, *BMJ: British Medical Journal*, where John Quin (2009) claims Updike was, "by some distance the most prodigiously gifted and prolific of contemporary American literary masters." His "metaphorical gifts were exceptional, and his observational skills led to conclusions" so "persistently correct" that his works were like "diagnostic procedure[s]" (242). In a playful eulogy, *Sports Illustrated* staff writer Stephen Cannella (2009) pokes fun at Updike's minimal golfing skills while celebrating his exceptional ability to capture the excitement and significance of sports in American life. *Beijing Review* contributor Zan Jifang (2009) reports that Updike "is deeply mourned" by Chinese readers, who discovered in the Rabbit novels "a window to American society" that "helped Chinese people know the true face of the lives and thinking of the American middle class." Zan includes in his article remarks by the Deputy Director of the Institute of Foreign Literature at the Chinese Academy of Social Sciences, who celebrates Updike as a "low-pitched writer" who "never expressed his political ideas or produced other stunts to attract the attention of others." Apparently Updike's fiction passed the Chinese Communist government's litmus test for appropriate social realism.

One of the most clever tributes—and certainly one that would likely have elicited a wry smile from Updike himself—appeared the day after his death on the website of the Seattle University *Spectator*. "World of Warcraft Mourns Updike's Death with Lunar Festival" (2009) is a lighthearted spoof suggesting that Blizzard Entertainment would commemorate Updike's death by inaugurating a "series of quest chains designed to immerse players deep within Updike's oft-used setting of middle class, small town banality." The new quests will allow warriors in the popular fantasy game to "experience adventure in a more subtle and complex way—through the acute and graceful interpretation of small shifts of affect"—before engaging in a fight against a new gang headed up by Running Rabbit the Vile Incarcerator.

A small number of commentators managed to express minor reservations. For example, Claire Messud (2009) observes that, while few writers "have so incisive an awareness, so frank and unsparing an eye, as did John Updike," many of his best works seem dated, largely because he could not "escape being a man of his time" (66). Anna Shapiro (2009) takes the occasion to restate the feminists' position that Updike was a misogynist whose portraits of females make women readers feel "like being splayed open on the examining table under the glare of medical lamps while satirical remarks were made." Worse still are Updike's portraits of men like Rabbit, who, despite abominable behavior, come off as "justified." That, Shapiro says, "is precisely what is unpalatable for female readers."

In another protest against the panegyrics to Updike's abilities, David Walsh (2009) asks pointedly whether Updike was really a great novelist—and answers "no." Although Updike consistently demonstrated "a great ability to transform intricate human behavior and details of social life and nature into language," Walsh argues that "a writer is not simply the sum total of his literary gifts." He must also have "in some fashion or other, 'great' things to say" and "some sharper, distinctive insight" into his times. Walsh believes Updike was too limited by his bourgeois upbringing; his "small-town, Protestant, lower middle class, rather smug background" and his "psychological predisposition made him vulnerable to prevailing orthodoxies." Updike is certainly worth reading, Walsh concludes, as long as one remembers that he has a tendency to "bend the truth" and "avoid certain realities," especially ones that expose America's real failings as a nation.

Final Volumes:
My Father's Tears and *Endpoint,* 2009

Obituary tributes were still being published when the last two volumes Updike prepared for publication were released by Knopf in March (*Endpoint and Other Poems*) and June (*My Father's Tears, and Other Stories*) of 2009. Almost immediately, reviewers recognized that Updike knew these books would be the last, or among the last, to appear during his lifetime. Both the poems and stories express an air of finality, a sense that the writer is dealing with matters of dying and death, including his own. Few reviewers had the temerity to criticize them too harshly. A notable exception is Martin Amis (2009), who thinks the stories show that Updike, "perhaps the greatest virtuoso stylist since Nabokov," was "in the process of losing his ear" (6). Amis believes the book may be Updike's "least distinguished" (6).

More typical are comments like those of Collette Bancroft (2009), who considers *My Father's Tears* "a moving, lovely coda" to Updike's career, because in it he turns his "lapidary eye" on the subject of death, offering extraordinary insights into the end of life. Simon Baker (2009) says Updike's final book of short stories is a fitting tribute to a writer who "continued to strive for freshness of expression after more than half a century of work." Baker says that "when Updike gets it right" the reader is "left with the sense of having encountered modern American fiction in its near-perfect state" (21). Reviewing *Endpoint*, Clive James (2009) says that Updike's tendency to belittle his skills as a poet has obscured the true value of his verse. The poems in *Endpoint* prove that Updike could have "reported the nation" through verse rather than fiction had he chosen to do so. J. P. Harrington (2011) also finds the poems in *Endpoint* a fitting finale to Updike's career. This is "a brilliant and incisive collection of heart-wrenching poems" which warns readers "that death and pain approach us."

In a joint critique of *Endpoint* and *My Father's Tears*, John McTavish (2010) calls the poems "elegant, thoughtful, and blessedly lucid," and suggests the stories are reminders of "how much there is to mourn" with Updike's death (524). Michiko Kakutani (2009) holds back from some of her usual caviling comments and instead says that Updike "writes in these stories and poems with the quiet assurance of someone in complete control of his craft" (C1). Giles Harvey (2009) suggests that, while "death, by and large, tends to be good to writers, and for them," one need not wax nostalgic about these stories and poems. They are, he admits, "a winding down, a farewell tour, with Updike revisiting for one last time the familiar haunts of his imagination." The tendency toward self-parody is ever-present, but only on occasion does Updike slip into sentimental nostalgia. On the whole, these last collections serve as a reminder that "inside the folksy, down-home Updike was always a meaner, angrier, more dangerous animal trying to escape"—and who did escape in the Rabbit novels, his finest literary productions, which reveal "slow-burning acrimony, resentment," and above all, "dread" (19).

In a lengthy combined retrospective review, Kevin Stevens (2009) suggests that Updike's short stories seem stronger than his novels—perhaps because they "take fewer formal risks" (000). Updike had uncanny ability to filter "the same phases of his life" through "his aesthetic consciousness" and constantly discover "fresh insights." No matter what he chose as his subject, "Updike was ever a brilliant observer who found just the right particulars (and then some) to convey the heft and shimmer of the materials world." In *My Father's Tears* these details "have been endowed with another stratum of feeling, a sense of physical accumulation that mocks the diminished time and capacity of the sentient, fading animal trying to make sense of them." Greg Johnson (2010) says *My Father's Tears* proves that, even in his advancing years, Updike did not lose the ability to "write masterful stories" (159). This collection is "a lovely and profound summation of this indispensable author's extraordinary career" (161). Julian Barnes (2009a) says these last two collections remind readers why Updike deserves the praise he is receiving now that he is gone. It is unfortunate, Barnes says, that Updike never won the Nobel Prize.

Valedictory Assessments

Because Updike's death prompted a number of general assessments of his career, it seems worthwhile to cite several that suggest how he may be viewed by future readers and scholars. In a long commentary, Andrew Rosenheim (2009) predicts that Updike is one of "a handful of American writers whose work in the second half of the last century will be read in the second half of this one" (38). Rosenheim admires Updike's continual willingness to experiment, but believes his best work was "reiterative"—the Bech books, the Rabbit novels. His "greatness" lies not in the "multiplicity of his talents" or in the "amazing amount he wrote," but "in the best of his novels, where he married his ever-astonishingly accomplished style to characters and situations that reach our hearts." Although his characters often seem outmoded, they reflect "America in an age when all seemed possible" (39).

Updike's death drove Julian Barnes back to the fiction (2009b), and his re-reading of the Rabbit novels reaffirms his belief that "the quartet was the best American novel of the postwar period" (20). However, the second reading produced a different impression on him. "Whereas my first reading I was overwhelmed by Updike's joy of description," Barnes says, "in my second I was increasingly aware of this underlying sense of things being already over, of the tug of dying and death" (20). Ben Myers (2009) calls Updike "the most *theological* novelist you'll ever come across," and claims "pastors and theologians today could still learn a great deal" from his fiction. He singles out *Roger's Version* as the best example of Updike's handling of theological issues, and declares that *In the Beauty of the Lilies* is "one of the most beautiful and insightful accounts" of the "disappearance (and, later, the disturbing reappearance) of faith in modern life." Even Updike's explicit treatment of sex can be justified, because "the relation between God and the human body is a central tenet of Christian faith."

The advantage of retrospective analysis is that it allows the critic to perform triage. Hence, Leo Robson (2009) sees Updike's career falling into three periods. The first, from the 1950s to the early 1980s, "comprises a run of ten fine novels." The second, "bookended by his regrettable visits to Eastwick" contains many novels "written on a whim," with only *Roger's Version* and *Rabbit at Rest* being of real value. The final period, he says, contains little of merit. Yet on the whole, Robson believes that over his career Updike contributed significantly to American literature: "a miraculous tetralogy, and two less accomplished though still estimable trilogies" (46). Sadly, Robson concludes, Updike always had "more talent than sense"—which grew to be a problem when he had nothing left to say (49). Similarly, Richard Brookhiser (2009) dismisses Updike's essays as "generous but bland," the poetry as "not good." Updike's principal interests, adultery and Christianity, "became, in large doses, tics" (43). But he could always write brilliant sentences, and while many of his characters are like himself, he could "vary his dramatis personae" when he wished. Brookhiser is also taken with Updike's "belief that the world was lovable"—a belief, Brookhiser says, that was always "combined with a doubt, against which he strove, that it might be a screen for nothing at all" (43–44).

An upbeat assessment appeared in the *Harvard Advocate* (2009), where Jessica Sequeira explores Updike's philosophy of the self. Working "from narrow to broad"—a lesson Updike said he learned in a seminar on the poetry of fellow Berks County native Wallace Stevens—Updike believed that "by digging deeply inward and knowing himself" he would be "better able to understand, in a metaphysical sense, those around him as well." Hence, Sequeira says, no contradiction exists "between Updike's acclaim as a genius of social description and the accusations leveled against him of solipsism." This Whitmanesque view of the world allowed him to "describe in exquisite detail what he knew best as a portal to greater truths." It "explains his reputation as a chronicler of the mundane eccentricities of middle America" and "accounts for his ambivalence toward social theory." It also explains his belief in God; he could not stop believing in God "because God was not something external," but was "inside himself." Far from being self-absorbed, Updike's "introspection was always in the service of something greater, a hope that by knowing himself he could know something of the rich and various world around him."

Even academic journals gave space to retrospective tributes. The summer 2009 issue of *Sewanee Review* included three articles on Updike's achievements. In the first, David Heddendorf (2009b) not only describes his long personal fascination with Updike's writing, but also comments about Updike's strengths and weaknesses as a regionalist and a realist who found life "neither as beautiful as he might have wished it to be, nor as ugly as his critics seemed to wish he would make it" (489). Bruce Allen (2009) celebrates Updike's versatility and his ability to capture in his writing the essence of American society over five decades. In the final brief commentary, Sanford Pinsker (2009) explains why he is fond of Updike's anti-heroes and why Updike was so successful in creating figures like Harry Angstrom. A year later in *Critique*, Donald Greiner's tribute (2010) describes Updike as "our literary Vermeer" (174) and offers a succinct summary of Updike's achievements, commenting that his "extraordinary accomplishment in so many venues, unprecedented in American letters, generated a wondering admiration that one artist could excel in such variety" (183).

One of the most personal retrospectives is Larry Woiwode's (2011). In a long essay heavily laced with insightful critiques of Updike's work, the poet and novelist offers a loving tribute to one whose work he says can be compared only to Henry James, Proust, and Joyce—with a dash of Henry Green—because "it is that good" (86). Woiwode, himself a man of faith, is not bothered by Updike's open profession of faith; he celebrates it as a distinct quality of his best work.

The "Last Word" from Updike: *Higher Gossip*, 2011

After Updike's death, his widow Martha commissioned Christopher Carduff to assemble a final collection of his nonfiction. In the introduction to *Higher Gossip*, Carduff (2011) reports that Updike himself simplified the task by placing copies of "recent and fugitive magazine pieces" (xvi) in a carton that he deposited at Harvard's Houghton Library. Carduff undertook the daunting task of compiling a volume that, if not coherent, at least has the distinction of being relatively complete in representing everything Updike wanted to include in a single book. Carduff's introduction provides a useful description of his principles for organizing and editing the collection, information that will undoubtedly be useful to scholars in the future.

Higher Gossip garnered accolades similar to those accorded earlier collections of nonfiction and was spared the more unsympathetic remarks that characterized some previous reviews of Updike's prose. Among enthusiastic reviewers, Catherine Holmes (2011) celebrates *Higher Gossip* as "a gift from the grave." Andrew Delbanco (2011) calls the collection "a deftly edited reminder of what a prodigy we have lost." Michiko Kakutani (2011) is gracious as well, observing that the volume "offers the reader plenty of palpable pleasures"—though it is "also filled out with disposable scraps of writing" (C1). Vince Cosgrove (2011) calls it "no small gift," because readers are once again allowed to experience "the beauty of style and clarity of thought" that consistently characterizes Updike's essays. However, both Cosgrove and Benjamin Schwarz (2011) feel the volume is not Updike's best. On balance, though, most agree with Danny Heitman (2011), who describes *Higher Gossip* as "a timely reminder of the graceful companionship that Updike offered to his readers—a presence that will be sorely missed."

The Future of Updike Studies: Some Observations

What does the future hold for Updike studies? Predictions are risky, unless, as Matthew Arnold reminds us in "To Shakespeare," one is talking about the Bard; everyone else, including Updike, must "abide our question." To predict what might happen in the near term, a review of some of the general appraisals offered upon Updike's death (surveyed above) and of recent critical commentary and developments in Updike studies may offer some hints about the direction "Updike studies" is likely to take and suggest how the next generation of critics may judge Updike's contributions to literature.

Although most criticism of Updike tends to focus on themes or social content, recently some critics have looked to his fiction to illustrate technical problems novelists face in the composition process. In a brief analysis of point of view and narrative authority in *Roger's Version*, James Silver (2010) argues that Updike "finds a new way to engage" an enduring set of problems—"literary realism, narrative authority, and point of view" in the novel—by granting his protagonist, a "subjective narrator," the "powers of a third-person, objective narrator" (4). In "Narrative Chromaticism of Youth and Age in John Updike's *Seek My Face*" (2009), Marta Moreno offers an imaginative reading that reveals how Updike's fascination with art shapes the novel. The rapport that develops between the two women protagonists over the course of the narrative can be "visualize[d]" as the "alignment of two lines in a painting moving in different directions" in a work that deals with youth and old age as "part of the same palette of colors" (175).

David Jarraway's highly theoretical analysis of the Rabbit tetralogy, "Future Interior Subjective (A)voidance" (2010), heavily reliant on Lacan, and Aristi Trendel's (2010) examination of two of Updike's late stories, "Sandstone Farmhouse" and "The Cats," informed by contemporary psychoanalytic theory, suggest that Updike's fiction may continue to be of interest to postmodern critics. Similarly, Jennie Stearns, Jennifer Sandlin, and Jake Burdick's (2011) reading of "A&P," a story they describe as an examination of how modern consumer culture is created and accepted or rejected by those exposed to it, provides evidence that Updike's fiction may prove fertile ground for broad cultural readings.

Another profitable avenue of study may be to relate Updike's work to broader literary traditions. That approach is taken by John Vickery, who includes a chapter on *The Centaur* in *The Prose Elegy* (2009), where he describes the novel as representative of the elegiac tradition in Western literature. In another analysis of Updike's relationship to literary tradition, Catherine Morley (2009) examines the Rabbit novels as examples of fiction that aspires, either consciously or unconsciously, to the epic. Morley examines "Updike's negotiation with the epic in its Joycean manifestations," with "the classical tradition of Homer and Virgil that Joyce sought to subvert," and the novels' relationship "between the epic of the everyday and the American literary tradition" (59). Just as Virgil uses the *Aeneid* to criticize Roman imperialism, Updike uses the Rabbit novels, collectively a "wonderfully ambiguous epic of the American people in the postwar era," to "deal with broad questions of state and people, geography and culture, politics and history, identity and empire" (83).

Undoubtedly, critics will continue to explore the religious aspects of Updike's work, perhaps offering more nuanced readings of familiar works. Two such analyses appeared in 2010. In a larger study of John Calvin's influence on American thought and writing, Kyle Pasewark (2010) examines the paradox inherent in the concept of freedom as it appears in Updike's fiction. In a study of the changing perceptions of Protestant ministers in American fiction, Douglas Alan Walrath (2010) comments on several of Updike's novels that feature ministers who seem ineffectual in combating the growing sense of godlessness in American society.

Other thought-provoking approaches to understanding Updike may well be forthcoming, as suggested by Kathleen Verduin's (2010) examination of the impact of reading and the ideology of the book on Updike's performance as a writer. Verduin argues that the "confessional impulse" of Updike's writing permits "reconstruction of his reading experience." That experience turns out to be "manifestly phenomenological, a witness to 'the falling away of the barriers' between self and book that was first theorized by Georges Poulet" (330). Carefully documenting what might be learned from understanding Updike's relationship to, and use of, books he read, Verduin concludes that, while he displays affinities with other readers in the consumer culture, his unique talents allowed him to use his reading to produce a body of work that will be of value to future readers.

One work that is sure to continue generating critical commentary is Updike's 9/11 novel, *Terrorist*. By 2011 several reassessments had already appeared. In what is certainly the most negative, "A Neo-Orientalist Narrative in John Updike's *Terrorist*" (2009), Mohammed Deyab argues that Updike is part of a reactionary movement which believes any account of Muslims "must begin and end with the fact that Muslims" are "violent, intolerant, and life haters" (3). Updike's research on Islam is faulty, Deyab says, and his portraits of Muslims little more than stereotypes. Decidedly more positive, Bob Batchelor (2011) says a close reading of *Terrorist* not only provides insight into ways fiction can be used to interpret history, but also represents "a near-complete reversal" of Updike's reputation as "the nation's foremost suburban and pro-American chronicler" (176). Though readers with preconceptions about Updike may be disoriented by this novel, *Terrorist* serves as a good example of the "role novels might play in depicting the terrorist attacks" and helping readers grasp the implications of a complex historical subject. Like Batchelor, Anna Hartnell (2011) gives Updike credit for attempting something different in his novel, trying to understand events of 9/11 from the point of view of the perpetrator. But by exploring "the discourse on morality" as a "clash of monotheistic religions" (477), he fails to be convincing because he is unable to "conceive of a meaningful relationship between faith and politics" (495) and continually falls back on stereotypes. He is better, however, in representing contemporary America, refusing to accept notions of triumphalism and revealing many flaws in the culture that make it vulnerable to attack from other ideologies. In an essay comparing *Terrorist* with Hany Abu-Assad's film *Paradise Now*, Samuel Thomas (2011) argues for the necessity of getting beyond the bickering that characterizes reviews of the novel to recognize that, despite its shortcomings as an examination of the mind and motivation of a suicide bomber, it reveals much about the American psyche and culture before and after 9/11. Clearly, the divergence among these four essays argues for further study of this controversial text.

There are certain to be new books about Updike that will enlighten future scholars about Updike's life and his place in American culture. Publisher HarperCollins has already commissioned Adam Begley to write a biography of Updike, due out (according to a recent prediction) sometime in 2013. In the same year Bob Batchelor will publish a study with the current working title *John Updike: A Literary Biography*. Based on Batchelor's dissertation, the book will provide extensive commentary on *Terrorist* and evaluate Updike's reputation. Both should be welcome additions to the list of critiques that have already shed light on Updike's accomplishments, and will help shape studies of his fiction and poetry in the future. One book already available is Bernard Rodgers's new collection of essays, *Critical Insights: John Updike* (2012). The volume contains original work by Derek Royal, James Schiff, James Plath, Jack De Bellis, and Rodgers himself, and thirteen reprints of previously published work.

Another guarantor of continuing interest in Updike is the new journal *The John Updike Review*, the first issue of which appeared in fall 2011. Edited by James Schiff, the *Review* promises to cover all aspects of Updike's work. It is sponsored by the John Updike Society, an organization formed in the spring of 2009, shortly after Updike died, with the express purpose of promoting interest in his work and serving as a forum for supporting conversation and research about him. Several essays in the inaugural issue of the *Review* were initially presented as papers at the first International Updike Society conference, which was held in October 2010 and received coverage in national publications like the *Wall Street Journal* (Paletta 2010) and the *Philadelphia Inquirer* (Timpane 2010). Reporting on the proceedings, Bruce Cordingly (2010) speculates about the possibility of Updike remaining of interest to future generations. Cordingly says the question was clearly on the mind of Society president James Plath, who asked, "Can an author survive without authorial champions? I don't think so." Updike himself seemed to share that view, Cordingly notes. In a 2008 interview he admitted that literary reputations are often left to the whims and tastes of future generations of readers and critics. The chances that Updike will be remembered are better, of course, since a Society of scholars has pledged (at least for the foreseeable future) to keep reading and studying his works. Further evidence of the seriousness of their purpose came in 2012, when the Society purchased John Updike's boyhood home in Shillington, Pennsylvania, which is expected to be converted into a museum (Williams 2012).

There have been suggestions that, had Updike written less, his work would have been better. Perhaps he would have captured the prize that eluded him, the Nobel. Unfortunately, such speculation is now pointless. We have more than three dozen volumes of fiction, eight of verse, ten of nonfiction, a play and a memoir. *John Updike Review* editor Schiff observes in the close of his Introduction to the inaugural issue (2011) that, "as much as any author of his time, Updike left us with an immense trove of elegant, playful, and intensely serious writings that are waiting to be read, reread, discussed, and debated" (4). For scholars, that should be—to borrow Harry Angstrom's famous last word—"Enough."

Major Works by John Updike

WITH THE EXCEPTION OF Updike's first volume of poetry, *The Carpentered Hen and Other Tame Creatures*, all volumes were originally published by Alfred A. Knopf, New York.

Novels

The Poorhouse Fair, 1959.
Rabbit, Run, 1960.
The Centaur, 1963.
Of the Farm, 1965.
Couples, 1968.
Bech, A Book, 1970.
Rabbit Redux, 1971.
A Month of Sundays, 1975.
Marry Me, 1977.
The Coup, 1978.
Rabbit Is Rich, 1981.
Bech Is Back, 1982.
The Witches of Eastwick, 1984.
Roger's Version, 1986.
S., 1988.
Rabbit at Rest, 1990.
Memories of the Ford Administration, 1992.
Brazil, 1994.
In the Beauty of the Lilies, 1996.
Toward the End of Time, 1997.
Bech at Bay, 1998.
Gertrude and Claudius, 2000.
Seek My Face, 2002.
Villages, 2004.
Terrorist, 2006.
The Widows of Eastwick, 2008.

Drama

Buchanan Dying, 1974.

Short Story Collections

The Same Door, 1959.
Pigeon Feathers, 1962.
Olinger Stories, 1964.
The Music School, 1966.
Museums and Women and Other Stories, 1972.
Problems and Other Stories, 1979.
Too Far to Go, 1979.
Trust Me, 1987.
The Afterlife and Other Stories, 1994.
Licks of Love, 2001.
The Early Stories: 1953–1975, 2003.
My Father's Tears and Other Stories, 2009.

Poetry

The Carpentered Hen, and Other Tame Creatures. New York: Harper, 1958.
Telephone Poles and Other Poems, 1963.
Midpoint, and Other Poems, 1969.
Tossing and Turning, 1977.
Facing Nature, 1985.
Collected Poems 1953–1993, 1993.
Americana and Other Poems, 2001.
Endpoint and Other Poems, 2009.

Nonfiction, Essays and Criticism

Assorted Prose, 1965.
Picked-Up Pieces, 1975.
Hugging the Shore, 1983.
Self-Consciousness: Memoirs, 1989.
Just Looking: Essays on Art, 1989.
Odd Jobs, 1991.
Golf Dreams: Writings on Golf, 1996.
More Matter, 1999.
Still Looking: Essays on American Art, 2005.
Due Considerations: Essays and Criticism, 2007.
Higher Gossip, 2011.

Works Cited

Abbey, Edward. 1987. "Reading Updike." *Nation*, March 28, 409–10.
Ableman, Paul. 1979. "Poetic Precision, Prose Breadth." *Spectator*, March 24, 18.
Abusharif, Ibrahim. 2006. "John Updike: Quranic Exegete?" *Altmuslim*, July 25. http://www.patheos.com/blogs/altmuslim/2006/07/john_updike_quranic_exegete/.
Ackroyd, Peter. 1975. "Wittery." *Spectator*, June 28, 781.
———. 1977. "Paradise Lost." *Spectator*, April 23, 22–23.
———. 1984. "The Spell of Modern American Psyches." *Times*, September 27, 9.
Adams, J. R. 1965. "Updike Best at Verse." *Rocky Mountain News*, February 14, 26A.
Adams, Phoebe. 1959. "The Poor and Unselfish." *Atlantic*, February, 100–101.
Adams, Robert Martin. 1966. "Without Risk." *New York Times Book Review*, September 18, 4–5.
Adelman, Richard. 1998. "A View from the Other Side." *Science*, February 6, 819.
Adler, Renata. (1963) 1982. "Arcadia, Pa." *New Yorker*, April 13, 182–88. Reprinted in Macnaughton 1982, 48–52.
Ahearn, Kerry. 1988. "Family and Adultery: Images and Ideas in Updike's Rabbit Novels." *Twentieth Century Literature* 34: 62–83.
Alden, John. 1997. "Updike's Latest a Mix of Syrupy Sci-Fi." *Cleveland Plain Dealer*, October 12, 13I.
Aldridge, John. (1966) 1987. "The Private Vice of John Updike." *Time To Murder and Create*, 164–71. New York: McKay. Reprinted in Bloom 1987, 9–13.
———. (1970) 1972. "An Askew Halo for John Updike." *Saturday Review*, June 27, 25–27, 35. Reprinted as "John Updike and the Higher Theology" in *The Devil in the Fire: Retrospective Essays in American Literature and Culture*, 195–201. New York; Harper's Magazine Press, 1972.
Allen, Brooke. 1995. "Intimations of Mortality." *New Criterion*, January, 62–67.
———. 1996. "Losing Faith." *New Criterion*, January, 57–60.
———. 1997. "Updike Redux." *New Leader*, December 1–15, 13–14.
———. 2000. "When 'To Be, or Not to Be' Was Yet to Be." *Wall Street Journal*, February 11, W13.

Allen, Bruce. 2009. "Updike and the Past Recaptured." *Sewanee Review* 117, no. 3 (Summer): 490–92.
Allen, Mary. 1976. "John Updike's Love of 'Dull Bovine Beauty.'" *The Necessary Blankness: Women in Major American Fiction of the Sixties*, 97–132. Urbana: University of Illinois Press.
Alter, Robert. (1972)1977. "Updike, Malamud, and the Fire This Time." *Commentary*, October, 68–74. Reprinted in *Defense of the Imagination*, 233–48. Philadelphia: Jewish Publication Society of America.
Alvarez, A. 1976. "Scraping the Barrel." *Observer*, March 21, 30.
Amidon, Stephen. 2005. "Unzipped." *New Statesman*, January 24, 51–52.
Amis, Martin. (1976) 2001. "Life Class." *New Statesman*, March 19, 368–69. Reprinted in Amis 2001, 369–72.
———. 1984. "Christian Gentleman." *Observer*, January 15, 48.
———. (1989) 2001. "In the Boiler-Room of the Self." *Observer*, May 14, 49. Reprinted in Amis 2001, 375–78.
———. (1990) 2001. "Death of the Typical American Heart." *Independent on Sunday*, October 28, 32. Reprinted in Amis 2001, 379–83.
———. 1991. "Magnanimous in a Big Way." *New York Times Book Review*, November 10, 7, 12. Reprinted in Amis 2001 384–88.
———. 2001. *The War Against Cliché*. London: Jonathan Cape.
———. 2009. "The Master's Voice." *Guardian*, July 4, 6.
Ancona, Francesco. 1986. "John Updike's *Rabbit Is Rich*." *Writing the Absence of the Father*, 81–91. Lanham, MD: University Press of America.
Anderson, David. 1963. "John Updike: An Introductory Appraisal." *Ivory Tower*, November 4, 10–13.
Anderson, Donald. 2000–2001. "Eccles Redux." *Journal of Modern Literature* 24, no. 2 (Winter): 327–36.
Anderson, Sam. 2009. "Three Pages a Day." *New York*, February 1.
Anderson, Sara. 1996. "*Rabbit at Rest* Beneath the Motions of Grace: Updike's Epigraph and the Spiritual Journey of Harry Angstrom" *Literature and Belief* 16, no. 1: 1–24.
Androne, Richard G. 2008. "'Never the Right Food': Eating and Irony in John Updike's Rabbit Angstrom Saga." In *You Are What You Eat: Literary Probes into the Palate*, edited by Annette Magid, 330–44. Newcastle, UK: Cambridge Scholars Press.
Angell, Roger. 2009. "The Fadeaway: An Editor's Note." *New Yorker*, February 9, 38.
"Answers to Questions Unasked." 1970. *Times Literary Supplement*, January 29, 104.
Armstrong, Charlotte. 1963. "Tale Blends Myth with the Modern." *Los Angeles Times*, January 20, M16.
Arnold, Martin. 2000. "Making Books: Literary Titans Face Reality." *New York Times*, June 8, E3.
Atwood, Margaret. 1984. "Wondering What It's Like to Be a Woman." *New York Times*, May 13, G1, G40.

———. 1997. "Memento Mori—But First, Carpe Diem." *New York Times Book Review*, October 12, 9–10.
Backscheider, Paula, and Nick Backscheider. 1974. "Updike's *Couples*: Squeak in the Night." *Modern Fiction Studies* 20, no. 1 (Spring): 45–52.
Bailey, Peter. 1981. "Notes on the Novel-as-Autobiography." *Genre* 14, no. 1 (Spring): 79–93.
———. 1991. "'Why Not Tell the Truth': The Autobiographies of Three Fiction Writers." *Critique* 32, no. 4 (Summer): 211–23.
———. 2006. *Rabbit (Un)Redeemed: The Drama of Belief in Updike's Fiction*. Madison, NJ: Fairleigh Dickinson University Press.
Baker, Carlos. 1975. "A Month of Sundays." *Theology Today* 32 (October): 335–36.
Baker, Nicholson. 1991. *U & I: A True Story*. New York: Random House.
Baker, Simon. 2009. "A Wry Eye on the American Condition." *Observer*, July 19, 21.
Balbert, Peter. 1983. "A Panoply of Metaphor: Exuberances of Style in Pynchon and Updike." *Studies in the Novel* 15 (Fall): 265–76.
Balliett, Whitney. (1959) 1982. "Writer's Writer." *New Yorker*, 7 February, 138–42. Reprinted in Macnaughton 1982, 39–41.
———. 1960. "The American Expression." *New Yorker*, November 5, 222–24.
Bamberger, Michael. 1996. "Rabbit Holes Out." *Sports Illustrated*, September 9, 12.
Bancroft, Collette. 2009. "John Updike's Posthumous Publication '*My Father's Tears*' Focuses on Aging Characters." *St. Petersburg Times*, June 7.
Banville, John. 2002. "Action Figure." *New York Times Book Review*, November 17, 10.
———. 2004. "Sentimental Education." *New York Review of Books*, December 16, 55–56.
Barnard, Judith. 1976. "Updike's Road Map to Wedded Harmony." *Chicago Daily News*, November 6, Panorama 6.
Barnes, Jane. 1981. "John Updike: A Literary Spider." *Virginia Quarterly Review* 57, no. 1 (Winter): 79–98.
Barnes, Julian. 1996. "Grand Illusion." *New York Times Book Review*, January 28, 9.
———. 2009a. "Flights." *New York Review of Books*, June 11, 8–9.
———. 2009b. "Running Away." *Guardian*, October 17, 20.
Barr, Donald. 1959. "A Stone's Throw Apart." *New York Times Book Review*, January 11, 4.
Barron, John. 2007. "Prolific Updike Shows No Signs of Stopping." *Chicago Sun-Times*, October 28, B11.
Batchelor, Bob. 2011. "Literary Lions Tackle 9/11." *Radical History Review* No. 111 (Fall): 175–83.
Batchelor, John. 1986. "The Hacker and the Heretic." *Washington Post Book World*, August 31, 1–2.

Baumann, Paul. 1989. "Beckoned by the Mother Tongue." *Commonweal*, August 11, 438–39.

Bawer, Bruce. 1989. "A Wordsmith's 'Careful' Life." *Wall Street Journal*, April 17, A10.

———. 1991. "He's Still Giving Praise." *Wall Street Journal*, November 21, A12.

———. 1992. "Academic Obsessions and Political Passions." *Washington Post Book World*, November 1, 1, 9.

———. 2000. "John Updike, Wordsmith." *Hudson Review* 53, no. 1 (Spring): 119–26.

Bayley, John. 1987. "Falling in Love with the Traffic Warden." *London Review of Books*, October 1, 6–8.

———. 1994. "Off the Map." *New York Review of Books*, May 12, 23–24.

———. 2000. "It Happened at Elsinore." *New York Review of Books*, March 23, 13–15.

Baym, Nina. 1984. Review of *The Witches of Eastwick*. *Iowa Review* 14, no. 3 (Fall): 165–70.

Becker, Stephen. 1983. "Updike the Critic: Shrewd, Stylish, Generous and Just." *Chicago Sun-Times*, September 11, 26.

Bedient, Calvin. 1975. "*Picked-up Pieces* by John Updike." *New Republic*, December 27, 28–29.

Begley, Adam. 2000. "Cuddly in his Rabbit Suit, Clever Updike Charms a Critic." *New York Observer*, November 20.

———. 2002. "Updike Picks Up His Brush, Whips Off a Dazzling Portrait." *New York Observer*, November 13, 23.

———. 2004. "It Takes a Village, Or Three." *New York Observer*, October 25, 10.

———. 2006. "Updike Does Islam: Colonizes New Jersey." *New York Observer*, May 31, 14.

Bell, Millicent. 2001. "Updike's Shakespeare." *Partisan Review* 68, no. 2 (Spring): 345–49.

Bell, Pearl. 1981. "Sequels." *Commentary*, October, 72–74.

Bell, Vereen. 1963. "A Study in Frustration." *Shenandoah* 14, no. 4 (Summer): 69–72.

Bellamy, John Stark. 1996. "Spiritual Saga Not Up to Snuff for John Updike." *Cleveland Plain Dealer*, January 21, Books: 10.

Ben-Bassat, Hedda. 2000. "John Updike's Postmodern Apocalypse at Midpoint: Bloom's Giants and their Barthian Double." *Prophets without Vision: Subjectivity and the Sacred in Contemporary American Writing*, 41–64. Lewisburg, PA: Bucknell University Press.

Bergonzi, Bernard. 1967. "Updike, Dennis, and Others." *New York Review of Books*, February 9, 28–30.

Berman, Paul. 2001. "Rabbit Undone." *New York Review of Books*, February 22, 4–6.

Berryman, Charles. 1986. "Updike and Contemporary Witchcraft." *South Atlantic Quarterly* 85, no. 1: 1–9.

"Bigger and Better." 1963. *Times Literary Supplement*, February 1, 73.
Billen, Andrew. 1994. "Supernatural Leap." *Literary Review*, April, 28–29.
Billings, J. Todd. 2003. "John Updike as Theologian of Culture: *Roger's Version* and the Possibility of Embodied Redemption." *Christianity and Literature* 52, no. 2 (Winter): 203–13.
Birkerts, Sven. 1990. "The Inner Rabbit." *Chicago Tribune Books*, September 30, 1, 4.
Blechner, Michael. 1980. "Tristan in Letters: Malory, C. S. Lewis, Updike." *Tristania* 6: 30–37.
Bloom, Alice. 1984–85. "Recent Fiction II." *Hudson Review* 37, no. 4 (Winter): 624–26.
Bloom, Harold, ed. 1987. *Modern Critical Views: John Updike*. Revised edition, 2001. New York: Chelsea House.
———, ed. 2001. *Bloom's Major Short Story Writers: John Updike*. Broomall, PA: Chelsea House.
Blotner, Joseph. 1982. "Updike Turns from 'Rabbit' to a Literary Lion." *Chicago Tribune*, October 10, Section 7: 1.
Blue, Adrianne. 1986. "Deus in Machina." *New Statesman*, October 10, 29.
———. 1987. "The Compassionate Wasp." *New Statesman*, September 18, 27–28.
Bodmer, George. 1986. "Sounding the Fourth Alarm: Identity and the Masculine Tradition in the Fiction of Cheever and Updike." In *Gender Studies: New Directions in Feminist Criticism*, edited by Judith Spector, 148–62. Bowling Green, OH: Bowling Green State University Press.
Bogan, Louise. (1959) 1983. "Books: Verse." *New Yorker* April 18, 170. Reprinted in Bruccoli 1983, 256.
Bolton Richard. 1989. "Cars of Our Years: The 'Diminished World' of *Rabbit Is Rich*." *Kansas Quarterly* 21, no. 4 (Fall): 97–104.
Borgman, Paul. 1977a. "Beyond Survival: Leisure, Stalemate and Redemption in the Later Fiction of John Updike and Walker Percy." *Reformed Journal*, September, 18–23.
———. 1977b. "The Tragic Hero of Updike's *Rabbit, Run*." *Renascence* 29, no. 2 (Winter): 106–12.
Boroff, David. (1960) 1983. "You Can't Really Flee." *New York Times Book Review*, November 6, 4, 43. Reprinted in Bruccoli 1983, 259–62.
Boswell, Marshall. 1998. "The Black Jesus: Racism and Redemption in John Updike's *Rabbit Redux*." *Contemporary Literature* 39, no. 1 (Spring): 99–132.
———. 1999. "The World and the Void: Creatio ex Nihilo and Homoeroticism in John Updike's *Rabbit Is Rich*." In Yerkes 1999b, 162–79.
———. 2001. *John Updike's Rabbit Tetralogy: Mastered Irony in Motion*. Columbia: University of Missouri Press.
Bottum, J. 1996. "Social Gospel." *Commentary*, April, 64–66.
Bowden, Christopher. 2001. "Sweet Land of Liberty . . . and Malls." *Christian Science Monitor*, April 26, 19.

Bowman, Diane. 1982. "Flying High: The American Icarus in Morrison, Roth, and Updike." *Perspectives on Contemporary Literature* 8: 10–17.

Boyer, Paul. 2001. "Notes of a Disillusioned Lover: John Updike's *Memories of the Ford Administration*." In *Novel History: Historians and Novelists Confront America's Past (And Each Other)*, edited by Mark Carnes, 45–57. New York: Simon & Schuster.

Boyers, Robert. (1997) 2005. "Towards the End of Time." *New Republic*, November 17, 38–42. Reprinted as "Bullets of Milk: John Updike" in *The Dictator's Dictation*, 59–68. New York: Columbia University Press, 2005.

Bradbury, Malcolm. 1977. "Made in Heaven." *New Statesman*, April 29, 568–69.

———. 1983. *The Modern American Novel*, 146–48. London: Penguin.

———. 1992. "A Vital American Realist." *Sunday Times*, January 19, Books 5.

———. 1998. "Home Truths on the Eve of the Apocalypse." *Times*, January 29, 38.

———. 1999. "An Ageing Writer's Great Revenge and Final Triumph." *Literary Review*, January, 37–38.

Braine, John. 1970. "Bourgeois Decadence." *Spectator*, October 24, 480–81.

Bremner, Charles. 1990. "Rabbit as Metaphor for America's Decline." *Times*, November 10, 23.

Brenner, Gerry. (1966) 1982. "*Rabbit, Run*: John Updike's Criticism of the 'Return to Nature.'" *Twentieth Century Literature* 12: 3–14. Reprinted in Macnaughton 1982, 91–104.

Brinnin, John. 1975. "John Updike: Erudite, Engaging." *Boston Globe*, December 21, A8.

Broer, Lawrence, ed. 1998. *Rabbit Tales: Poetry and Politics in John Updike's Rabbit Novels*. Tuscaloosa: University of Alabama Press.

Brookhiser, Richard. 1998. "Updike at an Angle." *National Review*, December 7, 61–62.

———. 2009. "Rabbit's Great Run." *National Review*, February 23, 43–44.

Brookner, Anita. 1986. "Deus in Machina." *Spectator*, October 11, 38–39.

———. 1987. "The Pleasures of the Suburbs." *Spectator*, September 19, 44–45.

———. 1988. "Getting Rid of the Garbage." *Spectator*, April 30, 35–36.

———. 1989. "Books: Happy Child Father to a Happy Man." *Spectator*, May 13, 37–38.

———. 1990. "Ending the Heartache." *Spectator*, October 27, 28–29.

———. 1993. "Looking Back in Sorrow." *Spectator*, February 27, 30.

———. 1998. "Magician of the Humdrum." *Spectator*, January 31, 39.

———. 2000. "Perpetual Youth and Effortless Artistry." *Spectator*, January 8, 32.

Brooks, Xan. 2001. "Rabbit Stew." *Guardian*, March 17.

Brophy, Brigid. 1976. "Love in the Garden State." *Harper's*, December, 80–82.

Brown, Brenda. 2001. "Mrs. Babbitt and Mrs. Rabbit." *Midwestern Miscellany* 29 (Fall): 55–64.
Brownworth, Victoria. 2007. "John Updike on Almost Everything: Brilliant, but Passion Isn't There." *Baltimore Sun*, October 28, 4F.
Broyard, Anatole. 1968. "Updike's Twosomes." *New Republic*, May 4, 28–30.
———. 1971. "Updike Goes All Out at Last." *New York Times*, November 5, 40.
———. 1975a. "Some Unoriginal Sins." *New York Times*, February 19, 30.
———. 1975b. "On a Spree with Updike." *New York Times*, December 2, 37.
———. 1981. "Ordinary People." *New York Times Book Review*, December 13, 43.
———. 1988. "Letters from the Ashram." *New York Times Book Review*, March 13, 7.
Bruccoli, Mary, ed. 1983. *Dictionary of Literary Biography: Documentary Series*, Volume 3. Detroit, MI: Gale.
Buchanan, John M. 2009. "Final Verses." *Christian Century*, November 3, 3.
Buchanan, Mark. 2003. "Rabbit Trails to God." *Christianity Today*, July, 42–44.
Buckley, William F., Jr. 1978. "Jungle Music." *New York*, December 18, 93.
Buitenhuis, Peter. 1963. "Pennsylvania Pantheon." *New York Times Book Review*, April 7, 4, 26.
———. 1965. "The Mowing of a Meadow." *New York Times Book Review*, November 14, 4, 34.
Burchard, Rachel. 1971. *John Updike: Yea Sayings*. Carbondale: Southern Illinois University Press.
Burgess, Anthony. (1966) 1982. "Language, Myth and Mr. Updike." *Commonweal*, February 11, 557–59. Reprinted in Macnaughton 1982, 55–58.
———. 1979. "Black Man's Burden." *Observer*, March 18, 36.
Burhans, Clinton S., Jr. (1973) 1982. "Things Falling Apart: Structure and Theme in *Rabbit, Run*." *Studies in the Novel* 5: 336–51. Reprinted in Macnaughton 1982, 148–62.
Burnett, Whit, ed. 1970. *America's 85 Greatest Living Authors Present: This Is My Best in the Third Quarter of the Century*. Garden City, NY: Doubleday.
Butcher, Fanny. 1959. "First Novel Talented, Tho Haphazard." *Chicago Sunday Tribune*, January 11: IV: 4.
Caldwell, Gail. 1987. "Updike Plumbs the Twilight Years." *Boston Globe*, April 26, 85–86.
———. 1994. "A Little Updike." *Boston Globe*, February 13, Books A1, A17.
———. 1997. "Autumn of the Patriarch." *Boston Globe*, October 19, P1, P4.
———. 1998. "Bech to His Old Tricks." *Boston Globe*, October 25, N1, N4.
———. 2000a. "*Hamlet*, Run." *Boston Globe*, February 6, C1, C4.
———. 2000b. "Rabbit in Absentia." *Boston Globe*, November 12, M1, M4.

———. 2006. "Gods and Monsters." *Boston Globe*, June 4, E4.
Caldwell, Mark. 1989. "This Is Your Life, John Updike." *Philadelphia Inquirer*, March 12, F1–2.
Calinescu, Matei. 1994. "Secrecy in Fiction: Textual and Intertextual Secrets in Hawthorne and Updike." *Poetics Today* 15, no. 3 (Fall): 443–65.
Campbell, Aidan. 2003. "*Seek My Face.*" *Culture Wars*, February. http://www.culturewars.org.uk/2003-02/updike.htm.
Campbell, James. 1980. "Front Lawn." *New Statesman*, 30 May, 821–22.
Campbell, Jeff. 1984. "Light on Your Fur: Regeneration in Updike's *Rabbit Is Rich*." *Lamar Journal of the Humanities* 10, no. 1 (Spring): 7–13.
———. 1987. *Updike's Novels: Thorns Spell a Word*. Wichita Falls, TX: Midwestern State University Press.
Cannella, Stephen. 2009. "John Updike: A Literary Master Had a Keen Eye for Sports." *Sports Illustrated*, February 9, 19.
Carduff, Christopher. 1994. "Shorter Notice." *New Criterion*, February, 77–78.
———. 2011. "Introduction." *Higher Gossip*, by John Updike, xv–xxiii. New York: Knopf.
Carnes, Mark. 1996. "Fictions and Fantasies of Early-Twentieth-Century Manhood." *Reviews in American History* 24: 448–53.
Cartwright, Justin. 2004. "How to Dice Up Your School Friends and Make a Rabbit." *Independent*, February 8, 16.
———. 2005. "Get 'Em Off, Love! It's All in the Name of Art." *Independent*, February 6, Features 33.
Casey, Florence. 1965. "Updike's Trap of Freedom." *Christian Science Monitor*, November 18, 15.
Charles, Ron. 2000a. "To Be or Not To Be a Good Parent, That Is the Question." *Christian Science Monitor*, February 3, 21.
———. 2000b. "Harry's Troubles Are Still Multiplying Like Rabbits." *Christian Science Monitor*, November 30, 19.
———. 2002. "A Splattering of Art History." *Christian Science Monitor*, December 5, 15.
Chase, Mary Ellen. 1959. "John Updike's Wise, Moving First Novel." *New York Herald Tribune Book Review*, January 11, 3.
———. 1962. "But Can He Communicate?" *New York Herald Tribune Book Review*, March 18, 4.
Chester, Alfred. 1962. "Twitches and Embarrassments." *Commentary*, July, 77–80.
Childers, Doug. 2006. "Updike's 'Terrorist' Misses the Mark." *Richmond Times-Dispatch*, June 11, K3.
Chipchase, Paul. 1982. "Reflections on a Sinking Ship." *Books & Bookmen*, March, 13–14.
Churchwell, Sarah. 2008. "What Happened Next to the *Witches of Eastwick*." *Times Literary Supplement*, October 29.
Clasen, Kelly. 2008. "In an Open Boat with Harry 'Rabbit' Angstrom." *Studies in American Naturalism* 3, no. 2 (Winter): 131–46.

Clausen, Jan. 1992. "Native Fathers." *Kenyon Review* New Series 14 (Spring): 44–55.
Clee, Nicholas. 1995. "Old-Timers' Reunion." *Times Literary Supplement*, January 27, 21.
Coale, Samuel. 1985. "John Updike: The Duality of Beauty." In *Hawthorne's Shadow: American Romance from Melville to Mailer*. Lexington: University Press of Kentucky.
Cockshutt, Rod. 1986. "Updike's Newest a Sprawling Mess." *Raleigh News and Observer*, September 21.
Cohen, Joseph. 1982. "Updike Holds Us in His Spell." *New Orleans Times-Picayune*, November 14, Sec. 3: 7.
Colgan, John-Paul. 2002/2003. "Going It Alone but Running Out of Gas: America's Borders in John Updike's 'Rabbit' Novels." *Irish Journal of American Studies* 11/12: 73–86.
"Community Feeling." 1968. *Times Literary Supplement*, November 7, 1245.
Conn, Peter. 1989. *Literature in America: An Illustrated History*. Cambridge: Cambridge University Press.
Cook, Bruce. 1962. "A Lesser Form." *Commonweal*, May 11, 184, 186.
Cook, Roderick. 1966. "*Of the Farm*." *Harper's*, January, 100.
Cooke, Judy. 1980. "Bull's Eye." *New Statesman*, October 10, 22–23.
Cooper, Rand Richards. 1991. "Rabbit Loses the Race: John Updike's 'Small Answer of a Texture.'" *Commonweal*, May 17, 315–21.
———. 1994. "Bungle in the Jungle." *Commonweal*, April 8, 18–20.
———. 2009. "To the Visible World: On Worshiping John Updike." *Commonweal*, May 8, 16–20.
Corbellari, Alain. 1999. "John Updike's *Tristanian* Passion." *Tristania* 19: 115–28.
Corbett, Edward. 1959 "*The Poorhouse Fair*." *America*, January 31, 528, 530.
Cordingly, Bruce. 2010. "John Updike, and the Curious Business of Sustaining Literary Reputations." www.themillions.com/2010/11/.john-updike-and-the-curious-business-of-sustaining-literary-reputations.html.
Cornwell, T. Bettina, and Bruce Keillor. 1996. "Contemporary Literature and the Embedded Consumer Culture: The Case of Updike's Rabbit." In *Empirical Approaches to Literature and Aesthetics*, edited by Roger Kreuz and Mary Sue MacNealy, 559–72. Norwood, NJ: Ablex Publishing.
Corwin, Phillip. 1984. "Oh, What the Hex." *Commonweal*, June 1, 340–41.
Cosgrove, Vince. 2011. "'Higher Gossip: Essays and Criticism': A Book Review." *Star-Ledger*, November 20.
Crane, Milton. 1959. "Young People with Time to Explore Their Souls." *Chicago Daily Tribune*, August 16, B3.
Crews, Frederick. 1986. "Mr. Updike's Planet." *New York Review of Books*, December 4, 7–10, 12, 14.
Crowley, John. 1996. "Varieties of Religious Experience." *Washington Post Book World*, February 4, 1.

Crowley, Sue Mitchell. 1977. "John Updike: 'the rubble of footnotes bound into Kierkegaard.'" *Journal of the American Academy of Religion* 45, no. 3 (September): 1011–35.

———. 1985. "John Updike and Kierkegaard's Negative Way: Irony and Indirect Communication in *A Month of Sundays*." *Soundings* 68, no. 2 (Summer): 212–28.

Cryer, Dan. 1986. "Updike: Serious and Hilarious on God and Sex." *Newsday*, September 7, 13, 16.

Culligan, Glendy. 1965. "Updike Is Back on the Farm with a Luminous Novel." *Washington Post*, November 23, A22.

Curley, Thomas. 1963. "Between Heaven and Earth." *Commonweal*, March 29, 26–27.

Curtler, Betsy. 1976. "Science, the Saving Grace of John Updike: *The Centaur* and *Couples*." *A Festschrift for Professor Marguerite Roberts*, edited by Frieda Penninger, 209–18. Richmond, VA: University of Richmond Press.

D'Evelyn, Thomas. 1986. "The 'Version' According to Updike." *Christian Science Monitor*, September 11, 23.

Danto, Arthur. 1989. "What MOMA Done Tole Him." *New York Times Book Review*, October 15, 12.

Davenport, Guy. 1963. "Novels with Masks." *National Review*, April 9, 287–88.

Davies, Howard. 1982. "Rabbiting On." *Literary Review*, February, 41–42.

Davies, Marie-Hélène. 1984. "Fools for Christ's Sake: A Study of the Clerical Figures in De Vries, Updike and Beuchner." *Thalia* 6 (Spring-Summer): 60–72.

Davies, Russell. 1980. "Modern Torments." *The Listener*, June 12, 771.

———. 1982. "Rabbit Knows He Is a Victim but He Fights On." *The Listener*, January 14, 21–22.

Davies, Serena. 2006. "A Novel Approach to Art." *Telegraph*, February 21.

Davis, Hope. 1988. "Distaff Doormat." *New Leader* 71, April 18, 20–21.

Davis, L. J. 1976. "Getting Too Full of Updike." *National Observer*, November 20, 25.

Davis, Robert. 1986. "Perversely Ingenious Morality." *New Leader*, October 20, 16–17.

De Bellis, Jack. 1964. "The Group and John Updike." *Sewanee Review* 72, no. 3–4 (July-September): 531–40.

———. 1989. "Oedipal Angstrom." *Wascana Review* 24 (Spring): 45–59.

———. (1993) 2005. "The 'Awful Power': John Updike's Use of Kubrick's *2001* in *Rabbit Redux*." *Literature/Film Quarterly* 21, no. 3: 209–17. Reprinted in De Bellis 2005, 82–94.

———. 1994. *John Updike, A Bibliography: 1967–1993*. Westport, CT: Greenwood.

———. 1995. "'It Captivates . . . It Hypnotizes': Updike Goes to the Movies." *Literature/Film Quarterly* 23, no. 3: 169–87.

———. 2000. *The John Updike Encyclopedia*. Westport, CT: Greenwood.

———. 2005. *John Updike: The Critical Responses to the 'Rabbit' Saga*. Westport CT: Praeger.
De Bellis, Jack, and Michael Broomfield. 2007. *John Updike: A Bibliography of Primary & Secondary Materials, 1948–2007*. New Castle, DE: Oak Knoll.
De Feo, Ronald. 1975. "Sex, Sermons, and Style." *National Review*, June 20, 679–80.
Deemer, Charles. 1973 "Exploring Suburbia." *New Leader*, January 22, 18–19.
Delbanco, Andrew. 2011. "How Updike Judged." *New York Times*, November 10.
Delrogh, Dennis. 1972. "Says the Rabbit, What's Updike? Masterful Major Author." *Village Voice*, January 27, 24–26.
De Mott, Benjamin. 1975. "Mod Masses, Empty Pews." *Saturday Review*, March 8, 20–21.
———. 1984. "Behold Updike, Bewitched." *New England Monthly*, June, 24–25.
Denby, David. 1989. "A Life of Sundays." *New Republic*, May 22, 29–33.
Detweiler, Robert. 1963. "John Updike and the Indictment of Culture-Protestantism." *Four Spiritual Crises in Mid-Century American Fiction*, 14–24. Gainesville: University of Florida Press.
———. (1971) 1982. "Updike's *Couples*: Eros Demythologized." *Twentieth Century Literature* 17: 235–46. Reprinted in Macnaughton 1982, 128–39.
———. 1972. *John Updike*. Revised edition, 1984. New York: Twayne.
———. 1979. "Updike's *A Month of Sundays* and the Language of the Unconscious." *Journal of the American Academy of Religion* 47, no. 4 (December): 611–25.
———. 1989. "John Updike's Sermons." *Breaking the Fall: Religious Readings of Contemporary Fiction*. New York: Harper & Row.
Deyab, Mohammad. 2008. "A Neo-Orientalist Narrative in John Updike's *Terrorist*." Paper presented at *Egypt at the Crossroads: Literary and Linguistic Studies, Proceedings of the 9th International Symposium on Comparative Literature*, Cairo, Egypt, 4 November 2008. 1–24.
Diamond, George. 1999. "Chaos and Society: Religion and the Idea of Civil Order in Updike's *Memories of the Ford Administration*." In Yerkes 1999b, 242–56.
Dicken, Thomas. 2004. "God and Pigment: John Updike on the Conservation of Meaning." *Religion & Literature* 36, no. 3 (Autumn): 69–87.
Didion, Joan. 1961. "Into the Underbrush." *National Review*, January 28, 54–56.
———. 1962. Review of *Pigeon Feathers and Other Stories*. *National Review*, June 19, 452.
Dilts, Susan. 1966. "Updike in a Deep Rut." *Baltimore Sunday Sun*, October 2, D9.
Dinnage, Rosemary. (1973) 1979. "At the Flashpoint." *Times Literary Supplement*, May 4, 488. Reprinted in Thorburn and Eiland 1979, 203–06.

———. 1980. "Guilt-Edged Entanglements." *Times Literary Supplement*, May 23, 575.

———. 1995. "The Downhill Slope." *New York Review of Books*, January 12, 20–21.

Dintenfass, Mark. 1979 "Updike Does it with Mirrors." *Milwaukee Journal*, January 7, Part 5:3.

Dirda, Michael. 1983. "John Updike: The Happy Critic." *Washington Post Book World*, September 18, 1.

———. 2000. Review of *Licks of Love*. *Washington Post Book World*, December 10, X15.

———. 2009. "John Updike, 1932–2009." *Chronicle of Higher Education Review*, February 13, B99.

Ditsky, John. 1969. "Roth, Updike and the High Expense of Spirit." *University of Windsor Review* 5, no. 1 (Fall): 111–20.

Donahue, Peter. 1996. "Pouring Drinks and Getting Drunk: The Social and Personal Implications of Drinking in John Updike's *Too Far to Go*." *Studies in Short Fiction* 33: 361–67.

Donald, Miles. 1978. "The Fate of the Traditional Novel: William Faulkner, John Updike." *The American Novel in the Twentieth Century*, 73–107. London: David Charles.

Donaldson, Scott. 1989. "Uniquely Updike." *Chicago Tribune*, February 26, Sec. 14: 1, 8.

Doner, Dean. (1962) 1979. "Rabbit Angstrom's Unseen World." *New World Writing 20*, 63–75. Philadelphia: Lippincott. Reprinted in Thorburn and Eiland 1979, 17–34.

Donnelly, Jerome. 1990. "*Just Looking*." *America*, February 24, 179–82.

Donoghue, Denis. 1970. "Silken Mechanism." *The Listener*, October 15, 524–25.

———. 1983. "The Zeal of a Man of Letters." *New York Times Book Review*, September 18, 1, 30–31.

———. 1991. "John Updike on the Books of the '80s." *Washington Post Book World*, November 17, 5.

Donovan, Laurence. 1970. "Updike Stands Still." *Miami Herald*, July 26, 7K.

Doody, Terrence. 1979. "Updike's Idea of Reification." *Contemporary Literature* 20, no. 2 (Spring): 204–20.

Doyle, Paul. 1964. "The Fiction of John Updike." *Nassau Review* 1: 9–19. Revised as "Updike's Fiction: Motifs and Techniques." *Catholic World*, September 1964, 356–62.

Drabble, Margaret. 1979. "Heroes of the Mundane." *Washington Post Book World*, October 21, 1, 4.

Duncan-Jones, Katherine. 2000. "Country Matters." *Washington Post Book World*, February 6, 3.

Duryea, Bill. 2006. "Updike's Take on 'Terrorism.'" *St. Petersburg Times*, June 4, 6P.

Duvall, John. 1991. "The Pleasure of Textual/Sexual Wrestling: Pornography and Heresy in *Roger's Version*." *Modern Fiction Studies* 37, no. 1 (Spring): 81–95.

———. 2000. "Cross-Confessing: Updike's Erect Faith in *A Month of Sundays*." In *Straight with a Twist: Queer Theory and the Subject of Heterosexuality*, edited by Calvin Thomas, 122–45. Urbana: University of Illinois Press.

———. 2006. "Conclusion: U(pdike) & P(ostmodernism)." In Olster 2006, 162–77.

Eberhart, John. 2001. "Faith for Breakfast, Doubt for Dessert." *Kansas City Star*, June 16, 22:15.

Eby, Lloyd. 1994. "Updike's Mixed Signals." *World & I*, July, 312–19.

Edelstein, J. M. 1960. "Down with the Poor in Spirit." *New Republic*, November 21, 17–18.

———. 1962. "The Security of Memory." *New Republic*, May 14, 30–31.

Eder, Richard. 1989. "Nothing to Declare." *Los Angeles Times Book Review*, March 12, 3, 5.

———. 1992. "Updike at Rest." *Los Angeles Times Book Review*, November 1, 3, 7.

———. 1996. "God and Mr. Updike." *Los Angeles Times Book Review*, January 28, 3, 10.

———. 2000. "Spoiled Rotten in Denmark." *New York Times Book Review*, February 27, 9.

Edwards, Lee R. 1972. "Says the Rabbit, What's Updike? As Pioneer, Most Wanting." *Village Voice*, January 27, 24, 26.

Edwards, Thomas. 1970. "*Bech: A Book*." *New York Times Book Review*, June 21, 1, 38.

———. 1975. "Busy Minister." *New York Review of Books*, March 3, 18–19.

———. (1981) 2005. "Updike's Rabbit Trilogy." *Atlantic*, October 1981, 94, 96, 100–101. Reprinted in De Bellis 2005, 106–12.

Ehrenpreis, Irvin. 1974. "Buchanan Redux." *New York Review of Books*, August 8, 6, 8.

Eichman, Erich. 1993. "Magic Is Not Enough." *New Leader*, December 27, 28–30.

Eiland, Howard. 1979. "Play in *Couples*." In Thorburn and Eiland 1979, 69–83.

———. 1982. "Updike's Womanly Man." *Centennial Review* 26, no. 4 (Fall): 312–23.

El Moncef, Salah. 1995. "Sounding the Black Box: Linear Reproduction and Chance Bifurcations in *Rabbit at Rest*." *Arizona Quarterly* 51, no. 4 (Winter): 69–108.

Ellison, James. 1981. "Rabbit Is Buying Krugerrands." *Psychology Today*, October, 110, 112, 115.

"Enemies of Promise." 1961. *Times Literary Supplement*, September 29, 648.

Engeman, Thomas. 2002. "The Technological Culture of Nihilism: John Updike's Protestant Pilgrimage and Walker Percy's Catholic Naturalism." In *Seers and Judges: American Literature as Political Philosophy*, edited by Christine Henderson, 135–57. Lanham, MD: Lexington.

Enright, D. J. (1965) 1966. "Updike's Ups and Downs." *Holiday*, November, 162, 164–65. Reprinted as "The Inadequate American: John Updike's Fiction." *Conspirators and Poets*, 134–40. London: Chatto & Windus, 1966.

———. 1984. "Rough Magic." *Listener*, September 27, 29–30.

Epstein, Joseph. 1965. "Mother's Day on the Updike Farm." *New Republic*, December 11, 23–25.

———. 1983. "John Updike: Promises, Promises." *Commentary*, January, 54–58.

Epstein, Seymour. 1972. "The Emperor's Blue Jeans." *University of Denver Quarterly* 6, no. 4 (Winter): 89–95.

Evanier, David. 1979. "An Affirmative Action." *National Review*, April 13, 490–91.

———. 1980. "Wearing Down." *National Review*, 22 February, 231–34.

Ewart, Gavin. 1985. "Making it Strange." *New York Times Book Review*, April 28, 18.

Falke, Wayne. 1974. "*Rabbit Redux*: Time/Order/God." *Modern Fiction Studies* 20, no. 1 (Spring): 59–76.

Farrell, Frank B. 2004. "John Updike and the Scene of Literature." *Why Does Literature Matter?* 217–41. Ithaca, NY: Cornell University Press.

Feeney, Mark. 1981. "Rabbit Running Down: Intimations of Mortality in Updike's Finest." *Boston Globe*, September 27, 1.

———. 1986. "God and Man at Flail—and Updike in the Middle." *Boston Globe*, August 24, A11–12.

———. 1989. "Updike: A Self-Portrait of the Artist." *Boston Globe*, March 5, B16, B18.

———. 1990. "Updike's Rabbit Makes his Final Run." *Boston Globe*, September 30, B43, 45.

Feinberg, Susan. 1983. "Anaclitic Love in John Updike's Novel *Of The Farm*." *Journal of Evolutionary Psychology* 4 (August): 163–68.

Feld, Ross. 1996. "Darkness and Doris Day." *Chicago Tribune*, February 4, 14:1, 9.

Fiedler, Leslie. 1964. *Waiting for the End*. New York: Stein & Day.

Finkelstein, Sidney. 1965. *Existentialism and Alienation in American Literature*. New York: International Publishers.

———. 1972. "The Anti-Hero of Updike, Bellow and Malamud." *American Dialog* 7, no. 2: 12–14, 30.

Fisher, Richard. 1962. "John Updike: Theme and Form in the Garden of Epiphanies." *Moderna Språk* 56, no. 3: 255–60.

Fitelson, David. 1959. "Conflict Unresolved." *Commentary*, March, 275–76.

Fleischauer, John. 1989. "John Updike's Prose Style: Definition at the Periphery of Meaning." *Critique* 30, no.1 (Summer): 277–90.

Flint, Joyce. 1968. "John Updike and *Couples*: The WASP's Dilemma." *Research Studies* 36, no. 4 (December): 340–47.

Flower, Dean. 1991. "Not Waving but Drowning." *Hudson Review* 44, no. 2 (Summer): 317–25.
———. 1998. "Looking Backward." *Hudson Review* 51, no. 1 (Spring): 241–49.
Forbes, Cheryl. 1975. "John Updike: Words, Words." *Christianity Today*, October 24, 16–18.
Forbes, Peter. 1987. "Master of Mimesis." *Poetry Review*, June, 22–23.
Ford, Mark. 1994. "Backside of the Tapestry." *Times Literary Supplement*, February 25, 21.
Foster, Richard. 1961. "What Is Fiction For?" *Hudson Review* 14, no. 1 (Spring): 132–49.
"Fragments of America." 1962. *Times Literary Supplement*, April 27, 277.
Freeman, John. 2000. "*Gertrude and Claudius.*" *Salon.com*. http://www.salon.com/books/review/2000/02/09/updike.
———. 2004. "Journey Through *Villages* Is a Cold One: Another Updike Hero Shaped by Women." *Hartford Courant*, October 10, G3.
Fremont-Smith, Eliot. 1965. "An Adventurer on Behalf of Us All." *New York Times*, June 22, 39.
———. 1968. "The Evidence in Tarbox." *New York Times*, March 25, 39.
———. (1981) 1983. "Rabbit Ruts." *Village Voice*, September 30–October 6, 35, 55. Reprinted in Bruccoli 1983, 315–20.
Fulford, Robert. 2006. "Explaining 9/11: Is Updike Up To It?" *National Post*, August 12, A16.
Fuller, Edmund. 1963a. "Chiron in Pennsylvania." *Wall Street Journal*, February 4, 14.
———. 1963b. "The Versatile Updike." *Wall Street Journal*, October 31, 15.
———. 1968. "Case for Celibacy." *Wall Street Journal*, May 13, 16.
———. 1971. "Return of Updike's Rabbit." *Wall Street Journal*, December 6, 12.
———. 1975. "A Fallen Minister Searches His Soul." *Wall Street Journal*, February 25, 16.
———. 1976. "Updike at the Top of His Form." *Wall Street Journal*, December 7, 22.
———. 1978. "Satiric Journey to the Heart of Darkness." *Wall Street Journal*, December 18, 28.
———. 1979. "Undisputed Masters of the Short Story." *Wall Street Journal*, December 10, 24.
Fyvel, T. R. 1983. "Jewish Anti-Hero." *Jewish Chronicle*, January 28.
Galgan, Gerald. 1976. "After Christianity, What?" *Commonweal*, November 5, 723–25.
Galloway, David. (1964) 1966. "The Absurd Man as Saint." *Modern Fiction Studies* 10 (Summer): 111–27. Revised and reprinted in *The Absurd Hero in American Fiction: Updike, Styron, Bellow, Salinger*, 21–50. Austin: University of Texas Press, 1966.
Gardiner, Harold. 1963. "Some Early Spring Novels." *America*, March 9, 340–41.

Gardner, James. 1996. "Our Country, 'Tis of Thee." *National Review*, February 26, 63–64.
Gardner, John. 1978. *On Moral Fiction*. New York: Basic Books.
Garrett, George. 1980. "Technics and Pyrotechnics." *Sewanee Review* 88, no. 3 (Summer): 412–23.
Gass, William. 1968. "Cock-a-doodle-doo." *New York Review of Books*, April 11, 3. Reprinted in *Fiction and the Figures of Life*, 20–21. New York: Knopf, 1970.
Gates, Ann. 1969. "John Updike—Wearing his Poet's Hat." *Christian Science Monitor*, August 15, 9.
Gayford, Martin. 2006. "John Updike, Man of American Letters, Is a Man of American Art, Too." *Sunday Telegraph*, February 19, 54.
Gessert, George. 1990. "Updike's Passage to India." *Northwest Review* 28, no. 2: 136–41.
Getlin, Josh. 1990. "Character Assassination." *Los Angeles Times*, November 4, E1, E12.
Gharraie, Jonathan. 2009. "John Updike" A Self Forever." *Oxonian Review* 8, no. 3 (February 9). http://www.oxonianreview.org/wp/category/issue/8-3/.
Ghosh, Amitav. 2006. "A Jihadist from Jersey." *Washington Post Book World*, June 4, 3.
Gilman, Richard. (1959) 1983. "A Last Assertion of Personal Being." *Commonweal*, February 6, 499–500. Reprinted in Bruccoli 1983, 256–59.
———. (1960) 1979. "A Distinguished Image of Precarious Life." *Commonweal*, October 28, 128–29. Reprinted in Thorburn and Eiland 1979, 13–16.
———. (1963) 1970. "Fiction: John Updike: The Youth of an Author." *New Republic*, April 13, 25–27. Reprinted in Gilman 1970, 62–68.
———. 1970. *The Confusion of Realms*. New York: Random House.
———. 1988. "The Witches of Updike." *New Republic*, June 20, 39–41.
Gindin, James. 1971. "Megalotopia and the WASP Backlash: The Fiction of Mailer and Updike." *Centennial Review* 15, no. 1 (Winter): 38–52.
Gingher, Robert. 1974. "Has John Updike Anything to Say?" *Modern Fiction Studies* 20, no. 1 (Spring): 97–105.
Glendinning, Victoria. 1983. "The Middle Age of an American Author." *Sunday Times*, January 9, 43.
"God Bless America." 1990. *Economist*, October 13, 157.
Goddard, Kevin. 2000. "'Looks Maketh the Man': The Female Gaze and the Construction of Masculinity." *Journal of Men's Studies* 9 (Fall): 23–39.
Godwin, Gail. 1984. "Wicked Witches of the North." *New Republic*, June 4, 28–29.
Gopnik, Adam. 2009. "Postscript." *New Yorker*, February 9, 35–36, 38.
Gordon, John. 1972. "Updike Redux." *Ramparts*, March, 56–59.
Gratton, Margaret. 1969. "The Use of Rhythm in Three Novels by John Updike." *University of Portland Review* 21 (Fall): 3–12.
Gray, Paul. 1986. "Theology and the Computer." *Time*, August 25, 67.

———. 1996. "We Lost It At the Movies." *Time*, January 29, 78.
Gray, Richard. 2004. *History of American Literature*. Malden, MA: Blackwell.
Gray, Simon. 1967. "Myth and Magic." *New Statesman*, June 16, 840.
Greenblatt, Stephen. 2000. "With Dirge in Marriage." *New Republic*, February 21, 32–38.
Greenfield, Josh. 1968. "A Romping Set in a Square New England Town." *Commonweal*, April 26, 185–87.
Greiner, Donald. 1981. *The Other John Updike: Poems/Short Stories/Prose/Play*. Athens: Ohio University Press.
———. 1983. "Pynchon, Hawkes, and Updike: Readers and the Paradox of Accessibility." *South Carolina Review* 16, no. 1 (Fall): 45–51.
———. 1984a. *John Updike's Novels*. Athens: Ohio University Press.
———. 1984b. "Updike Moves Sorcery to Suburbia." *Charlotte Observer*, May 27, 5F.
———. 1985. *Adultery in the American Novel: Updike, James, and Hawthorne*. Columbia: University of South Carolina Press.
———. 1987. "Updike on Hawthorne." *Nathaniel Hawthorne Review* 13, no. 1 (Spring): 1–4.
———. 1988. "Updike's Witches." In *Selected Essays: International Conference on Wit and Humor, 1986*, edited by Dorothy Joiner, 20–25. West Georgia International Conference.
———. 1989. "Body and Soul: John Updike and *The Scarlet Letter*." *Journal of Modern Literature* 15, no. 4 (Spring): 475–95.
———. 2006. "Updike, Rabbit, and the Myth of American Exceptionalism." In Olster 2006, 149–61.
———. 2007. "John Updike, Don DeLillo, and the Baseball Story as Myth." In Schiff 2007, 44–53.
———. 2010. "John Updike: The Literary Vermeer." *Critique* 51, no. 2 (Winter): 177–84.
Griffith, Albert. 1974. "Updike's Artist's Dilemma: 'Should Wizard Hit Mommy?'" *Modern Fiction Studies* 20, no. 1 (Spring): 111–115.
Gross, John. 1999. "Breaking the Rules." *Commentary*, January, 63–66.
Grumbach, Doris. 1975. "John Updike, With a Critical Eye." *Washington Post*, December 16, C4.
Hall, Joan. 1975. "A Month of Sundays." *New Republic*, February 22, 29–30.
Hall, Linda. 1996. "Rabbit, Researched." *New York*, January 15, 52–53.
Hallissy, Margaret. 1981. "Updike's *Rabbit, Run* and Pascal's *Pensees*." *Christianity and Literature* 30, no. 2 (Winter): 25–32.
Hamilton, Alice. 1969. "Between Innocence and Experience: From Joyce to Updike." *Dalhousie Review* 49, no. 4 (December): 102–09.
Hamilton, Alice, and Kenneth Hamilton. 1967. *John Updike*. Contemporary Writers in Christian Perspective. Grand Rapids, MI: Eerdmans.
———. 1970a. *The Elements of John Updike*. Grand Rapids, MI: Eerdmans.
———. (1970b) 1982. "Metamorphosis through Art: John Updike's *Bech: A Book*." *Queen's Quarterly* 77: 624–36. Reprinted in Macnaughton 1982: 115–27.

———. 1970c. "Theme and Technique in John Updike's *Midpoint*." *Mosaic* 4, no. 3 (Fall): 79–106.

———. 1972. "John Updike's Prescription for Survival." *Christian Century*, July 5–12, 740–44.

———. 1973. "Mythic Dimensions in Updike's Fiction." *North Dakota Quarterly* 41, no. 3 (Summer): 54–66.

———. 1974. "John Updike's *Museums and Women and Other Stories*." *Thought* 49: 56–71.

Hamilton, Kenneth. 1967. "John Updike: Chronicler of 'the Time of the Death of God.'" *Christian Century*, June 7, 745–48.

Hardwick, Elizabeth. 1961. "The New Books." *Harper's*, January, 104–05.

Harper, Howard M. 1967. "John Updike: The Intrinsic Problem of Human Existence." In *Desperate Faith: A Study of Bellow, Salinger, Mailer, Baldwin and Updike*, 162–90. Chapel Hill: University of North Carolina Press.

Harrington, J. P. 2011. "Updike's Grand and Tantalizing Final Act." *Dartmouth Review*, February 3. http://dartreview.com/arts-culture/2011/2/3/updikes-grand-and-tantalizing-final-act.html.

Hartle, Terry. 2005. "Rabbit Runs—Straight to the Fine Arts Exhibit." *Christian Science Monitor*, December 20, 15.

Hartnell, Anna. 2011. "Violence and the Faithful in Post-9/11 America: Updike's *Terrorist*, Islam, and the Specter of Exceptionalism." *Modern Fiction Studies* 57, no. 3 (Fall): 477–500.

Harvey, Giles. 2009. "The Last Scoop of Ice Cream." *Times Literary Supplement*, July 10, 19.

Hawthorne, Nathaniel. *The Scarlet Letter: A Romance*. Boston: Ticknor, Reed, and Fields, 1850.

Healey, Robert. 1959. "John Updike with a Packet of Stories." *New York Herald Tribune*, August 16, 3.

Heddendorf, David. (2000) 2005. "Rabbit Reread." *Southern Review* 36, no. 3 (Summer): 641–47. Reprinted in De Bellis 2005, 237–42.

———. 2008. "The Modesty of John Updike." *Sewanee Review* 116, no. 1 (Winter): 108–16.

———. 2009a. "Learned Critic, Working Stiff." *Sewanee Review* 117, no. 3 (Summer): xliii–xliv.

———. 2009b. "The Pennsylvanian." *Sewanee Review* 117, no. 3 (Summer): 487–90.

Heidenry, John. 1972. "The Best American Novel in a Decade." *Commonweal*, January 7, 332–33.

Heitman, Danny. 2011. "Higher Gossip." *Christian Science Monitor*, November 9.

Hendin, Josephine. (1976) 1979. "Updike as Matchmaker." *Nation*, October 30, 437–39. Reprinted in Thorburn and Eiland 1979, 99–106.

———. 1978. "The Victim as Hero." *Vulnerable People: A View of American Fiction Since 1945*, 88–115. New York: Oxford University Press.

Henricks, Thomas. 1988. "Social Science Meets Updike: The Passion for Sport as Personal Regression." *Aethlon* 5, no. 2 (Spring): 131–45.

Hensher, Philip. 1995. "Another Guided Tour-de-Force." *Spectator*, January 21, 34–35.
Heyen, William. 1970. "Sensibilities." *Poetry* 115 (March): 426–29.
Hicks, Granville. (1959) 1970. "Novels in Limbo." *Saturday Review*, January 17, 58–59. Reprinted in Hicks 1970, 109.
———. (1960) 1970. "A Little Good in Evil." *Saturday Review*, November 5, 28. Reprinted in Hicks 1970, 110–13.
———. (1962) 1970. "Mysteries of the Commonplace." *Saturday Review*, March 17, 21–22. Reprinted in Hicks 1970, 113–16.
———. (1963a) 1970. "Generations of the Fifties: Malamud, Gold, and Updike." In *The Creative Present*, edited by Nona Balakian 1963, 217–37. Garden City, NJ: Doubleday.
———. (1963b) 1970. "Pennsylvania Pantheon." *Saturday Review*, February 2, 27–28. Reprinted in Hicks 1970, 116–20.
———. (1965) 1970. "Mothers, Sons, and Lovers." *Saturday Review*, November 13, 41–42. Reprinted in Hicks 1970, 109.
———. (1966) 1970. "Domestic Felicity?" *Saturday Review*, September 24, 31–32. Reprinted in Hicks 1970, 126–28.
———. (1968) 1970. "God Has Gone, Sex Is Left." *Saturday Review*, April 6, 21–22. Reprinted in Hicks 1970, 126–32.
———. 1970. *Literary Horizons*. New York: New York University Press.
Hicks, Thomas. 1992/93. "Updike's Rabbit Novels: An American Epic." *Sacred Heart University Review* 13, no. 1 (Fall/Spring): 65–70.
Hill, John S. 1969. "Quest for Belief: Theme in the Novels of John Updike." *Southern Humanities Review* 3, no. 2 (September): 166–75.
Hill, William B. 1968. "*Couples*." *America*, June 8, 757.
———. 1975. "A Month of Sundays." *America*, April 26, 3.
Hitchens, Christopher. 1988. "The Karmic Polymorphous Perverse." *Times Literary Supplement*, April 22–28, 453.
———. 1994. "Writing Out of His Skin, and Not Ashamed of It." *Evening Standard*, April 8, 12.
———. 2006. "No Way: John Updike's Latest Novel Reveals His Tin Ear for Critical Times." *Atlantic Monthly*, June, 114–17.
———. 2007. "Mr. Geniality." *New York Times Book Review*, November 4, 1.
———. 2009. "Farewell to a Much-Misunderstood Man." *Slate*, February 2. http://www.slate.com/id/2210302/.
Hoag, Ronald. 1979. "A Second Controlling Myth in John Updike's *Centaur*." *Studies in the Novel* 11: 446–53.
———. 1980. "*The Centaur*: What Cures George Caldwell?" *Studies in American Fiction* 8, no. 1 (Spring): 88–98.
Hodgart, Matthew. 1978. "Family Snapshots." *Times Literary Supplement*, October 13, 1158.
Hogan, Robert. 1980. "Catharism and John Updike's *Rabbit, Run*." *Renascence* 32, no. 4 (Summer): 229–39.
Hogan, William. 1962. "The Incandescent Updike at Work." *San Francisco Chronicle*, March 22, 39.

Holleran, Andrew. 1981. "Rabbit Resplendent." *New York*, October 5, 64.
Holmes, Catherine. 2011. "Gift from Updike: 'Higher Gossip' Offers Thoughts from Late Writer." *Post and Courier*, November 20.
Hoover, Bob. 2004. "John Updike Boxes Himself into a Familiar Corner when Writing about Relationships." *Pittsburgh Post-Gazette*, October 17, B4.
Hope, Francis. 1973. "Too Much." *New Statesman*, April 27, 626.
Hopkin, James. 2000. "Bard Times." *Guardian*, July 1.
Horner, Avril and Sue Zlosnik. 2000. "'Releasing Spirit from Matter': Comic Alchemy in Spark's *The Ballad of Peckham Rye*, Updike's *The Witches of Eastwick* and Mantel's *Fludd*." *Gothic Studies* 2, no. 1: 136–47.
Horvath, Brooke. 1988. "The Failure of Erotic Questing in John Updike's Rabbit Novels." *University of Denver Quarterly* 23, no. 2 (Fall): 70–89.
Hough, Henry. 1958. "Readings Put to Jazz." *Denver Post*, April 27, Roundup: 12.
Howard, Maureen. 1976. "Jerry and Sally and Richard and Ruth." *New York Times Book Review*, October 31, 2.
Hubler, Richard. 1966. "Updike Dazzles Until It's Boresome." *Los Angeles Times*, September 25, M28.
Hulbert, Dan. 2000. "Updike: We Know Him Well." *Atlanta Journal-Constitution*, February 20, L12.
Hume, Kathryn. 2000. *American Dream, American Nightmare: Fiction Since 1960*. Urbana: University of Illinois Press.
Hunsinger, George. 1987. "Updike's Version." *New York Review of Books*, February 12, 41.
Hunt, George W., S.J. 1975. "John Updike's Sunday Sort of Book." *America*, June 21, 477–80.
———. 1977a. "Kierkegaardian Sensations into Real Fiction: John Updike's 'The Astronomer.'" *Christianity and Literature* 26, no. 3: 3–17.
———. 1977b. "*Marry Me: A Romance*." *America*, January 8, 18–19.
———. 1978. "Updike's Pilgrims in a World of Nothingness." *Thought* 53: 384–400.
———. (1979a) 1982. "Reality, Imagination, and Art: The Significance of Updike's 'Best' Story." *Studies in Short Fiction* 16: 219–29. Reprinted in Macnaughton 1982, 207–16.
———. 1979b. "Updike's Omega-Shaped Shelter: Structure and Psyche in *A Month of Sundays*." *Critique* 19, no. 3: 47–60.
———. 1980a. *John Updike and the Three Great Secret Things: Sex, Religion, and Art*. Grand Rapids, MI: Eerdmans.
———. 1980b. "The Problems of John Updike." *America*, March 8, 187–88.
———. 1981a. "Religious Themes in the Fiction of John Updike and John Cheever." *New Catholic World*, November/December, 248–51.
———. 1981b. "Updike's Rabbit Returns." *America*, November 21, 321–22.
———. 1982. "Bech Is Back!" *America*, November 20, 314–16.

———. 1983. "Hugging the Shore." *America*, December 31, 437.
———. 2006. "Ahmad's Plot." *America*, July 3–10, 23–25.
Hunt, Russell. 1979. "Review: *The Coup*, by John Updike." *The Dooryard Post* 1, no. 3 (Summer): 25–26.
Huston, Warner. 2006. "John Updike and Why Libs Will Never 'Get' the War on Terror." *Conservative Voice*, 5 June. Reprinted in *Renew America*. http://www.renewamerica.com/columns/huston/060605.
Hyman, Stanley. 1962. "The Artist as a Young Man." *New Leader*, March 19, 22–23.
———. (1963) 1966. "Chiron at Olinger High." *New Leader*, February 4, 20–21. Reprinted in *Standards*, 128–32.
———. *Standards*. 1966. New York: Horizon Press.
———. (1968) 1978. "Couplings." *New Leader*, May 20, 20–21. Reprinted in *The Critic's Credentials*, edited by Phoebe Pettingell. New York: Atheneum, 1978, 107–11.
Iannone, Carol. 1988. "Adultery, from Hawthorne to Updike." *Commentary*, October, 55–59.
Inglis, Fred. 1989. "On Being a Dud." *Nation*, July 10, 59–61.
Jackson, Edward. 1985. "Rabbit Is Racist." *CLA Journal* 28, no. 4 (June): 444–51.
Jacobsen, Josephine. 1966. Review of *The Music School*. *Commonweal*, December 9, 299–300.
James, Clive. 2009. "Final Act." *New York Times Book Review*, May 3, 15.
Janowitz, Henry D. 2003. "'Master Eustace' and *Gertrude and Claudius*: Henry James and John Updike Rewrite *Hamlet*." *Hamlet Studies* 25: 189–99.
Jarraway, David. 2010. "Future Interior Subjective (A)voidance in John Updike's 'Rabbit' Novels." *Canadian Review of American Studies* 40, no. 1: 45–62.
Jay, Elisabeth. 2005. "'Who Are You, Gentle Reader?': John Updike's *A Month of Sundays*." *Literature & Theology* 19, no. 4 (November): 346–54.
Johnson, Charles. 1992. "The Virgin President." *New York Times Book Review*, November 1, 11.
Johnson, Diane. 1984. "Warlock." *New York Review of Books*, June 14, 3–4.
Johnson, Greg. 1999. "Updike, Discoursing on Things that Matter." *Atlanta Journal-Constitution*, October 3, L13.
———. 2010. "Reputations and Renewals." *Georgia Review* 64, no 1 (Spring): 158–67.
Johnson, Jeffrey. 2009. "Updike's Passions." *Christian Century*, March 24, 12–13.
Johnson, Roger A. 1995. "Soul-Loss, Sex Magic, and Taboos in Contemporary America: The Death of Rabbit Angstrom." In *On Losing the Soul: Essays in the Social Psychology of Religion*, edited by Richard Fenn and Donald Capps, 195–212. Albany: SUNY Press.

Johnston, Robert. 1977. "John Updike's Theological World." *Christian Century*, November 16, 1061–66.

———. 1978. "The 'Wisdom' of John Updike." *Duke Divinity School Review* 43, no. 1 (Spring): 112–27.

"John Updike: His Other Hand." 1994. *Economist*, January 29, 92.

Jones, D. A. N. 1979. "Kismet Kush." *The Listener*, March 15, 390, 392.

Jones, Nicolette. 1994. "The Order of Merit: Who Is the Greatest Living Novelist Writing in English?" *London Sunday Times*, March 13, 8–9.

Jong, Erica. 1979. "*Too Far to Go.*" *New Republic*, September 15, 36–37.

Kakutani, Michiko. 1981a. "Be More Like Graham Greene, Dear." *New York Times Book Review*, August 16, 3.

———. 1981b. "Turning Sex and Guilt into an American Epic." *Saturday Review*, October, 14–15, 20–22.

———. 1988. "Updike's Struggle to Portray Women." *New York Times*, May 5, C29.

———. 1990. "Just 30 Years Later, Updike Has a Quartet." *New York Times*, September 25, C13, C17.

———. 1991. "The Magic Act of a Novelist." *New York Times*, October 25, C29.

———. 1994a. "Of Time, Loss and Death: The Vista Is Lengthening." *New York Times*, November 8, C17.

———. 1994b. "Tristan and Iseult as Latin Lovers." *New York Times*, January 25, C19.

———. 1996a. "Bad Sports." *New York Times Magazine*, August 25, 24.

———. 1996b. "Seeking Salvation on the Silver Screen." *New York Times*, January 12, C1, C32.

———. 1997. "On Sex, Death and the Self: An Old Man's Sour Grapes." *New York Times*, September 30, E1, E8.

———. 1999. "Making a Thing Real by Pinning It Down in Words." *New York Times*, September 21, E8.

———. 2000a. "Run, Gerutha, Run: Elsinore, Aye, Has Gone Suburban." *New York Times*, February 8, E1, E8.

———. 2000b. "Updike Takes Another Shot at Rabbit." *New York Times*, November 7, E7.

———. 2002. "Roman à Clef Sketches Jackson Pollock's Downward Spiral." *New York Times*, November 12, E1, E6.

———. 2003. "Writer Run: Early Years of the Updike Marathon." *New York Times*, November 21, E31, E41.

———. 2004. "Another Updike Trip to His Kind of Suburbia." *New York Times*, October 22, E33, E43.

———. 2006. "A Homegrown Threat to Homeland Security." *New York Times*, June 6, E1, E8.

———. 2008. "Old Black Magic Is Old, and so Are These Witches." *New York Times*, October 20, C1.

———. 2009. "Memory Arpeggios in Updike's Sunset." *New York Times*, May 26, C1.

———. 2011. "Last Notes from a Man of Letters." *New York Times*, November 29, C1.
Kanon, Joseph. 1972. "Satire and Sensibility." *Saturday Review*, September 30, 77–78.
Kapp, Isa. 1982. "Updike in a Foreign Country." *New Leader*, December 13, 5–7.
———. 2004. "Sex and the Small Town." *New Leader*, September/October, 33–34.
Karl, Frederick. 1983. *American Fictions 1940/1980*. New York: Harper & Row.
Kauffmann, Stanley. 1966. "Onward with Updike." *New Republic*, September 24, 15–17.
Kay, Jane. 1965. "Casuals by Updike." *Christian Science Monitor*, June 26, 9.
Kazin, Alfred. 1968. "Updike: Novelist of the New, Post-Pill America." *Chicago Tribune Book World*, April 7, 1, 3.
———. 1971. "Professional Observers: Cozzens to Updike." *Bright Book of Life: American Novelists and Storytellers from Hemingway to Mailer*, 95–124. Boston: Little, Brown.
———. (1976) 1982. "Alfred Kazin on Fiction." *New Republic*, November 27, 22–23. Reprinted in Macnaughton 1982, 79–80.
———. 1981. "Easy Come, Easy Go." *New York Review of Books*, November 19, 3.
———. 1992. "The Middle Way." *New York Review of Books*, December 17, 45–46.
Keenan, John. 2005. "Updike on Empty." *January Magazine*, February. http://januarymagazine.com/fiction/villages.html.
———. 2008. "Why John Updike Is a Virtual Shadow of His Old Self." *Guardian*, August 22.
Keener, Brian. 2005. *John Updike's Human Comedy: Comic Morality in The Centaur and the Rabbit Novels*. New York: Peter Lang.
"Keeping it Short." 1967. *Times Literary Supplement*, 24 August, 757.
Kehe, Marjorie. 2009. "John Updike: A Look Back." *Christian Science Monitor*, January 27.
Kemp, Peter. 1995. "Thanks for the Memories." *Times*, February 5, 13.
———. 1996. "Voice of America." *Sunday Times*, April 21, Books 1–2.
———. 2005. Review of *Villages*. *Sunday Times*, January 23, 52.
Kennedy, Douglas. 2006. "Not a Bang but a Whimper." *Times*, August 5, 5.
Kennedy, Eugene. 1986. "John Updike Seeks God in a Computer." *Chicago Sun-Times*, August 31, Book Week: 1–2.
Kennedy, William. 1968. "Updike Explores Antics of Oversexed Generation." *National Observer*, April 15, 19.
Kennedy, X. J. 1963. "A Light Look at Today." *New York Times Book Review*, September 22, 10, 12.
———. 1993. "Orphan Asylum." *New Criterion*, April, 62.
Kermode, Frank. 1979. "Fiction in Focus." *Guardian*, March 19, 10.
———. 1999. "Overflow." *London Review of Books*, January 21, 23–24.

Kidder, Gayle. 1994. "Updike's Latest: It's a Dirty Shame." *San Diego Union-Tribune*, February 6, Books 4.

Kielland-Lund, Erik. 1993 "The Americanness of *Rabbit, Run*: A Transatlantic View." In Trachtenberg 1993, 77–94.

King, Francis. 2001. "Rabbit Is Dead." *Spectator*, March 31, 42.

Kingsolver, Barbara. 1994. "Desire Under the Palms." *New York Times Book Review*, February 6, 1, 26–27.

Kirklighter, Cristina. 1994. "No Roads to Freedom: The Unfulfilled Quests in Updike's Rabbit Novels." *Lamar Journal of the Humanities* 20, no. 1 (Spring): 61–73.

Kirn, Walter. 2004. "Swing Time." *New York Times Book Review*, October 31, 13.

Kirsch, Robert. 1975. "Pieces of the Vintage Updike." *Los Angeles Times*, November 14, G15.

Klausler, Alfred. 1961. "Steel Wilderness." *Christian Century*, February 22, 245–46.

Klinkowitz, Jerome. 1995. "Toward a New American Mainstream: John Updike and Kurt Vonnegut." In *Traditions, Voices, and Dreams: The American Novel since the 1960s*, edited by Melvin Friedman and Ben Siegel, 150–67. Newark: Univrsity of Delaware Press.

Koenig, Rhoda. 1984. "That Old White Magic." *New York*, May 14, 76–77.

———. 1986. "Soul on Ice." *New York*, September 8, 76.

———. 1989. "The Watchful I." *New York*, March 13, 66.

———. 1991. "Swell's Lettres." *New York*, November 4, 130–31.

———. 1994. "Rio Is Rich." *New York*, January 31, 62–63.

Koeppel, Fredric. 1986. "Updike Disappoints Fans." *Memphis Commercial Appeal*, September 7, J4.

———. 1990a. "Updike: '*Rabbit at Rest*' Ends Noted Author's Series." *Memphis Commercial Appeal*, September 16, G1–2.

———. 1990b. "Versatile Writer Sits Atop World of American Letters." *Memphis Commercial Appeal*, September 16, G1–2.

———. 1996. "Saga of Kin and Country Shatters the Updike Mold." *Memphis Commercial Appeal*, February 11, G1, G4.

Kort, Wesley. 1966. "A Confession of Debt." *Christian Century*, January 19, 82.

———. 1968. "Desperate Games." *Christian Century*, October 23, 1340–42.

———. 1999. "Learning to Die: Work as Religious Discipline." In Yerkes 1999b, 180–91.

Kramer, Hilton. 1986. "A High-Tech Shrine to Sex and Society." *Wall Street Journal*, September 24, 30.

———. 1989. "Every Picture Tells a Story." *Washington Post Book World*, November 26, 9.

Kuehl, Linda. 1970. "The Risks in Putting on a Put-On." *Christian Science Monitor*, July 23, 7.

Kunkel, Francis. 1975. "John Updike: Between Heaven and Earth." *Passion and the Passion: Sex and Religion in Modern Literature*, 75–98. Philadelphia: Westminster.
La Course, Guerin. 1963. "The Innocence of John Updike." *Commonweal*, February 8, 512–14.
La Salle, Peter. 1978. "More Than Are Dreamt of in Your Philosophy." *America*, December 23, 482.
Laird, Nicholas. 2003. "A Life in Art." *Times Literary Supplement*, April 25, 21–22.
Lambirth, Andrew. 2007. Review of *Still Looking: Essays on American Art*. *Art Book* 14, no. 1 (February): 30–31.
Lanchester, John. 1988. "Be a Lamp Unto Yourself." *London Review of Books*, May 5, 20–21.
Larsen, Richard. 1972–73. "John Updike: The Story as Lyrical Meditation." *Thoth* 13: 33–39.
Larson, Janet. 1975. "A Man Out of the Cloth." *Christian Century*, April 30, 445–47.
Lask, Thomas. 1963. "End Papers." *New York Times*, September 21, 19.
Lasseter, Victor. 1989. "*Rabbit Is Rich* as a Naturalistic Novel." *American Literature* 61, no. 3 (October): 429–45.
Lathrop, Kathleen. 1985. "*The Coup*: Updike's Modernist Masterpiece." *Modern Fiction Studies* 31, no. 2 (Summer): 249–62.
Lawson, Lewis. 1974. "Rabbit Angstrom as a Religious Sufferer." *Journal of the American Academy of Religion* 42, no. 2 (June): 232–46.
Leader, Zachary. 1990. "No Mercy in the Death State." *Times Literary Supplement*, October 26–November 1, 1145–46.
———. 2001. "Nelson's Dad." *Times Literary Supplement*, March 23, 8.
Leckie, Barbara. 1991. "'The Adulterous Society': John Updike's *Marry Me*." *Modern Fiction Studies* 37, no. 1 (Spring): 61–79.
LeClair, Thomas. 1975. "Updike's Anti-Metafiction." *Fiction International* 4/5: 130–32.
———. 1977. "Updike and Gardner: Down from the Heights." *Commonweal*, February 4, 89–90.
Lee, Hermione. (1990) 2005. "The Trouble with Harry." *New Republic*, December 24, 34–37. Reprinted in De Bellis 2005, 167–73.
Lehmann-Haupt, Christopher. 1970. "Updike: A Mensch." *New York Times*, June 11, 43.
———. 1988. "In John Updike's Latest, The Woman Called 'S.'" *New York Times*, March 7, C16.
———. 1989. "A Man of Letters and the Pull of Visual Arts." *New York Times*, October 9, C18.
———. 1992. "A Heroic Then, a Realistic Now." *New York Times*, October 22, C25.
———. 1996. "How One Small Ball Holds the Whole Universe." *New York Times*, September 19, C17.

Leigh, David J., S.J. 2002. "Ironic Apocalypse in John Updike's *Toward the End of Time*." *Religion & Literature* 34, no. 1 (Spring): 51–65. Revised and reprinted as "The Ultimate Self: Death and Dying in John Updike and Charles Williams." *Apocalyptic Patterns in Twentieth-Century Fiction*, 152–66. Notre Dame, IN: University of Notre Dame Press, 2008.

Leonard, John. 1981. "Books of the Times." *New York Times*, September 22, C13.

———. 1989. "Bad-Boy Books." *Ms. Magazine*, January-February, 124.

———. 2006. "Rabbit Is Radical." *New York*, May 28, 71–72.

Lindroth, James. 1972. "*Rabbit Redux*." *America*, January 29, 102, 104.

Linford, E. H. 1965. "Updike's Essays Lack Original Flavor." *Salt Lake Tribune*, May 30, W9.

Lipsius, Frank. 1975. "Yankee Saints and Sinners." *Books and Bookmen*, September, 28.

Lipsky, David. 1988. "S.-Trogen." *National Review*, May 13, 58–59.

———. 1993. "Memories of U." *National Review*, February 1, 58–60.

"The Loathly Glass." 1989. *Economist*, May 13, 98, 101.

Locke, Richard. (1971) 1983. "Rabbit Returns: Updike Was Always There— It's Time We Noticed." *New York Times Book Review*, November 14, 1–2, 12–16, 20–21. Reprinted in Bruccoli 1983, 284–91.

Lodge, David. 1962. "Instant Novel." *Spectator*, May 11, 628.

———. (1970) 1971. "Post-Pill Paradise Lost: John Updike's *Couples*." *New Blackfriars*, November, 511–18. Reprinted in Lodge 1971, 237–44.

———. 1971. *The Novelist at the Crossroads, and Other Essays on Fiction and Criticism,*. Ithaca, NY: Cornell University Press.

———. 1979. "The King's Head." *New Statesman*, March 23, 404–05.

———. 1986. "Chasing After God and Sex." *New York Times Book Review*, August 31, 1, 15.

———. (1998) 2002. "Bye-Bye Bech?" *New York Review of Books*, November 19, 8–10. Reprinted in Lodge 2002, 234–47.

———. 2002. *Consciousness and the Novel*. Cambridge, MA: Harvard University Press.

Loercher, Diana. 1979. "Updike's Romance with Language." *Christian Science Monitor*, November 7, 7.

Loudermilk, Kim. 2004. "'Weak Sisters': Feminism and *The Witches of Eastwick*." In *Fictional Feminism: How American Bestsellers Affect the Movement for Women's Equality*, 99–122. New York: Routledge.

Lurie, Alison. 1988. "The Woman Who Rode Away." *New York Review of Books*, May 12, 3–4.

———. 2009. "Widcraft." *New York Review of Books*, January 15.

Luscher, Robert. (1988) 1995. "John Updike's Olinger Stories: New Light Among the Shadows." *Les Cahiers de la Nouvelle (Journal of the Short Story in English)* No. 11 (Autumn): 99–117. Reprinted in *Modern American Short Story Sequences*, edited by J. Gerald Kennedy, 151–69. Cambridge, England: Cambridge University Press, 1995.

———. 1993. *John Updike: A Study of the Short Fiction*. New York: Twayne.

Lynn, Kenneth. 1982. "Bunny Stuff." *National Review*, December 10, 1558.
Lyons, Eugene. 1972. "John Updike: The Beginning and the End." *Critique* 14, no. 2 (Spring): 44–59.
Lyons, Gene. 1979. "Cultural Deformations." *Nation*, February 3, 117–19.
———. 1981. "The Way We Are." *Nation*, November 7, 477–79.
Mabe, Chauncey. 1996. "A Flawed Beauty." *Fort Lauderdale Sun-Sentinel*, February 25, 8D.
Mack, Mehammed. 2006. "The Spider and the Wasp." *Los Angeles Weekly*, May 31.
Macnaughton, William, ed. 1982. *Critical Essays on John Updike*. Boston: G. K. Hall.
Magaw, Malcolm. 1992. "From Vermeer to Bonnard: Updike's Interartistic Mode in *Marry Me*." *Midwest Quarterly* 33, no. 2 (Winter): 137–50.
———. 1995. "The Geographical and Spatial Correlative in Updike's *Marry Me*." *Midwest Quarterly* 36, no. 3: 250–64.
Mailer, Norman. 1963. "Norman Mailer vs. Nine Writers." *Esquire*, July, 63–69, 105.
Mallon, Thomas. 1981. "Rabbit, Jog." *National Review*, November 13, 1356–58.
Malone, David. 1999. "Updike 2020: Fantasy, Mythology, and Faith in *Toward the End of Time*." In Yerkes 1999b, 80–98.
Manning, Margaret. 1978. "Updike Presents a Puzzle of Beauty, Irony, Cruelty." *Boston Sunday Globe*, December 10, A8.
———. 1979. "Updike: Sometimes Radiant, Dazzling." *Boston Globe*, November 4, A7.
———. 1982. "John Updike Redux." *Boston Sunday Globe*, March 21, A19.
———. 1984. "Updike Heats the Caldron to a Steamy Boil." *Boston Globe*, May 20, B1, B3.
Mano, D. Keith. (1974) 1982. "Doughy Middleness." *National Review*, 20 August 1974, 987. Reprinted in Macnaughton 1982, 74–76.
Manuel, Bruce. 1990. "Rabbit Is Still Running on Empty." *Christian Science Monitor*, November 29, 13.
Marcus, James. 2007. "'Due Considerations: Essays and Criticism' by John Updike." *Los Angeles Times*, October 28.
Mariani, Paul. 2001. "Travels and Travails." *America*, December 3, 24–25.
Maristed, Kai. 2008. "In Eastwick, a Sinful Trio Returns." *Los Angeles Times*, October 27.
Markle, Joyce. 1973. *Fighters and Lovers: Theme in the Novels of John Updike*. New York: New York University Press.
———. 1982. "*The Coup*: Illusions and Insubstantial Impressions." In Macnaughton 1982, 281–301.
Markovits, Benjamin. 2003. "A Load of Pollocks." *New Statesman*, May 5, 41–42.
Markovitz, Irving. 1980. "John Updike's Africa." *Canadian Journal of African Studies* 14: 536–45.
Mars-Jones, Adam. 1999. "Make Yourself a Tome." *Observer*, December 12.

———. 2001. "You Can't Keep a Good Rabbit Down." *Observer*, March 25, 15.

———. 2003. "How Many Artists Does it Take to Paint a Portrait?" *Observer*, April 27, 15.

Martin, John. 1982. "Rabbit's Faith: Grace and the Transformation of the Heart." *Pacific Coast Philology* 17: 103–11.

"A Master of Craft." 1992. *Economist*, February 1, 100.

Matson, Elizabeth. 1967. "A Chinese Paradox but Not Much of One: John Updike in His Poetry." *Minnesota Review* 8: 157–67.

Matthews, Charles. 2002. "Updike's '*Seek My Face*' Wanders Off Course and Goes On Too Long." *San Jose Mercury News*, November 17, Books 1.

Matthews, John. 1983. "The Word as Scandal: Updike's *A Month of Sundays*." *Arizona Quarterly* 39, no. 4 (Winter): 351–80.

———. 1985. "Intertextuality and Originality: Hawthorne, Faulkner, Updike." In *Intertextuality in Faulkner*, edited by Michel Gresset and Noel Polk, 144–57. Jackson: University Press of Mississippi.

Mayne, Richard. 1962. "Instant Literature." *New Statesman*, April 27, 606–07.

———. 1966. "Epicures, etc." *New Statesman*, February 4, 169.

Mazurek, Raymond. 1989. "'Bringing the Corners Forward': Ideology and Representation in Updike's Rabbit Trilogy." In *Politics and the Muse: Studies in the Politics of Recent American Literature*, edited by Adam Sorkin, 142–60. Bowling Green, OH: Bowling Green State University Press.

McCarthy, Abigail. 1979. "The Master of the Minor." *New York*, November 19, 97.

McCarthy, Desmond. 1997. *Reconstructing the Family in Contemporary American Fiction*. New York: Peter Lang.

McCord, David. 1958. "Trivia of Life." *Saturday Review*, August, 32.

McCormack, Ed. 2006. "John Updike: The Art Book as Belles Lettres." *Gallery & Studio*, February/March, 10–11.

McCoy, Robert. 1974. "John Updike's Literary Apprenticeship on *The Harvard Lampoon*." *Modern Fiction Studies* 20, no. 1 (Spring): 3–12.

McEwan, Ian. 1995. "Updike's Intimations of Mortality." *Financial Times*, February 4, Books: 13.

———. 1996. "A Spiritual Legacy from Disbelief to Cultism." *Financial Times*, April 20, 15.

McGuiness, Frank. 1961. "In Extremis." *New Statesman*, September 29, 439–40.

McKenzie, Alan. 1974. "'A Craftsman's Intimate Satisfactions': The Parlor Games in *Couples*." *Modern Fiction Studies* 20, no. 1 (Spring): 53–58.

McPherson, William. 1975. "Sacramental Relations." *Washington Post Book World*, February 16, 1.

———. 1978. "John Updike in the Land of Kush." *Washington Post Book World*, November 26, 1.

———. 1979. "Too Far To Go: The Maples Stories." *Washington Post Book World*, March 18, E1, E6.
McTavish, John. 1996. "John Updike: A Novelist for Curious Christians." *Presbyterian Record*, March 1, 22–23.
———. 2000. "The Theological Dimension in John Updike's Fiction." *Theology Today* 57 (April): 66–74.
———. 2010. Review of *Endpoint and Other Poems* and *My Father's Tears and Other Stories*. *Theology Today* 66 (January): 524–26.
Mehl, Duane. 1987. "The Downward Trajectory of John Updike." *National Review*, February 13, 53–54, 56.
Meinke, Peter. 1966. "Yearning for Yesteryear." *Christian Century*, December 7, 1512.
Mellard, James. (1979) 1982. "The Novel as Lyric Elegy: The Mode of Updike's *The Centaur*." *Texas Studies in Literature and Language* 21: 112–27. Reprinted in Macnaughton 1982, 217–30.
Menand, Louis. 1990. "Rabbit Is Dead." *Esquire*, November, 93, 97.
———. 2003. "Pursuits of Happiness." *New Yorker*, December 1, 104–10.
Merkin, Daphne. 1978. "Updike in Africa." *New Leader*, December 4, 21–22.
Messud, Claire. 2009. "The Alchemist of the Mundane." *Newsweek*, February 9, 66–67.
Meyer, Arlin. 1974. "Selected Checklist of Criticism." *Modern Fiction Studies* 20, no. 1 (Spring): 121–33.
Michie, James. 1997. "It's Not Just a Game." *Spectator*, May 3, 41–42.
Milazzo, Lee. 1978. "Updike's *The Coup* Should Be Just That." *Dallas Morning News*, December 3, 5G.
———. 1984. "Bewitched! John Updike's Newest Novel Works Like Magic." *Dallas Morning News*, June 10, 4G.
———. 1986. "A Complex, Dazzling New Novel by Updike." *Dallas Morning News*, September 14, 11C.
———. 1995. "A Growth Spurt after Maturity." *Dallas Morning News*, January 22, 8J.
Millard, Kenneth. 2000. "John Updike: *Memories of the Ford Administration*." *Contemporary American Fiction*, 233–39. New York: Oxford University Press.
Miller, Alicia. 1994. "An Updike Gone Astray." *Cleveland Plain Dealer*, January 30, Books: 13.
Miller, D. Quentin. 1997. "Updike's Rabbit Novels and the Tragedy of Parenthood." In *Family Matters in the British and American Novel*, edited by Andrea Herrera, Elizabeth Nollen, and Sheila Foor, 195–216. Bowling Green, OH: Bowling Green Popular Press.
———. 2001. *John Updike and the Cold War: Drawing the Iron Curtain*. Columbia: University of Missouri Press.
———. 2005. "Deeper Blues, or the Posthuman Prometheus: Cybernetic Renewal and the Late-Twentieth-Century American Novel." *American Literature* 77, no. 2 (June): 379–406.

———. 2006. "Updike, Middles, and the Spell of 'Subjective Geography.'" In Olster 2006, 15–28.
Miller, Jonathan. 1982. "Off-Centaur." *New York Review of Books*, 1 November 1963, 28. Reprinted in Macnaughton, 53–55.
Miller, Karl. 1977. "*Couples.*" *New York Review of Books*, February 3, 38–41.
Miller, Miriam. 1984. "A Land Too Ripe for Enigma: John Updike as Regionalist." *Arizona Quarterly* 40, no. 3 (Autumn): 197–218.
Miller, Norman. 1961. "Three of the 'Best.'" *Antioch Review* 21, no. 2 (Spring): 118–28.
Mills, Nicolaus. 2009. "An American Balzac." *Guardian*, January 28. http://www.guardian.co.uk/commentisfree/cifamerica/2009/jan/28/john-updike-death-american#history-link-box.
Miracky, James J. 1998. "*Toward the End of Time.*" *America*, January 17, 25–26.
Mishra, Pankaj. 1999. "More of the Same." *New Statesman*, February 12, 55–56.
Mitsch, Ruthmarie. 1994. Review of *Brazil*. *Arthuriana* 14, no. 2 (Summer): 200–201.
Mizener, Arthur. (1962) 1982. "Behind the Dazzle Is a Knowing Eye." *New York Times Book Review*, March 18, 1, 29. Reprinted in Macnaughton 1982, 45–47.
———. 1964. "The American Hero as High-School Boy." *The Sense of Life in the Modern Novel*, 247–66. Boston: Houghton Mifflin.
"Mocking Feminism." 1984. *Glamour*, June, 118.
Montrose, David 1984. "Non-Slip Polish." *New Statesman*, 20 January, 23–24.
Moore, Arthur. 1986. "God, Ideas, and John Updike." *Christianity and Crisis*, December 8, 443–45.
———. 1989. "Updike's Updike." *Christianity and Crisis*, May 22, 173–74.
Moore, Caroline. 2008. "*The Widows of Eastwick.*" *Telegraph*, October 26.
Moore, Jack. 1984. "Africa Under Western Eyes: Updike's *The Coup* and Other Fantasies." *African Literature Today* 14: 60–67.
Moore, Lorrie. 2003. "Home Truths." *New York Review of Books*, November 20, 16–18.
Moran, Joseph. 2000a. "John Updike's *Self-Consciousness* and Literary Fame." *a/b: Auto/Biography Studies* 15, no. 2 (Winter): 298–309.
———. 2000b. *Star Authors: Literary Celebrity in America*. London: Pluto.
"*More Matter*: Essays and Criticism." 1999. *Missoula Independent*, October 21.
Moreno, Marta. 2009. "Narrative Chromaticism of Youth and Age in John Updike's *Seek My Face*." *Journal of Aging, Humanities, and the Arts* 3: 175–98.
Morey, Ann-Janine. 1986. "Updike's Sexual Language for God." *Christian Century*, November 19, 1036–37.

Morey-Gaines, Ann-Janine. 1983. "Religion and Sexuality in Walker Percy, William Gass, and John Updike: Metaphors of Embodiment in the Androcentric Imagination." *Journal of the American Academy of Religion* 51, no. 4 (December): 595–609.

Morley, Catherine. 2009. *The Quest for Epic in Contemporary American Fiction: John Updike, Philip Roth, and Don De Lillo*. New York: Routledge.

Morrissey, Daniel. 1975. "*A Month of Sundays*." *Commonweal*, 6 June, 187–88.

Mosher, Howard. 1988. "S. is Updike's Funniest Novel Yet." *Chicago Sun-Times*, March 6, Book Week 1.

Mosley, Nicholas. 1992. "Magnanimous Wasp of Letters." *Times*, January 16, Books: 12.

"Mother's Boy." 1966. *Times Literary Supplement*, April 14, 321.

Moyer, Linda. 1986. "In the Nature of Women." *Christianity and Crisis*, April 21, 140, 144.

Mudrick, Marvin. 1972. "Fiction and Truth." *Hudson Review* 25, no. 1 (Spring): 142–56.

Muradian, Thaddeus. 1965. "The World of Updike." *English Journal* 54, no. 7 (October): 577–84.

Murphy, Richard. 1962. "In Print: John Updike." *Horizon*, March, 84.

Murray, Michele. 1968. "*Couples* All Surface: 'Updike has Narrowed his Vision to the Bed.'" *National Catholic Reporter*, May 1, 11.

———. 1970. "Profile of a Literary Hustler." *National Catholic Reporter*, July 24, 13.

———. 1971. "Rabbit Runs in Circles." *National Catholic Reporter*, December 10, 13.

Myers, Ben. 2009. "John Updike, 1932–2009: A Glance at his Theology." *Faith and Theology*. http://www.faith-theology.com/2009/01/john-updike-1932-2009-glance-at-his.html.

Myers, David. 1971. "The Questing Fear: Christian Allegory in John Updike's *The Centaur*." *Twentieth Century Literature* 17: 73–82.

Mysak, Joe. 1983. "Gossip of a Higher Sort." *National Review*, November 11, 1426.

"A Mythical Animal." 1963. *Times Literary Supplement*, September 27, 728.

Nadeau, Robert. 1981. "John Updike." *Readings from the New Book of Nature*, 95–120. Boston: University of Massachusetts Press.

Neary, John M. 1986. "*The Centaur*: John Updike and the Face of the Other." *Renascence* 38, no. 3 (Summer): 228–44.

———. 1989. "'Ah: Runs': Updike, Rabbit, and Repetition." *Religion & Literature* 21, no. 1 (Spring): 89–110.

———. 1992. *Something and Nothingness: The Fiction of John Updike and John Fowles*. Carbondale: Southern Illinois University Press.

Negrea, Irina. 2005. "'He. She. Sleeps.': Media and Entropy in *Rabbit Redux*." In De Bellis 2005, 94–101.

Newman, Judie. 1988. *John Updike*. Macmillan Modern Writers. London: Macmillan.

———. 2005. "Updike's Golden Oldies: Rabbit as Spectacular Man." In *Literature and the Visual Media*, edited by David Seed, 123–41. *Essays and Studies*, vol. 55. Cambridge: D. S. Brewer.

Neyfakh, Leon. 2009. "The *Observer's* Own Adam Begley to Write Updike Bio for HarperCollins." *New York Observer*, February 19.

Nordell, Roderick. 1963. "An Updike Mythology." *Christian Science Monitor*, February 7, 7.

———. 1978. "Updike's Lightest Africa." *Christian Science Monitor*, December 13, 21.

Novak, Frank G., Jr. 2005. "The Satanic Personality in Updike's *Roger's Version*." *Christianity and Literature* 55, no. 1 (Fall): 3–24.

Novak, Michael. 1963a. "*Pigeon Feathers*." *Commonweal*, February 22, 577.

———. (1963b) 1979. "Updike's Quest for Liturgy." *Commonweal*, May 10, 192–95. Reprinted in Thorburn and Eiland 1979, 183–91.

———. (1968) 1982. "Son of the Group." *The Critic* 26 (June-July): 72–74. Reprinted in Macnaughton 1982, 59–61.

Nussbaum, Emily. 2008. "Updike and the Women: *The Witches, The Widows*, and the Ambiguous Bliss of Misogyny." *New York*, October 19.

Oates, Joyce Carol. (1975) 1979. "Updike's American Comedies." *Modern Fiction Studies* 21, no. 2 (Fall): 459–72. Reprinted in Thorburn and Eiland 1979, 53–68.

———. (1979a) 1982. "*The Coup* by John Updike." *New Republic*, January 6, 32–35. Reprinted in Macnaughton 1982, 80–86.

———. 1979b. "Nostalgic But Not Sentimental." *Mademoiselle*, December, 44–45.

———. (1990) 1999. "So Young!" *New York Times Book Review*, September 30, 1, 43. Reprinted as "John Updike's Rabbit" in *Where I've Been, And Where I'm Going*, 161–65. New York: Plume, 1999.

———. 1997. "Future Tense." *New Yorker*, December 8, 116–17.

O'Brien, Michael. 1996. "Rabbit in the Rough." *Times Literary Supplement*, November 22, 11.

O'Connell, Mary. 1996. *Updike and the Patriarchal Dilemma: Masculinity in the Rabbit Novels*. Carbondale: Southern Illinois University Press.

O'Connell, Shaun. 1983. "Updike as Critic: Essays that Live, Range and Shine." *Boston Sunday Globe*, September 11, A13, A15.

O'Connor, William Van. 1964. "John Updike and William Styron: The Burden of Talent." In *Contemporary American Novelists*, edited by Harry T. Moore, 205–21. Carbondale: Southern Illinois University Press.

O'Farrell, Mary Ann. 2001. "*Self-Consciousness* and the Psoriatic Personality: Considering Updike and Potter." *Literature and Medicine* 20, no. 2 (Fall): 133–50.

Oldsey, Bernard. 1972. "Rabbit Run to Earth." *Nation*, January 10, 54, 56.

O'Leary, Theodore. 1987. "Stories in 'Trust Me' Bring Out the Best in Updike." *Kansas City Star*, May 17, 11D.

———. 1992. "Updike Proves an Apt 'Historical Novelist.'" *Kansas City Star*, November 29, K9.
Olivas, Michael. 1975. *An Annotated Bibliography of John Updike Criticism, 1967–1973, and a Checklist of His Works*. New York: Garland.
Olster, Stacey. (1991) 2005. "Rabbit Rerun: Updike's Replay of Popular Culture in *Rabbit at Rest*." *Modern Fiction Studies* 37, no. 1 (Spring): 45–59. Reprinted in De Bellis 2005, 174–86.
———. 1992. "Rabbit Is Redundant: Updike's End of an American Epoch." In *Neo-Realism in Contemporary American Fiction*, edited by Kristiaan Versluys, 111–20. Amsterdam: Rodopi.
———. 1993. "Unadorned Woman, Beauty's Home Image: Updike's *Rabbit, Run*." In Trachtenberg 1993, 95–118.
———, ed. 2006. *The Cambridge Companion to John Updike*. Cambridge, England: Cambridge University Press.
"On Not Rocking the Boat." 1970. *Times Literary Supplement*, October 16, 1183.
Opdahl, Keith. 1987. "The Nine Lives of Literary Realism." In *Contemporary American Fiction*, edited by Malcolm Bradbury and Sigmund Ro, 1–15. London: Arnold.
Oriard, Michael. 1982. "Intimations of Mortality: Youth and Age in American Sports Fiction." *Dreaming of Heroes: American Sports Fiction, 1868–1980*, 160–69. Chicago: Nelson Hall.
Osborne, John. 1959. "The Light and the Dark." *Times Literary Supplement*, November 13, 663.
Ozick, Cynthia. 1970. "Ethnic Joke." *Commentary*, November, 106–14. Reprinted with a postscript as "Bech, Passing" in *Art and Ardor*, 114–29. New York: Knopf, 1983.
———. (2003) 2006. "God Is in the Details." *New York Times Book Review* November 30, 8–9. Reprinted as "John Updike: Eros and Death" in *The Din in the Head*, 47–53. Boston: Houghton Mifflin, 2006.
Paletta, Anthony. 2010. "Keystone to Updike's Imagination." *Wall Street Journal*, October 5, D5.
Parini, Jay. 1994. "All His Wives Are Mother." *New York Times Book Review*, November 6, 7.
———. 1996. "Faith after the Fall." *World & I*, June, 240–47.
———. 1999. "Man Thinking." *Times Literary Supplement*, December 10, 6.
Parks, John. 2005. "The Need of Some Imperishable Bliss: John Updike's *Toward the End of Time*." *Renascence* 57, no. 2 (Winter): 151–57.
Pasewark, Kyle. 1996. "The Troubles with Harry: Freedom, America, and God in John Updike's Rabbit Novels." *Religion and American Culture* 6, no. 1 (Winter): 1–33.
———. 2010. "Cold Comforts: John Updike, Protestant Thought, and the Semantics of Paradox." In *John Calvin's American Legacy*, edited by Thomas Davis, 257–66. New York: Oxford University Press.
Patchett, Ann. 2002. "Brushes with Greatness." *Washington Post Book World*, November 17, T8.

Pate, Nancy. 1987. "The Ground Is Shaky on Updike Turf." *Orlando Sentinel*, May 10, F8.
———. 1997. "Weak 'End of Time' Paints a Bleak Future." *Orlando Sentinel*, November 9, F10.
Pawley, Daniel. 1982. "Updike's Rich Rabbit: Suffocating in Sin." *Christianity Today*, November 12, 100–101.
Pearce, Edward. 2000. "You're Not So Vain." *Prospect*, March, 64–66.
Pearson, Gabriel. 1972. "Rabbit Rerun." *Guardian Weekly*, April 15, 22.
Pearson, Michael. 1997. "Man Out of Time" *Atlanta Journal-Constitution*, October 5, L10.
Peden, William. 1959. "Minor Ills that Plague the Human Heart." *New York Times Book Review*, August 16, 5.
Peter, John. 1968. "The Self-Effacement of the Novelist." *Malahat Review*, no. 8 (October): 119–28.
Peters, Margaret. 1984. "Country Coven: Sorcery in the Suburbs." *Wall Street Journal*, June 20, 28.
Petter, Henri. (1969) 1982. "John Updike's Metaphoric Novels." *English Studies* 50: 197–206. Reprinted in Macnaughton 1982, 105–14.
Phillips, Robert. 1967. "The Wizard of Ooze." *North American Review*, January, 39–40.
Pinsker, Sanford. 1991. "John Updike and the Distractions of Henry Bech, Professional Writer and Amateur American Jew." *Modern Fiction Studies* 37, no. 1 (Spring): 97–111.
———. 1993. "Restlessness in the 1950s: What Made Rabbit Run." In Trachtenberg 1993, 53–76.
———. 1995. "Joyce's Poldy/Updike's Rabbit: Popular Culture and the Problem of Consciousness." *Cimarron Review*, no. 110 (January): 92–101.
———. 2000. "Is John Updike a Dinosaur?" *American Scholar* 69, no. 1 (Winter): 150–53.
———. 2009 "John Updike, Harry (Rabbit) Angstrom, and I." *Sewanee Review* 117, no. 3 (Summer): 492–94.
Plagman, Linda. 1976. "*Eros* and *Agape*: The Opposition in Updike's *Couples*." *Renascence* 28, no. 2 (Winter): 83–93.
Plath, James, ed. 1994. *Conversations with John Updike*. Jackson: University Press of Mississippi.
Podhoretz, John. 1982. "Thinking Big." *New Criterion*, December, 84.
Podhoretz, Norman. 1959. "Novels: Style and Substance." *The Reporter*, January 22, 42–44.
———. (1963) 1964. "A Dissent on Updike." *Show*, April, 49–52. Reprinted in *Doings and Undoings*, 251–57. New York: Farrar, Straus, 1964.
———. 1988. "Salute to a Pair of Older—and Wiser—American Novelists." *New York Post*, February 8, 69–70. Reprinted as "Updike and Roth: Serious at Last." *Washington Post*, March 15, A23.
Pollitt, Katha. 1984. "Bitches and Witches." *Nation*, June 23, 773–75.

Porter, Gilbert. 1988. "From Babbitt to Rabbit: The American Materialist in Search of a Soul." In *American Literature in Belgium*, edited by Gilbert Debusscher and Marc Maufort, 195–96. Amsterdam: Rodopi.
Potter, Dennis. 1968. "Into His Own Trap." *Times*, November 9, 23.
Powers, Peter. 1994. "Scribbling for a Life: Masculinity, Doctrine, and Style in the Work of John Updike." *Christianity and Literature* 43, no. 3–4 (Spring-Summer): 329–46.
Prescott, Orville. 1963. "Books of the Times." *New York Times*, February 4, 7.
Prescott, Peter. (1976) 1983. "To Have and To Hold." *Newsweek*, November 8, 103. Reprinted in Bruccoli, 1983, 305–06.
Pritchard, William. 1987. "Updike's Version." *New York Review of Books*, February 12, 41.
———. 1990. "The Right American Stuff." *Boston Review* 15, no. 6 (December): 26–27.
———. 1997. "A Journey into the Future." *Wall Street Journal*, October 8.
———. 1999. "His Own School of Criticism." *New York Times Book Review*, September 26, 7.
———. 2000. *Updike: America's Man of Letters*. South Royalton, VT: Steerforth Press.
———. 2007. "Updike Experimenting: *The Music School*." In Schiff 2007, 35–44.
———. 2009. "Rough Magic." *Boston Globe*, February 1.
Pritchett, V. S. 1981. "Updike." *New Yorker*, November 9, 201–6.
Prose, Francine. 1988. "Men Who Read Women's Minds." *Savvy*, August, 18–20.
Prosser, Jay. 2001a. "The Thick-Skinned Art of John Updike: 'From the Journal of a Leper.'" *Yearbook of English Studies* 31: 182–91.
———. 2001b. "Under the Skin of John Updike: *Self-Consciousness* and the Radical Unconscious." *PMLA* 116, no. 3 (May): 579–93.
———. 2006. "Updike Race, and the Postcolonial Project." In Olster 2006, 76–90.
Pryor, Felix. 2000. "*Hamlet* for the Outdoor-Minded." *Spectator*, July 8, 32.
Quin, John. 2009. "Diagnostician of the Human Condition." *BMJ: British Medical Journal*, July 20, 242.
Ra'ad, Basem L. 1991. "Updike's New Versions of Myth in America." *Modern Fiction Studies* 37, no. 1 (Spring): 25–32.
Raban, Jonathan. 1970. "Talking Head." *New Statesman*, October 16, 494. Reprinted in Macnaughton 1982, 62–63.
———. 1990. "Rabbit's Last Run." *Washington Post Book World*, September 30, 1.
———. 2006. "The Good Soldier." *New York Review of Books*, July 13, 8, 10–11.
Raine, Craig. 1984. "Sisters with the Devil in Them." *Times Literary Supplement*, September 28, 1084.

———. 1990 "Updike's Innocence." *London Review of Books*, January 25, 12–13.
Ratcliff, Carter. 2001. "*Just Looking*: Essays on Art by John Updike." *Art & Auction*, February, 88, 90.
Ratcliffe, Michael. 1983. "Breathtaking Comic Virtuosity." *Times*, January 13, 8.
Regan, Robert. 1974. "Updike's Symbol of the Center." *Modern Fiction Studies* 20, no. 1 (Spring): 77–96.
Richardson, Jack. 1970. "Keeping Up with Updike." *New York Review of Books*, October 22, 46–48.
Ricks, Christopher. 1963. "Tennysonian." *New Statesman*, February 8, 208.
———. 1964. "Spotting Syllabics." *New Statesman*, May 1, 584–85.
———. 1971. "Flopsy Bunny." *New York Review of Books*, December 16, 7–9.
———. 1977. "The Members of the Wedding." *Sunday Times*, April 24, 41.
Riggan, William. 1984. "Shallow Drafts: John Updike's *Hugging the Shore*." *World Literature Today* 58, no. 3 (Summer): 380–83.
Ristoff, Dilvo. 1988. *Updike's America: The Presence of Contemporary American History in John Updike's Rabbit Trilogy*. New York: Peter Lang.
———. 1998. *Updike's Rabbit at Rest: Appropriating History*. New York: Peter Lang.
———. 1999. "When Earth Speaks to Heaven: The Future of Race and Faith in Updike's *Brazil*." In Yerkes 1999b, 64–79.
Robb, Christina. 1977. "Updike's Poetry Accompanies Him Everywhere." *Boston Globe*, June 10, 25.
Roberts, Preston. 1963. "Horror Made Habitable." *Christian Century*, April 10, 463–64.
Roberts, Tom. 1995. "John Updike and the Three Great Secret Things." *National Catholic Reporter*, May 26, 28–29.
Robinson, Marilynne. 1987. "At Play in the Backyard of the Psyche." *New York Times Book Review*, April 26, 1, 44.
Robinson, Sally. 1998. "'Unyoung, Unpoor, Unblack': John Updike and the Construction of Middle America." *Modern Fiction Studies* 44, no. 2 (Summer): 331–63.
Robson, Leo. 2009. "More Talent than Sense." *New Statesman*, July 6, 46, 48–49.
Rodgers, Bernard. 2004. "Civilization and Its Discontents." *World & I*, May, 229–34.
———, ed. 2012. *Critical Insights: John Updike*. Pasadena, CA: Salem Press.
"*Roger's Version* by John Updike." 1987. *Radio-Electronics*, May, 137.
Rogers, W. G. 1965. "The Many Sides of Updike." *Philadelphia Sunday Bulletin*, Books & Art, May 16, 3.
Rohrbach, Peter. 1972. Review of *Museums and Women and Other Stories*. *America*, December 16, 535–36.
Roiphe, Anne. 2000. "Rabbit." *For Rabbit, with Love and Squalor: An American Read*, 109–39. New York: Free Press.

Romano, John. 1979. "Updike's People." *New York Times Book Review*, October 28, 1.
Rosa, Alfred. 1974. "The Psycholinguistics of Updike's 'Museums and Women.'" *Modern Fiction Studies* 20, no. 1 (Spring): 107–111.
Rosenbaum, Ron. 2000. "Updike's *Gertrude and Claudius*: It's His Valentine to Eve." *New York Observer*, February 14, 22–23.
Rosenheim, Andrew. 2009. "John Updike: Writer Who Chronicled the Poetry of Everyday Life in Post-War Middle America." *Independent*, January 29, 38–39.
Rotella, Guy. 1985. "Updike as Poet: Serious, yet Joyous." *Boston Sunday Globe*, March 10, A13.
Rovit, Earl. 1994. "Updike, the Family Romance, and the Novel Today." *Sewanee Review* 102, no. 4 (Fall): 676–82.
Rowland, Stanley. 1962. "Limits of Littleness." *Christian Century*, July 4, 840–41.
Royal, Derek. 2002. "An Absent Presence: The Rewriting of Hawthorne's Narratology in John Updike's *S*." *Critique* 44, no. 1 (Fall): 73–85.
Rubin, Merle. 1984. "John Updike's '*Witches of Eastwick*': An Overbrewed Allegory That Doesn't Gel." *Christian Science Monitor*, 18 July, 21.
———. 1988. "A 'Scarlet Letter' with Neither Victim, Heroine—nor Martyr." *Christian Science Monitor*, 5 April, 20.
———. 1992. "Updike's Vintage 'Memories.'" *Christian Science Monitor*, November 27, 13.
———. 1994. "Updike's South American Fantasy." *Christian Science Monitor*, February 14, 15.
———. 1996. "One Man's Family Struggles with a Century of Change." *Christian Science Monitor*, February 29, B3.
Rudman, Mark. 1990. "An Erotics of Contemplation." *Art News*, February, 104.
Rumens, Carol. 1982. "The Tackier Textures of Success." *Times Literary Supplement*, January 15, 48.
"Run from Rabbit." 1960. *America*, November 19, 257–58.
Rupp, Richard. 1967. "John Updike: Style in Search of a Center." *Sewanee Review* 75, no. 4 (Autumn): 693–709. Reprinted in *Celebration in Postwar American Fiction*, 41–57. Coral Gables, FL: University of Miami Press, 1970.
Russell, John. 1976. "Praising and Sharing." *Times Literary Supplement*, March 19, 309.
———. 2003. "Geniuses Together." *New York Review of Books*, March 27, 37–38.
Russell, Mariann. 1973. "White Man's Black Man: Three Views." *CLA Journal* 17, no. 1 (September): 93–100.
"Rustic and Urbane." 1964. *Times Literary Supplement*, 20 August, 748.
Ryle, John. 1979. "Going with the Current." *Times Literary Supplement*, November 30, 77.

Sage, Lorna. 1984. "At the Confectionery Counter." *Times Literary Supplement* 20 January 1984.
———. 1986. "Narrator-Creator Data." *Times Literary Supplement*, October 24, 1189.
Sale, Roger. 1963. "Gossips and Storytellers." *Hudson Review* 16, no. 1 (Spring): 141–49.
———. 1966. "High Mass and Low Requiem." *Hudson Review* 13, no. 1 (Spring): 124–34.
———. 1981. "Rabbit Returns." *New York Times Book Review*, September 27, 1, 32–34.
Samuels, Charles T. (1966a) 1979. "*The Music School*: A Place of Resonance." *Nation*, October 3, 328. Reprinted in Thorburn and Eiland 1979, 192–95.
———. 1966b. "The Question of Updike." *Kenyon Review* 25, no. 2 (March): 268–76.
———. 1969. *John Updike*. Minneapolis: University of Minnesota Press.
———. (1971) 1982. "Updike on the Present." *New Republic*, November 20, 29–30. Reprinted in Macnaughton 1982, 63–67.
Sauerländer, Willibald. 2006. "The Novelist in the Gallery." *New York Review of Books*, June 22, 60–61, 64–65.
Savu, Laura. 2003. "In Desire's Grip: Gender, Politics, and Intertextual Games in Updike's *Gertrude and Claudius*." *Papers on Language and Literature* 39 (Winter): 22–48.
Schiff, James. 1992a. "Updike's *Roger's Version*: Re-Visualizing *The Scarlet Letter*." *South Atlantic Review* 57 (November): 59–76.
———. 1992b. "Updike's *Scarlet Letter* Trilogy: Recasting an American Myth." *Studies in American Fiction* 20 (Spring): 17–31. Reprinted in *The New Romanticism: A Collection of Critical Essays*, edited by Eberhard Alsen, 159–75. New York: Garland, 2000.
———. 1992c. *Updike's Version: Rewriting The Scarlet Letter*. Columbia: University of Missouri Press.
———. 1995. "Updike Ignored: The Contemporary Independent Critic." *American Literature* 67, no. 3 (September): 531–52.
———. 1998. *John Updike Revisited*. New York: Twayne.
———. 1999. "The Pocket Nothing Else Will Fill: Updike's Domestic God." In Yerkes 1999b, 50–63.
———, ed. 2007. *Updike in Cincinnati*. Athens: Ohio University Press.
———. 2011. "Introduction." *John Updike Review* 1, no. 1 (Fall): 1–4.
Schlesinger, Arthur, Jr. (1974) 1983. "The Historical Mind and the Literary Imagination." *Atlantic*, June, 54–59. Reprinted in Bruccoli 1983, 294–98.
Schneiderman, Leo. 1992. "Updike: Fiction and the Writer's Access to Contradictory Ego States." *American Journal of Psychoanalysis* 52, no. 2 (June): 149–59.

Schopen, Bernard. (1978) 1982. "Faith, Morality, and the Novels of John Updike." *Twentieth Century Literature* 24, 1978: 523–35. Reprinted in Macnaughton 1982, 195–206.

Schueller, Malini. 1991. "Containing the Third World: John Updike's *The Coup*." *Modern Fiction Studies* 37, no. 1 (Spring): 113–28.

Schwartz, Sanford. 1983. "Top of the Class." *New York Review of Books*, November 24, 26–30, 35.

Schwarz, Benjamin. 2011. "The Greatest Gossip." *Atlantic*, December, 101–3.

Scott, A. O. 1996. "God Goes to the Movies." *Nation*, February 12, 25–28.

Searles, George. 1982. "*The Poorhouse Fair*: Updike's Thesis Statement." In Macnaughton 1982, 231–36.

———. 1985. *The Fiction of Philip Roth and John Updike*. Carbondale and Edwardsville: Southern Illinois University Press.

———. 1988. "S." *Christian Century*, May 18–25, 508, 510.

———. 1990. "Angst Up to the End." *New Leader*, October 1–15, 21–22.

See, Carolyn. 1987. "Updike: Suburban Punch, No Knockout." *Los Angeles Times*, May 25, 1, 6.

———. 1988. "'S': John Updike Puts Seriocomic Spin on Sex, Sin and Salvation." *Chicago Tribune*, Books, February 28, 1, 9.

Selden, Raman. (1989) 1993. "Narrative Theory: John Updike." *Practicing Theory and Reading Literature: An Introduction*, 61–66. Lexington: University Press of Kentucky. Reprinted in Luscher 1993, 201–6.

Sequeira, Jessica. 2009. "Pinhole of Light: John Updike's Philosophy of the Self." *Harvard Advocate Online*. Spring. http://www.theharvardadvocate.com/content/pinhole-light-john-updikes-philosophy-self.

Sethuraman, Ramchandran. 1993a. "Updike's *The Centaur*: On Aphanisis, Gaze, Eyes, and the Death Drive." *Literature and Psychology* 39, no. 3: 38–65.

———. 1993b. "Writing Woman's Body: Male Fantasy, Desire, and Sexual Identity in Updike's *Rabbit, Run*." *Literature Interpretation Theory* 4, no. 2: 101–22.

Sexton, David. 1986. "The Crotch of the Matter." *Literary Review*, October, 6–7.

Shainin, Jonathan. 2006. "The Plot Against America." *Nation*, July 10, 27–30.

Shapiro, Anna. 2009. "Updike's Women." *Guardian*, January 28. www.guardian.co.uk/commentisfree/2009/jan/28/john-updike-women#history-link-box.

Shapiro, James. 1998. "Settling Old Scores." *New York Times Book Review*, October 25, 7.

Shaw, Patrick W. 1986. "Checking Out Faith and Lust: Hawthorne's 'Young Goodman Brown' and Updike's 'A & P.'" *Studies in Short Fiction* 23: 321–23.

Shechner, Mark. 1996. "An Overdone Epic of Faith and Fortunes." *Buffalo News*, February 18, 7B.

Sheed, Wilfrid. 1968. "Play in Tarbox." *New York Times Book Review*, April 7, 1, 30–33. Reprinted as "John Updike, *Couples*" in *The Morning After*, 36–42. New York: Farrar, Straus & Giroux, 1971.
Shetley, Vernon. 1986. Review of *Facing Nature*. *Poetry* 147: 297–99.
Shone, Tom. 1994. "Going Native." *Times Literary Supplement*, April 1, 21.
Siegel, Lee. 2003. "*The Early Stories* Render the Author's Self-Delusion and the Pathos of Memory." *Los Angeles Times*, November 16, 16–18.
Siegle, Robert. 1986. *The Politics of Reflexivity: Narrative and the Constitutive Poetics of Culture*. Baltimore, MD: Johns Hopkins University Press.
Sigal, Clancy. 1982. "Return of the Kvetch." *New York*, November 1, 70.
Silver, James. 2010. "The Problem of Omniscience in John Updike's *Roger's Version*." *Notes on Contemporary Literature* 40, no. 3 (May): 4–6.
Simmons, Tracy Lee. 1994. "Books in Brief: *The Afterlife, and Other Stories*." *National Review*, December 31, 64–65.
———. 2006. "Jihad on the Turnpike." *National Review*, September 25, 50–51.
Simon, John. 1983. "Plying a Periplus." *New Republic*, November 21, 34–37.
Singh, Sukhbir. 1996. "Fire, Rain, Rooster: John Updike's Christian Allegory in *Couples*." *International Fiction Review* 23: 36–41.
———. 2005. "Rewriting the American Wasteland: John Updike's *The Centaur*." *American Notes & Queries* 18, no. 1 (Winter): 60–64.
Sissman, L. E. 1970. "John Updike: Midpoint and After." *Atlantic*, August, 102–04.
Slavitt, David. 1985. "Smoke and Mirrors, Or Making an Elephant Appear: Strategies in the Novels of Updike and Heller." *Michigan Quarterly Review* 24, no. 1 (Winter): 134–39.
Slethaug, Gordon. 1982. "*Rabbit Redux*: 'Freedom Is Made of Brambles.'" In Macnaughton 1982, 237–53.
Smee, Sebastian. 2004. "Both Deep and Dazzling." *Spectator*, January 17, 33–34.
———. 2006. "The Fine Art of Appreciation." *Spectator*, March 4, 47.
Sokoloff, B. A., and David E. Arnason. 1971. *John Updike: A Comprehensive Bibliography*. Folcroft, PA: Folcroft.
Sokolov, Raymond. 1988. "Mom's Troubles at the Ashram." *Wall Street Journal*, March 29, 28.
Solomon, Deborah. 1989. "Reader, Run." *New Criterion*, November, 70–73.
Sorrentino, Gilbert. (1976) 1982. "Never on Sunday." *Partisan Review* 43, no. 1 (Winter): 119–21. Reprinted in Macnaughton 1982, 77–79.
Southern, Terry. 1960. "New Trends and Old Hats." *Nation*, November 19, 380–83.
Spector, Judith Ann. 1993. "Marriage, Endings, and Art in Updike and Atwood." *Midwest Quarterly* 34, no. 4 (Summer): 426–45.
Spice, Nicholas. 1986. "Underparts." *London Review of Books*, November 6, 8–9.
Stade, George. 1975. "The Resurrection of Reverend Marshfield." *New York Times Book Review*, February 23, 4.

Stafford, William T., ed. 1974. "John Updike." Special issue, *Modern Fiction Studies* 20, no. 1 (Spring).
Standley, Fred. 1967. "*Rabbit, Run*: An Image of Life." *Midwest Quarterly* 8, no. 4 (Summer): 371–86.
Stearns, Jennie, Jennifer A. Sandlin, and Jake Burdick. 2011. "Resistance on Aisle Three?: Exploring the Big Curriculum of Consumption and the (Im)Possibility of Resistance in John Updike's 'A & P.'" *Curriculum Inquiry* 41, no. 3: 394–415.
Steiner, George. 1975. "Scarlet Letters." *New Yorker*, March 10, 116–18. Reprinted in Bruccoli 1983, 299–302.
———. 1996. "Supreme Fiction." *New Yorker*, March 11, 105–06.
Stern, Richard. 1994. "Rio Redux." *New Republic*, March 21, 40–41.
Stevens, Kevin. 2009. "Increments of Uncertainty." *Dublin Review of Books*, October 6. http://www.drb.ie/more_details/09-10-06/Increments_of_Uncertainty.aspx.
Stevick, Philip. 1993. "The Full Range of Updike's Prose." In Trachtenberg 1993, 31–52.
Steyn, Mark. 2006. "Why John Updike's Book Is a Bomb." *Macleans*, July 25, 58–59.
Stone, Robert. 1997. "The Croatians Are Coming." *New York Review of Books*, December 4, 32.
———. 2006. "Updike's Other America." *New York Times Book Review*, June 18, 1, 8.
Storey, Celia. 1997. "You're Getting Sleepy, Sleepy." *Little Rock Arkansas Democrat-Gazette*, November 9, J6.
Stout, Cushing. 1990. "In Hawthorne's Shadow: The Minister and the Woman in Howells, Adams, Frederic, and Updike." *Making American Tradition: Visions and Revisions from Ben Franklin to Alice Walker*, 22–39. New Brunswick, NJ: Rutgers University Press.
Strandberg, Victor. (1978) 1982. "John Updike and the Changing of the Gods." *Mosaic* 12, no. 1 (Fall): 157–75. Reprinted in Macnaughton 1982, 175–94.
Straub, Peter. 1975. "Wise Women." *New Statesman*, January 10, 50.
Strawson, Galen. 1992. "Lies, Damned Lies and Critical Statistics." *Independent*, January 19, 26.
———. 1993. "Coupling like Rabbits." *Times Literary Supplement*, February 26, 19.
———. 2003. "The Beauty of Being Oneself." *Guardian*, April 19, 9.
Stubbs, John. 1968. "The Search for Perfection in *Rabbit, Run*." *Critique* 10: 94–101.
Stuckey, William J., ed. 1991. "John Updike." Special issue, *Modern Fiction Studies* 37, no. 1 (Spring).
Suderman, Elmer. 1969. "The Right Way and the Good Way in *Rabbit, Run*." *University Review* 26 (October): 13–21.
Sullivan, Mary Rose. 1984. "Updike's Witches." *San Diego Magazine*, June, 112–13.

Sullivan, Richard. 1965. "A Quartet of Tangled Actors." *Chicago Tribune*, November 28, 6.
Sutherland, John. 1999. "How to Enrage the Critics." *Sunday Times*, Art & Books, January 3, 5.
Swindell, Larry. 1978. "A Different Updike, but Really the Same." *Philadelphia Inquirer*, December 10, 24G.
Symons, Julian. 1972. "Warren Report." *Sunday Times*, April 9, 7.
Tallent, Elizabeth. 1982. *Married Men and Magic Tricks: John Updike's Erotic Heroes*. Berkeley, CA: Creative Arts Book Company.
Tandon, Bharat. 1999. "Bye-Bye Bech?" *Times Literary Supplement*, January 1, 20.
Tanenhaus, Sam. 2008. "Mr. Wizard." *New York Times*, October 26.
———. 2010. "Literary Ore of Updike, Do-It-Yourself Man of Letters." *New York Times*, June 20.
Tanner, Tony. 1968. "Hello, olleh." *Spectator*, November 8, 658–59.
———. 1971. "A Compromised Environment." *City of Words*, 273–94. New York: Harper & Row.
———. (1972) 1982. "The Sorrow of Some Central Hollowness." *New York Times Book Review*, October 22, 5, 24. Reprinted in Macnaughton 1982, 71–74.
Tate, Sister M. Judith. 1964. "Of Rabbits and Centaurs." *The Critic* 22 (February–March): 44–47, 49–51.
Taubman, Robert. 1963. "God Is Delicate." *New Statesman*, September 27, 406.
———. 1982. "Nobody Is God." *London Review of Books*, February 4–18, 19–20.
Taylor, C. Clarke. 1968. *John Updike: A Bibliography*. Kent, OH: Kent State University Press.
Taylor, John. 2002. Review of *Americana and Other Poems*. *Poetry* (February): 294–95.
Taylor, Larry. 1971. *Pastoral and Anti-Pastoral Patterns in John Updike's Fiction*. Carbondale: Southern Illinois University Press.
"That Long Atlantic Crossing." 1966. *Times Literary Supplement*, February 17, 124.
Theroux, Paul. 1971. "A Has-Been, Ten Years Later." *Chicago Tribune Book World*, November 14, 3, 10.
———. 1977. "A Marriage at the End of Its License." *Guardian*, April 21, 14.
———. 1978. "Updike in Africa." *Book Views*, December, 36–37.
———. 1979. "A Marriage of Mixed Blessings." *New York Times Book Review*, April 8, 7. Reprinted in Macnaughton 1982, 86–88.
Thomas, Samuel. 2011. "Outtakes and Outrage: The Means and Ends of Suicide Terror." *Modern Fiction Studies* 57, no. 3 (Fall): 425–49.
Thompson, John. 1961. "Other People's Affairs." *Partisan Review* 27 (January-February): 117–24.
———. 1968. "Updike's *Couples*." *Commentary*, May, 70–73.

———. 1978. "Updike le Noir." *New York Review of Books*, December 21, 3–4.
Thorburn, David and Howard Eiland, eds. 1979. *John Updike: A Collection of Critical Essays*. Englewood Cliffs, NJ: Prentice Hall.
Thorne, Matt. 2008. "A Slow Sequel that Fails to Cast a Spell." *Independent*, October 31.
Timpane, John. 2010. "First Global Gathering of Updike Cheerleaders." *Philadelphia Inquirer*, 3 October, B1.
Todd, Richard. 1972. "Updike and Barthelme: Disengagement." *Atlantic*, December, 126–32.
———. 1976. "A Ladies' Man." *Atlantic*, November, 115–16.
Tomalin, Claire. 1979. "State of Africa." *Punch*, March 28, 552–53.
———. 1980. "Guilty Man." *Sunday Times*, May 25.
———. 1984. "That Old Black Magic." *Sunday Times*, September 30.
Towers, Robert. (1978) 1979. "Updike in Africa." *New York Times Book Review*, December 10, 1, 55. Reprinted in Thorburn and Eiland 1979, 157–61.
———. 1979. "Cuisine Minceur." *New York Review of Books*, November 8, 18–20.
Trachtenberg, Jeffrey, ed. 1993. *New Essays on Rabbit, Run*. Cambridge, England: Cambridge University Press.
Trendel, Aristi. 2010. "The Resurgence of the Repressed in John Updike's Homecoming Stories 'The Sandstone Farmhouse' and 'The Cats.'" *Psychoanalytic Review* 97, no. 1 (February): 163–74.
Trevor, William. 1972. "All Right, Sort Of." *New Statesman*, April 7, 462–63.
———. 1992. "Discourse Most Eloquent Musing." *Spectator*, February 8, 29–30.
Trilling, Diana. 1968. "Updike's Yankee Traders." *Atlantic*, April, 129–31.
Turner, Kermit. 1975. "Rabbit Brought Nowhere: John Updike's *Rabbit Redux*." *South Carolina Review* 8, no. 1 (Fall): 35–42.
Umphlett, Wiley. 1975. "The Agony of Rabbit Angstrom: The Search for a Secure Self." *The Sporting Myth and the American Experience*, 145–56. Lewisburg, PA: Bucknell University Press.
"Updike, Lettrist." 1966. *Times*, January 27, 15.
Uphaus, Suzanne. 1977a. "*The Centaur*: Updike's Mock Epic." *Journal of Narrative Technique* 7: 24–36. Reprinted in Macnaughton 1982, 163–74.
———. 1977b. "The Unified Vision of *A Month of Sundays*." *University of Windsor Review* 12, no. 2 (Spring-Summer): 5–16.
———. 1980. *John Updike*. New York: Frederick Ungar.
Vanderwerken, David. 1975. "Rabbit 'Re-Docks': Updike's Inner Space Odyssey." *College Literature* 2: 73–78.
Vargo, Edward. 1973a. "The Necessity of Myth in Updike's *The Centaur*." *PMLA* 88, no. 3 (May): 452–60.

———. 1973b. *Rainstorms and Fire: Ritual in the Novels of John Updike*. New York: Kennikat Press.
Vaughan, Philip. 1981. *John Updike's Images of America*. Reseda, CA: Mojave Books.
Verduin, Kathleen. 1982. "Fatherly Presences: John Updike's Place in a Protestant Tradition." In Macnaughton 1982, 254–68.
———. 1985. "Sex, Nature, and Dualism in *The Witches of Eastwick*." *Modern Language Quarterly* 46, no. 3 (September): 293–315.
———. 2006. "Updike, Women, and Mythologized Sexuality." In Olster 2006, 61–75.
———. 2010. "Imprinting Mortality: Updike Reading Books." *Modern Language Quarterly* 71, no. 3 (September): 329–66.
Vickery, John. 1974. "*The Centaur*: Myth, History, and Narrative." *Modern Fiction Studies* 20, no. 1 (Spring): 29–44.
———. 2009. *The Prose Elegy: An Exploration of Modern American and British Fiction*. Baton Rouge: Louisiana State University Press.
Vidal, Gore. (1996) 2001. "Rabbit's Own Burrow: The Comfortable Patriotism of John Updike and his Fiction." *Times Literary Supplement*, April 26, 3–7. Reprinted in *The Last Empire: Essays 1992–2000*, 87–113. New York: Doubleday, 2001.
"View from the Catacombs." 1968. *Time*, April 26, 66–68, 73–75.
Vigilante, Richard. 1989. "The Observer Observed." *National Review*, May 19, 51–52, 54–55.
Vincent, Norah. 2000. "Not to Be." *National Review*, March 20, 57–58.
Wackerman, Daniel. 1996. "Mind's Eye." *America*, November 30, 5.
Wagner, Joseph. 1978. "John Updike and Karl Barth: An Insistent 'Yes.'" *Cithara* 18, no. 1: 61–69.
Walden, George. 2004. "The Human Bind." *New Statesman*, January 19, 48–50.
———. 2006. "American Beauty." *New Statesman*, March 6, 50–51.
Waldmeir, Joseph. 1974. "It's the Going That's Important, Not the Getting There: Rabbit's Questing Non-Quest." *Modern Fiction Studies* 20, no. 1 (Spring): 13–28.
———. 1996. "Rabbit's Four-Stage Quest to Learn the Way and Figure Out the Destination—Then Get There." In *Powerless Fictions? Ethics, Cultural Critique, and American Fiction in the Age of Postmodernism*, edited by Ricardo Alfonso, 203–21. Atlanta: Rodopi.
Waldron, Randall H. 1984. "Rabbit Revised." *American Literature* 56, no. 1 (March): 51–57.
Wall, James. 1996. "Among the Lilies." *Christian Century*, March 6, 251–52.
———. 2001. "Rabbit Lives." *Christian Century*, January 3–10, 36.
Wallace, David Foster. 1997. "Twilight of the Great Literary Beasts." *New York Observer*, October 13, 1, 21.
Waller, Bret. 1990. "Looking, But Not Seeing." *Journal of Museum Education* 15, no. 1 (Winter): 25–26.

Waller, G. F. 1972. "Updike's *Couples*: A Barthian Parable." *Research Studies* 40, no. 1 (March): 10–21.

Waller, Gary. 1982. "Stylus Dei or the Open-Endedness of Debate?: Success and Failure in *A Month of Sundays*." In Macnaughton 1982, 269–80.

Walrath, Douglas Alan. 2010. *Displacing the Divine: The Minister in the Mirror of American Fiction*. New York: Columbia University Press.

Walsh, David. 2006. "John Updike's *Terrorist*." *World Socialist Web Site*, August 25. http://www.wsws.org/articles/2006/aug2006/updi-a25.shtml.

———. 2009. "Novelist John Updike Dead at 76: Was He a 'Great Novelist'?" *World Socialist Web Site*. January 29. http://www.wsws.org/articles/2009/jan2009/updi-j29.shtml.

Walsh, William. 1980. "American Ambitions." *Books and Bookmen*, May, 38–39.

Walter, Natasha. 1995. "Glossy Shins and Spots of Light." *Independent*, Books, January 28, 27.

Walton, James. 1998. "Narcissus Still Trying Hard in his Old Age." *Literary Review*, February, 23–24.

Ward, J. A. 1962. "John Updike's Fiction." *Critique* 5, no. 1 (Spring–Summer): 27–40.

———. 1963. "John Updike: *The Centaur*." *Critique* 6, no. 2 (Fall): 109–14.

Watman, Max. 2004. "Worse Yet, Real Life." *New Criterion*, November, 54–55.

Waxman, Robert. 1977. "Invitations to Dread: John Updike's Metaphysical Quest." *Renascence* 29, no. 4 (Summer): 201–10.

"Ways of the World." 1959. *Times Literary Supplement*, March 20, 157.

Webb, Stephen. 2008. "John Updike and the Waning of Mainline Protestantism." *Christianity and Literature* 57, no. 4 (Summer): 583–93.

———. 2009. "In Praise of John Updike." *Christianity and Literature* 58, no. 3 (Spring): 500.

Weber, Brom. 1971. "*Rabbit Redux*." *Saturday Review*, November 27, 54–55.

Weeks, Edward. 1966. "He and She." *Atlantic*, November, 154, 156.

Weintraub, Stanley. 1974. "Closet Drama." *New Republic*, June 22, 26.

Weldon, Fay. 2004. "Carnal Knowledge." *Washington Post Book World*, October 24, 3.

Whetter, Darryl. 2006. "The First Real Novel about 9/11." *Toronto Star*, June 4, D5.

Whitaker, Jennifer. 1979. "*A Bend in the River; The Coup*." *Foreign Affairs* 58, no. 1 (Fall): 206.

White, Edmund. 1976. "Lyrics of Lust in a Song of the Suburbs." *Washington Post Book World*, November 14, L1–2.

Wilhelm, Albert. 1982. "The Search for Meaningful Work in John Updike's Fiction." In *Perspectives on American Business*, edited by Don Harkness, 27–33. Tampa, FL: American Studies Press.

Will, George. (1990) 1994. "Rabbit Is Mortal, But Is the U.S.?" *Washington Post*, October 28, C7. Reprinted as "Rabbit Angstrom: At Rest, At Last." *The Leveling Wind*, 401–2. New York: Viking, 1994.

Williams, David. 1982. "Updike Is Richer." *Punch*, February 3, 201–2.

Williams, John. 2012. "John Updike Society Buys Author's Boyhood Home for $200,000." *New York Times*, May 14.

Williams, Wirt. 1968. "America's Most Explicitly Sexual Novel Ever." *Los Angeles Times*, April 7, D43.

Williamson, Chilton, Jr. 1990. "Harry's End." *National Review*, November 19, 51–53.

Wills, Garry. 1990. "Long-Distance Runner." *New York Review of Books*, October 25, 11–14.

Wilson, Matthew. 1991. "The Rabbit Tetralogy: From Solitude to Society to Solitude Again." *Modern Fiction Studies* 37, no. 1 (Spring): 5–24.

Wilson, Raymond J., III. 1989. "*Roger's Version*: Updike's Negative-Solid Model in *The Scarlet Letter*." *Modern Fiction Studies* 35, no. 2 (Summer): 241–50.

"Witty, Wise, Then Weary." 2000. *Economist*, February 19, 3–4.

Woiwode, Larry. 2011. *Words Made Flesh: Essays on Literature and Culture*, 85–125. Wheaton, IL: Crossway.

Wolcott, James. 1981. "Running on Empty." *Esquire*, October, 20, 22–23.

———. 2009. "Caretaker/Pallbearer." *London Review of Books*, January 1, 9–10.

Wood, James. 1990. "The Beast in the American Ice Cream Parlour." *Guardian*, October 25, 25.

———. 1992. "The Professional Image." *Times Literary Supplement*, January 24, 21.

———. 1994. "Ever So Comfy." *London Review of Books*, March 24, 22–23.

———. 1996. "Under the Aspect of Serenity." *New Republic*, May 27, 29–33.

———. (1999a) 2000. "John Updike's Complacent God." *The Broken Estate: Essays on Literature and Belief*, 192–99. New York: Random House. New York: Modern Library, 2000: 208–15.

———. 1999b. "The Professional." *New Republic*, October 11, 41–48.

———. 2001. "Gossip in Gilt." *London Review of Books*, April 19, 30–31.

———. 2006. "Jihad and the Novel." *New Republic*, July 3, 25–30.

Wood, Michael. 1987. "Hiding the Harm Away." *Times Literary Supplement*, October 9–15, 1106.

———. 1989. "Out of Harm's Way." *New Statesman and Society*, May 12, 34.

Wood, Peter. 2008. "Extra-Curricular Updike." *NAS: National Association of Scholars*, 1 December. http://www.nas.org/articles/Updike_at_Rest.

Wood, Ralph. (1982) 2005. "John Updike's Rabbit Saga: A Celebration of Human Ambiguity and Acceptance." *Christian Century*, January 20, 50–54. Reprinted in De Bellis 2005, 117–24.

———. 1984. "Updike: Evil as Sexual Sorcery." *Christian Century*, July 18–25, 715–17.

———. 1988. *The Comedy of Redemption: Christian Faith and Comic Vision in Four American Novelists.* Notre Dame, IN: University of Notre Dame Press.

———. 1989a. "Karl Barth, John Updike and the Cheerful God." *Books and Religion* 16 (Winter): 5, 26, 29–31.

———. 1989b. "Updike's Song of Himself." *Christian Century*, May 17, 526–28.

———. (1990) 2005. "Rabbit Runs Down." *Christian Century*, November 21, 1099–1101. Reprinted in De Bellis 2005, 158–62.

———. 1996. "Into the Void: Updike's Sloth and America's Religion." *Christian Century*, April 24, 452–55, 457.

"World of Warcraft Mourns Updike's Death with Lunar Festival." 2009. *Seattle University Spectator*, January 28. http://blog.su-spectator.com/index.php?s=Updike.

Wright, Derek. 1991. "Mapless Motion: Form and Space in Updike's *Rabbit, Run.*" *Modern Fiction Studies* 37, no. 1 (Spring): 35–44.

Wyatt, Bryant. 1967. "John Updike: The Psychological Novel in Search of Structure." *Twentieth-Century Literature* 13 (July): 89–96.

Yardley, Jonathan. (1982) 1991. "Rabbit Isn't Rich." *Washington Post*, April 26, C1. Reprinted in Yardley 1991, 11–15.

———. 1987. "John Updike: For Better, For Worse." *Washington Post Book World*, May 10, X3.

———. 1991. *Out of Step: Notes from a Purple Decade.* New York: Villard Books.

———. 1994. "Updike as Always." *Tampa Tribune*, November 20, 6.

———. 1998. "Henry the Third." *Washington Post Book World*, October 18, 3.

Yates, Norris. 1965. "The Doubt and Faith of John Updike." *College English* 26 (March): 469–74.

Yerkes, James. 1997. "Beyond Time, Death, and the Cosmos." *Christian Century*, November 16–26, 1079, 1081–83.

———. 1999a. "A Dark Thread Runs Through It." *Christian Century*, November 17–24, 1132–34.

———, ed. 1999b. *John Updike and Religion: The Sense of the Sacred and the Motions of Grace.* Grand Rapids, MI: Eerdmans.

———. 2000. Review of *Gertrude and Claudius. Christian Century*, February 23, 220–21.

———. 2002. "Beyond a Doubt." *Christian Century*, October 9–22, 30–31.

———. 2003. "Saying the Unsayable." *Christian Century*, December 13, 44–45.

———. 2004. "It Takes a Village." *Christian Century*, December 28, 32–33.

Zan, Jifang. 2009. "Booking His Place in History." *Beijing Review*, February 19.

Zender, Karl. 1993. "Where Is Yoknapatawpha County? William Faulkner, John Updike and Postwar America." In *Faulkner, His Contemporaries, and His Posterity*, edited by Waldemar Zacharasiewicz, 284–300. Tübingen, Germany: Francke.

Zipp, Yvonne. 2006. "Ahmad, Run." *Christian Science Monitor*, June 13, 14, 17.
Zverev, Aleksei. 1995. "Nabokov, Updike, and American Literature." In *The Garland Companion to Vladimir Nabokov*, edited by Vladimir Alexandrov, 536–48. New York: Garland.

Index

Abbey, Edward, 91, 197
Ableman, Paul, 55, 197
Abu-Assad, Hany, 192
Abusharif, Ibrahim, 171, 197
Ackroyd, Peter, 42, 51, 76, 197
Adams, J. R., 16, 197
Adams, Nick (Hemingway character), 110
Adams, Phoebe, 7, 197
Adams, Robert Martin, 19, 197
Adler, Renata, 13, 197
adultery (in Updike's novels), 31, 78, 83, 86–87, 123, 124, 153, 156, 182, 188
Aeneid, The (Virgil), 190
Africa (Africans), 53–56, 64, 96
African Americans (Blacks), 42, 47, 62, 85, 118, 120, 163
Ahearn, Kerry, 111, 197
Airport (Arthur Hailey), 27
Albee, Edward, 2
Alden, John, 138, 197
Aldridge, John, 1, 18, 35, 145, 197
Allen, Brooke, 121, 133, 137, 149, 197
Allen, Bruce, 188, 198
Allen, Mary, 59, 107, 126, 144–45, 198
Alter, Robert, 62, 198
Alvarez, Alfred, 45, 198
America (in Updike's fiction), 8, 9, 10, 11, 16, 20, 24, 25, 27, 28, 29, 30, 31, 33, 34, 35, 36, 38, 40, 42, 44, 47, 48, 50, 53, 54, 55, 56, 58, 60, 70, 71, 72, 75, 77, 81, 82, 83, 84, 85, 86, 90, 93, 97, 102, 103, 104, 105, 110, 111, 112, 116, 117, 124, 126, 131–35, 142, 144, 145, 147, 148, 151, 152, 153, 154, 155, 157, 158, 159, 160, 163, 164, 165, 166, 171, 172, 173, 174, 176, 177, 178–79, 183, 184, 185, 187, 188, 190, 191, 192
American Book Award, 68, 69
American Pastoral (Philip Roth), 161
Amis, Martin, 1, 45, 74, 99, 103, 115, 185, 198
Ancona, Francesco, 109, 198
Anderson, David, 163, 198
Anderson, Donald, 165, 198
Anderson, Sam, 183, 198
Anderson, Sara, 145–46, 198
Androne, Richard G., 180, 198
Angell, Roger, 183, 198
Angstrom, Harry "Rabbit" (Updike character), 23–24, 47–48, 52, 68–71, 84–86, 101–5, 111, 124, 126–27, 140, 144–45, 151–53, 164–65, 179–80, 188, 193
Angstrom, Janice (Updike character), 48
Apollinaire, Guillaume, 169
Armstrong, Charlotte, 13, 198
Arnason, David E., 2, 216
Arnold, Martin, 151, 198
Arnold, Matthew, 62, 189
Astraea Redux (John Dryden), 38
Atwood, Margaret, 77, 124, 136, 198–99
Augustine (St. Augustine, Bishop of Hippo), 181
Austen, Jane, 56, 167, 183

Babbitt (Sinclair Lewis), 38, 70, 165
Babbitt, George (Sinclair Lewis character), 38, 112, 145
Backscheider, Nick, 48, 199
Backscheider, Paula, 48, 199

Bailey, Peter, 180–81, 199
Baker, Carlos, 42, 199
Baker, Nicholson, 4, 122, 199
Baker, Simon, 185–86, 199
Balbert, Peter, 82, 199
Baldwin, James, 2
Balliett, Whitney, 7, 10, 199
Balzac, Honore de, 145, 152, 182
Bamberger, Michael, 135, 199
Bancroft, Collette, 185, 199
Banville, John, 154, 158, 199
Barfield, Owen, 143
Barnard, Judith, 51, 199
Barnes, Jane, 82, 199
Barnes, Julian, 132, 186, 187, 199
Barr, Donald, 7, 199
Barron, John, 174, 199
Barth, Karl, 25, 34, 60, 61–62, 66, 84, 91, 106, 110, 128, 132, 146, 147, 160, 163
Barthes, Roland, 63, 123
Barton, Ralph, 163
Batchelor, Bob, 191, 192, 199
Batchelor, John, 91, 199
Baudelaire, Charles, 169
Baudrillard, Jean, 179
Baumann, Paul, 98, 200
Bawer, Bruce, 99, 116, 117, 141–42, 200
Bayley, John, 94, 120, 149, 200
Baym, Nina, 77, 200
Becker, Stephen, 73–74, 200
Bedient, Calvin, 45, 200
Begley, Adam, 152–53, 154, 158, 170, 182, 200
Bell, Millicent, 150, 200
Bell, Pearl, 68, 200
Bell, Vereen, 14, 200
Bellamy, John Stark, 134, 200
Bellow, Saul, 2, 51, 108, 114
Ben-Bassat, Hedda, 160, 200
Bergonzi, Bernard, 18, 200
Berks County, Pennsylvania, 82, 188
Berman, Paul, 152, 200
Berryman, Charles, 78, 200
Bible, 34, 61, 112
Bildungsroman, 157
Billen, Andrew, 119, 201

Billings, J. Todd, 165, 201
Billy Bathgate (E. L. Doctorow), 161
Birkerts, Sven, 102, 201
Blechner, Michael, 143, 201
Blithedale Romance, The (Nathaniel Hawthorne), 32
Bloom, Alice, 77, 201
Bloom, Harold, 107–8, 201
Blotner, Joseph, 72, 201
Blue, Adrianne, 92–94, 201
Bodmer, George, 109, 201
Bogan, Louise, 6, 201
Bolton, Richard, 112, 201
Book of the Month Club, 120
Borgman, Paul, 61, 63–64, 201
Boroff, David, 9, 201
Boswell, Marshall, 163–64, 201
Bottum, J., 134, 201
Bovary, Emma (Flaubert character), 150
Bowden, Christopher, 153, 201
Bowman, Diane, 82, 202
Boyer, Paul, 162, 202
Boyers, Robert, 138, 202
Bradbury, Malcolm, 51, 82, 115, 137, 139, 202
Braine, John, 33, 202
Bremner, Charles, 103, 202
Brinnin, John, 45, 202
Broadway (New York theater), 27
Broer, Lawrence, 145, 202
Bronowski, Jacob, 84, 202
Brookhiser, Richard, 139, 187–88, 202
Brookner, Anita, 91, 94, 95, 98, 103, 114, 117, 136, 140, 202
Brooks, Xan, 151–52, 202
Broomfield, Michael, 1, 2, 206
Brophy, Brigid, 52, 202
Brown, Brenda, 165, 203
Brownworth, Victoria, 175, 203
Broyard, Anatole, 29, 37, 42, 45, 70, 203
Bruccoli, Mary, 203
Buchanan, James (15th president of the United States), 41–42, 116–17
Buchanan, John M., 183, 203
Buchanan, Mark, 155, 203

Buckley, William F., Jr., 54, 203
Buitenhuis, Peter, 1, 13, 17, 203
Bumppo, Natty (James Fenimore Cooper character), 86
Burchard, Rachel, 37, 62, 203
Burgess, Anthony, 17, 54, 203
Burhans, Clinton S., Jr., 47, 203
Burke, Kenneth, 111, 203
Burnett, Whit, 2, 203
Butcher, Fanny, 7, 203

Caldwell, Gail, 93–94, 119, 138, 139, 148, 151, 170, 203–4
Caldwell, George (Updike character), 13, 14, 63
Caldwell, Mark, 98, 204
Calinescu, Matei, 128–29, 204
Campbell, Aidan, 154, 204
Campbell, James, 59, 204
Campbell, Jeff, 85, 107, 204
Camus, Albert, 63, 107
Cannella, Stephen, 184, 204
Capital (Karl Marx), 152
Capote, Truman, 2, 37
Carduff, Christopher, 118, 182, 189, 204
Carnes, Mark, 133, 204
Cartwright, Justin, 156, 204
Casey, Florence, 17, 204
Cathars (religious sect), 64
Cather, Willa, 157
Caulfield, Holden (Salinger character), 145
character studies, 25, 33–34, 62, 63, 68, 83, 86, 88, 101, 112, 122, 159, 162, 163, 179
Charles, Ron, 148, 151, 154, 204
Chase, Mary Ellen, 7, 11, 204
Cheever, John, 83, 176
Chekhov, Anton, 95
Chester, Alfred, 12, 204
Childers, Doug, 171, 204
Chillingworth, Roger (Hawthorne character), 90
Chinese Academy of Social Sciences, 184
Chinese Institute of Foreign Literature, 184

Chipchase, Paul, 68, 204
Christian (Christianity), 21, 23, 26, 29, 35–36, 37, 42, 43, 48, 56, 60, 61, 79, 84, 91, 93, 105–6, 110, 136, 138, 146, 153, 155, 165, 166, 173, 174, 178, 180, 181, 183, 187, 188
Churchwell, Sarah, 176, 204
Clasen, Kelly, 179, 204
Claudius (Shakespeare character), 148–50, 162
Claudius (Updike character), 148–50, 162
Clausen, Jan, 124, 205
Clavell, James, 27
Clee, Nicholas, 121, 205
Coale, Samuel, 87, 205
Cockshutt, Rod, 93, 205
Cohen, Joseph, 71–72, 205
Cold War, 131, 159–60
Colgan, John-Paul, 164, 205
Collector, The (John Fowles), 13
Comedie Humaine (Honore de Balzac), 145, 152
comedy (literary genre), 7, 54, 55, 56, 79, 92, 102, 103, 110, 136, 175, 176, 179
Commentary (periodical), 8, 30, 72, 140
Conn, Peter, 108, 205
Conrad, Joseph, 107, 170
conservative (conservatism), 22, 29, 50, 54, 62, 64, 88, 99, 101, 104, 111, 112, 119, 135, 147, 173–74
consumerism, 38, 68, 86, 144, 190, 191
Cook, Bruce, 11, 205
Cook, Roderick, 17, 205
Cooke, Judy, 54, 205
Cooper, James Fenimore, 47
Cooper, Rand Richards, 102–3, 120, 183–84, 205
Corbellari, Alain, 143, 205
Corbett, Edward, 7, 205
Cordingly, Bruce, 192, 205
Cornwell, T. Bettina, 144, 205
Corwin, Phillip, 78, 205
Cosgrove, Vince, 189, 205

Crane, Milton, 8, 205
Crane, Stephen, 179
Crews, Frederick, 4, 105–7, 120, 205
Crowley, John, 133, 205
Crowley, Sue Mitchell, 60, 84, 206
Cryer, Dan, 91–92, 206
Culligan, Glendy, 17, 206
cultural criticism, 43, 56, 87, 110, 112, 125, 134, 135, 139, 141, 144, 145, 159–60, 164, 166, 167, 180, 190
Curley, Thomas, 13, 206
Curtler, Betsy, 62, 206

Damnation of Theron Ware, The (Harold Frederic), 113
Danto, Arthur, 100, 206
Danvers, Massachusetts, 182
Davenport, Guy, 13, 206
Davies, Howard, 68, 206
Davies, Marie-Hélène, 84, 206
Davies, Russell, 58, 70, 206
Davies, Serena, 168, 206
Davis, Hope, 96, 206
Davis, L. J., 52, 206
Davis, Robert, 92, 206
De Bellis, Jack, 1, 2, 13, 32, 112, 125, 159, 179, 192, 206–7
De Feo, Ronald, 43, 207
De Mott, Benjamin, 44, 75, 207
De Rougemont, Denis, 64
De Tocqueville, Alexis, 163
Debord, Guy, 180
deconstruction, 108–9, 115, 117, 127, 161
Deemer, Charles, 41, 207
Delbanco, Andrew, 189, 207
Delrogh, Dennis, 40, 207
Denby, David, 99, 207
Derrida, Jacques, 63, 108, 127
Detweiler, Robert, 23, 36, 45–46, 63, 80, 88, 110–11, 207
Deyab, Mohammad, 191, 207
Diamond, George, 147, 207
Dicken, Thomas, 165–66, 207
Dickens, Charles, 101, 147
Didion, Joan, 10, 11, 207
Dilts, Susan, 19, 207

Dinnage, Rosemary, 41, 59, 121, 207–8
Dintenfass, Mark, 55, 208
Dirda, Michael, 73, 152, 182, 208
dissertations (on Updike), 2, 24, 123, 192
Ditsky, John, 31, 208
Divorce (in Updike's fiction), 31, 58, 75, 82, 86
Doctor Zhivago (Boris Pasternak), 7
Don Juan, 36
Donahue, Peter, 143–44, 208
Donald, Miles, 64, 208
Donaldson, Scott, 98, 208
Doner, Dean, 23, 208
Donne, John, 38
Donnelly, Jerome, 100, 208
Donoghue, Denis, 32, 73, 115–16, 208
Donovan, Laurence, 33, 208
Doody, Terence, 63, 208
Dos Passos, John, 2, 145
Dostoevsky, Fyodor, 170
Doyle, Paul, 21, 208
Drabble, Margaret, 59, 208
Dryden, John, 38
Duncan-Jones, Katherine, 149, 208
Duryea, Bill, 171, 208
Duvall, John, 123, 165, 177, 209

Eberhart, John, 153, 209
Eby, Lloyd, 120, 209
Eco, Umberto, 128
Edelstein, J. M., 10, 11–12, 209
Eder, Richard, 98–99, 116, 134, 149, 209
Edwards, Lee R., 40, 209
Edwards, Thomas, 33, 43, 70, 209
Ehrenpreis, Irvin, 42, 209
Eichman, Erich, 119–20, 209
Eiland, Howard, 63, 65, 66, 83, 209, 239
El Moncef, Salah, 129, 209
elegy (literary genre), 63, 102, 103, 155, 158, 190
Ellellou, Colonel (Updike character), 54–55, 64, 86
Ellison, James, 68, 209
Emerson, Ralph Waldo, 37

Engeman, Thomas, 166, 209–10
Enright, D. J., 24, 78–79, 210
epic (literary genre), 11, 65, 70, 126, 132, 146, 190
Epstein, Joseph, 18, 72, 210
Epstein, Seymour, 38, 210
Erikson, Erik, 111
Evanier, David, 54, 58, 210
Ewart, Gavin, 79, 210
existentialism (existentialist philosophy), 21, 24, 38, 85, 166
Exodus (Leon Uris), 7

Falke, Wayne, 48, 210
Farrell, Frank B., 160–61, 210
fatalism, 60
Faulkner, William, 20, 23, 37, 64, 82, 87, 90, 107, 110, 124, 145, 157
Feeney, Mark, 70, 91, 98, 102, 210
Feinberg, Susan, 82–83, 210
Feld, Ross, 132, 210
feminism (feminist criticism), 50, 59, 76, 77, 78, 79, 83, 84, 88, 92, 95, 96, 109–10, 122, 124, 128, 137, 144–45, 152, 161, 162, 164, 175, 178, 185
Fiedler, Leslie, 15, 210
film, Updike's relation to, 125, 141, 192
Finkelstein, Sidney, 24, 39, 210
Finn, Huckleberry (Twain character), 110, 179
First World, 56
Fisher, Richard, 20, 210
Fitelson, David, 8, 210
Fitzgerald, F. Scott, 157
Flaubert, Gustave, 152, 159
Fleischauer, John, 108, 210
Flint, Joyce, 31, 210
Flower, Dean, 104, 137, 211
Forbes, Cheryl, 42, 211
Forbes, Peter, 93, 211
Ford, Mark, 118, 211
formalism (formalist criticism), 46, 82, 123, 163
Forster, E. M., 34
Forsyte Saga (John Galsworthy), 132
Foster, Richard, 10, 20, 211
Foucault, Michel, 129, 161, 180

Fowles, John, 13, 127
Franklin, Benjamin, 112
Frederic, Harold, 113
Freeman, John, 148–49, 157, 211
Fremont-Smith, Eliot, 16, 28, 71, 211
French theorists, 88, 92, 108, 129
Freud, Sigmund, 12, 31, 82, 83
Fulford, Robert, 174, 211
Fuller, Edmund, 13, 16, 30, 38, 44, 50, 55, 57, 87
futurist fiction, 136, 138
Fyvel, T. R., 72, 211

Galgan, Gerald, 60, 211
Galloway, David, 24, 211
Galsworthy, John, 132
Gardiner, Harold, 14, 211
Gardner, James, 133, 212
Gardner, John, 65, 212
Garrett, George, 57, 212
Gass, William, 29
Gates, Ann, 32, 212
Gatsby, Jay (Fitzgerald character), 145, 179
Gayford, Martin, 168, 212
gender studies, 109, 162, 165
German literary theorists, 129
Gertrude (Shakespeare character), 148–51, 162
Gertrude (Updike character), 148–51, 162
Gessert, George, 96, 212
Getlin, Josh, 102, 212
Getty, J. Paul, Museum, 101
Gharraie, Jonathan, 183
Ghosh, Amitav, 171, 212
Gilman, Richard, 7, 11, 15, 97, 212
Gindin, James, 36, 212
Gingher, Robert, 49, 212
Glasgow, Ellen, 23
Glendinning, Victoria, 67, 212
God, 22, 23, 25, 30, 31, 35, 36, 37, 38, 40, 43, 51, 60, 61, 62, 63, 65, 70–71, 79, 84, 87, 90–93, 98, 99, 110, 126, 128, 132, 134–35, 138, 143, 144, 146, 154, 155, 157, 163, 165–66, 170, 173, 180, 187, 188

Goddard, Kevin, 165, 212
Godwin, Gail, 75–76, 212
Gold, Herbert, 22, 212
Gopnik, Adam, 183, 212
Gordon, John, 38, 212
Gratton, Margaret, 34, 212
Gray, Paul, 91, 133, 212
Gray, Richard, 148, 213
Gray, Simon, 19, 213
Green, Henry, 189
Greenberg, Clement, 169
Greenblatt, Stephen, 149–50, 213
Greenfield, Josh, 30, 213
Greiner, Donald, 4, 26, 79, 80–81, 84, 86–87, 89, 127, 142, 177, 188, 213
Griffith, Albert, 49, 213
Gross, John, 140, 213
Group, The (Mary McCarthy), 13
Grumbach, Doris, 44–45, 213

Hailey, Arthur, 27
Hall, Joan, 43, 213
Hall, Linda, 133, 213
Hallissy, Margaret, 84, 213
Hamilton, Alice, 4, 25–26, 34–35, 39, 41, 48, 61, 107, 110, 181, 213–14
Hamilton, Kenneth, 4, 25–26, 34–35, 39, 41, 48, 61, 107, 110, 181, 213–14
Hamlet (William Shakespeare), 148–50
Hamlet (Shakespeare character), 148–50
Hamlet (Updike character), 148–50
Hard Times (Charles Dickens), 147
Hardwick, Elizabeth, 10, 214
Hardy, Thomas, 82
Harper, Howard M., 24, 214
Harrington, J. P., 186, 214
Hartle, Terry, 168–69, 214
Hartnell, Anna, 191–92, 214
Harvard Lampoon, 49
Harvard University, 56, 182, 189
Harvey, Giles, 186, 214
Hawthorne, Nathaniel, 22, 23, 27–28, 32, 44, 86–87, 89, 90, 93, 95–97, 112–13, 123–24, 128, 132, 148, 162–63, 214
Healey, Robert, 8, 214
Heddendorf, David, 164–65, 174, 181, 188, 214
Hefner, Hugh, 73
Heidegger, Martin, 163, 166
Heidenry, John, 37, 214
Heitman, Danny, 189, 214
Heller, Joseph, 23, 51
Hemingway Hero (literary term), 53
Hendin, Josephine, 52, 59–60, 214
Henricks, Thomas, 111, 214
Hensher, Philip, 122, 215
Hesse, Herman, 62
Heyen, William, 32, 215
Hicks, Granville, 7, 10–11, 13, 17, 22, 29, 59, 215
Hicks, Thomas, 126, 215
Hill, John S., 31, 215
Hill, William B., 28, 42, 215
historical novel, 133–35
Hitchens, Christopher, 95, 119, 172, 174, 184, 215
Hoag, Ronald, 63, 215
Hodgart, Matthew, 53, 215
Hogan, Robert, 64, 215
Hogan, William, 11, 215
Holleran, Andrew, 70, 216
Holmes, Catherine, 189, 216
Homer, 190
Hoover, Bob, 158, 216
Hope, Francis, 41, 216
Hopkin, James, 150, 216
Horner, Avril, 161, 216
Horvath, Brooke, 111–12, 216
Hough, Henry, 6, 216
Houghton Library (Harvard University), 189
Howard, Maureen, 51, 216
Howells, William Dean, 148
Hubler, Richard, 18–19, 216
Huizinga, Johan, 111
Hulbert, Dan, 150, 216
Human Comedy. See *Comedie Humaine*
humanism, 23, 33, 40, 48, 71, 115

Humbert, Humbert (Nabokov character), 92
Hume, Kathryn, 164, 216
Hunsinger, George, 106–7, 216
Hunt, George W., S.J., 48, 51, 58, 65–66, 71, 73, 83, 145, 170, 216
Hunt, Russell, 56, 217
Huston, Warner, 173–74, 217
Hyman, Stanley, 12, 14, 30, 217

Iannone, Carol, 97, 216
Iliad, The (Homer), 180
Indecent Obsession, An (Colleen McCullough), 67
Inglis, Fred, 99, 217
Irony (in Updike's work), 25, 38, 41, 45, 49, 55, 56, 69, 75, 79, 81, 108, 110, 111, 112, 119, 132, 151, 163–64, 165, 172, 176, 181
Ishmael (Melville character), 145
Islam, 170–74, 191
Islamist militants, 170–74

Jackson, Edward, 85, 217
Jacobsen, Josephine, 18, 217
Jakes, John, 67
James, Clive, 186, 217
James, Henry, 19, 73, 183, 189
Jameson, Frederic, 111
Janowitz, Henry D., 162, 217
Jarraway, David, 190, 217
Jay, Elisabeth, 178, 217
Jewish writers, 7, 29, 71–72, 139–40
Jihad (jihadists), 170, 172
John Updike Review, 192, 193
Johnson, Charles, 116, 217
Johnson, Diane, 77–78, 217
Johnson, Greg, 141, 186, 217
Johnson, Jeffrey, 183, 217
Johnson, Mark, 84
Johnson, Roger A., 127, 217
Johnston, Robert, 61, 218
Jones, D. A. N., 56, 218
Jones, Nicolette, 114, 218
Jong, Erica, 57, 218
Joyce, James, 8, 13, 14, 34, 71, 82, 101, 107, 125, 189, 190

Kakutani, Michiko, 3, 70, 89, 96, 102, 115, 120, 121, 131–32, 136, 138, 140, 150, 151, 154, 156, 159, 171, 174, 175, 186, 189, 218–19
Kanon, Joseph, 41, 219
Kant, Immanuel, 49
Kapp, Isa, 72, 158, 219
Karl, Frederick, 81–82, 123, 219
Kauffmann, Stanley, 19, 219
Kay, Jane, 16, 219
Kazin, Alfred, 29, 36, 51–52, 70, 117, 219
Keenan, John, 158, 176, 219
Keener, Brian, 179, 219
Kehe, Marjorie, 182–83, 219
Keillor, Bruce, 144, 219
Kemp, Peter, 121, 132, 158, 219
Kennedy, Douglas, 171, 219
Kennedy, Eugene, 91, 219
Kennedy, William, 28, 219
Kennedy, X. J., 118, 219
Kermode, Frank, 56, 139–40, 219
Keyes, Frances Parkinson, 7
Kidder, Gayle, 120, 220
Kielland-Lund, Erik, 126, 220
Kierkegaard, Søren, 21, 25, 34, 60, 66, 84, 109, 110, 163, 166
King, Francis, 151, 220
Kingsolver, Barbara, 119, 220
Kirklighter, Cristina, 126, 220
Kirn, Walter, 158, 220
Kirsch, Robert, 45, 220
Klausler, Alfred, 10, 220
Klinkowitz, Jerome, 124–25, 220
Knopf, Alfred A., publisher, 6, 57, 182, 185
Koenig, Rhoda, 77, 92–93, 99, 116, 118, 220
Koeppel, Frederic, 92, 104–5, 132, 220
Kohlberg, Lawrence, 111
Koran, 171, 172
Kort, Wesley, 17, 28–29, 147, 220
Kramer, Hilton, 93, 100, 220
Krasner, Lee, 154
Kristeva, Judith, 87
Kubrick, Stanley, 125

Kuehl, Linda, 33, 220
Kunkel, Francis, 48, 221
Künstlerroman, 127

La Course, Guerin, 21, 221
La Salle, Peter, 54, 221
Lacan, Jacques, 63, 109, 127, 128
Laird, Nicholas, 154, 221
Lakoff, George, 84
Lambert, Roger (Updike character), 90, 92, 123, 178
Lambirth, Andrew, 169, 221
Lanchester, John, 97, 221
Larsen, Richard, 40, 221
Larson, Janet, 43, 221
Lask, Thomas, 16, 221
Lasseter, Victor, 112, 179, 221
Lathrop, Kathleen, 86, 221
Lawson, Lewis, 47, 221
Leader, Zachary, 103, 151, 221
Leaves of Grass (Walt Whitman), 152
Leavis, F. R., 147
Leckie, Barbara, 123, 221
LeClair, Thomas, 44, 52, 221
Lee, Hermione, 103, 221
Lehmann-Haupt, Christopher, 32, 96, 100, 116, 136, 221
Leigh, David J., S.J., 165, 222
Leonard, John, 69, 96, 170, 222
Levi-Strauss, Claude, 152
Lewis, C. S., 143
Lewis, Sinclair, 70, 112, 165, 183
Library of Congress, 2
Lindroth, James, 38, 222
Linford, E. H., 16, 222
Lipsius, Frank, 42, 222
Lipsky, David, 95, 117, 222
Locke, Richard, 37, 222
Lodge, David, 8, 31–32, 55, 93, 139, 222
Loercher, Diana, 58, 222
Lolita (Vladimir Nabokov), 7, 55
Loman, Willie (Arthur Miller character), 38, 112, 145
Loudermilk, Kim, 161, 222
Love in the Western World (Denis De Rougemont), 64
Ludlum, Robert, 67

Lurie, Alison, 95, 175, 222
Luscher, Robert, 127, 222
Lutheran (Lutheranism), 70, 147
Lynn, Kenneth, 72–73, 223
Lyons, Eugene, 39, 223
Lyons, Gene, 56, 69–70, 223

Mabe, Chauncey, 133, 223
Mack, Mehammed, 170–71, 223
Macnaughton, William, 26, 81, 223
Magaw, Malcolm, 125, 223
Mailer, Norman, 2, 4, 10, 22, 23, 37, 223
Malamud, Bernard, 2, 22
Mallon, Thomas, 71, 223
Malone, David, 147, 223
Malraux, Andre, 170
Manning, Margaret, 56, 57, 67, 77, 223
Mano, D. Keith, 48, 223
Manuel, Bruce, 104, 223
Maples (couple in Updike's fiction), 57, 143–44
Marcel, Gabriel, 58
March, Augie (Bellow character), 86
Marcus, James, 174, 223
Mariani, Paul, 153, 223
Maristed, Kai, 175, 223
Markle, Joyce, 46, 81, 223
Markovits, Benjamin, 154, 223
Markovitz, Irving, 64, 223
Marriage (in Updike's work), 35, 50, 51, 57, 58, 72, 79, 82, 83, 124, 144, 154
Marshfield, Reverend Thomas (Updike character), 43, 84, 90
Mars-Jones, Adam, 141, 152, 154, 223–24
Martin, John, 84, 224
Marx, Karl, 63, 152
Marxist criticism, 24, 39, 112
Massachusetts Bay Colony, 171
Matson, Elizabeth, 32, 224
Matthews, Charles, 154, 224
Matthews, John, 87–88, 224
Mayne, Richard, 8, 16, 224
Mazurek, Raymond, 112, 224
McCarthy, Abigail, 58, 224

McCarthy, Desmond, 143, 224
McCarthy, Mary, 13
McCaslin, Ike (Faulkner character), 110
McCord, David, 6, 224
McCormack, Ed, 169, 224
McCoy, Robert, 49, 224
McCullough, Colleen, 67
McEwan, Ian, 114, 121, 132, 224
McGuffey reader, 112
McGuiness, Frank, 10, 224
McKenzie, Alan, 48, 63, 224
McLuhan, Marshall, 179
McPherson, William, 42, 53, 57, 224–25
McTavish, John, 146, 165, 186, 225
McTeague (Frank Norris), 112
Mehl, Duane, 93, 225
Meinke, Peter, 19, 225
Mellard, James, 63, 225
Melville, Herman, 1, 22, 23, 129
Menand, Louis, 103, 156, 225
Meredith, George, 56
Merkin, Daphne, 54–55, 225
Messud, Claire, 184–85, 225
Metaphysical poets, 32
Michie, James, 136, 225
Milazzo, Lee, 54, 76, 91, 121, 225
Millard, Kenneth, 161–62, 225
Miller, Alicia, 120, 225
Miller, Arthur, 2, 112
Miller, D. Quentin, 159–60, 177, 178, 225–26
Miller, J. Hillis, 109
Miller, Jonathan, 14, 226
Miller, Karl, 52, 226
Miller, Miriam, 82, 226
Miller, Norman, 10, 226
Mills, Nicolaus, 182, 226
Miracky, James J., 137, 226
Mishra, Pankaj, 140, 226
misogyny, 50, 67–89, 90, 96, 120, 122, 126, 142, 149, 152, 157, 161, 175, 178, 185
Mitsch, Ruthmarie, 119, 226
Mizener, Arthur, 12, 22, 226
Modern Fiction Studies, 20, 48, 123, 144

Montrose, David, 74, 226
Moore, Arthur, 91, 98, 226
Moore, Caroline, 175, 226
Moore, Jack, 85–86, 226
Moore, Lorrie, 155, 226
Moran, Joseph, 166–67, 226
Moreno, Marta, 190, 226
Morey, Ann-Janine, 84, 92, 226–27
Morey-Gaines, Ann-Janine. *See* Morey, Ann-Janine
Morley, Catherine, 190, 227
Mosher, Howard, 95, 227
Mosley, Nicholas, 115, 227
Moyer, Linda, 76, 227
Mudrick, Marvin, 38, 227
Muradian, Thaddeus, 23, 227
Murphy, Richard, 20, 227
Murray, Michele, 20, 33, 39, 130, 227
Museum of Modern Art (New York City), 100
Muslims, 168, 171, 173, 191
Myers, Ben, 187, 227
Myers, David, 35–36, 227
Mysak, Joe, 74, 227
myth criticism, 34–36, 62, 63, 123
mythology (Updike's use of), 12–15, 17, 18, 28, 34, 38, 45–46, 48–49, 77, 82, 86, 108, 118–21, 126, 143, 147, 178–79

Nabokov, Vladimir, 54, 55, 92, 125, 132, 176, 183, 185
Nadeau, Robert, 80, 227
National Association of Scholars, 181
National Book Award, 15, 68
National Book Critics Circle Award, 68
Neary, John M., 108–9, 127, 146, 227
Negrea, Irina, 179, 227
New Criticism, 31
New England (in Updike's fiction), 26, 36, 53, 75
New York Times bestseller list, 7, 12, 16, 41, 50, 90, 94, 101, 131
New Yorker, 2–3, 8, 12, 15, 16, 20, 56, 121, 176, 183
Newman, Judie, 107, 180, 228
Neyfakh, Leon, 182, 228

Nietzsche, Friedrich, 109, 166
Nobel Prize, 105, 186, 193
Nordell, Roderick, 14, 56, 228
North and South (John Jakes), 67
Novak, Frank G., Jr., 178, 228
Novak, Michael, 22, 29, 228
Nussbaum, Emily, 176, 228

Oates, Joyce Carol, 4, 49, 55, 57–58, 102, 136, 228
O'Brien, Michael, 135, 228
O'Connell, Mary, 144–45, 228
O'Connell, Shaun, 73, 228
O'Connor, William Van, 22, 228
Oedipal complex, 52, 112
O'Farrell, Mary Ann, 166, 228
Oldsey, Bernard, 38, 228
O'Leary, Theodore, 93, 117, 228–29
Olivas, Michael, 2, 229
Olster, Stacey, 126, 177, 229
Opdahl, Keith, 108, 229
"Open Boat, The" (Stephen Crane), 179
Oprah Book Club, 151
Oriard, Michael, 85, 229
Osborne, John, 58, 229
Ozick, Cynthia, 33, 156–57, 229

Pale Fire (Vladimir Nabokov), 55
Paletta, Anthony, 192, 229
Paradise Now (Hany Abu-Assad), 192
Parini, Jay, 121, 132, 141, 229
Parks, John, 177–78, 229
Pascal, Blaise, 62, 84
Pasewark, Kyle, 144, 191, 229
Patchett, Ann, 154, 229
Pate, Nancy, 94, 136, 230
Pawley, Daniel, 71, 230
Pearce, Edward, 141, 230
Pearson, Gabriel, 40, 230
Pearson, Michael, 137, 230
Peden, William, 8, 230
Pennsylvania (in Updike's fiction), 33, 41, 53, 66, 82, 116
Pensees (Blaise Pascal), 84
Peter, John, 31, 230
Peters, Margaret, 76, 230
Petter, Henri, 31, 230

Peyton Place (Grace Metallious), 28
Phillips, Robert, 24, 230
philosophical criticism, 33, 35, 55, 60, 83–84, 159–60, 166
Piaget, Jean, 111
Pinsker, Sanford, 123, 125, 126, 142, 230
Plagman, Linda, 60, 230
Plath, James, 129, 192, 230
Playboy (magazine), 73, 114
Podhoretz, John, 72, 230
Podhoretz, Norman, 7–8, 15, 86, 107, 230
Pollock, Jackson, 154
Pollitt, Katha, 77, 230
Porter, Gilbert, 112, 231
Porter, Katherine Anne, 2
postcolonial(ism), 55, 123, 177
postmodern(ism), 33, 36, 88, 101, 110–11, 115, 117, 119, 120, 127, 129, 134, 141, 149, 161, 162, 163, 166, 169, 177, 180, 190
poststructural(ist), 109
Potter, Dennis, 29, 231
Potter, Harry (J. K. Rowling character), 151
Poulet, Georges, 191
Powers, Peter, 128, 231
Prescott, Orville, 14–15, 231
Prescott, Peter, 50–51, 231
Pritchard, William, 3, 102, 106, 107, 136, 140, 148, 152–53, 177, 182
Pritchett, V. S., 70, 231
Prodigal Daughter, The (Robert Ludlum), 67
Prose, Francine, 109–10, 231
Prosser, Jay, 148, 166, 177, 231
Protestant (Protestantism), 36, 42, 43, 61, 81, 88, 99, 133, 147, 155, 181, 185, 191
Proust, Marcel, 107, 182, 183, 189
Pryor, Felix, 149, 231
psoriasis, 166
psychological criticism, 31, 33, 58, 105, 111, 112, 121, 170, 185
Pulitzer Prize, 68, 101
Puritans, 31, 161
Pynchon, Thomas, 63

Quin, John, 184, 231

Ra'ad, Basem L., 123, 231
Raban, Jonathan, 33, 101, 171–72, 231
Raine, Craig, 76, 100, 231–32
Ratcliff, Carter, 101, 232
Ratcliffe, Michael, 71, 232
realism (realist fiction), 13, 15, 18, 22, 23, 28, 34, 36, 38, 47, 48, 51, 55, 58, 64, 71, 74, 80, 82, 86, 88, 100, 101, 108, 109, 115, 116, 119–20, 121, 124, 127, 129, 131, 136, 137, 141, 147, 163, 176, 177, 184, 188, 190
Regan, Robert, 49, 232
religion, 12, 20, 21, 22, 23, 25, 26, 28–29, 34, 35, 36, 41, 42, 43, 46, 47, 48, 51, 52, 61, 62, 65, 71, 79, 81, 83, 84, 88, 90–93, 95–98, 105, 107, 108, 110, 120, 123, 128, 132, 133, 134, 135, 138, 141, 143, 144, 146–47, 155, 158, 164, 165, 170, 172, 173, 180–81, 183, 191
Renault, Mary, 7, 27
Richardson, Jack, 33, 232
Richardson, Samuel, 124
Ricks, Christopher, 11, 16, 38, 52, 232
Ricoeur, Paul, 84
Riggan, William, 74, 232
Ristoff, Dilvo, 111, 145, 147, 232
Robb, Christina, 53, 232
Roberts, Preston, 13, 232
Roberts, Tom, 130, 232
Robinson, Marilynne, 94, 232
Robinson, Sally, 145, 232
Robson, Leo, 187, 232
Rodgers, Bernard, 155, 192, 232
Rogers, W. G., 16, 232
Rohrbach, Peter, 41, 232
Roiphe, Anne, 104, 232
romance (literary genre), 50–53, 87, 88, 118–20, 123, 133
Romano, John, 58, 233
Rosa, Alfred, 49, 233
Rosenbaum, Ron, 149, 233

Rosenheim, Andrew, 3, 187, 233
Rosenthal Family Foundation, 8
Rosetta Stone, 74
Rotella, Guy, 79, 233
Roth, Philip, 4, 87, 114, 161
Rovit, Earl, 120–21, 233
Rowland, Stanley, 12, 233
Royal, Derek, 162–63, 233
Rubin, Merle, 76–77, 96–97, 116, 120, 133, 233
Rudman, Mark, 100, 233
Rumens, Carol, 68, 233
Rupp, Richard, 25, 105, 233
Rushdie, Salman, 170
Ruskin School of Drawing and Fine Art (Oxford University), 100
Russell, John, 44, 233
Russell, Mariann, 47, 233
Russian literary theorists, 129
Ryle, John, 55, 233

Sage, Lorna, 73, 92, 234
Sale, Roger, 13, 17–18, 20, 69, 234
Salinger, J. D., 2, 176
Samuels, Charles T., 19–20, 34, 38, 234
Sandlin, Jennifer A., 190, 234
satire, 35, 42, 54, 56, 71, 72, 79, 85, 93, 95, 97, 135, 139, 182, 185
Sauerländer, Willibald, 169, 234
Savu, Laura, 162, 234
Scarlet Letter, The (Nathaniel Hawthorne), 28, 44, 87, 90, 92, 94–97, 112, 113, 123, 127, 142, 163, 165
Schiff, James, 4, 123–24, 129–30, 142, 146, 177, 192, 234
Schlesinger, Arthur, Jr., 42, 234
Schneiderman, Leo, 128, 234
Schopen, Bernard, 61, 235
Schueller, Malini, 123, 235
Schwartz, Sanford, 75, 235
Schwarz, Benjamin, 189, 235
science (in Updike's work), 62, 80, 90–93, 107, 138, 146
science fiction, 74, 137, 147
Scott, A. O., 133, 235
Searles, George, 81, 87–88, 95, 102, 235

Second World War, 165, 177
secular (secularism), 22, 29, 45, 48, 61, 71, 83, 141, 155, 177, 180
See, Carolyn, 94, 97, 235
Selden, Raman, 109, 235
self, concept of, 9, 11, 25, 32–33, 47, 48, 58, 60, 80, 83, 85, 97–99, 109, 123, 124, 128, 136, 154, 156, 160, 161, 162, 166, 180, 183, 191
sentimentality (in Updike's fiction), 14, 15, 30, 38, 52, 57, 60, 69, 76, 104, 108, 134, 136, 140, 168, 186
September 11, 2001. *See* terrorism
Sequeira, Jessica, 188, 235
Sethuraman, Ramchandran, 127–28, 235
sex (in Updike's fiction), 9, 10, 28–32, 33, 35, 36, 39, 43, 48, 51, 52, 53, 60, 61, 62, 63, 64, 66, 68, 69, 72, 77, 78, 79, 80, 83, 84, 85, 88, 90, 91, 92, 93, 97, 105, 108, 110, 113, 118, 120, 126, 127, 128, 131, 136, 146, 150, 156, 157–58, 161, 164, 167, 177, 181, 183, 187
Sexton, David, 91, 235
Shainin, Jonathan, 172, 235
Shakespeare, William, 112, 148–50, 162, 183, 189
Shapiro, Anna, 185, 235
Shapiro, James, 140, 235
Shaw, Patrick W., 113, 235
Shechner, Mark, 134, 235
Sheed, Wilfrid, 28, 236
Shetley, Vernon, 79–80, 236
Shillington, Pennsylvania, 193
Shone, Tom, 119, 236
Siegel, Lee, 156, 236
Siegle, Robert, 109, 236
Sigal, Clancy, 72, 236
Silver, James, 190, 236
Simmons, Tracy Lee, 121–22, 170, 236
Simon, John, 74–75, 236
Singh, Sukhbir, 146, 178–79, 236
Sissman, L. E., 33, 236
Sister Carrie (Theodore Dreiser), 112
Skeeter (Updike character), 47
Slavitt, David, 75, 236
Slethaug, Gordon, 81, 236
Smee, Sebastian, 155, 168, 236
sociological criticism, 29, 31, 51, 56, 88, 127, 143, 170, 180
Sokoloff, B. A., 2, 236
Sokolov, Raymond, 95, 236
Solomon, Deborah, 101, 236
Sorrentino, Gilbert, 44, 236
Sound and the Fury, The (William Faulkner), 20
Southern, Terry, 10, 236
Southern Illinois University Press, 36
Spector, Judith Ann, 124, 236
Spice, Nicholas, 92, 236
Stade, George, 43, 236
Stafford, William T., 48, 123, 237
Standley, Fred, 23, 237
Stearns, Jennie, 190, 237
Steinbeck, John, 2
Steiner, George, 44, 132, 237
Stern, Richard, 118–19, 237
Stevens, Kevin, 186, 237
Stevens, Wallace, 65, 188
Stevick, Philip, 126, 237
Stewart, Mary, 27
Steyn, Mark, 172, 237
Stone, Robert, 136–37, 172, 237
Storey, Celia, 138, 237
Stout, Cushing, 113, 237
Strandberg, Victor, 62, 237
Straub, Peter, 41–42, 237
Strawson, Galen, 115, 116, 154, 237
Stubbs, John, 23, 237
style (in Updike's work), 4, 6, 8, 9, 13, 16, 17, 18, 21, 22, 24, 25, 29, 30, 33, 35, 38, 43, 44, 45, 48, 57, 65, 69, 71, 82, 97, 101, 103, 105, 106, 108, 122, 125, 129, 131, 133, 135, 164, 171, 187, 189
Styron, William, 22
suburbs (in Updike's fiction), 19, 22, 29, 41, 42, 53, 55, 56, 57, 85, 88, 95, 108, 144, 156, 182, 191
Suderman, Elmer, 34, 237
Sullivan, Mary Rose, 78, 237
Sullivan, Richard, 17, 238
Sutherland, John, 139, 238
Swindell, Larry, 56, 238

symbolism (in Updike's work), 22, 30, 31, 35, 46, 49, 56, 57, 69–70, 85, 86, 105, 111, 124, 125, 154, 161, 180
Symons, Julian, 37–38, 238

Tales of Burning Love (Louise Erdrich), 161
Tallent, Elizabeth, 83, 238
Tandon, Bharat, 139, 238
Tanenhaus, Sam, 175, 238
Tanner, Tony, 29, 36, 41, 123, 238
Tarbox (Updike's fictional town), 28, 55
Tarkington, Booth, 90
Tate, Sister M. Judith, 23, 238
Taubman, Robert, 14, 69, 238
Taylor, C. Clarke, 2, 238
Taylor, John, 153, 238
Taylor, Larry, 36–37, 238
Tennyson, Alfred, 62
terrorism (terrorist attack on United States), 168–74
theme (in Updike's work), 4, 14, 17, 19, 20, 21, 22, 23, 24, 27, 31, 36, 37, 41, 43, 46, 50, 52, 57, 58, 60, 65, 66, 68, 76, 78, 81, 83, 86, 92, 99, 102, 107, 108, 111, 123, 127, 134, 136, 137, 141, 145, 147, 149, 150, 151, 153, 154, 158, 162, 175, 178, 179, 183, 190
Theroux, Paul, 38–39, 51, 55, 57, 238
Third World, 54, 56
Thomas, Samuel, 192, 238
Thompson, John, 20, 30, 54, 238–39
Thorburn, David, 65–66, 239
Thoreau, Henry David, 37
Thorne, Matt, 176, 239
Tillich, Paul, 34, 163
Timpane, John, 192, 239
"To Shakespeare" (Matthew Arnold), 189
Todd, Richard, 41, 52–53, 239
Tolstoy, Leo, 62
Tomalin, Claire, 54, 58, 78, 239
Towers, Robert, 53–54, 58, 239
Trachtenberg, Jeffrey, 125–26, 239

tragedy, 10, 28, 70, 85, 104, 110, 120, 148, 170
Trendel, Aristi, 190, 239
Trevor, William, 38, 114–15, 239
Trilling, Diana, 30, 239
Tristan and Iseult (Isolde) (fictional characters), 36, 118–20, 143
Turner, Kermit, 48, 239
Twayne U.S. Authors series, 45, 80, 142

Umphlett, Wiley, 47, 239
United States foreign policy, 173
Updike, John, works by: "A & P," 113, 190; *Afterlife and Other Stories, The*, 114, 121–22, 180; *Americana and Other Poems*, 153; *Assorted Prose*, 16, 44; "Astronomer, The," 60, 65; *Bech at Bay*, 139–40; *Bech Is Back*, 71–73; *Bech, A Book*, 27, 32–33, 34; *Brazil*, 114, 118–21, 136, 143, 146, 147, 150; *Buchanan Dying*, 27, 41–42; *Carpentered Hen and Other Tame Creatures, The*, 6, 67; "Cats, The," 190; *Centaur, The*, 12–15, 18, 23, 34, 35–36, 48–49, 62, 63, 65, 66, 69, 108–9, 127–28, 178–79, 180, 190; *Collected Poems 1953–1993*, 117–18; *Coup, The*, 50, 53–56, 64, 66, 81, 85, 86, 96, 118, 123; *Couples*, 25, 26, 27–33, 36, 37, 40, 43, 48, 51, 52, 60, 62, 63, 66, 73, 127, 139, 146, 157, 158; "Dogwood Tree, The," 65; *Due Considerations: Essays and Criticism*, 174–75; *Early Stories: 1953–1975*, 155–57; *Endpoint and Other Poems*, 185–86; *Facing Nature*, 67, 79–80; *Gertrude and Claudius*, 148–51, 162; *Golf Dreams: Writings on Golf*, 135–36; *Higher Gossip*, 189; *Hoping for a Hoopoe*, 6; *Hugging the Shore*, 73–75; *In the Beauty of the Lilies*, 131–36, 143, 149, 187; *Just Looking: Essays on Art*, 100–101, 168; *Licks of Love*, 151–53; *Marry Me*, 50–53, 123, 125;

Updike, John, works by—*(continued)*
Memories of the Ford Administration, 114, 116–17, 136, 146, 147, 161–62; *Midpoint, and Other Poems*, 27, 32, 34, 107, 177; *Month of Sundays, A*, 27, 42–44, 50, 52, 60, 63, 65, 81, 84, 88, 90, 110, 165, 178; *More Matter*, 141–42; *Museums and Women and Other Stories*, 27, 41–42, 57; *Music School, The*, 18–19; *My Father's Tears and Other Stories*, 185–86; *Odd Jobs*, 114–16, 140; *Of the Farm*, 16–18, 34, 82–83; *Olinger Stories*, 127; *Picked-Up Pieces*, 42, 44–45; *Pigeon Feathers*, 11–12, 22; *Poorhouse Fair, The*, 6–8, 9, 10, 14, 18, 45, 136; *Problems and Other Stories*, 57–59; *Rabbit at Rest*, 90, 101–5, 114, 116, 125, 126, 127, 129, 132, 145, 149, 152, 170, 187, 190; *Rabbit Is Rich*, 67–73, 85, 90, 102, 112, 165, 180–81; *Rabbit Redux*, 27, 37–41, 45, 47–48, 50, 52, 62, 68–71, 85, 102, 106, 125, 165, 179; "Rabbit Remembered," 151–53; *Rabbit, Run*, 6, 9–12, 13, 14, 18, 22, 23, 24, 37, 38, 39, 47, 48, 50, 64, 66, 69, 70, 71, 72, 84, 85, 102, 109, 112, 123, 125–26, 144, 164, 165, 179; *Roger's Version*, 90–94, 105, 106, 110, 113, 123, 140, 143, 165, 173, 178, 187, 190; *S.*, 94–98, 110, 146, 150, 163; *Same Door, The*, 8–9; "Sandstone Farmhouse," 190; *Seek My Face*, 154–55, 166, 190; *Self-Consciousness: Memoirs*, 97–99, 166, 180; *Still Looking: Essays on American Art*, 168–69; "Should Wizard Hit Mommy?" 109; *Telephone Poles and Other Poems*, 16; *Terrorist*, 168, 169–74, 191–92; *Too Far to Go*, 57; *Tossing and Turning*, 53; *Toward the End of Time*, 136–39, 146, 147, 157, 160, 165, 177; *Trust Me*, 93–94; "Varieties of Religious Experience," 170; *Villages*, 157–59; *Widows of Eastwick, The*, 168, 175–76; *Witches of Eastwick, The*, 67, 75–79, 83, 90, 110, 113, 149, 161, 168, 175–76

Updike Figure (literary term), 52–53
Updike Society, 192–93
Uphaus, Suzanne, 65, 239
Uris, Leon, 27
USA Trilogy (John Dos Passos), 145
Utopian fiction, 31

Vanderwerken, David, 47–48, 239
Vargo, Edward, 46–47, 63, 239–40
Vaughan, Philip, 80, 240
Verduin, Kathleen, 81, 83, 177, 191, 240
Vickery, John, 48–49, 190, 240
Victorian fiction, 11, 127, 142
Vidal, Gore, 135, 240
Vietnam War, 99, 135, 173–74, 184
Vigilante, Richard, 99, 240
Vincent, Norah, 150, 240
Virgil (Publius Virgilius Maro), 190
Vonnegut, Kurt, 124

Wackerman, Daniel, 135, 240
Wagner, Joseph, 61–62, 240
Wagnerian drama (Richard Wagner), 119
Walden, George, 157, 169, 240
Waldmeir, Joseph, 48, 144, 240
Waldron, Randall H., 85, 240
Wall, James, 132–33, 152, 240
Wallace, David Foster, 4, 138, 240
Wallace, Irving, 27
Waller, Bret, 101, 240
Waller, G. F., 36, 241
Waller, Gary, 81, 241
Walrath, Douglas Alan, 191, 241
Walsh, David, 1, 173, 185, 241
Walsh, William, 59, 241
Walter, Natasha, 122, 241
Walton, James, 137, 241
Ward, J. A., 15, 20–21, 241
Waste Land, The (T. S. Eliot), 179
Watman, Max, 158–59, 241
Waxman, Robert, 62, 241

Webb, Stephen, 181, 182, 241
Weber, Brom, 38, 241
Weeks, Edward, 18, 241
Weintraub, Stanley, 41, 241
Weldon, Fay, 157, 241
Wheelwright, Philip, 84, 241
Whetter, Darryl, 170, 241
Whistler, James McNeill, 169
Whitaker, Jennifer, 2, 241
White, Edmund, 51, 241
Wilhelm, Albert, 82, 241
Will, George, 104, 242
Williams, David, 69, 242
Williams, John, 193, 242
Williams, Ted, 183
Williams, Tennessee, 2
Williams, Wirt, 28, 242
Williamson, Chilton, 101, 242
Wills, Garry, 104, 242
Wilmot family (Updike characters), 133
Wilson, Edmund, 75, 148, 183
Wilson, Matthew, 123, 242
Wilson, Raymond J., III, 113, 242
Woiwode, Larry, 188–89, 242
Wolcott, James, 68, 176, 242
Wolfe, Thomas, 23

Wood, James, 104, 115, 118, 134–35, 141, 143, 153, 173, 242
Wood, Michael, 94, 98, 242
Wood, Peter, 181, 242
Wood, Ralph, 70–71, 79, 99, 102, 110, 242–43
World Trade Center, 169
Worth, Sarah (Updike character), 94–96
Wright, Derek, 123, 243
Wyatt, Bryant, 25, 243

Yardley, Jonathan, 69, 94, 122, 139, 145, 243
Yates, Norris, 23, 243
Yerkes, James, 137–38, 141, 146, 147, 149, 155, 157, 243
Yoknapatawpha (Faulkner's fictional county), 124, 145
"Young Goodman Brown" (Nathaniel Hawthorne), 113

Zan, Jifang, 184, 243
Zender, Karl, 124, 243
Zipp, Yvonne, 171, 244
Zlosnik, Sue, 161, 216
Zverev, Aleksei, 125, 244

www.ingramcontent.com/pod-product-compliance
Lightning Source LLC
Chambersburg PA
CBHW021659230426
43668CB00008B/672